Great Rivers – Great Hatches

GREAT RIVERS–
GREAT HATCHES

Charles Meck
and Greg Hoover

STACKPOLE
BOOKS

Copyright © 1992 by Charles R. Meck and Gregory A. Hoover

Published by
STACKPOLE BOOKS
Cameron and Kelker Streets
P.O. Box 1831
Harrisburg, PA 17105

Printed in the United States of America

Interior layout by Margaret N. Schmidt

First Edition

10 9 8 7 6 5 4 3 2 1

Library of Congress Cataloging-in-Publication Data

Meck, Charles R.
  Great rivers—great hatches / Charles Meck and Greg Hoover.
    p.   cm.
  Includes bibliographical references and index.
  ISBN 0-8117-1282-6
  ISBN 0-8117-1526-4
  1. Fly fishing—United States. 2. Trout fishing—United States.
3. Aquatic insects—United States. I. Hoover, Greg. II. Title.
SH463.M42   1992
799.1'755--dc20
                                                          92-3957
                                                          CIP

To my wife, Shirley, for her patience and understanding while I was away doing research for the book.

Charles R. Meck

To my parents, Owen and Helen Hoover, to whom I attribute my focus on matters that are important in life and professional growth. Thank you for all of your support through the years.

And to my wife, Deb, whose unending patience and tremendous assistance with this project have gone far beyond what a husband could ever expect.

Gregory A. Hoover

Contents

Acknowledgments

There have been many people who have contributed to the successful completion of *Great Rivers—Great Hatches*. Here are a few of them.

Garry Sandstrom of the Morning Hatch in Tacoma, Washington, and Richard Turner, an attorney and avid fly fisher also of Tacoma. Craig Shuman, an entrepreneur from Fort Collins, Colorado, and an accomplished angler, helped considerably with the information and the trip to Washington state. George Cook, a representative of Sage Rods, was a congenial host at the Isaak Ranch near Moses Lake, Washington. Much of the information on the Yakima River was obtained from two expert guides on the river, Dean Stephenson and Mike Kuffler.

In Oregon the following guides helped considerably: Ken Helfrich on the McKenzie River, Craig Lacy and Alan Stewart on the Deschutes River, and Ed Miranda on the Williamson River. Others who helped were Gary Kish, without whose knowledge the insect emergence chart for the Metolius River couldn't have been completed; Bob Zagorin of the Oregon Guides and Packers Association; Denny Rickarts of Rocky Point Lodge near Klamath Falls; and Steve and Judy Carothers and Paul Pursell of Chiloquin.

In Montana and Wyoming Dave Blackburn helped on the Kootenai

River; Nick Nicklas on the Firehole, Yellowstone, and Madison rivers; Pat Elam and Mike Bay on the Missouri River; Brian Nelson on the Bitterroot River; Richie Montella on the Bighorn River; Rod Walinchus on the North Platte River; and Phil Phillips on the Wind and Bighorn rivers.

In Idaho Mike Lawson helped with the Henry's Fork, Brett Drummond with Silver Creek, and Doug Brearey and Todd Van Bramer with the Big Wood River.

In West Virginia and Maryland Paul Kurincak assisted on the Savage River, and Paul and Gary Lang helped with the Cheat River system and the Elk River. Rob Gilford and his father, Jim Gilford, assisted with history and the hatches on Big Hunting Creek in Maryland. Wally Vait of Monkton, Maryland, and Steve Snyder of York, Pennsylvania, gave us information on the Gunpowder Falls River in Maryland. Thanks also to the Maryland Chapter of Trout Unlimited for sharing their macroinvertebrate sampling data with us.

In Virginia Harry Murray gave us background and hatches on the Rapidan, North Fork of the Moormans, and Rose rivers, and Bob Cramer helped with Mossy Creek.

Phil Camera of Woodland Park, Colorado, the creator of Larva Lace, assisted us on the South Platte and Arkansas rivers; Don Puterbaugh and Bill McMillen of Salida, Colorado, fished and coached on the Arkansas River; and Roy Palm of Frying Pan Anglers of Basalt, Colorado, assisted on the Fryingpan and Roaring Fork rivers.

Thanks also to Kenton Williams, Hank Boehm, Chris Kunkel, Farrell Hirst, Phyllis Hirst, and Mark Forslund for providing information on the Green River in Utah.

On the White River in Arkansas we had assistance from Bob Gartner and fly-fishing guides Hank Weir and Shawn Taylor.

Tom Maxwell, cofounder of Thomas and Thomas, and Jim Krul, owner of English Angling Trappings in New Fairfield, Connecticut, were of great assistance on the Housatonic River. And on the Farmington River a great deal of assistance was provided by Jim Stack and Dick Lowery, a professional fly tyer and guide.

Guidance on the Deerfield River in Massachusetts was provided by Marc Aroner, a bamboo fly-rod builder; Bob Olszewski, a fly-shop owner; and Bill Latrel, president of the Deerfield River Watershed Association.

In the Au Sable region of Michigan Rusty Gates, Mike and Jim Calvin, Scott Rob, Charlie Weaver, and Craig Perry, all of Gates Lodge and Pro Shop, provided many useful insights on rivers of the area. Tim Roodvoets and Charles Chlysta provided additional insight into quality trout water in the region. George Griffiths, cofounder of Trout Unlimited, gave a tremendous amount of insight on the fly-fishing history of the Au Sable River. Additional assistance on the Manistee River was provided by fisheries biologist Joe Kutkuhn. On the Pere Marquette River John Kestner, Jim Empie, and Tom and Jim Johnson at Johnson's Lodge and Fly Shop in Baldwin, Michigan, were helpful in explaining difficult hatches on this river. Larry Demmink and Charles Belt also shared some fly-fishing experiences on the Pere Marquette with us.

Thanks to Ron Manz, owner of Brule River Classics near Brule, Wisconsin, who was very helpful and shared his experiences with rivers of northwestern Wisconsin.

In Missouri fisheries biologist Spencer Turner and fly-fishing guide Shawn Taylor of Taylormade River Treks in Tecumseh provided information on trout rivers of the Ozark region. Aquatic entomologist Lynden Trial provided information on aquatic insects in rivers in southern Missouri, and in southwestern Missouri Ray Krouscup was a tremendous help on Crane Creek.

The intricacies of New Hampshire's Saco River were explained by Dick Stewart, publisher, and Jack Russell, editor, of *American Angler* magazine and Fred Abbruzzese, co-owner of North Country Angler. On the Connecticut River in northern New Hampshire Grant Woodbury, president of the Abenaki Chapter of Trout Unlimited, and Bob Pierce of Pittsburg shared some of their experiences from the past forty years.

As always, Fran Betters of the Adirondack Fly Shop near Wilmington, New York, was very insightful on the hatches and changes occurring on the West Branch of the Ausable River.

Al Hines, owner of High Country Fly Fishing, and Stuart McCormac, an employee at the fly shop, shared many of their observations on quality trout water in western North Carolina.

Both Doug Suddreth and Al Hines shared their knowledge on hatches and fly fishing the South Fork Holston River in eastern Tennessee.

Comments on fly fishing and hatches on the Batten Kill in Vermont were made by Gloria Jordan, wife of the late Wes Jordan and fly-shop owner and rod builder, and Dan Reid at Orvis in Manchester.

In California Andy Burk of the Fly Shop in Redding helped considerably on Hat Creek and Fall River. Thanks also to Bill Sunderland of San Jose.

Thanks to Phil Baldacchino of Kettle Creek Tackle shop, who suggested the idea for *Great Rivers – Great Hatches*.

Lew and Jon Scheckler of Scheckler Photographics in State College, Pennsylvania, performed their magic in developing black-and-white photographs. Ralph Frankenberger also helped with photo development, and John Swinton made editorial comments. Both live in State College, Pennsylvania.

Thanks to Chris Jung, illustrator, for her wonderful talents that are evident in the pages of this book.

Appreciation to Virginia Eby, head programmer with the Expert System Development Group at the Pennsylvania State University, for merging our two word processing applications.

Without the help of those mentioned, this book could never have been completed. Thanks to all of them and also to the many state agencies who assisted.

Charles R. Meck
Pennsylvania Furnace, Pennsylvania

Gregory A. Hoover
Lemont, Pennsylvania

1

Introduction

Can you remember your most satisfying fly-fishing adventures? Those days when nothing went wrong? When trout took your imitations on almost every cast? We'll bet most of those successful days and evenings revolved around a particular hatch—mayfly, stonefly, caddisfly, or some other insect—that you matched with just the right imitation. Memorable days on our favorite streams and rivers almost always include a terrific hatch, trout rising to that hatch, and a fly that perfectly imitates it.

But how many times have you been fly fishing a river for a few hours with not much happening? Oh, the trout occasionally rose to a surface insect and you caught a couple of them, but it just wasn't the fly fishing you had hoped for. Then, in what seemed like just seconds, insects began to appear on the surface in front of you. First a few, then hundreds, then thousands; and where just a few minutes earlier you had seen only a few trout feeding, dozens were gorging themselves on a sudden food supply. What happened? What happened was a hatch.

Let me tell you about several similar events across the United States that were transformed into memorable fly-fishing experiences for us when the hatches appeared.

One day in early July Charles Meck stopped on the bank of the

Bitterroot River just below Missoula, Montana. It still flowed 2 feet higher with snowmelt from the range to the west. It was his first time ever on western water, and he wondered how he'd ever catch a trout in that swollen river. Nothing happened for a half hour or so, and Charles grew increasingly doubtful. Then, around 10:00 A.M. he noticed a large mayfly struggling to become airborne. Soon a second one emerged. Gradually, dozens more of these insects – western green drakes – appeared on the surface. A major hatch had begun, and more than a dozen heavy Bitterroot rainbows began to feed right in front of him. Within minutes the barren surface had been transformed into an extremely productive one.

Here's another example. One day in early September Charles Meck had just fished over a spinner fall of tricos on the Colorado River near Kremmling, Colorado. The water turned quiet. Around 6:00 P.M. he moved downriver to the area just above Gore Canyon and waited. A single trout fed near the far shore. Just before 8:00 P.M. thousands of ginger quill spinners appeared just above the surface, and the trout went crazy – several came completely out of the water chasing the low flyers. The action continued past dusk as the trout fell steadily for a #14 Ginger Quill.

How about the great trip on the McKenzie River in Oregon? It was a cold, misty day, and Ken Helfrich, Mike Manfredo, and Charles Meck drifted for more than 3 miles along this normally productive river without seeing one rising trout. Around 2:00 P.M. they came to a pool 3 miles above the Willamette River where thousands of mayflies began emerging in the riffle and rainbows fed freely on the emerging duns. Because the air temperature never rose above the high forties, these mayflies never took flight, and trout fed freely on them. The three entered the Willamette and two hours later caught and released more than fifty trout rising to the western march brown hatch.

How about that evening Charles Meck fly fished on the Yellowstone River near Corbin Springs, Montana? He checked the low-growing willows near the river's edge and found each branch saturated with huge salmon flies. Charles waited by the river until dusk, when these huge stoneflies returned to the river to lay eggs. Huge trout fed freely on this food, and a #6 down-wing performed very well for him during that memorable event.

And recently Charles waited for the sulphur hatch to appear on the Little Juniata River in Pennsylvania. For two hours only an occasional trout took a gray fox or a sulphur, but neither hatch appeared in the numbers necessary to create the frenzied feeding that he was hoping for. By 8:15 P.M. many of the uninformed anglers had already left the river, but Charles still waited for the sulphur hatch. Moments later sulphurs appeared by the thousands on the surface, and the trout went crazy. Approximately fifty trout rose in front of him right in the same area where for the two previous hours he had seen maybe only three fish surface.

What do these and many other fly-fishing events have in common? What made them memorable events?

Ask some great western fly fishermen – people like Craig Shuman of Fort Collins or Phil Camera of Woodland Park, Colorado – what one change has occurred in western fly fishing in the past couple decades. They agree on one significant change with western anglers. Twenty years ago most anglers fishing western rivers might have used a Goofus or large Wulff Royal Coachman to coax trout to the surface, but more recently serious anglers fish the hatches – they realize that if they're going to succeed, they have to match the hatch.

This book, *Great Rivers – Great Hatches*, will help you enjoy more memorable days like the ones just described by providing detailed information about these great hatches and rivers.

Chapter 2 provides an emergence chart of all the major hatches – as well as several stonefly and caddisfly species – across the United States. You'll find some new species and some new names mentioned there.

Many great rivers across the country have become associated with certain hatches: Michigan's Au Sable is famous for its Michigan caddis and brown drake hatches; New York's Beaverkill and Pennsylvania's Penns Creek boast fantastic green drake hatches; and Henry's Fork of the Snake River in Idaho holds prolific pale morning dun and western green drake hatches. Some of these rivers and where to locate their hatches are examined in chapter 3.

Why do the tricos on Colorado's South Platte seem to be several sizes larger in July and August than in September and October? Why is the little blue-winged olive dun larger in April than in September? How many days can you expect the white fly to appear after it starts to emerge? You'll find the answers to these questions and more also in chapter 3, as well as new findings on some of the hatches. You'll find interesting and useful discussions of the white fly, trico, and others that will help you recognize and respond to these hatches.

Have you ever wondered just what hatches rise off the Batten Kill in Vermont? Or maybe you'd like to fish the Beaverkill in New York in late June and would like to know what hatches might appear at that time of year. Chapter 4 discusses these rivers and some of the other famous and productive trout streams and rivers in the East. In chapter

5 you'll learn about the better trout rivers of Michigan, Wisconsin, Arkansas, and Missouri. In chapter 6 you'll find a discussion of such western rivers as the Deschutes in Oregon, the Madison in Montana, and the North Platte in Wyoming. In these three chapters we'll examine more than sixty of the best trout streams in the country along with the major hatches on each. You'll also find the special regulations that apply on some of the rivers. In these special regulations, you'll find tackle restrictions, size and creel limits, and boundaries of the regulated water. These regulations can change from year to year, however, so make sure to check the current state regulations when you buy your license.

Earlier in this chapter you read how weather affected the western march brown on the McKenzie and Willamette rivers. Charles Meck has confronted inclement weather just about every time he's floated the McKenzie in Oregon during the western march brown hatch. In chapter 7 Charles Meck describes how weather affects the hatches and how to enjoy success on those apparently futile fishing days.

In the past two decades more innovations in fly tying have come from the West than any other section of the country. Crystal Comparaduns, caddis patterns with trailing shucks, Larva Lace, Z-lon, and dozens of other patterns and materials have emanated from this region, and in chapter 8 some of these innovations are listed.

Many organizations and clubs devote their energies to protecting our streams and rivers, and these groups need your support. Chapter 9 discusses forming organizations and other ways that you can help to preserve our great fishing waters.

Even though we title the book *Great Rivers–Great Hatches,* we have included some information on lake, pond, and stream fly fishing.

In chapter 3 you'll find information about speckle-winged hatches on eastern ponds. In chapter 6, Charlie Meck talks about fly fishing on some of Washington state's desert lakes like Nunnally and Lenore. We also examine some small waters and creeks in Pennsylvania, New York, Maryland, Virginia, North Carolina, Missouri, and Washington.

Understanding and anticipating the best hatches across the country, learning the streams and rivers on which these hatches appear, recognizing which patterns match what hatches – all of these important fundamentals make up the practical foundation for this book.

2

Insect Emergence

Are the hatches predictable enough to list approximate dates for them? What about the diversity in the West?

Gary Kish met Dick Turner, Jay Kapolka, and Charles Meck at the Metolius River in Oregon on May 23 to fish while a tremendous hatch of pale morning duns and western green drakes appeared. Several days later, on May 29, Jay Kapolka and Charles fly fished this great river again. This time they saw heavy hatches of western green drakes, pale morning duns, and blue-winged olive duns (*Drunella flavilinea*).

On June 24 of the same year Jerry and Charles Meck fished over a superb pale morning dun hatch on the Kootenai River in northwestern Montana. Their guide on the river for the day, Dave Blackburn, said that this was the first hatch of pale morning duns of the season. Just a couple days before, on June 21, Jerry and Charles had seen the first few western green drakes of the season emerge on Henry's Fork. That's almost a month's difference between the beginning of the pale morning duns' appearance on the Metolius and Kootenai rivers.

Look at the salmon fly emergence throughout the West. Charles Meck first hit the hatch on May 25 on the Deschutes River in central

Slate drake (*Isonychia* sp.) nymphal shucks on a rock. *Greg Hoover.*

Oregon. That same year the salmon fly didn't emerge on the Yellow-stone until July 8. Talk about seasonal variability.

With these cautions in mind, emergence charts can be useful tools in your quest for a better understanding of meeting and fishing the hatches. In fact, with knowledge of local emergence times you can plan to fish certain hatches for several weeks.

Following is an emergence chart for hatches in the United States. It's in two parts—eastern and midwestern hatches, and western hatches. The dates are approximate for these regions, but they will be useful in planning to meet and fish the hatches.

HATCHES OF THE UNITED STATES

Eastern and Midwestern Hatches

Hatch and match	Emergence date (dates are only rough guides and should not be followed rigidly)	Time of day for Dun and Spinner	Hook size
Paracapnia species (stonefly) Little Black Stonefly	March 1	Morning and afternoon	18
Baetis tricaudatus (mayfly) Dun: Little Blue-Winged Olive Dun Spinner: Rusty Spinner	March 15	10:00 A.M. to 6:00 P.M.	16–20
Callibaetis skokianis (mayfly) Dun: Speckle-Winged Dun Spinner: Speckle-Winged Spinner	April 1	Morning and afternoon	14–16
Strophopteryx fasciata (stonefly) Early Brown Stonefly	April 10	Afternoon	14
Paraleptophlebia adoptiva (mayfly) Dun: Dark Blue Quill Spinner: Dark Brown Spinner	April 10	11:00 A.M. to 4:00 P.M. Heaviest: 2:00 to 4:00 P.M. Spinner: 4:00 to 7:00 P.M.	18
Brachycentrus solomoni (caddisfly) Grannom	April 12	Morning and afternoon	10
Epeorus pleuralis (mayfly) Dun: Quill Gordon Spinner: Red Quill Spinner	April 18	1:00 to 3:00 P.M. Spinner: 11:30 A.M. to 2:00 P.M.	14
Rhithrogena jejuna (mayfly) Dun: Dark Quill Gordon Spinner: Quill Gordon Spinner	April 18	1:00 to 3:00 P.M.	14

Hatch and match	Emergence date (dates are only rough guides and should not be followed rigidly)	Time of day for Dun and Spinner	Hook size
Siphloplecton basale (mayfly) Dun: Great Speckled Olive Dun Spinner: Great Speckled Spinner	April 18	1:30 P.M.	10 or 12
Brachycentrus numerosus (caddisfly) Grannom	April 23	Morning and afternoon	12
Ephemerella subvaria (mayfly) Male dun: Red Quill Female dun: Hendrickson Spinner: Red Quill	April 23	2:00 to 4:00 P.M. Spinner: 3:00 to 8:00 P.M.	12–16
Leptophlebia cupida (mayfly) Dun: Black Quill Spinner: Early Brown Spinner	April 25	2:00 to 4:00 P.M. Spinner: 1:00 to 6:00 P.M.	12 or 14
Chimarra atterima (caddisfly) Little Black Caddis	April 26	11:00 A.M. to 6:00 P.M.	16 or 18
Psilotreta species (caddisfly) Tan Caddis	April 26	Morning and afternoon	14
Isoperla signata (stonefly) Light Stonefly	May 8	Afternoon	12 or 14
Ephemerella rotunda (mayfly) Dun: Pale Evening Dun Spinner: Pale Evening Spinner	May 10	2:00 to 8:00 P.M. Spinner: 6:00 to 8:00 P.M.	14 or 16
Pseudocloeon species (mayfly) Dun: Blue Dun Spinner: Rusty Spinner	May 10	Afternoon and evening	20

Hatch and match	Emergence date (dates are only rough guides and should not be followed rigidly)	Time of day for Dun and Spinner	Hook size
Rhyacophila lobifera (caddisfly) Green Caddis	May 10	4:00 to 9:00 P.M.; caddisfly appears later (around dusk) in June and July	14
Baetis flavistriga (mayfly) Dun: Little Blue-Winged Olive Dun Spinner: Rusty Spinner	May 10	Morning Evening	20
Brachycentrus numerosus (caddisfly) Grannom	May 10	3:00 to 7:00 P.M.	12
Stenonema fuscum (mayfly) Dun: Gray Fox Spinner: Ginger Quill Spinner	May 15	Dun emerges sporadically throughout chance of heaviest hatches 4:00 to 8:30 P.M. Spinner: 7:00 to 8:30 P.M.	12
Baetis quebecensis (mayfly) Dun: Little Blue-Winged Olive Dun Spinner: Rusty Spinner	May 15	Morning Evening	20
Ephemerella septentrionalis (mayfly) Dun: Pale Evening Dun Spinner: Pale Evening Spinner	May 18	8:00 P.M.	14 or 16
Leucrocuta (Heptagenia) aphrodite (mayfly) Dun: Pale Evening Dun Spinner: Pale Evening Dun	May 18	8:00 P.M.	16
Ephemerella invaria (mayfly) Dun: Pale Evening Dun Spinner: Pale Evening Spinner	May 20	3:00 to 8:00 P.M. Spinner: 7:00 to 8:30 P.M.	16 or 18

Hatch and match	Emergence date (dates are only rough guides and should not be followed rigidly)	Time of day for Dun and Spinner	Hook size
Stenonema vicarium (mayfly) Dun: American March Brown Spinner: Great Red Spinner	May 20	10:00 A.M. to 7:00 P.M. Spinner: 8:00 P.M.	12
Symphitopsyche slossanae (caddisfly) Spotted Sedge	May 23	1:00 to 6:00 P.M.	14 or 16
Eurylophella (Ephemerella) bicolor (mayfly) Dun: Chocolate Dun Spinner: Chocolate Spinner	May 25	Late morning and early afternoon	16
Siphlonurus quebecensis (mayfly) Dun: Gray Drake Spinner: Brown Quill Spinner	May 25	Evening	14
Stenonema ithaca (mayfly) Dun: Light Cahill Spinner: Light Cahill	May 25	Evening	12 or 14
Isonychia sadleri (mayfly) Dun: Slate Drake Spinner: White-Gloved Howdy	May 25	Evening	12
Epeorus vitreus (mayfly) Male dun: Light Cahill Female dun: Pink Cahill Spinner: Salmon Spinner	May 25	Evening	14
Stenacron interpunctatum interpunctatum (mayfly) Dun: Light Cahill Spinner: Light Cahill	May 25	Evening	14

Hatch and match	Emergence date (dates are only rough guides and should not be followed rigidly)	Time of day for Dun and Spinner	Hook size
Stenacron interpunctatum canadense (mayfly) Dun: Light Cahill Spinner: Light Cahill	May 25	Sporadic during day but mainly 6:00 to 8:30 P.M. Spinner: 7:00 P.M. to 9:00 P.M.	12 or 14
Litobrancha recurvata (mayfly) Dun: Dark Green Drake Spinner: Brown Drake	May 25	1:00 to 8:00 P.M. Spinner: 7:00 P.M.	8 or 10
Ephemera simulans (mayfly) Dun: Brown Drake Spinner: Brown Drake	May 25	8:00 P.M.	10 or 12
Ephemera guttulata (mayfly) Dun: Green Drake Spinner: Coffin Fly	May 25	8:00 P.M.	8 or 10
Stenonema modestum (mayfly) Dun: Cream Cahill Spinner: Cream Cahill Spinner	May 25	Evening	14 or 16
Drunella (Ephemerella) cornuta (mayfly) Dun: Blue-Winged Olive Dun Spinner: Dark Olive Spinner	May 25	Sporadic during day. Morning with a possible spurt at 11:00 A.M. to 12:00 N. Spinner: 7:00 to 9:00 P.M.	14
Isonychia bicolor (mayfly) Dun: Slate Drake Spinner: White-Gloved Howdy	May 30	Sporadic, but mainly 7:00 P.M. Spinner: 8:00 P.M.	12
Ephemerella needhami (mayfly) Dun: Chocolate Dun Spinner: Chocolate Spinner	May 30	Afternoon (early) and morning (late). Spinner: afternoon and evening	14 or 16

Hatch and match	Emergence date (dates are only rough guides and should not be followed rigidly)	Time of day for Dun and Spinner	Hook size
Agnetina capitata (stonefly) Perlid Stonefly	June 1	Evening	12
Ephemerella dorothea (mayfly) Dun: Pale Evening Dun Spinner: Pale Evening Dun	June 1	8:00 P.M.	16 or 18
Serratella (Ephemerella) deficiens (mayfly) Dun: Dark Blue Quill Spinner: Dark Brown Spinner	June 1	Evening	20
Paraleptophlebia mollis (mayfly) Dun: Dark Blue Quill Male spinner: Jenny Spinner Female spinner: Dark Brown Spinner	June 3	10:00 A.M. to 4:00 P.M.	18
Hexagenia limbata (mayfly) Dun: Michigan Caddis or Great Olive-Winged Drake Spinner: Great Olive-Winged Spinner	June 5	Dusk to dark	6 or 8
Paraleptophlebia strigula (mayfly) Dun: Dark Blue Quill Male spinner: Jenny Spinner Female spinner: Dark Brown Spinner	June 5	Early morning to midafternoon	18 or 20
Attenella (Ephemerella) attenuata (mayfly) Dun: Blue-Winged Olive Dun Spinner: Dark Olive Spinner	June 5	Sporadic during day, often with a heavy burst at 11:00 A.M.	14 or 16
Isoperla bilineata (stonefly) Yellow Stonefly	June 5	Morning and afternoon	14

Hatch and match	Emergence date (dates are only rough guides and should not be followed rigidly)	Time of day for Dun and Spinner	Hook size
Alloperla imbecilla (stonefly) Little Green Stonefly	June 5	Morning and afternoon	16
Psilotreta frontalis (caddisfly) Dark Blue Sedge	June 8	8:00 P.M.	12
Leptophlebia johnsoni (mayfly) Dun: Iron Blue Dun Male spinner: Jenny Spinner Female spinner: Blue Quill Spinner	June 9	11:00 A.M. Spinner: evening	14 or 16
Dannella (Ephemerella) lata (mayfly) Dun: Blue-Winged Olive Dun Spinner: Dark Olive Spinner	June 12	Morning and afternoon	16
Serratella (Ephemerella) simplex (mayfly) Dun: Blue-Winged Olive Dun Spinner: Dark Olive Spinner	June 15	Morning (sometimes afternoon) Spinner: evening	20
Baetis brunneicolor (mayfly) Dun: Little Blue-Winged Olive Dun Spinner: Rusty Spinner	June 15	Morning and afternoon Evening	18 or 20
Stenacron interpunctatum heterotarsale (mayfly) Dun: Light Cahill Spinner: Light Cahill	June 15	Evening	14
Heptagenia marginalis (mayfly) Dun: Light Cahill Spinner: Olive Cahill Spinner	June 15	8:00 P.M.	12

Hatch and match	Emergence date (dates are only rough guides and should not be followed rigidly)	Time of day for Dun and Spinner	Hook size
Stenonema pulchellum (mayfly) Dun: Cream Cahill Spinner: Cream Cahill Spinner	June 15	Sporadic, from midday to evening. Spinner: evening	12 or 14
Siphlonurus alternatus (mayfly) Dun: Gray Drake Spinner: Brown Quill Spinner	June 15	Morning and afternoon	10
Ephemera varia (mayfly) Dun: Yellow Drake Spinner: Yellow Drake	June 22	8:00 to 9:15 P.M.	10 or 12
Leucrocuta (Heptagenia) hebe (mayfly) Dun: Pale Evening Dun Spinner: Pale Evening Dun	June 22	8:00 P.M.	16
Paraleptophlebia guttata (mayfly) Dun: Dark Blue Quill Male spinner: Jenny Spinner Female spinner: Dark Brown Spinner	June 25	Sporadic during day. Spinner: morning and afternoon	18
Anthopotamus (Potamanthus) distinctus (mayfly) Dun: Golden Drake Spinner: Golden Spinner	June 25	9:00 P.M.	12
Tricorythodes stygiatus (mayfly) Dun: Pale Olive Dun Female spinner: Reverse Jenny Spinner or Trico Spinner Male spinner: Dark Brown Spinner	July 23	7:00 to 9:00 A.M. Spinner: 8:00 to 11:00 A.M.	24

Hatch and match	Emergence date (dates are only rough guides and should not be followed rigidly)	Time of day for Dun and Spinner	Hook size
Tricorythodes atratus (mayfly) Dun: Pale Olive Dun Male spinner: Dark Brown Spinner Female spinner: Reverse Jenny Spinner or Trico Spinner	July 23	7:00 to 9:00 A.M. Spinner: 8:00 A.M.	24
Caenis species (mayfly) Dun: Little White Mayfly Spinner: Little White Spinner	July 15	Evening	26
Isonychia harperi (mayfly) Dun: Slate Drake Spinner: White-Gloved Howdy	July 20	Sporadic during day, but mainly 7:00 P.M.	12
Acerpenna (Baetis) pygmaea (mayfly) Dun: Little Blue-Winged Olive Dun Spinner: Rusty Spinner	August 1	Morning and afternoon	22
Ephoron leukon (mayfly) Dun: White Mayfly Spinner: White Mayfly	August 15	7:00 P.M.	12–16
Ephoron album (mayfly) Dun: White Mayfly Spinner: White Mayfly	August 15	Evening	12
Hexagenia atrocaudata (mayfly) Dun: Big Slate Drake Spinner: Dark Rusty Spinner	August 18	8:00 P.M. Spinner: 6:00 to 7:00 P.M.	6 or 8

Western Hatches

Hatch and match	Emergence date (dates are only rough guides and should not be followed rigidly)	Time of day for Dun and Spinner	Hook size
Rhithrogena morrisoni (mayfly) Dun: Western March Brown Spinner: Dark Tan Spinner	February 25	Afternoon	14
Baetis tricaudatus (mayfly) Dun: Little Blue-Winged Olive Dun Spinner: Light Rusty Spinner	March through October	Morning and afternoon[1] Spinner: early morning and evening	16–20
Baetis intermedius (mayfly) Dun: Little Blue-Winged Olive Dun Spinner: Dark Rusty Spinner	April through October	Morning and afternoon. Spinner: early morning and evening	18 or 20
Skwala parallela (stonefly) Olive Stonefly	April 5	Afternoon	10 or 12
Strophopteryx occidentalis (stonefly) Early Brown Stonefly	May 1	Afternoon	14
Brachycentrus occidentalis (caddisfly) Grannom	May 10	Morning and afternoon	12–16
Pteronarcys californica (stonefly) Salmon Fly	May 20	Emergence often occurs in the morning; egg laying can occur almost any time of the day	4
Rhyacophila bifila (caddisfly) Green Sedge	May 20	Afternoon and evening	12 or 14
Ephemerella inermis[2] (mayfly) Dun: Pale Morning Dun Spinner: Pale Morning Spinner	May 25	Morning, afternoon, and evening. Spinner: morning and evening	16 or 18

Hatch and match	Emergence date (dates are only rough guides and should not be followed rigidly)	Time of day for Dun and Spinner	Hook size
Baetis bicaudatus (mayfly) Dun: Pale Olive Dun Spinner: Light Rusty Spinner	June through October	Morning and afternoon. Spinner: morning and evening	20
Calineuria californica (stonefly) Golden Stonefly	June through September	Afternoon	6
Hesperoperla pacifica (stonefly) Willow Fly	June and July	Variable	6
Callibaetis americanus[1,2] (was *C. nigritus* and *C. coloradensis*) (mayfly) Dun: Speckle-Winged Dun Spinner: Speckle-Winged Spinner	May through September	Late morning	14 or 16
Cinygmula ramaleyi (mayfly) Dun: Dark Red Quill Spinner: Red Quill Spinner	May 25	Late morning. Spinner: midday	16
Drunella (Ephemerella) grandis (mayfly) Dun: Western Green Drake Spinner: Great Red Spinner	May 25	Late morning and afternoon. Spinner: evening	2
Paraleptophlebia heteronea (mayfly) Dun: Blue Quill Spinner: Dark Brown Spinner	June 1	Morning and afternoon	3
Isoperla species (stonefly) Little Yellow Stonefly	June 5	Afternoon	14 or 16
Arctopsyche grandis (caddisfly) Dark Brown Caddis	June 5	Morning and afternoon	14

Hatch and match	Emergence date (dates are only rough guides and should not be followed rigidly)	Time of day for Dun and Spinner	Hook size
Serratella (Ephemerella) tibialis (mayfly) Dun: Red Quill Spinner: White-Gloved Howdy	June 5	Midday Spinner: evening	16 or 18
Ephemera simulans (mayfly) Dun: Brown Drake Spinner: Brown Drake	June 10	Evening	10
Hydropsyche cockerellia and H. occidentalis (caddisfly) Spotted (Tan) Sedge	June 12	Evening	12 or 14
Hexagenia limbata (mayfly) Dun: Michigan Caddis or Great Olive-Winged Drake Spinner: Great Olive-Winged Spinner	June 12	Dusk and later	8
Epeorus longimanus (mayfly) Dun: Quill Gordon Spinner: Red Quill Spinner	June 12	Late morning and afternoon	12 or 14
Drunella (Ephemerella) doddsi (mayfly) Dun: Western Green Drake Spinner: Great Red Spinner	June 15	Late morning and afternoon	12
Drunella (Ephemerella) flavilinea (mayfly) Dun: Blue-Winged Olive Dun Spinner: Dark Olive Spinner	June 15	Morning and evening (heaviest hatches seem to appear in the evening)	14 or 16
Alloperla species (stonefly) Little Olive Stonefly	June 15	Afternoon	14

Hatch and match	Emergence date (dates are only rough guides and should not be followed rigidly)	Time of day for Dun and Spinner	Hook size
Heptagenia elegantula (mayfly) Dun: Pale Evening Dun Spinner: Pale Evening Spinner	June 20	Late afternoon and evening. Spinner: evening	14
Diphetor (Baetis) hageni (mayfly) Dun: Dark Brown Dun Spinner: Dark Brown Spinner	June 20	Late morning, afternoon, and early evening. Spinner: early morning and evening	20
Ephemera compar (mayfly) Dun: March Brown or Brown Drake Spinner: March Brown Spinner	July 1	Evening	10
Cheumatopsyche campyla (caddisfly) Little Sister Sedge	July 1	Evening	14 or 16
Ephemerella infrequens[2] (mayfly) Dun: Pale Morning Dun Spinner: Rusty Spinner	July 1	Late morning and afternoon. Spinner: morning and evening	18
Paraleptophlebia memorialis (mayfly) Dun: Dark Blue Quill Spinner: Dark Brown Spinner	July 1	Morning and afternoon	18
Rhithrogena futilis (mayfly) Dun: Quill Gordon Spinner: Quill Gordon	July 1	Late morning and afternoon. Spinner: evening	12
Cinygmula reticulata (mayfly) Dun: Pale Brown Dun Spinner: Dark Rusty Spinner	July 5	Late morning and afternoon. Spinner: early morning	14
Paraleptophlebia vaciva (mayfly) Dun: Dark Blue Quill Spinner: Dark Brown Spinner	July 5	Morning and afternoon	18

Hatch and match	Emergence date (dates are only rough guides and should not be followed rigidly)	Time of day for Dun and Spinner	Hook size
Heptagenia solitaria (mayfly) Dun: Gray Fox Spinner: Ginger Quill Spinner	July 5	Late afternoon and evening. Spinner: late morning and evening	12 or 16
Epeorus albertae (mayfly) Dun: Pink Lady Spinner: Salmon Spinner	July 5	Evening	12
Paraleptophlebia debilis (mayfly) Dun: Dark Blue Quill Spinner: Dark Brown Spinner	July 5	Morning and afternoon	18
Siphlonurus occidentalis (mayfly) Dun: Gray Drake Spinner: Gray Drake Quill Spinner	July 5	Late morning and afternoon; heaviest appear around 3:00 P.M. Spinner: morning and evening; evening seems to be heavier	10 or 12
Cinygma dimicki (mayfly) Dun: Light Cahill Spinner: Light Cahill	July 5	Evening	12
Timpanoga (Ephemerella) hecuba (mayfly) Dun: Great Red Quill Spinner: Great Brown Spinner	July 5	Afternoon	10
Rhithrogena hageni (mayfly) Dun: Pale Brown Dun Spinner: Dark Tan Spinner	July 10	Late morning and afternoon. Spinner: morning and evening	12 or 14
Ameletus cooki (mayfly) Dun: Dark Brown Dun Spinner: Dark Brown Spinner	July 10	Late morning and afternoon	14

Hatch and match	Emergence date (dates are only rough guides and should not be followed rigidly)	Time of day for Dun and Spinner	Hook size
Rhithrogena undulata (mayfly) Dun: Quill Gordon Spinner: Red Quill or Dark Red Quill	July 10	Morning and afternoon. Spinner: afternoon and evening	12
Tricorythodes minutus (mayfly) Dun: Pale Olive Dun Male spinner: Reverse Jenny Spinner or Trico Spinner Female spinner: Dark Brown Spinner	July 15	Morning	24
Pseudocloeon edmundsi[2] (mayfly) Dun: Blue Dun Spinner: Rusty Spinner	August 1	Evening	20
Drunella (Ephemerella) coloradensis (mayfly) Dun: Dark Olive Dun or Autumn Green Drake Spinner: Dark Brown Spinner	August 1	Midday Spinner: evening	12
Ephoron album (mayfly) Dun: White Mayfly Spinner: White Mayfly	August 15	Evening	12
Paraleptophlebia bicornuta (mayfly) Dun: Dark Blue Quill Spinner: Dark Brown Spinner	September 10	Morning and afternoon	18
Dicosmoecus jucundus (caddisfly) October Caddis	September 10	Late morning, afternoon, and early evening	12

[1] More than one hatch per year
[2] Color of species varies considerably

MATCHING THE FLOWER

The brown drake once appeared by the thousands on Pine Creek in north-central Pennsylvania. Charles Meck anticipated this great hatch each and every year around the end of May. More than most other mayflies, however, there's an obstacle to fishing this profuse hatch – it usually appears on the water for four or fewer days. By the time Charles heard that the hatch was on, it had disappeared for another year. Soon he noted that the height of the brown drake hatch on Pine Creek occurred when the rhododendron and peony in his backyard were in full bloom. Several years later, on Henry's Fork in Idaho, he noted the brown drake appearing on this productive river when peonies bloomed near Island Park, Idaho.

Charles began to make some additional observations. The quill gordon emerged when forsythia located near the stream just began to flower. The hendrickson appeared on the surface when the forsythia was in full bloom.

Entomologists recognize this phenomenon called plant phenology. They make pest management decisions based upon a comparison of insect and plant development. For example, entomologists know that a pest of turf is first susceptible to control when black locust is just starting to bloom. A second time when this same pest species is susceptible to management occurs when rose of sharon is in first bloom.

How is this information useful to you as a fly fisherman? By recognizing plants or flowers along your favorite river or the one you plan to fly fish, you too can take advantage of phenology. We've included a chart of some of the more important hatches for your reference so that you can get started. Within a couple years you will be able to adapt these to observations you make on your own favorite trout fisheries.

East and Midwest

Common name	Species	Flowers appearing when the hatch appears
Quill Gordon	*Epeorus pleuralis*	Forsythia just opening
Blue Quill	*Paraleptophlebia adoptiva*	Forsythia just opening
Hendrickson	*Ephemerella subvaria*	Forsythia in full bloom
Sulphur	*Ephemerella rotunda*	Lilac in first bloom
Gray Fox	*Stenonema fuscum*	Dame's rocket just opening
Green Drake	*Ephemera guttulata*	Black locust in full bloom
Slate Drake	*Isonychia bicolor*	Oxeye daisy first bloom
Yellow Drake	*Ephemera varia*	Chickory and elderberry first bloom
Trico	*Tricorythodes atratus*	Queen Anne's lace first blooming or spotted knapweed just opening
White Fly	*Ephoron leukon*	New England aster just opening

West

Pale Morning Dun	*Ephemerella inermis*	Lilac in full bloom
Western Green Drake	*Drunella grandis*	Lilac well past full bloom Black locust just past full bloom
Salmon Fly	*Pteronarcys californica*	Lilac just past full bloom
Trico	*Tricorythodes minutus*	Baby's breath just opening

Remember, emergence can vary widely from river to river even within the same state. Use these emergence charts to better understand the sequence of hatches around you.

3

A Closer Look at Some of the Great Hatches

Ed Gunnett of Williamsburg, Pennsylvania, called on August 27. The white mayfly hatch on the Little Juniata River had begun in the Petersburg area. Ed, Danny Deters, and hundreds of other locals look forward to this last great hatch of the season in the East. For the past several years Charles has spent hours at the river researching the white mayfly. After several years he has deduced that on average the white mayfly on the Little Juniata emerges in fishable numbers at a specific location for twelve nights (Figure 1). The projection held up again this year, and Ed and I met and fished the hatch until September 8.

Three weeks later and 2,000 miles west, Mike Manfredo, Don Rodriguez, and Charles stood on a cliff 2,000 feet above the canyon rimming the North Fork of the Cache la Poudre River in northern Colorado. The early-morning sun had not yet reached the valley floor below. Charles had convinced the other two that they should meet at the canyon early so they might see a hatch on this mid-September morning. After forty minutes hiking down the winding, narrow trail, the group arrived at the Poudre. Guess what? In front of them and 20 feet above the surface thousands of tricos formed a mating swarm over the river. That day they fished a hatch that few others knew about.

Mike headed upriver and began casting to some heavy browns

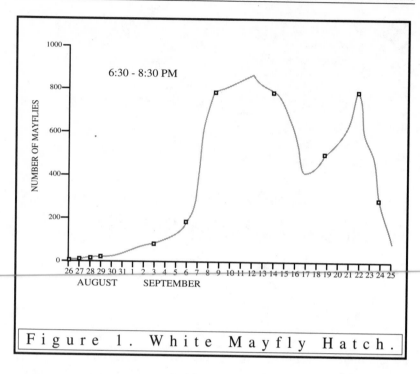

Figure 1. White Mayfly Hatch.

with a Wulff Royal Coachman, but after a few frustrating minutes casting that attractor over rising trout he switched to a pattern copying the trico. He quickly landed four browns on the pattern while the naturals still floated past him.

The next morning Mike, Craig Shuman, and Charles planned to fish the main stem of the Cache la Poudre downriver about 10 miles. Again Charles suggested that they arrive at the river early – around 8:00 A.M. – so they could see if it also held a trico hatch. By the time the trio arrived, there were already hundreds of spinners in the air above the river, and they got into position for the expected spinner fall. Soon Mike called Charles downriver to fly fish over a pod of about a dozen trout feeding on tricos, and they picked up four trout before the hatch waned. The group didn't see one other person on the river that day enjoying the rewards of fishing the hatches.

What do these examples prove? They show that any fly fisherman who knows more details about the traits of specific hatches should be able to meet more hatches and catch more trout. If you know that the white fly appears in a certain area for twelve days, you can make your fishing plans accordingly.

If you fly fish for a long period in all parts of the United States, you'll find nearly three hundred species of mayflies, four hundred species of stoneflies, and one thousand species of caddisflies. That's a total of seventeen hundred different aquatic insect species that can cause trout to feed. Add to that the spinners of the mayflies, crane flies, midges, other aquatic or semiaquatic insects, and crustaceans, olive tannish trailing Z-lon shuck tied over the tail, and we both began and you can see that you have an impossible number of sizes, shapes, and colors to copy.

If you've ever fished often spectacular hatches like the western green drake, green drake, brown drake, Michigan caddis (or *Hexagenia limbata*), hendrickson, white fly, sulphur, or pale morning dun, you'll never forget them. Then there are dozens of other hatches that on a cold, miserable day develop into great hatches as a result of the weather. (You'll read more about these inclement weather hatches in chapter 7.) In this chapter we'll examine some of the major hatches across the United States and where you can find them. We'll even examine a chironomid hatch on a western river.

As in chapters 4 through 6, the responsibilities here have been divided up. Charles Meck describes the *Tricorythodes*, white fly, sulphur, western green drake, little blue-winged olive dun, gray fox, pale morning dun, western march brown, chironomid, specklewing, and salmon fly. Greg Hoover writes about the march brown, green drake, and *Hexagenia limbata*.

When Charles Meck speaks at Trout Unlimited and Fly Fishers Federation banquets, he often starts these talks with a quiz on recent scientific findings that have significance for fly fishermen. Studies on the tricos, white mayfly (*Ephoron* species), slate drake (*Isonychia*), green drake, and many other mayflies have appeared in scientific literature in recent years. Many of these findings have importance for fly fishermen, and included here is some of the latest information. With the knowledge from these studies, you will be better able to fish the hatches and see rising trout.

TRICOS *(TRICORYTHODES)*

After years of fishing I'm convinced that two or three trico species are extremely common throughout the United States. Whether you fish on East Coast streams and rivers like the Delaware or the Beaverkill, the Au Sable in the Midwest, the Cache la Poudre in the Rockies, or the McKenzie River or Rocky Ford Creek in the Far West, you'll see heavy trico hatches. I've seen these small insects on small, foot-wide streams like Mail Creek in Fort Collins, Colorado, and huge rivers like the Missouri in Montana.

George Harvey has studied tricos on Falling Springs Branch Creek in south-central Pennsylvania since 1927 and has spent hours watching the duns emerge, the mating flight, and the spinner fall. He tied his first female trico dun copy in 1932. When the hatch began, George switched to a pale olive dun to match the emerging imagoes. An hour later when the female spinners fell onto the water after laying their eggs, he matched the female. Finally, near the end of the spinner fall some males fell onto the surface, and he matched the dark brown spinner. George did exceptionally well when the trico appeared on Falling Springs Branch Creek. Few other fly fishermen in 1932 bothered with this small hatch.

More recently, with the fly-fishing season extended well into fall in most states, many anglers have begun fishing to trico hatches. Why bother matching this diminutive mayfly? First, it's a challenge to catch trout on a #24 fly, but it's also an effective method. George Harvey can tell about days when he's caught more than fifty trout during a hatch of tricos. Hit a stream or river with a heavy hatch and you can find pods of a dozen or more trout feeding on the spent spinners.

For the past fifteen years George has fished the tremendous trico hatch and spinner fall on Spruce Creek in central Pennsylvania almost daily. After more than sixty years of observation, George has some important and fascinating theories on the trico. In 1978 Ronald Hall received his doctorate from the University of Minnesota. His dissertation centered around one mayfly species: *Tricorythodes atratus*. What follows is a combination of George's sightings, the results of Dr. Hall's studies, and my own observations.

Life Cycle

Ron Hall's study found that *Tricorythodes atratus* on the upper Mississippi River has the following typical life cycle (Figure 2). Male duns emerge on July 20, usually from 10:00 P.M. to 2:00 A.M., and transform into spinners around 4:30 A.M. Female duns emerge on July 21 from 4:30 A.M. to 9:00 A.M. and change into spinners within a few minutes after they emerge. They then enter the mating swarm. The male spinners form a mating swarm over riffles in sections where the stream has little overhead canopy. You'll find mostly males at the top of the swarm, females and males in the middle, and mated females with egg sacs in the lower third of the swarm. The mated female spinners leave the swarm and look for a place to deposit their eggs.

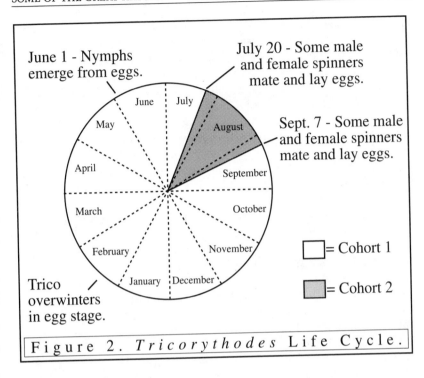

June 1 - Nymphs emerge from eggs.

July 20 - Some male and female spinners mate and lay eggs.

Sept. 7 - Some male and female spinners mate and lay eggs.

Trico overwinters in egg stage.

☐ = Cohort 1

▨ = Cohort 2

Figure 2. *Tricorythodes* Life Cycle.

They land on the surface and drop dark olive egg sacs, which have from 150 to 600 eggs each in them, with a good average being about 470.

You can predict fairly accurately when female spinners will start falling onto the surface by studying the swarm. If you don't find any female spinners with egg sacs in the lower third of the swarm, it will be a while until the first female falls. If you see a few female spinners, the fall should occur within a half hour. If you see thousands of fertilized females with some moving away from the swarm, then the fall will begin momentarily.

For the major part of the spinner fall you'll see female spinners on the water. Then you'll see female and male spinners in equal numbers for a while. Toward the end of the spinner fall you'll find mostly male spinners on the water.

The eggs change into nymphs within a few days. The nymphs grow quickly, and to accommodate this rapid enlargement, they shed their nymphal skin through a series of instars (a period of growth between the shedding of nymphal or larval skins). Forty-nine days later, around September 7, male duns emerge at night and female duns at dawn. These duns are considered the second generation, or cohort 2. Anglers often find that this second generation is not quite as large as cohort 1. On the South Platte River in Colorado cohort 1 can be matched with a #18–20 imitation. When matching the size of cohort 2, anglers find they have to use a #22 or #24.

This second cohort of female spinners lays eggs. These eggs don't develop into nymphs like the first batch but, rather, go into diapause (a period of physiological dormancy between periods of activity) until next year. Tricos overwinter in the egg stage on many streams and rivers in the United States, so you won't find trico nymphs in these waters. Around the beginning of June these eggs develop into nymphs and the cycle begins again.

The first cohort of tricos usually appears from early July until late August, and the second generation emerges from mid-August until late October. The two generations overlap to some extent.

How does this information help the fly fisher? How does it improve your chances to catch more trout? First, you wouldn't use a trico nymph during winter or spring because you won't find the natural on most streams and rivers. Second, you would almost never use the imitation of a male trico dun, since they emerge from 10:00 P.M. to 2:00 A.M. Third, once you study the mating swarm, you know when the spinner fall will occur. Fourth, when the spinner fall occurs, you'll automatically use an imitation of the female spinner first, then toward the end of the fall you'll change over to the male spinner.

Where will you find some of the best trico hatches? Probably the heaviest hatch in the United States occurs on the Missouri River near Craig, Montana, and on the South Platte River in central Colorado. Other spectacular trico hatches appear on the North Platte in Wyoming, the North Branch of the Au Sable in Michigan, Mossy Creek in Virginia, Falling Springs in Pennsylvania, the West Branch of the Ausable in New York, and hundreds of other streams and rivers in the United States.

One of the most memorable hatches for me occurred on the South Platte River in Colorado, just below Spinney Reservoir. Phil Camera wanted us to be on the river, ready to fish the hatch, at 7:30 A.M., but we arrived an hour late. Cloudy skies and a cool mid-August morning saved us by delaying the hatch. Duns covered the water as we waded into the winding river, and trout fed freely on the small emergers. I tied on a conventional dun pattern, and in a half hour of casting over feeding fish I couldn't hook even one of the browns or rainbows. Fishing pressure is extremely heavy on the South Platte–anglers filled almost every available spot on the river to fish the hatch. Trout under these circumstances get exceedingly leader shy and carefully inspect every artificial before they strike. Phil says that the trout in the South Platte during a trico hatch count the number of tails on a pattern.

Phil and I tied on #20 Crystal Compara-dun Tricos, which have an to catch trout – trout that had just refused the conventional pattern. (See chapter 8 for tying directions on this pattern.)

Duns continued to appear for almost two hours. Not until 10:30 A.M. did the spinners begin to fall to the surface. I tied on a #20 male Trico Spinner and cast to a pod of a half dozen risers, each slowly scooping the surface and in one gulp taking in maybe a dozen spent spinners. I also tied on a 4-foot piece of 6X tippet to help prevent immediate drag. On maybe the fourth or fifth perfect drift one of the heavy trout slowly sucked in the artificial. I hooked maybe one in five of the strikes – the small hook gave way in the other four.

At noon the spinner fall finally quit and only a few heavy trout took scattered trico spinners.

Fishing the trico hatch and spinner fall on the South Platte taught me several lessons. First, on rivers with heavy hatches, get there early and fish the dun emergence. When fishing over emerging trico duns, try a Sparkle Trico Compara-dun or a parachute pattern with a trailing shuck. When fishing the hatch or spinner fall in very slow water, use a long, fine tippet, preferably 6X or smaller. Finally, don't give up if a fish refuses the pattern. Try several times with drag-free floats before moving to another trout.

Some Rivers with Trico Hatches

McKenzie River – Oregon

Deschutes River – Oregon

Rocky Ford Creek – Washington

Yakima River – Washington

Williamson River – Oregon

South Platte River – Colorado

Green River – Utah

Big Wood River (spotty) – Idaho

Henry's Fork – Idaho

Silver Creek – Idaho

Bitterroot River – Montana

Missouri River – Montana

Bighorn River – Montana

Bighorn River – Wyoming

Madison River – Montana

Yellowstone River – Montana

Smith River – Montana

North Platte River – Wyoming

Fishing Creek – Pennsylvania

Spring Creek – Pennsylvania

Little Juniata River (spotty) – Pennsylvania

Penns Creek – Pennsylvania

Yellow Breeches Creek – Pennsylvania

Beaverkill River – New York

Delaware River – New York

Mossy Creek – Virginia

Au Sable River – Michigan

Manistee River – Michigan

North Fork of the White River – Missouri

Fall River – California

Hat Creek – California

THE WHITE MAYFLY

Why include the white mayfly (*Ephoron leukon* and *E. album*) in a book on trout fishing? Doesn't this mayfly particularly inhabit warm rivers with smallmouth bass? Sure, you'll find this insect on many of the major rivers, like the Potomac, Susquehanna, Delaware, Youghiogheny, Allegheny, and White in the East, but what about trout waters? J. W. Leonard and F. A. Leonard, in *Mayflies of Michigan Trout Streams*, mention *Ephoron* briefly, saying that these mayflies "occur in warm waters of southern Michigan."

For years I also thought that these mayflies only frequented warm bass waters. Then, ten years ago Ed Koch and Ed Shenk wrote about a great hatch of white mayflies they had found on Yellow Breeches Creek in south-central Pennsylvania. Other fly fishermen found the same hatch on the Housatonic River in Connecticut. While completing *Pennsylvania Trout Streams and Their Hatches*, Charles Meck found the same hatch on Oil, Muddy, and Yellow creeks and on the Delaware and Little Juniata rivers—all bona fide trout waters.

Now that we know that the white mayfly appears on some trout waters, let's look at some of the characteristics of the hatch. Eggs are laid by the female dun in late August or early September. The female doesn't change from dun to spinner but lays its eggs as a mated dun. The male does not change from dun to spinner on the wing. Often you'll see male spinners carrying their pellicle (skin of the dun) still attached behind them. Seldom do these mayflies fly more than a few feet above the surface of the water. Males appear first and move up and downstream a foot or two above the surface searching for females. When the females appear, the males mate with them. The females then move to the surface to lay their eggs.

The white mayfly overwinters in the egg stage, and the fertilized eggs of this burrowing species don't hatch until May of the following year. This might easily account for the lack of a fishable hatch for some years on some streams. If the river or stream experiences high winter floods, many of the eggs might be washed miles downriver, thus losing the hatch on the upper part.

Nymphs appear when the water temperature reaches middle to high fifties in May. Nymphs burrow, feed, and grow, shedding their outer skin many times (instars) and continuing to grow until they emerge in late summer.

The tan nymph emerges from its burrow from 6:30 P.M. to 9:30 P.M., and trout often actively chase the nymph as it emerges. Trout also often come completely out of the water for the low-flying duns and spinners that fly inches above the surface. The nymph rises rapidly to the surface, changes into a dun almost immediately, and the dun quickly lifts off from the surface. The legs of the dun are atrophied (male front legs are an exception), so the dun will fall over if it can't take flight promptly. The emergence of the white mayfly is a continuous process of the nymph shedding its skin and the dun flying from the surface. Often you'll see trout that had followed the nymph to the surface coming out of the water after the insect.

With the action fast and furious during a hatch, you often don't know whether to use a pattern copying the nymph, the emerger, or the dun. When I get frustrated, I tie on a special rig. I tie a weighted nymph onto the tippet, an emerger pattern onto the first dropper, and a dry fly onto the second dropper. I call this way of fishing frustrating hatches "the cycle." When you use the cycle method, you've effectively copied all the important food phases and should quickly be able to determine what the trout are feeding on.

In Pennsylvania the hatch first appears on the Susquehanna River near Harrisburg around the middle of July. It reaches the Juniata River at Lewistown around the middle of August and the Little Juniata River by the last week in August. Duns first appear around 7:00 P.M. and on warm nights can continue well after dark. Often trout will delay feeding on the surface flies until it's almost dark.

Try the bi-cycle setup discussed in chapter 8. Tie a #16 White Fly nearest the rod and a #14 tan nymph on the tippet. Tie the nymph to the bend of the hook of the dry fly with an improved clinch knot.

Some Rivers with White Mayfly Hatches

Little Juniata River – Pennsylvania

Yellow Breeches Creek – Pennsylvania

Delaware River – New York

Housatonic River – Connecticut

Farmington River – Connecticut

North Platte River – Wyoming

Yellowstone River – Montana

Au Sable River – Michigan

Namekagon River – Wisconsin

THE MARCH BROWN

Recently, Sam Bricker, Bill Palmer, Paul Rebarchak, and I experienced and fished an excellent march brown spinner fall. We had arrived on Penns Creek near Coburn, Pennsylvania, early one evening in mid-May. Small trout were surfacing to #16 tan caddisflies as we approached. I managed to land and release two wild browns on a #16 Elkhair Caddis imitation. Paul and Bill decided to fish nymphs in some heavy riffles and runs while Sam and I fished dry flies in the water below. The water was quite low for that time in Pennsylvania's trout season. I studied the water, and all of a sudden a large, brown silhouette slid past me in about 3 feet of water. My heart raced with the hope that it was a monster brown trout. Would this be the chance at a huge fish in the diminishing light? A closer examination revealed that this underwater form had a tail, but the tail was oriented horizontally, opposite that of a fish. At that point I knew I was looking at a beaver, not a trout!

At 8:12 P.M. march brown spinners began to alight on the water. Soon after, the flow of water was interrupted by many rising trout, and Sam and I took fish on March Brown Polywing Spinners. Later that evening all four of us got together to compare notes. Paul stated that the spinners fell in the area where he and Bill were fishing at 8:14 P.M. During our time on Penns Creek, not one of us had observed any march brown duns on the wing. That night proved to be the best fishing that Paul has ever had on Penns Creek. He fought the urge to fish on top and did very well with his nymphal imitation of the march brown. In fact, it was an unforgettable trip for all of us.

The widely distributed march brown, *Stenonema vicarium*, may be one of the most common mayflies on trout waters in the East and Midwest. It is known to occur from southern Canada to the mountain rivers of North Carolina. Generally speaking, hatches in the southern mountains can occur in early May and can taper off until Memorial Day. In Pennsylvania hatches usually begin early to mid-May and will sometimes last into the first week of June. March browns appear later in the New England states and continue almost until late June. Emergence in most of Michigan and Wisconsin occurs in early June, and they may first appear in Michigan's Upper Peninsula, Wisconsin, and Minnesota during the second week of June.

Stenonema vicarium is a member of the family Heptageniidae, which also includes the rock clingers. I am sure that fly fishermen who study the aquatic biota of their favorite trout stream have observed these nymphs. They are the clinging forms, with body and thorax structures that are flattened from top to bottom, but they are wider and less flattened than many other heptageniid mayflies. They avoid the light, are quite agile, and quickly scurry across the rocks when exposed to sunlight.

March brown nymphs are generally dark reddish brown on their dorsal surfaces, with dark ribbing apparent at each abdominal segment. Males have body lengths of 12 millimeters (#12 hook), while females can measure 18 millimeters (#8–10 hook). In productive trout streams the tails may be longer than the total length of the nymph, and long tails should be built into the patterns you design for your favorite water.

Relatively high oxygen demand plays an important part in this mayfly's selection of suitable nymphal habitat. The march brown nymph's delicate gills are shielded by covers. *Stenonema* nymphs are usually found in fast water, although some individuals may be found in association with bottom debris and aquatic vegetation in well-oxygenated rivers.

Some fly-fishing authors suggest that march brown nymphs migrate from the riffles and currents into the shallows in order to prepare for emergence. Emergence of the march brown is slow, usually occurring sporadically throughout the day, starting about 9:30 A.M. Hatching can continue until early evening. During cold or rainy weather march brown duns often have difficulty escaping their nymphal skins, and emerging march browns often drift surprising distances before escaping their skins. Each of these factors should be kept in mind by the fly tyer and fly fisher.

Newly emerged duns are not strong fliers, and they may rest on the water surface for long durations, sometimes fluttering their wings in an attempt to escape the surface tension. Not all duns successfully emerge from their nymphal shucks.

Unlike many mayflies, the march brown egg-laying behavior makes this species more available to trout. Each female makes many short floats on the surface before she is finished depositing her eggs. When egg laying is complete, the exhausted spinners fall to the water.

Like the fluttering of the hatching march brown duns, the egg-laying behavior of the spinners can trigger explosive rises. The spinner is spectacular in its mating flight. Its body is somewhat more slender than the dun's, its tails grow longer in its final molt, and its wings are transparent, with veins darkly outlined. The big spinners stimulate the trout to rise aggressively, completely unlike the sipping rises associated with most mayfly spinner falls.

Movement of mature nymphs, their drift at time of hatch, and behavior need to be considered at the tying bench. Weighted imitations fished dead-drift work well before, during, and after the emergence. Trout move to feed on these nymphs before and during their emergence. Movement imparted to the fly when fished near the edge of the river may prove very effective.

Imitations of the emerging nymphs should be fished in the surface film. It may come as a surprise to most that the march brown emergence is more complicated than other mayfly species imitated by a fly fisherman.

Mating swarms of the march brown are important even on infertile trout streams. Most females lay eggs in riffles, and trout feed on them in runs immediately below heavy water. Try to time your next midseason fly-fishing trip to coincide with activity of the march brown. The rewards of meeting and fishing to this mayfly will be memorable.

In 1979 A. F. Bednarik and W. P. McCafferty published research in the *Canadian Bulletin of Fisheries and Aquatic Sciences*. In their study they found that nymphs they had identified as gray foxes keyed out as march browns when adults. In 1968 another ephermopterist, R. W. Koss, could find very little difference in eggs of the march brown and the gray fox. Therefore, based upon their research, Bednarik and McCafferty placed the gray fox (*Stenonema fuscum* and one other species) as the same species as the march brown (*S. vicarium*). This research may assist with the many questions that fly fishers have posed regarding the identity of these mayflies emerging on their favorite trout water during midseason.

Some Rivers with March Brown Hatches

Beaverkill River– New York

Fishing Creek – Pennsylvania

Big Hunting Creek – Maryland

Savage River – Maryland

Gunpowder Falls River – Maryland

Cheat River – West Virginia

Elk River – West Virginia

Farmington River – Connecticut

Housatonic River – Connecticut

Deerfield River – Massachusetts

Rose River – Virginia

North Fork Moormans River – Virginia

Rapidan River – Virginia

Delaware River – New York

THE SULPHUR HATCH ON THE LITTLE JUNIATA RIVER

After years of neglect the water quality in the Little Juniata River has improved impressively and rapidly. Within a few years the river has evolved from one of dark brown color and pungent sulfurous odor to a typically healthy limestone river with a chalky appearance and no offensive odor. Even at its nadir, however, the river held a huge population of wild brown trout, and some anglers who didn't worry about aesthetics fished the river during those mediocre years. They even

A #16 Cut Wing Sulphur used to imitate *Ephemerella rotunda* on the Little Juniata River. *Greg Hoover.*

reported that they saw mayflies emerge in the polluted water. Reports stated that the river even contained a huge population of sulphurs *(Ephemerella rotunda)*.

By 1972 the river had recovered from man's mistreatment, and that year I first fly fished this evolving river. That same year, however, the Little Juniata River suffered another setback from a flood caused by Hurricane Agnes, and not until late July did the water recede enough to attempt to fish. On that very first trip I noted four species of mayflies. But more important than that, I caught more than twenty trout over 15 inches long in less than two hours of fishing. What a potentially great river! And it was a great river until the word got out to all those who would kill every trout they caught. Within weeks dozens of anglers filled the banks of this river – most with creels bulging from the big trout they had killed.

Not until 1973 did I start meeting and fishing the hatches on this river. I visited it almost every night to catalog the ever-increasing number of aquatic insects the river contained. One mid-May afternoon I sat at the pool below the barn on the Espey Farm. About 3:00 P.M. several sulphurs appeared at the head of the pool, and within a half hour a full-fledged hatch started.

For a few minutes I sat in disbelief at this heavy hatch on this newly rejuvenated river, and in those few minutes trout began to feed on this surprise, late-afternoon appearance. I spotted an unusually heavy fish just at the head of the pool and near the railroad bank on the far shore. This lunker seemed to suck in two and three duns on each rise to the surface. I covered the rise one, two, three times before he took the lifelike pattern. But this heavy brown didn't like the hook. It shook, jumped, and then made a run toward the far bank. After five minutes I was no closer to landing that fish than I was when I first hooked it. Five minutes more and the brown came to the surface, shook violently, and the hook flew loose. I sat back on the bank, shaking from the vicious fight put up by this heavy, wild trout. I estimate conservatively that this sulphur-feeding trout weighed nearly 6 pounds and would have measured 2 feet or more in length. The hatch continued for more than an hour while I sat back and watched.

Often when the sulphur first appears in mid-May, it will appear during the afternoon for a day or two, then after a couple days the hatch resorts to its normal time late in the evening. Also look for this hatch to appear during daylight hours when you experience dreary, cold, cloudy, drizzly days in May. Read chapter 7 for more information on this hatch and others that may appear during inclement weather.

Anglers often combine this hatch with other closely related species (*Ephemerella invaria, E. dorothea,* and *E. septentrionalis*) and call all of them sulphurs or pale evening duns. Add to this group others (many *Heptagenia* species), and you see that this group and the sulphur imitation can be important.

Most of the sulphurs appear in May and June. One of the smallest *(E. dorothea)* emerges from early June until late July. If you're fortunate enough to find this hatch in any abundance, you'll find great fishing for as long as six weeks. You'll find many *Heptagenia* species appearing nightly throughout the summer. Mayflies of this genus most often appear on marginal water, and by the time they appear, water temperatures have warmed above 70 degrees on most of the streams and rivers they inhabit.

With the exception of the first emergence of *E. rotunda* in early afternoon, most of these species are evening emergers. You can expect to see most of these related hatches just before dusk. The sizes of the sulphurs vary from #14 and #16 (*E. rotunda* and *E. septentrionalis*) to #18 *(E. dorothea)*.

Spinners or mating adults of many of these species can be as important to match as the duns. With *E. rotunda* it's difficult to pre-determine which phase will take on more importance each evening.

Be prepared to switch from a copy of the dun to one imitating the spinner. I tie some of the Sulphur Spinners with upright wings made of poly yarn. I also tie some that have a body color halfway between the dun and the spinner. The body of the dun is creamish yellow with a hint of olive; the spinner has a tannish orange body. After the spinner exudes its eggs into an egg sac, the body becomes a tan color. I tie some of the spinners with an orangish tan body.

The sulphur hatches are widespread in the East and Midwest. Many Michigan and Wisconsin streams and rivers hold at least one of these species. Hatches also are important in the Northeast and appear on the Ausable, Beaverkill, Delaware, and on many of the other rivers and streams in the East and Midwest that we discuss in chapters 4 and 5. Additionally, don't overlook the limestone streams of central and south-central Pennsylvania. Falling Springs Branch Creek near Chambersburg holds an excellent hatch.

Be prepared for the first evening hatch of the new trout season. Take plenty of sulphur dun and spinner imitations with you on your trips to the great rivers and streams of the East and Midwest. When you find water with this great mayfly, you're in for an extended period of matching the hatches. And you, too, might get a chance to tangle with a lunker during a sulphur hatch.

Some Eastern and
Midwestern Rivers with Sulphur Hatches

Little Juniata River – Pennsylvania

Fishing Creek – Pennsylvania

Yellow Breeches Creek – Pennsylvania

Spring Creek – Pennsylvania

Youghiogheny River – Pennsylvania

Penns Creek – Pennsylvania

Savage River – Maryland

Gunpowder Falls River – Maryland

Cheat River System – West Virginia

Rose River – Virginia*

Rapidan River – Virginia*

North Fork Moormans River – Virginia

Mossy Creek – Virginia

Beaverkill River – New York

Delaware River – New York

South Fork Holston River – Tennessee

South Toe River – North Carolina

Farmington River – Connecticut

Deerfield River – Massachusetts

Au Sable River – Michigan

Manistee River – Michigan

*Smaller pale evening dun *(Ephemerella dorothea)*

THE GREEN DRAKE ON PENNS CREEK

I have been fly fishing to green drake emergences for almost eighteen years, and this species always amazes me with its beauty and abundance. This past season I was able to meet and fish to this mayfly once again, and I wondered if it would be the year to land a 2-foot brown on a dry fly at night. As in the past several years I fished this emergence with Bill Botts and Glenn Barder, both members of the Lykens Valley Camp on Penns Creek near Poe Paddy State Park. I met Bill at the lower part of the Broadwater section in the catch-and-release area on Penns Creek. I arrived late and found fish rising to gray fox spinners and some male green drake spinners already starting their mating dance. Bill took a few fish while I waited for additional risers to work in front of me. As darkness began to fall, the fish started working on green drake spinners. When this shift in feeding takes place, you can audibly note the difference. Trout started working behind me near the bank where I entered Penns. Although there were several good fish rising around Bill and me, we only managed to take a few on our Green Drake imitations. This seems to be the norm for most people who meet and fish this hatch.

The following evening I traveled upstream to water near Coburn. The emergence was moving along quite quickly with the low water and high temperatures of this season. Around 10:00 P.M. I hooked a good fish that made a loud splash. Immediately after the fish broke the surface, I heard another loud splash upstream from me. An angler had fallen into the creek and was struggling to get out of the water. Thank goodness two fishermen came to his assistance and pulled him out of the creek. Even though fly fishing to this hatch can be intense, one still must pay close attention while wading unfamiliar water at night.

Interestingly, most angling literature states that imitating burrowing mayfly nymphs is of little or no importance, but Glenn Barder will attest to the fact that one can have a ten- to twenty-fish morning on patterns that imitate the green drake nymph. He is one of the best nymph fishermen I know, and he has taken several good fish on my green drake nymph pattern. You may want to examine a green drake nymph on your favorite water and develop your own effective imitation, which should be fished just before and early into this mayfly's emergence.

The family Ephemeridae includes the fossorial (burrowing) mayflies of the genus *Ephemera*. Ephemerids include some of the largest mayflies present in our lakes and streams today. These mayflies inhabit the larger lakes and streams of the world, and the ephemerid nymphs spend most of their life cycle buried in the sediment, although they can sometimes be seen swimming freely in the water around the time of molting.

Ernest Schweibert, in his excellent book *Nymphs*, tells us that pollution, extensive use of pesticides to protect our eastern forests, and the scouring of river bottoms by flooding have seriously depleted eastern populations of *Ephemera* mayflies. Therefore, the presence or absence of *Ephemera* mayflies can be used as indicators of water quality. In 1970 Vince Marinaro stated in *Modern Dry-Fly Code* that Penns Creek is famous for its large green drake emergences, and I have witnessed prodigious hatches of *E. guttulata* there. This particular *Ephemera* mayfly is of great nutritional importance to fish populations in Penns Creek. Many anglers take advantage of this well-known emergence, fly fishing for trout that surface to feed upon this large mayfly.

There is a very limited amount of biological information about *E. guttulata*. In 1926 some basic biological research was conducted on the nymphal stage of the green drake, but much of the biological data that has been collected on this species has been gathered by fly fishermen.

There are many trout waters in the United States (eastern and southeastern states) that support populations of *E. guttulata*. I have collected green drake nymphs on both Kettle and Penns creeks in Pennsylvania. It became apparent to me that the finer the substrate, the more male nymphs were gathered; and if the substrate was slightly coarse, more female nymphs were collected. This would make sense because of the size difference between mature male and female green drake nymphs. Female nymphs are much larger than the males and, therefore, require more interstitial space between the substrate particles in order to respire properly.

Eastern green drake *(Ephemera guttulata)* **female dun (subimago) on Penns Creek.** *Greg Hoover.*

Nymphs may vary greatly in size. The nymphs on Penns Creek in Pennsylvania are on average about 7 mm larger than those found in freestone streams such as Kettle Creek. This size is probably a reflection of the food availability on each stream.

Preliminary investigations of gut contents have revealed the presence of diatoms, some detrital material, and some mineral material. In 1973 the presence of mineral particles was speculated by Ken Cummins, a nationally recognized aquatic ecologist, as a substitute for a gizzard structure that is lacking in green drake nymphs. That is to say, the mineral particles may grind up the diatoms and detrital material during the digestive process.

Initially in my research I had hoped to rear the green drake in the laboratory to determine how long its life cycle lasts. I collected eggs from female spinners that I captured in an aerial net on Penns Creek. The females were placed in a tub of water, where they expelled their fertilized eggs. These eggs were then taken back to the laboratory and were placed in tubs of Penns Creek water with substrate. The water temperature was kept at about 60 degrees Fahrenheit. Egg hatch occurred from twenty-seven to thirty-two days after fertilization. Similar egg hatch time was also noted with another burrowing mayfly.

While studying the green drake on Penns Creek, I found that the life cycle requires two years. Through extensive sampling during the year I would find in almost equal numbers the midinstar (developmental phase) nymphs as well as nymphs that were preparing to emerge in the coming months.

I've counted the number of eggs per female subimago (dun) on Penns Creek, and the average number of eggs was found to be 4,597. The average length (head to tip of abdomen) of a female dun on Penns Creek is 29.7 mm. The production of eggs as well as the size of the adults may well be a result of the kind and quantity of food available during the nymphal stage of the green drake.

Wing blotching is known to vary from stream to stream and seems to be more extensive on streams in northern Pennsylvania (less alkaline) such as Cedar Run and Kettle Creek and less extensive on Penns and White Deer creeks. William P. McCafferty, Department of Entomology at Purdue University, believes that this blotching may be the result of a genetic expression specific for a particular population of green drakes. This blotching may even be the result of a food substance causing increased or decreased pigmentation in the wings.

The green drake offers the fly fisher the opportunity to hook large trout on a dry fly. What a way to introduce someone to the art of fly fishing. Additionally, experiencing the emergence and mating flights of this important mayfly is truly one of the many wonders of the aquatic insect world.

Some Streams with Green Drake Hatches

Penns Creek – Pennsylvania

Fishing Creek – Pennsylvania

Little Juniata River – Pennsylvania

Big Hunting Creek – Maryland

Savage River – Maryland

Cheat River – West Virginia

Elk River – West Virginia

Connecticut River – New Hampshire

Delaware River – New York

Beaverkill River – New York

Housatonic River – Connecticut

Farmington River – Connecticut

THE WESTERN GREEN DRAKE ON HENRY'S FORK AND
THE BITTERROOT—A HATCH YOU DON'T WANT TO MISS

I landed at Missoula, Montana, and had a week to fly fish the Bitterroot River before I had to travel to Yellowstone Park. This was my first trip past the western border of Pennsylvania, I had no guide, I didn't know anything about the Bitterroot, and I certainly didn't expect much in the way of hatches or large trout.

I headed up to a section of the river near Florence, asked a rancher for permission to fish, and headed down to the swollen river. Snowmelt from the 10,000-foot range to the west by the same name still filled the river. How would I catch any trout under these adverse conditions?

No sooner did I arrive at the river's edge in late morning than I noticed some large mayflies struggling to free themselves from the raging current. I grabbed one of the stragglers and identified it as a western green drake. Within the first couple of minutes on my first trip to a western river I met my first hatch—and a great one at that. I had prepared for the hatch and had tied a #12 imitation. But would any trout rise in this high water?

I didn't have to wait long. Within minutes a heavy Bitterroot rainbow took a struggling dun just out from the far bank. On the second cast I covered the rise, and the fish took my pattern. The rainbow headed up through the rapids above the pool into the tail of the pool above. There I turned him and headed the 16-inch trout into my net. That wasn't bad—ten minutes of waiting and a heavy trout. Soon more drakes appeared, and they continued for more than two hours. By the time the hatch had waned, more than a dozen heavy trout had taken my imitation. Not bad for my first trip to a western river.

For more than a week I came back to the Bitterroot to fish over stragglers of this large mayfly and caught trout rising to them.

The following year I met Al Gretz on Henry's Fork for a week of great fly fishing. That was before Henry's Fork acquired its lofty fly-fishing reputation and before the water became filled with anglers anxious to match the hatch. Al and I met on the river the last few days of June, and in the next few days we fished over hatches of blue-winged olive duns, pale morning duns, dark brown duns, brown drakes, and, yes, western green drakes. These hatches weren't your normal sporadic hatches; many of them were spectacular, with plenty of rainbows rising freely to duns and spinners.

Al and I headed down the Railroad Ranch a couple miles from the upper end ostensibly to fish over a pale morning dun hatch. There was no need to hurry—it was early morning and the hatch wouldn't appear for another hour or two. By the time Al and I got into place, some duns had already started to emerge, and a few trout were feeding. Al and I talked about strategies and delayed fishing for a few minutes. By that time the pale morning dun hatch had diminished. Fish began feeding on another larger, darker mayfly – the western green drake. It continued to appear on the surface that day for more than three hours. Trout fed on this large mayfly almost continuously until the hatch ended in midafternoon. Trout fed so consistently on the hatch that Al and I began to pick and choose the trout that we wanted to catch, casting only over what we thought were fairly large trout.

For five days we had very predictable matching-the-hatch events over the western green drake on Henry's Fork. When trout refused our dun patterns, we switched to emerger patterns and took more trout.

Scientists have found not only one subspecies of *Ephemerella grandis*, but several. Additionally, they have changed the genus from *Ephemerella* to a new one named *Drunella*. *Drunella grandis grandis* is the subspecies that appears on Henry's Fork.

The western green drake can be found on many of the great streams and rivers of the West. The color of this species varies tremendously from stream to stream. On the Bitterroot River you'll find an almost black drake with olive reflections on its body *(D. grandis ingens)*. This subspecies often appears to be somewhat darker than *D. grandis grandis*. On Henry's Fork the drake has more green to its body color. Other rivers with good *D. grandis ingens* hatches include the Alsea in Oregon and the Green River in Washington.

The time of year that the drake appears varies considerably from area to area in the West. Along the West Coast and for some miles inland the western green drake can appear as early as middle to late May. Hatches on the McKenzie and Metolius rivers in Oregon normally appear around May 28. Those hatches appearing in the Rockies, like the one on the Bitterroot River, Henry's Fork, and the Flathead River above Kalispell, appear near the end of June. You'll find western green drakes still emerging on the Fryingpan River in central Colorado into mid-August.

You'll find a western green drake pattern listed in chapter 8. It also works well when the common *Drunella doddsi* emerges on Rock Creek in Montana.

If you can plan your fishing trip to fly fish over a hatch of western green drakes, do it. This great hatch is common on many western waters. When it appears, large trout lose their timidity and feed on the surface freely. The hatch can last for a week or two at any given location. This is one great hatch of the West that you don't want to miss.

Some Western Rivers with
Western Green Drake Hatches

Metolius River – Oregon

Deschutes River – Oregon

McKenzie River – Oregon

Fryingpan River – Colorado

Roaring Fork River – Colorado

Henry's Fork – Idaho

Kootenai River – Montana

Bitterroot River – Montana

Madison River – Montana

Yellowstone River – Montana

Firehole River – Wyoming

Yakima River – Washington

Williamson River – Oregon

Fall River – California

Hat Creek – California

THE LITTLE BLUE-WINGED OLIVE DUN ON
THE BIGHORN RIVER

Baetis species, commonly called little blue dun or little blue-winged olive dun, often appear in the morning but may continue into the afternoon. With many species of this genus the heaviest hatches often occur in the afternoon. *Baetis hageni (parvus)* (dark brown dun), *B. bicaudatus* (pale olive dun), and *B. intermedius* (little blue dun) are three *Baetis* species that can be important to meet and fish on many summer and fall afternoons on western waters. *B. hageni* is one of the most important hatches I have ever experienced in the West. But even more important is the little blue-winged olive dun *(B. tricaudatus)*. The latter has two generations each year and is very common on many streams and rivers throughout the United States. You'll find fantastic little blue-winged olive hatches on the Arkansas River near Salida, Colorado, but the hatch found on the Bighorn River in south-central Montana is one of the finest.

For several years Mike Manfredo had tried to get me to fish with him on the Bighorn River just south of Billings, Montana. He and thousands of other anglers had discovered an oasis chock-full of heavy trout and great hatches. So, a few years ago I agreed to fish with him on the river, and we decided on the first day of October.

We hit an early fall snowstorm on our drive from the Billings airport to Fort Smith. Would this ruin our five-day trip to this hot spot of fly fishing? We'd soon find out.

We entered our drift boat just below the dam at Fort Smith, and I wasn't impressed with the number of other anglers entering the water at the same time. By the time we started drifting, we saw a half dozen boats in front of us and another dozen behind us. As soon as we could, Mike and I disembarked onto an island. A fairly heavy trico spinner hatch occurred while we waited for many of the upriver boats to pass us. I caught several trout on a Trico, but nothing very large. Only a half dozen trout rose to the spinners.

Later we got back into the boat again and floated downriver another 5 miles before stopping for a midafternoon snack. As we sat on the bank and watched a pool above, we saw dozens of heavy trout begin to feed. I walked to the water's edge and saw dazed little blue-winged olive duns unable to take flight. Trout took two, three, and four of these on one rise. At the height of the hatch more than twenty lunkers fed on the duns in front of me. Matching the little blue-winged olive dun wasn't easy. The small olives covered the surface, and the trout were highly selective. Finally I got a strike, then another. After two fantastic hours of matching the hatch, the olives subsided. What a hatch – more than two hours of fishing over this #20 mayfly on the highly productive Bighorn.

Little blue-winged olives aren't found only on the Bighorn. This is one of a handful of mayfly species found in all three regions of the United States. I've seen good hatches in April on the Arkansas River just west of Pueblo, Colorado. In the East many of the limestone streams boast great hatches of this mayfly.

You'll first encounter a *B. tricaudatus* hatch in March or April, and the second generation may be met in September and October. The hatch occurs in good numbers on central Pennsylvania's Falling Springs Branch Creek. Here and many other places members of the first generation are larger than those of the second generation. I've heard Gene Macri say that he uses a #16 Little Blue-Winged Olive Dun to match the March/April hatch and a #20 to match the September/October one.

Where can you find little blue-winged olive duns in the West other than the Bighorn River? Just about every well-known river in the West holds a good September hatch of *Baetis*. Anglers fish great hatches on the Missouri, Green, South Platte, Kootenai, and dozens of other rivers.

Some Eastern and Midwestern Streams with Little Blue-Winged Olive Dun Hatches

Beaverkill River – New York

Delaware River – New York

Spring Creek – Pennsylvania

Little Juniata River – Pennsylvania

Yellow Breeches Creek – Pennsylvania

Savage River – Maryland

Big Hunting Creek – Maryland

Gunpowder Falls River – Maryland

Cheat River System – West Virginia

Mossy Creek – Virginia

South Fork Holston River – Tennessee

North Fork of the White River – Missouri

Pere Marquette River – Michigan

Au Sable River – Michigan

Manistee River – Michigan

Some Western Rivers with Little Blue-Winged Olive Dun Hatches

Bighorn River – Montana

Bitterroot River – Montana

Kootenai River – Montana

Madison River – Montana

Missouri River – Montana

Yellowstone River – Montana

Green River – Utah

Bighorn River – Wyoming

Firehole River – Wyoming

North Platte River – Wyoming

Williamson River – Oregon

Arkansas River – Colorado

Fryingpan River – Colorado

Roaring Fork River – Colorado

San Juan River – New Mexico
Yakima River – Washington
Henry's Fork – Idaho
Big Wood River – Idaho
Silver Creek – Idaho

THE GRAY FOXES ON THE COLORADO
AND DELAWARE RIVERS

Two great trout rivers of the United States flow thousands of miles apart, but both rivers hold spectacular hatches with plenty of rising trout. Both rivers have several blue quill hatches, a good trico hatch, and yes, a gray fox hatch.

On the Delaware River in the East, the Gray Fox copies a very common mayfly *(Stenonema fuscum)*, which is found on many eastern and midwestern waters around the end of May. On the Namekagon River in Wisconsin, on the Au Sable River in Michigan, on Pine Creek in Pennsylvania, and on the Delaware River between New York and Pennsylvania you'll find good hatches of this often sporadic light-colored mayfly.

Most eastern gray foxes emerge from 2:00 to 8:00 P.M. On some streams you'll see heightened activity from 4:00 to 8:00 P.M. Spinners mate and lay their eggs around 8:30 P.M.

The same pattern you use to copy the hatch in the East and Midwest can be used to copy another important hatch *(Heptagenia solitaria)* in the West. The hatch on western waters emerges later in the year – you'll often see these mayflies appearing as late as mid-September. On the Cache la Poudre and Colorado rivers in Colorado and on the North Platte River in southern Wyoming you'll see these duns emerge around 6:30 P.M. The spinners become active around 10:30 A.M. and again in the evening.

Other than being slightly smaller, the western gray fox is almost identical in both the dun and spinner stages. Fly fishers copy spinners of the eastern and midwestern species with the Ginger Quill. That same spinner imitation also copies the western spinner.

I've fished many great gray fox hatches in the East, but the one on Pine Creek in central Pennsylvania and the one on the Delaware near Hancock, New York, are two of the more concentrated. For more than ten years I anticipated the hatch on Pine Creek. On several occasions Fred Templin, Vince Gigliotti, and I hit this late-May emergence correctly, and we fished over emerging duns and rising trout for several hours. On one afternoon trip to fish this hatch several of us caught more than fifty trout copying the duns that appeared on the surface. Recently, the hatch on Pine Creek has diminished dramatically. Many anglers blame this drastic decline on mine acid seepage from an upstream tributary. Other hatches, like the hendrickson and brown drake, have also been affected in the same area.

I recently had an opportunity to fish the Delaware River in New York with Bob Sentiwany. Bob had fly fished this river long before it became a popular matching-the-hatch haven for fly fishermen. He caught heavy rainbows back in the 1970s. We hit several areas of the river from Callicoon to Balls Eddy to get a flavor for the activity and the hatches. We headed to a section of the river just above the junction of the east and west branches of the river, two miles below Hancock. We arrived at what Bob claimed to be a hot spot around 6:00 P.M. As we waded into this tailwater I could already see a sporadic gray fox hatch. I tied on a #12 imitation and waited for surface action. Trout on the Delaware River are extremely difficult to catch. I suggest that the only time to fish this fickle river is when you're matching a hatch. Then and only then can you increase your chances of coming away with success. Fish this same river when there is no hatch, and you'll likely come away frustrated.

I didn't have to wait long for the fish to take some of the sluggish duns. Within minutes one trout rose 50 feet from me in a heavy riffle. After a couple false attempts I covered the heavy fish and it took the floating fly. Soon two more trout fed on clumsy duns. For the next two hours Bob and I fly fished over a sporadic hatch of gray foxes and rising trout. Some of the trout that took the Gray Fox imitation weighed over 4 pounds.

Duns appear as early as the second week in May and may last into late June on many waters. The heaviest hatch of the species usually occurs from late May to mid-June, depending on the location. On occasion I've hit a concentrated hatch of gray foxes just at dusk.

The spinner of the species, the ginger quill, appears over the water around 8:30 P.M. Don't overlook this phase. Female spinners can create some great rises for a half hour or so.

In early September, 2,000 miles away, I fly fished on the Colorado River near Kremmling. In the morning I hit a respectable trico hatch, with trout rising to these as well as several other hatches. Around 10:30 A.M. dark brown spinners gathered where just a few minutes before the tricos had performed their mating ritual. Little did I know that these dark brown spinners, commonly called ginger quills, were a harbinger of things to come that evening a few miles downriver.

By 6:00 P.M. the same evening I had arrived at a point on the river a few hundred feet above Gore Canyon. Anglers had told me that this section held some heavy fish and some great hatches. I planned to come back the next morning to hit the trico hatch because I didn't expect to see anything during the evening that late in the year.

After scanning the surface and deciding what I'd do for the rest of the evening, I noticed first a few spinners, then hundreds of what looked like the same spinners I had encountered a few miles upriver that morning. Ten minutes after the spinners first arrived at the surface, the trout went crazy. They splashed and jumped at spinners, trying to take them in the air.

I hurriedly tied on a #14 Ginger Quill and began casting. I didn't specifically cast to one fish, but aimed the fly in the general direction of five or six feeding trout. (It's the same problem I have with quail hunting. When a cover flushes, I try to hit several rather than aiming at one.) After several false attempts I covered a rising trout and caught it. Before the spinner fall had ended that evening, I had caught a dozen trout on the Ginger Quill.

Two tremendous hatches, 2,000 miles apart on two great rivers of the United States, both copied by the same dun and spinner patterns – the Gray Fox and Ginger Quill. What memorable events these matching-the-hatch episodes evoke!

Gray Fox Hatches in the East

Penns Creek – Pennsylvania

Little Juniata River – Pennsylvania

Delaware River – New York

Beaverkill River – New York

Gray Fox Hatches in the West

Colorado River – Colorado

Cache la Poudre River – Colorado

North Platte River – Wyoming

THE PALE MORNING DUN ON THE KOOTENAI RIVER

I had just successfully wrapped up a matching-the-hatch session with the yellow pale morning dun at the Railroad Ranch on Henry's Fork in Idaho and was headed upriver to the Box Canyon area to look for late-afternoon and evening hatches. I didn't have to wait long—within a half hour a #16 reddish brown mayfly appeared. What was it? The belly had a pale yellowish olive cast with some red, and the back of the mayfly was dark reddish brown. I captured several male duns, let them change to spinners overnight in a Styrofoam cup, and shipped them off to an entomologist, Will Flowers, who later told me that the reddish brown insects were pale morning duns *(Ephemerella inermis)*. He added that this mayfly more than any other often has considerable color variations from river to river. To substantiate his statement I later sent several male duns that were a pale olive color. These were also identified as pale morning duns.

I didn't think much of Will's comments until I fished the Kootenai a few miles above Libby, Montana. This productive tailwater holds good hatches and teems with heavy rainbows. Vince Gigliotti, Al Gretz, and I hit the river after our evening meal, and around 7:00 P.M. a medium-sized mayfly appeared on the surface. Soon the number of these insects brought some heavy trout to the surface for the food. Before I tied on a pattern, I captured one of the flies. The #16 (6–8 mm) mayfly had a light olive body. What was it? From earlier identifications I assumed it was another pale morning dun.

I had no #16 pale olive pattern to copy the emerging dun so I tied on a yellow version and cast to a heavy fish at the head of a half-mile pool. This trout fed almost continuously on struggling duns in the riffle. Trout that feed almost uninterrupted are often easier to catch than those taking an occasional surface insect. The heavy feeder took my imitation of the dun after five or six direct floats over it. It headed deep, then came to the surface, shook violently, and the fly came flying back towards me.

Several other heavy rainbows took up positions for some of the floating duns. Before nightfall I landed three of those heavy rainbows, all over 4 pounds.

Three years later I was back on the Kootenai River hoping to fish over another spectacular pale morning dun hatch. This time Jerry Meck and I were there in late June. Our guide for the float trip from the Libby Dam downriver to the town was Dave Blackburn. Dave has guided thousands of fly fishermen on the same river for the past ten years. He knows it and its hatches extremely well. But Dave had bad news for us when we arrived at his place on June 24—the hatches were a week later than normal because of the unusually cold spring. Dave had not encountered any major hatch of morning duns or rising trout so far that season.

The bad news continued for most of the morning and afternoon.

As we entered the river, a light drizzle gave way to a heavy shower. Jerry and I tied on heavy weighted Woolly Buggers trying to take a rainbow or two off the bottom of the Kootenai. We caught a half dozen by noon, when we stopped at the Haul Bridge to eat. There we began seeing a few pale morning duns on the surface. Within an hour these few duns turned into a full-blown hatch. First just a few rainbows responded by rising. By 5:00 P.M., however, we not only had a full-blown hatch but also a dozen rising trout between the boat and the shore. Jerry and I caught a half dozen, and Dave drifted us to the next pod of risers.

The action continued for more than two hours until the cool wind slowed down the hatch. What a spectacular event. What a great, great day of fly fishing over the pale morning dun on the Kootenai River in northwestern Montana.

Here are some important guidelines to remember for the pale morning dun hatch:

1) I've seen colors of tannish orange, some pale olive, and olive yellow, so carry a variety of patterns in #16 and #18 with you. The most common color of this insect is a pale yellow with an olive tint. The color pattern listed in chapter 8 was taken from a hatch on Henry's Fork in Idaho. The color varies so much – even on the same stream – that it's important to carry imitations with bodies of tan, reddish brown, olive, and the most common color, pale yellow with an olive cast. Since the color is so variable, I have not suggested one specific pattern. Nymphs also vary from light brown to dark brown.

2) The best time to fish the hatch is during July. I've seen pale morning duns appear as early as late May on the Metolius River and late June on the Kootenai in Montana, but the majority of these mayfly hatches appear in early to late July.

3) Hatches vary according to the time of day. On Henry's Fork I saw these on the water in the morning and through early afternoon. On the Metolius I saw the heaviest hatches around 3:00 P.M. On the Kootenai the heaviest emergence is in the early evening hours.

At least three mayfly species combine to be called pale morning duns – *Ephemerella inermis, E. laccutrus,* and *E. infrequens.* The first of these by a wide margin seems to be the most important and most varied species and is probably the most widespread western mayfly hatch you'll see. It is found in Washington, Oregon, California, Idaho, Montana, Nevada, Arizona, New Mexico, Colorado, and Utah. The hatch is also found through much of western Canada and southern Alaska.

You'll find the pale morning dun on almost every important river and stream in the West. Because it's widespread and appears for several weeks each year, the pale morning dun probably takes precedence as the number-one hatch to match in the West.

Pale Morning Dun Hatches in the West

McKenzie River – Oregon

Metolius River – Oregon

Williamson River – Oregon

Deschutes River – Oregon

Rocky Ford Creek – Washington

Yakima River – Washington

Silver Creek – Idaho

Henry's Fork – Idaho

Bitterroot River – Montana

Kootenai River – Montana

Madison River – Montana

Yellowstone River – Montana

Bighorn River – Montana

Missouri River – Montana

Firehole River – Wyoming

North Platte River – Wyoming

Bighorn River – Wyoming

Green River – Utah

San Juan River – New Mexico

South Platte River – Colorado

Arkansas River – Colorado

Fryingpan River – Colorado

Roaring Fork – Colorado

THE WESTERN MARCH BROWN ON
THE McKENZIE RIVER

How would you like to fish a hatch that appears on the water on some western rivers for almost three months? How would you like to catch trout rising to mayflies almost every late-winter and early-spring afternoon around 2:00 P.M.? Try the spectacular western march brown in the Pacific Northwest.

The western march brown *(Rhithrogena morrisoni)* first makes its appearance on Willamette Valley rivers and streams while the Midwest and East are still blanketed in snow. Anxious anglers can meet and fish while the hatch of this #14 or #16 mayfly appears as early as late February. For several years Mike Manfredo, who at that time lived in Corvallis, Oregon, bragged about this great hatch. Now, in late April, Mike and I set off on a float trip on the lower McKenzie hoping to fish the hatch. Ken Helfrich of nearby Springfield served as our guide for the 5-mile float. We entered the water just above Eugene and planned to float downriver 2 miles below the McKenzie's juncture with the Willamette River.

The Northwest at this time of year can hold some early-spring surprises for you, and it did for us that day. When we met Ken at 10:00 A.M., we donned our cold-weather gear and raincoats. A fine drizzle was falling as we drifted for the first couple of uneventful miles. While we were waiting for the projected hatch, Ken taught us the recast method of fly fishing from a McKenzie boat. First you cast your dry fly forty-five degrees downriver from the boat, then lift the fly upriver the distance of your leader and let it float back downriver. We tied Ken's favorite pattern, a parachute Western March Brown dry fly, to the tippet and a wet-fly version of the imitation on the dropper. I later used this same technique on eastern waters when I had no idea whether trout were taking the nymph, emerger, or dun during a white fly hatch. I tied the nymph on the tippet, the emerger on the first dropper, and an oversized dry fly on the second dropper. The large dry fly acted as a bobber, or strike indicator, and I could see when trout struck my nymph or emerger.

We drifted through three sets of rapids and pools before we had any indication that that day would be one of those memorable ones. About 2:00 P.M. and at the fourth riffle we noticed a few rainbows rising at the head of the pool. I scanned the surface and saw dozens of sluggish duns resting before they took flight. The drizzle and cold air temperature delayed any rapid takeoff. Air temperature at midafternoon still remained in the midforties.

Within minutes the sporadic western march brown hatch transformed into a concentrated one that brought dozens of trout to the surface. On almost every cast over a rising trout Mike and I had a strike or a hookup. For the next two hours and five sets of pools and riffles, we saw plenty of rising trout. Even after we entered the Willamette, we saw insects on the surface and caught trout. After more than two hours and fifty trout, the hatch finally subsided

What a pity for most fly fishermen on the McKenzie. Until two years ago you couldn't legally fish the McKenzie for trout until May. Many anglers illegally fished the hatch in February, March, and April. With some foresight Oregon Fish and Wildlife opened the lower section of the McKenzie. A 10-mile section from near the Hayden Bridge to its mouth is now open the entire year.

You might have the impression that the western march brown inhabits a very small area of the Northwest. That is not true! You'll find respectable, fishable hatches in California, Washington, Idaho, and the western half of Montana. On the Kootenai River near Libby, Montana, the species appears much later than it does near the coast—best hatches on the Kootenai appear in early May. Remember, hatches of the same species occur as much as a month later in Idaho, Colorado, Wyoming, and Montana than they do in the Pacific Coast states.

You can hit hatches of the western march brown as late as late April on Willamette Valley rivers in central Oregon. However, the best hatches of this mayfly occur in March and April. Early members of the genus appear a size larger than those appearing later. In February and March you can match the hatch with a #14; in May the hatch can best be matched with a #16 Western March Brown.

Other great rivers and streams of the Northwest also hold good populations of this and other similar *Rhithrogena* species. The Yakima River in south-central Washington boasts a hatch in April and May, and the Kootenai River in northwestern Montana and eastern Idaho produces a spectacular hatch in May. You'll find the hatch fairly common in Oregon, Washington, Idaho, and the western part of Montana.

Read the incident on the western march brown in chapter 7. Often the best time to fish this early-season hatch is on a cold day when the insects have difficulty taking off from the surface. I've hit the same hatch on a warm May afternoon, when most of the mayflies escaped rapidly from the surface and few trout rose.

Western March Brown Hatches in the West

McKenzie River – Oregon

Metolius River – Oregon

Yakima River – Washington

Kootenai River – Montana

Henry's Fork – Idaho

Bighorn River – Wyoming

Deschutes River – Oregon

CHIRONOMIDS ON THE CACHE LA POUDRE

Hatches appear early – sometimes as early as late February – on coastal waters of the West, but nothing really happens on inland waters in the Rockies until late May or June. No worthwhile hatch emerges on Rocky Mountain waters until the appearance of blue-winged olive duns and pale morning duns in late April and May. At least that's what is generally thought. But nothing could be further from the truth! Look at the San Juan River in New Mexico or the Cache la Poudre in Colorado. On the tailwater of the San Juan you can often fish from December through April to profuse, predictable, but some-times frustrating midge or chironomid hatches daily. The same goes for the nontailwater Cache la Poudre River near Fort Collins, Colorado.

Eric Pettine, Jim Garrett, Craig Shuman, and I recently fly fished the Cache la Poudre just below the hatchery in the 4-mile catch-and-release area. Craig is a local entrepreneur in Fort Collins, a good friend, and an avid fly fisherman. Eric is a dentist in Fort Collins and one of Colorado's top fly fishermen. Jim runs Garrett and Duffy Orvis Shop in Fort Collins and fishes the black chironomid hatch on the Poudre at least once a week throughout the winter. Jim knows as much about the Colorado rivers in general and the Poudre and its hatches as anyone in the area. He prepares for the midge hatch with plenty of emergers to match the #24 chironomids. If the Poudre Valley experiences a mild winter and the water is open, Jim fly fishes the hatch from December through April.

We left Fort Collins in the middle of April in a cold, misty rain with the temperature at 38 degrees Fahrenheit – no way to fish an early spring hatch. But as we traveled the 40 miles to our final destination, the overcast gave way to a bright blue sky.

We arrived at the Poudre at 9:15 A.M. and as the four or us headed down the path to the river, Jim pointed out the remains of a cabin that had been used for the filming of the television epic "Centennial." At the river we noted dozens of browns and rainbows already feeding on the thousands of chironomids on the water. By 9:30 A.M. thousands and thousands of midges covered the surface. As soon as we began casting, I realized a meaningful problem: why would trout take a copy of the midge when thousands of naturals dotted the surface? Jim and Eric caught an occasional trout in the first half hour of fishing with an emerger pattern, but I struck out.

Mid-April on the Poudre often means low water conditions. All three anglers – who had frequented the Poudre for years – commented that they had never seen the river lower at this time of year. Add the low water and a 30-mile-an-hour wind to the great hatch, and no wonder that the midge hatch that day grew frustrating. The wind blew chironomids in my face, down my neck, and into my mouth.

I headed downriver to try my luck over trout that maybe hadn't been fished over daily for the past few weeks. In front of me twenty or more trout took midge emergers. I tied on a #20 gray chironomid with a gray quill body and began casting over a pod of more than ten sippers. Finally, one of the rainbows sucked in the midge dry fly. In the next half hour more than ten trout took that imitation. I hurried up-river to get Craig, Jim, and Eric and have them come downriver. When I arrived where they were fly fishing, all three were landing trout. It seems their success ratio had also increased over the past half hour. The three skilled anglers had hooked and released more than thirty trout while I was downriver. Craig and Jim caught their trout on an emerger, whereas Eric and I caught ours on a floating one. Eric used a #20 Griffith's Gnat.

Why all of a sudden did we begin catching trout when we had had few rises to our imitations before? Fewer midges now emerged, and with less competition, trout seemed more ready to take our dry- and wet-fly patterns.

Four hours after we arrived on the Poudre we decided to quit for the day. Ecstatic by our early-season success, we talked about the chironomid hatch all the way back to Fort Collins. What the midge lacked in size on the Poudre it certainly made up in numbers.

Don't overlook emerging pupa patterns. You'll find tying directions in chapter 7 for these small insects. If you prefer to use a second fly rather than a strike indicator, you can attach a large attractor pattern nearer the rod. Tie a piece of tippet material to the attractor at the bend of the hook and secure it with an improved clinch knot. Tie your pupa pattern on the tippet. This worked extremely well on the Green River in Utah.

Don't overlook these winter and early-spring hatches. You'll find chironomids on hundreds of streams, rivers, and lakes in the West, Midwest, and East. Carry emerger and floating patterns in #12–24 with cream, gray, black, and olive bodies (see chapter 8 for some tying directions). Look for the hatches especially from December through April, when these tiny insects make up an important food supply for trout.

SPECKLEWINGS ON EASTERN PONDS AND LAKES

In *Meeting and Fishing the Hatches* I wrote about a great hatch of speckle-winged mayflies that I encountered on a western lake in the

Bob Marshall Wilderness Area just south of Glacier National Park. This hatch began about midmorning in July and continued unabated for several hours. Spinners came back to the thirty-five-acre lake around noon to lay their eggs, and the grayling and rainbow trout in the impoundment actively fed on both phases. Trout fed indiscriminately on duns and spinners for more than two hours. Al Gretz, Vince Gigliotti, and I caught more than fifty trout matching the hatch and spinner fall.

I've encountered excellent hatches of specklewings on other lakes of the West and some rivers and creeks with slow water. Rocky Ford Creek in Washington has an especially respectable hatch. If you didn't know better, at many spots along the stream you'd think you were fishing a small pond.

But with some minor exceptions I've never encountered a hatch of specklewings on any waters outside the West worthwhile matching. That is, until recently. Not long ago Rich Meyers called me about just such a hatch on a small lake at Big Moore's Run Lodge just south of Coudersport, Pennsylvania. The lodge is one of two Orvis-endorsed lodge east of the Mississippi River, and it encompasses two lakes and a small fertile stream, Big Moore's Run. The lakes contain a generous

Speckle-winged dun (*Callibaetis* sp.) male spinner (imago) from an eastern lake. *Greg Hoover.*

supply of browns, brooks, and rainbows—some in the 8- to 9-pound category—and some of the rainbows are Kamloops. Rich fished the lake in late April and encountered a hatch of specklewings that lasted for hours. Rich called me after the hatch and urged me to corroborate it.

I had to witness this unexpected hatch for myself, so I visited with the proprietors, Bill and Barb Haldaman. I arrived at the lake on a late April morning around 11:00 A.M. The weather didn't act like it was late April. The temperature hovered in the low forties and a winterlike north wind blew across the lake and right into my face. As I anxiously headed for the lake, I could already see dozens of swallows picking up insects off the surface, and several hefty trout were surface feeding. I scanned the windblown shoreline near me and saw a half dozen dazed specklewings. Trout throughout the lake were feeding on the stunned duns that were unable to fly.

Duran Knapp, a professional guide for Bill Haldaman, tied on a #14 Blue Dun to copy the hatch and cast it into the wind and let it float back towards him. After several futile attempts a heavy rainbow struck the fly. Duran landed a 4-pound rainbow matching that specklewing hatch in the East.

Bill Haldaman said the hatch became heavy about four years ago after he had emptied the lake and limed the bottom. The hatch normally begins in early April and lasts for more than a month on the lake. The specklewing resembles those of the West with its medium to dark gray body, tan tail and legs, and dark wings that are heavily barred. The hatch at Big Moore's Run Lodge can last for several hours each day.

Specklewing is a name used interchangeably for members of the genus *Callibaetis*, which closely resemble each other in general body coloration. Members of this genus usually have several generations each year. When the female spinner lays its eggs, they almost instantaneously hatch out as live nymphs, which prefer aquatic vegetation and develop rapidly. Each generation appears about five or six weeks apart.

Can you imagine matching a hatch and catching Kamloop rainbows up to 8 pounds on a dry fly? You can do it in northern Pennsylvania during the emergence of the speckle-winged dun.

THE SALMON FLY ON THE DESCHUTES

I arrived at the Corbin Springs area on the Yellowstone River on July 9. I had no guide—no local expert to help me. I stood at the huge boiling snow-fed river and wondered how I'd ever catch a trout under these no-hatch conditions. Soon I saw a huge stonefly flutter over the river, then another. I scanned the bushes near the shore and saw thousands of these down-wings on the branches and leaves. At 9:00 P.M. first a few, then thousands of egg-laying females moved back towards the water. Where the surface had seemed barren just minutes before, it had now come alive with trout chasing returning egg-laden female stoneflies. I tied on a Salmon Fly tied by Al Troth and caught several heavy trout before I quit.

If you're fortunate enough to hit the hatch just as it begins, you'll find success with the nymph. On May 25 Jay Kapolka and I drifted down the Deschutes River with Craig Lacy of nearby Bend, Oregon, guiding us through a series of riffles and glides until we stopped for lunch. As we sat by the bank, Craig pointed to several adult stoneflies that had just climbed out of the water. We looked along the bank farther upriver and found hundreds more that had just emerged. On the rest of our float downriver to Trout Run Jay and I used the Grindle Stonefly, a copy of the *Pteronarcys* nymph, and we landed more than a dozen heavy rainbows.

If you fly fish western waters for any length of time from late May into mid-July, you'll probably run across a salmon fly hatch. When you do, you'll never be the same fly fisherman you were before. These huge stoneflies have the same effect on trout that the green drake, Michigan caddis, and western green drake do in the East, Midwest, and West respectively. The migrating nymphs entice trout to a feeding frenzy. Once the hatch begins, you can expect to see some unbelievable matching-the-hatch fly fishing. These huge downwings bring lunkers to the surface.

If you know the rivers and the approximate dates that the salmon fly appears on them, you can fish the hatch for a long time. Mike Lawson of Henry's Fork Anglers often follows the hatch from one river to another. Salmon flies first appear on the Box Canyon area of Henry's Fork, Rock Creek in Montana, and as early as late May on the Deschutes River in Oregon. The salmon fly next appears on the Big Hole in Montana around the middle of June. If you arrive in late June or early July, you still can find salmon flies emerging. You'll find the salmon fly appearing on the Madison River near the end of June and early July and on the Yellowstone and Gallatin rivers around or shortly after July 1.

The best adult stonefly imitation I've seen is the one tied by Nick Nicklas of West Yellowstone, Montana. The pattern, the Simple Salmon, has outfished more than a dozen other imitations I've tested. You'll find a description for the pattern in chapter 8.

HEXAGENIA LIMBATA ON THE AU SABLE
RIVER IN MICHIGAN

During the third week of June I traveled to this famous midwestern stream hoping to meet and fish to the Michigan caddis. I have read numerous articles on this huge burrowing mayfly. Analogies of this hatch can be made to that of the green drake on Penns and other creeks in the East. Would I experience all that the fly-fishing articles promised? I have heard about large trout feeding to green drakes on Penns Creek, but would I find myself in the middle of an emergence of this huge burrowing mayfly in Michigan?

When I arrived in Michigan, I quickly found out that the "Hex," or Michigan caddis, is also known as the fishfly, sandfly, or just mayfly in areas in the midwestern part of the United States. Michigan, Wisconsin, and Minnesota have rivers that provide prodigious hatches of this mayfly. Emergence of *Hexagenia limbata* generally starts between mid-June and mid-July. In addition to the Au Sable in Michigan, the Pere Marquette and Manistee rivers also support this giant mayfly, as well as rivers in the Upper Peninsula. Surprisingly, the hatch starts in the upper reaches of the Au Sable and progresses to the South Branch of the Au Sable. Eventually it emerges above the Mio Dam on lower stretches of the main stem. This hatching sequence is very different from most others we're accustomed to seeing as fly fishermen. Most of the hatches we meet and fish, such as the green drake, start in the lower reaches and progress upstream.

Nymphs of this species are some of the largest known to occur in North America. To determine if you have a *Hexagenia* or an *Ephemera* population on your river, you can examine the front part of the head of a mature nymph. If the projection from the head is rounded, chances are you have a *Hexagenia* nymph. If the projection is deeply forked, this is an indication that you may be looking at a species of *Ephemera*.

Hexagenia limbata nymphs live in mudbanks along the edges of the Au Sable. In this oxygen-deficient environment the nymphs move their feathery gills to obtain oxygen in their burrows. It usually takes two years for these nymphs to mature.

Nymphs leave their burrows around dusk and wiggle to the surface, making them vulnerable to trout. Many angling authors have suggested that imitating burrowing mayfly nymphs is not important, but many successful fly fishermen will attest to the fact that imitations of *H. limbata* nymphs fished early in the emergence can be very effective.

Duns escape their nymphal shucks and fly to objects within 100–200 yards of the water's edge. In this life stage they are 15–38

Michigan caddis or "Hex" *(Hexagenia limbata)* female dun (subimago) from the South Branch of the Au Sable River in Michigan. *Greg Hoover.*

millimeters in total length. When duns are on the water early in the emergence, trout rise to take them with little caution, but as the emergence progresses, the trout become more selective. This may be the result of most of the fish becoming filled up on these large mayflies later in the hatch. Individuals will be duns for about one to three days. Upon molting, the fully developed adult or spinner is ready to mate.

Mating flights of the spinners and the consequent spinner fall take place between 9:00 P.M. and midnight, and the spinner flights are some of the most spectacular that I have witnessed in the world of mayflies. Once mated, one female will lay over three thousand eggs.

In mid-June I met Charlie Chlysta at Gates Lodge and Pro Shop near Grayling. Charlie is a biology teacher in Ohio and has been fishing to this giant mayfly on the Au Sable for over ten years. He is a night fisherman and prefers to float tube his favorite stretches of the river. When fishing to *H. limbata* activity, he targets pools with mudbanks that support this burrowing mayfly. Charlie's night-fishing techniques are unusual and truly unique. He has landed and released many heavy browns during his fly-fishing tenure on the Au Sable.

When preparing to fish this hatch, you will need to dress your imitations on large hooks, preferably #6. Gary LaFontaine's imitation—known as the Mess—works well. Another effective pattern is Robert's Yellow Drake. I managed to take several good fish one evening on the lower main stem on a Robert's Yellow Drake. Other local dry-fly patterns consistently yielded heavy trout during the hex hatch. Imitations of the spinners work well, especially later on in the evening in eddies associated with large pools in the river.

If you have never fished to this hatch, I strongly recommend that you put meeting and fishing it on your agenda. If you are not intimidated by night fishing, you will be in for a memorable fly-fishing experience when casting large dry flies to surface-feeding brown trout. I was not disappointed with my first encounter with this colossal mayfly.

Some Rivers with a *Hexagenia* Hatch

Au Sable River – Michigan

Namekagon River – Wisconsin

Manistee River – Michigan

Pere Marquette River – Michigan

South Branch of the Au Sable River – Michigan

Williamson River – Oregon

Fall River – California

4

Great Rivers of the East
and Their Hatches

American fly fishing was started on the fabled great rivers of the East. Many well-known fly fishers were schooled in the art on rivers such as the Ausable and Beaverkill in New York, the Batten Kill in Vermont, and Penns Creek in Pennsylvania. The variety of trout water at that time put the tackle available to the fly fisherman to the test.

Hatches were reported to be blizzardlike. The green drake, march brown, quill gordon, and hendrickson were very abundant. Today, many of these hatches are still intact but with a decrease in abundance being noted by anglers and scientists alike. Some rivers – like the Housatonic in Connecticut, the Connecticut in New Hampshire, and the Deerfield in Massachusetts – are in need of a more constant flow of cold water that will sustain trout and the organisms on which they feed.

With new approaches to fisheries management, Maryland and North Carolina are developing some exciting trout water within their boundaries. The Savage River is a remarkable trout river, as are the Beaverkill and West Branch of the Ausable in New York. Many great hatches, like the hendrickson, green drake, and slate drake, remain on these high-quality waters.

Well-organized action groups are forming in an attempt to improve

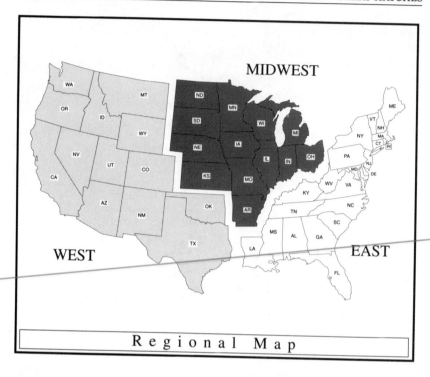

MIDWEST

WEST

EAST

R e g i o n a l   M a p

or maintain the quality of fisheries that currently exist in each state. New Hampshire, Massachusetts, and Connecticut all have angler/ conservation organizations that are starting to effectively sway politi- cally motivated decisions in favor of high-quality water. After all, isn't that what all of us require, including trout?

We divided the United States into three regions (see map). Charles covered rivers in the West, while Greg covered those in the Midwest. In the East, Charles describes rivers in New York, Pennsylvania, Maryland, West Virginia, and Virginia. Greg was responsible for those in New Hampshire, Vermont, Connecticut, Massachusetts, New York, North Carolina, and Tennessee.

Let's spend some time on the great rivers in the East. Traveling from north to south, we will examine blue-ribbon trout waters from the New England states through Pennsylvania, Maryland, Virginia, West Virginia, North Carolina, and Tennessee. Interestingly, we found little angling pressure on some excellent trout rivers in the southeast- ern United States. You may have fished some of them. Others that we discuss will be new to you. Sit back and let us share some of our insights and experiences on the great rivers and hatches in the East.

NEW HAMPSHIRE

Where else can you fly fish for trout and observe loons and moose going about their daily routines? Cold, steep-gradient trout rivers are available in this beautiful state. We will assess two of New Hampshire's quality trout waters.

Connecticut River

Connecticut River Regulations (for that portion of the river between New Hampshire and Vermont): "Connecticut River" means all waters of the river including the bays, setbacks, and tributaries to the first highway bridge crossing said tributaries on the Vermont and New Hampshire sides.

Licenses: All New Hampshire and Vermont fishing licenses are valid for the taking of fish in the Connecticut River lying between New Hampshire and Vermont, including all bays, setbacks, and tributaries to the first upstream highway bridge.

— Freshwater Fishing Guide,
New Hampshire Fish & Game Department

The large yellow signs along the road stated: "Brake for moose, it could mean your life." One hundred and seventy collisions had already occurred during the season along roads that parallel the upper Connecticut River. There are over four thousand moose in the northern White Mountains of New Hampshire. I didn't want to meet one of those animals with my Subaru, so I proceeded with caution.

The Connecticut River starts at its source at Second Lake near the Quebec, Canada, border. It flows in and out of three other impoundments before it reaches Pittsburg, New Hampshire. The upper Connecticut River is very scenic, offering a wilderness setting like no other trout water in the East. Below Lake Francis and the 100-foot-high Murphy Dam the Connecticut is a big river with adequate hatches. It is a tailwater fishery, since summer release temperatures are in the low fifties. Additionally, springs at several points along its course provide more cold water for the river. At this point it flows through the serene Connecticut River valley.

The upper Connecticut can be accessed from U.S. Route 3 at several points north of Pittsburg. In this region you will find the river to have a steep gradient with large boulders and pocket water throughout.

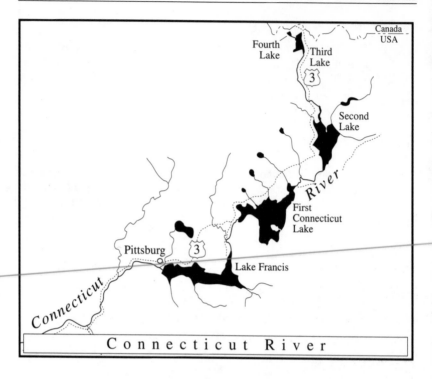

Grant Woodbury, president of the Abenaki Chapter of Trout Un-limited, has been fly fishing the region for approximately forty years and has guided many float trips on the Connecticut. He feels that with additional minimum flow requirements the Connecticut River could be as good or better than any trout river in the West. He is also concerned about the impact that logging could potentially have on this trout fishery. Aquatic resource managers and professional foresters need to work together to ensure the quality of the Connecticut.

At the request of Bob Pierce of Pittsburg, whose home is situated above a large pool below Murphy Dam, Grant and I visited the release site from Lake Francis late one afternoon in August. Bob told us that he thought the water had been turned off at the lake. We thought that surely he must be wrong, but to our displeasure and disappointment we found that Bob was indeed right – the gates were closed on the discharge into the river. How could anyone with any sense of responsi-bility subject an aquatic resource to such abuse? I had been at this same site the previous day, and the ground literally vibrated beneath my feet with the volume of water being discharged from the lake. Grant stated that this was the lowest he had ever seen the Connecticut

River in all the years he has been monitoring it. What impact could this event have on trout and the organisms that sustain them? We turned over a few rocks and found *Stenonema* nymphs exposed to the elements. We obviously didn't see any trout. We returned to Bob's house overlooking the Connecticut and observed a fly fisherman wading right across the middle of a huge, deep pool in front of Bob's house. Bob's reply was that you would never be able to do that with normal flows.

The Connecticut River above Lake Francis near Pittsburg, New Hampshire. *Greg Hoover.*

Even with this neglect of a high-quality resource, hatches such as the quill gordon, hendrickson, march brown, and blue-winged olive have maintained their populations on the Connecticut. If fly fishermen are to enjoy this resource, managers will have to examine the current flow schedules on the Connecticut River.

Best Times to Fly Fish

May 16–June 15
Quill Gordon: #12–14, afternoon
Hendrickson/Red Quill: #14, afternoon and early evening
Blue-Winged Olive: #16–18, morning and evening
Gray Caddis: #14, afternoon and evening
Tan Caddis: #14–16, afternoon and evening
Olive Caddis: #14–16, afternoon and evening

June 16–July 15
March Brown: #10–12, afternoon and evening
Hendrickson/Red Quill: #14, afternoon and early evening
Blue-Winged Olive: #16–18, morning and evening
Gray Caddis: #14, afternoon and evening
Tan Caddis: #14–16, afternoon and evening
Olive Caddis: #14–16, afternoon and evening
Green Drake: #8–10, evening

July 16–August 15
Gray Caddis: #14, afternoon and evening
Tan Caddis: #14–16, afternoon and evening
Olive Caddis: #14–16, afternoon and evening
Slate Drake: #10–12, afternoon and evening
Trico: #22–26, morning
Golden Drake: #12, evening

August 16–September 15
Gray Caddis: #14, afternoon and evening
Tan Caddis: #14–16, afternoon and evening
Olive Caddis: #14–16, afternoon and evening
Slate Drake: #10–12, afternoon and evening
Trico: #22–26, morning

September 16–October 15
Small White Caddis: #18, afternoon
Small Black Caddis: #18, afternoon

Saco River

As I traveled north on State Route 16 toward the town of North Conway, I listened to the radio announcer commenting on the fact that Hurricane Bob was about to hit the Rhode Island coast. A gentle rain was beginning to fall, but the worst was yet to come.

In North Conway Fred Abbruzzese, co-owner of North Country Angler, provided me with an excellent tour of the river, then we decided to take a break for lunch. As we discussed the river, the rain got heavy and the winds increased – the force of Hurricane Bob had come to this beautiful region. Fred alluded to the fact that the Saco is very susceptible to runoff: it rises rapidly with snowmelt (each winter an average of 150 inches of snow falls in the Northern White Mountains) and rainfall events. He stated that the river would be unfishable the next day. Regrettably, he was right. The Saco had come up about 3 feet in less than six hours.

This beautiful valley is shadowed by Mount Washington in the Presidential Range of the White Mountains, and the tributaries of the Saco River drain these picturesque mountains. Over the last ten years,

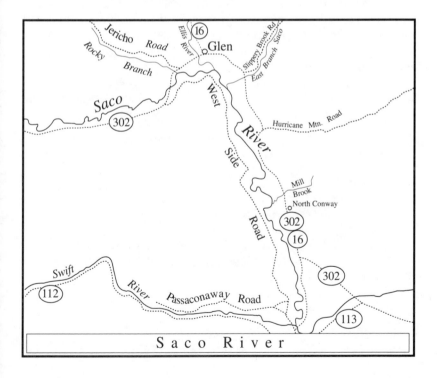

however, development has come to the valley, and this has impacted the quality of water in the Saco.

The river begins at Saco Lake at a 1,900-foot elevation and flows for about 40 miles in New Hampshire. In its headwaters the Saco River is a fast-flowing, boulder-laden fishery, and the substrate is comprised mainly of schist, granite, and other igneous rocks.

Fred has done some snorkeling in the Saco River to observe trout behavior and has witnessed many interesting displays by large browns. He feels that every pool in the Saco contains some very heavy trout.

Both Dick Stewart, publisher, and Jack Russell, editor, of *American Angler* magazine in Intervale feel that the gray drake is one of the most important hatches on the Saco. Brown and rainbow trout will surface to feed on this mayfly species from May 20 through June 20. Dick is actively pursuing the identity of the significant species in the genus *Siphlonurus*. He has made several important observations on these mayflies and has authored an article entitled "The Mirus Spinner" in the winter 1988 issue of their magazine. Gray foxes and sulphurs also cause trout to feed on the surface of the Saco.

My first impressions of the Saco River will be lasting ones. It is a huge western-style river with a great deal of holding capacity, and I have no reason to doubt Fred's observations on heavy trout in this river. But I am concerned about the continued development in this sensitive river valley.

Karl Swendsen at North Country Anglers said that the Saco offers a scenic experience for any fly fisherman who wishes to cast a fly in solitude on its waters.

Best Times to Fly Fish

May 15–June 15
> Black Quill: #12–14, afternoon and evening
> Quill Gordon: #12, afternoon and evening
> Red Quill *(Rhithrogena)*: #14, afternoon and evening
> Gray Drake *(Siphlonurus)*: #12–14, morning and evening
> Dark Green Drake *(Litobrancha recurvata)*: #6–8, afternoon and
> early evening
> March Brown: #10–12, afternoon and evening
> Sulphur: #14, evening

June 16–July 15
> Gray Drake *(Siphlonurus)*: #12–14, morning and evening

Dark Green Drake *(Litobrancha recurvata)*: #6–8, afternoon and
  early evening
March Brown: #10–12, afternoon and evening
Gray Fox: #12, afternoon and evening
Sulphur: #14, evening
Blue Quill: #16–18, afternoon and evening
Yellow Drake: #10, evening
Little Blue-Winged Olive Dun: #18, morning and evening

July 16–August 15
Blue Quill: #16–18, afternoon and evening
Yellow Drake: #10, evening
Little Blue-Winged Olive Dun: #18, morning and evening

August 16–September 15
Little Blue-Winged Olive Dun: #18, morning and evening

VERMONT

Many anglers rate fly fishing in the Green Mountain State as excellent,
but many fly fishermen have been frustrated while fishing for trout in
Vermont because the hatches seem to be somewhat irregular. The
Little and Dog rivers, however, yield some excellent brown trout. We
will examine just one of Vermont's finest, the Batten Kill.

The Batten Kill

If you ask most fly fishermen where they would fish if they spent time
in Vermont, most would say that they would fish the Batten Kill. Its
reputation is a national one, and the scenic beauty of this river as it
flows along the base of the Green Mountains is awesome year-round.
Surprisingly, the Batten Kill remains a cold-water fishery throughout
the season, getting an abundance of cold water directly from springs
and other groundwater sources.

The headwaters of the Batten Kill are located near the town of
Peru, and the river winds its way 25 miles toward New York State. The
Batten Kill can be accessed off of U.S. Route 7 between Manchester
and Arlington and State Route 313 between Arlington and the New
York State boundary. The trout season ends October 31 in the Green
Mountain State, so plan your trips to fly fish this river accordingly.

The Batten Kill is a brook- and brown-trout fishery with the lower
reaches often yielding heavy browns. Brown trout in the Batten Kill
are truly wild – no stocking of this species has occurred since 1971.

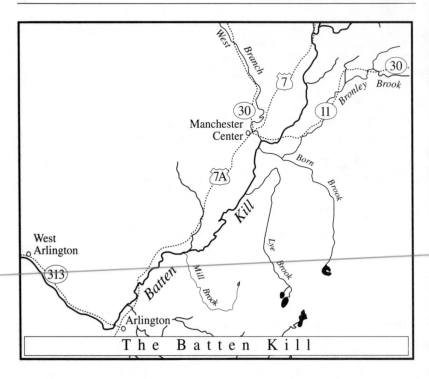

The Batten Kill

Brook trout reproduction occurs throughout the Batten Kill watershed. These fish run small, but their beauty makes up for their lack of
size. This river is subject to a lot of fishing pressure, but if you fly fish it
in August, you will see fewer fishermen. Trout in the "Kill" (Dutch
word meaning "creek") are especially difficult to catch during summer
months.

Gloria Jordan, wife of the late Wes Jordan, fly-shop owner, and rod
builder, is truly dedicated to fishing the Batten Kill. She has fly fished
for thirty-one years and guides fly fishermen on this quality trout river.
According to both Gloria and Dan Reid of the Orvis Fly Shop in Manchester, hatches on the river have been declining during the past
fifteen years, but the hendrickson, light cahill, and tricos remain as
important hatches. They also enjoy fly fishing to caddis emergences in
late May and early June and also cast terrestrial imitations during July.

Fly fishers should be aware that the pristine quality of the Batten
Kill easily may be reduced by man's activities. A landfill downriver of
Manchester could pose a threat to the Batten Kill. Bulldozing of
streambeds is also a concern of those who monitor this watershed, and

certain recreation uses could also threaten the quality of this trout fishery. If the Batten Kill is to remain a blue-ribbon trout river, vigilance on this river must be practiced by Vermont residents and nonresidents alike.

Best Times to Fly Fish

April 1–May 15
Little Black Caddis: #18–20, afternoon and early evening
Blue Quill: #16–18, afternoon and early evening
Hendrickson/Red Quill: #12–14, afternoon and early evening

May 16–June 15
Hendrickson/Red Quill: #12–14, afternoon and early evening
March Brown: #12, afternoon and evening
Tan Caddis: #14–16, afternoon and evening
Green Caddis: #14–16, afternoon and evening
Light Cahill: #12–16, late afternoon and evening
Dark Red Quill: #14–16, afternoon

June 16–July 15
Trico: #24, morning
Blue-Winged Olive: #18, morning and evening
Golden Drake: #12, evening
Sulphur: #18, evening
Little Blue-Winged Olive Dun: #18–20, afternoon and early evening
Light Cahill: #12–16, late afternoon and evening
Dark Red Quill: #14–16, afternoon
Yellow Drake: #10–12, evening

July 16–August 15
Trico: #24, morning
Little Blue-Winged Olive Dun: #18–20, afternoon and early evening
Ants: #14–18, afternoon
Light Cahill: #14–16, late afternoon and evening

August 16–September 15
Trico: #24, morning

September 16–October 15
Trico: #24, morning

MASSACHUSETTS

This New England state offers some fine fly fishing for trout, and you have the choice of fishing large water or small brooks. You'll find deep pools and fast runs to test your fly-fishing skills, and catch-and-release areas are available in the East Branch of Westfield, Quashnet, and Swift rivers. We will examine another river, which has two catch-and-release areas – the Deerfield River.

Deerfield River

Catch-and-release area (artificial lures only, no bait in possession): Fife Brook Dam to Hoosac Tunnel and the section extending from Pelham Brook to the Mohawk Campground.

– Abstracts of the Fish & Wildlife Laws,
Commonwealth of Massachusetts,
Division of Fisheries & Wildlife

One morning I found myself on the upper Deerfield River with Marc Aroner, who has spent twenty years on the river and is an excellent bamboo-rod builder from Conway. Bob Olszewski, owner of Sugarloaf Tackle Company in South Deerfield, accompanied us. He also has had experience on this river. We were fishing the upper catch-and-release area in a pool known as the Aquarium. I decided to fish nymphs, while Marc cast dry flies in Long Pool downstream from me. Both Bob and Marc cautioned me about how quickly the river rises at this point. I believed them, but not with the degree of interest that they had hoped. About forty-five minutes after we started to fish the large boulder-strewn area, I thought I noticed an increase in the sound of the water flowing through the gorgelike setting. Sure enough, the water was coming up more rapidly than I ever could have believed. I worked my way downriver toward Marc, and he was already backing out of Long Pool. In a short while the river had come up 2 feet, and whitewater enthusiasts came floating by us. Please heed the warnings along the Deerfield that indicate this rapid rise in water levels. You don't want to be caught in it. Also, when fishing the Deerfield, we strongly advise wearing felt-soled waders, and the use of a wading staff is suggested because the rocks are very slippery.

There are two regulated sections on the Deerfield. To access them, go west on State Route 2 toward North Adams. Go past Charlemont Center 2.2 miles, turn right on Zoar Road toward the Yankee Atomic

The Deerfield River in the upper catch-and-release area. *Greg Hoover.*

Power Plant, drive approximately 4 miles to a fork in the road, bear left under the railroad underpass and over a bridge. The Deerfield is now on your right. Travel approximately 4 miles more and you will reach Hoosac Tunnel and the B & M Railroad tressel. There are signs indicating the Deerfield River Catch-and-Release Area along the highway.

Brown and rainbow trout can be caught in this section of the river. According to Bob and Marc, Elkhair Caddis, Adams, Light Cahill, and Blue Quill are popular patterns to fish on the Deerfield. Terrestrial patterns prove to be productive during midsummer.

Pools with names like Fife Brook, Beaver, Shady, Crib, and Cold River provide some excellent tests of your fly-casting skills on the Deerfield.

Bill Latrel, president of the Deerfield Watershed Association, is quite knowledgeable on the flows associated with the Deerfield. He stated that there is probably more electricity generated per river mile on the Deerfield than any other river in the country. The watershed association has started an inventory of the aquatic insects in the Deerfield, hoping to establish some baseline information in preparation for requests for relicensing of these hydroelectric dams. Hydropsychid caddisflies (free-living species) are most common in their samples to date.

With several of the dams scheduled for relicensing in the coming years, the future of the river rests in the hands of resource managers, conservation groups like the watershed association, concerned citizens, and managers of utility companies. We can only hope that their decisions will be for the benefit of all, including the water quality of the Deerfield.

Best Times to Fly Fish

April 1–May 15
Early Brown Stonefly: #14, afternoon
Little Black Caddis: #18–20, afternoon and early evening
Gray Caddis: #12–16, afternoon and evening

May 16–June 15
March Brown: #12, afternoon and evening
Gray Caddis: #12–16, afternoon and evening
Sulphur: #16, evening
Tan Caddis: #12–16, afternoon and evening
Light Cahill: #14, later afternoon and evening
Blue Quill: #16, afternoon and early evening
Black Quill (on lower stretches): #14, afternoon

June 16–July 15
Pale Evening Dun: #16–18, evening
Sulphur: #16, evening
Tan Caddis: #12–16, afternoon and evening
Gray Caddis: #12–16, afternoon and evening
Light Cahill: #14, late afternoon and evening
Golden Drake: #12, evening

July 16–August 15
Light Cahill: #14, late afternoon and evening

CONNECTICUT

A fly fisher would not normally equate trout with densely populated Connecticut, but it contains several quality rivers. We will examine two of these trout fisheries – the Farmington and Housatonic rivers.

Farmington River

> Trout management areas are established to allow the implementation of special management concepts in areas judged to be unique trout habitat. The ultimate goal is to enhance recreational fishing and provide a variety of opportunities for Connecticut's trout anglers.
>
> *Barkhamsted–New Hartford, from the State Route 318 bridge downstream to the State Route 219 bridge*: There is no closed season for trout and charr in this area and the daily creel limit for trout and charr is zero. All trout and charr caught must be immediately returned, without avoidable injury. Possession of trout or charr in the waters or on the shores of this area is prohibited.
>
> *—Connecticut Angler's Guide,*
> Connecticut Department of Environmental Protection,
> Bureau of Fisheries and Wildlife

What could a river that is a thirty-minute drive from a population of almost one million people offer you? Well, if it's the Farmington River with all its natural, scenic beauty, it can offer you plenty. Over three hundred years ago the river was teaming with salmon; they were so abundant that the Indians depended more on fish than game for their survival. But the industrial revolution, with its associated papermills, tanneries, foundries, and sawmills, spelled an end to the high quality of water in the Farmington.

However, as pollution decreased in the northern Farmington, the trout began to repopulate the river. In the early to mid-1900s dams were constructed on branches of this river to eliminate the effects of major flooding. Now, according to Bill Hyatt, fisheries biologist with the Department of Environmental Protection in Connecticut, nearly every sport fish species presently existing in Connecticut can be found in the Farmington. Trout dominate much of the fishery from the U.S. Route 202 bridge downstream to State Route 4.

I met Jim Stack of Wethersfield early one morning. He spends most of his trout-fishing hours on the Farmington. We fished to an excellent spinner fall of tricos, and both of us caught and released many heavy trout during the morning. Jim feels that bottom releases of cold water into the Farmington are critical to maintaining this high-quality trout fishery. The temperature of the river on this August day was 66 degrees Fahrenheit.

David Gooley and Mike Motyl of Classic & Custom Fly Shop in New Hartford are very knowledgeable about the hatches of the

Farmington, and they feel that caddisfly emergences and egg laying are important to the fly fisher.

Dick Lowrey, fly tyer and fishing guide for ten years on the Farmington, is in love with the river. He should be – he's president of the Farmington River Anglers Association and is a strong advocate of these waters. Jim Stack and I fished with Dick later in the evening and we all released several good trout on polywing spinners. When we left the river in darkness, we traveled up a trail for a short distance and encountered a beaver feeding on a small branch. Dick suggested that we detour around this thirty-pounder to make our way back to our vehicles.

Even though the Farmington is situated so close to a dense population, it still offers a wildernesslike experience in its upper reaches. Just about any fly fisherman will enjoy testing his skills on the many great hatches that occur on this great river.

Best Times to Fly Fish

April 1–May 15
 Early Brown Stonefly: #14, afternoon
 Little Black Caddis: #18–20, afternoon and early evening
 Quill Gordon: #12–14, afternoon
 Little Blue-Winged Olive Dun: #18, afternoon and early evening
 Hendrickson/Red Quill: #10–12, afternoon and evening
 Blue Quill: #16–18, afternoon and early evening
 Early Brown Stonefly: #14, afternoon

May 16–June 15
 Hendrickson/Red Quill: #10–12, afternoon and evening
 March Brown: #10–12, afternoon and evening
 Sulphur: #14–16, evening
 Green Drake: #10, evening
 Light Cahill: #12–18, late afternoon and evening

June 16–July 15
 Light Cahill: #12–18, late afternoon and evening
 Golden Drake: #10–12, evening
 Sulphur: #18, evening
 Little Orange Crane Fly: #16, evening

July 16–August 15
 Trico: #22–24, morning
 Golden Drake: #10–12, evening
 Slate Drake: #12–14, afternoon and evening
 Bright Green Caddis: #20–22, evening

Ants: #18–22, afternoon
Leafhoppers: #20–24, afternoon
Beetles: #16–18, afternoon

August 16–September 15

Slate Drake: #12–14, afternoon and evening
Little Blue-Winged Olive Dun: #20–24, afternoon
Little Dark Blue Dun: #22–26, afternoon
White Fly: #12–14, evening
Ants: #18–22, afternoon
Leafhoppers: #20–24, afternoon
Beetles: #16–18, afternoon

September 16–November 15

Little Blue-Winged Olive Dun: #20–24, afternoon
Little Dark Blue Dun: #22–26, afternoon

Housatonic River

Trout management areas are established to allow the implementation of special management concepts in areas judged to be unique trout habitat. The ultimate goal is to enhance recreational fishing and provide a variety of opportunities for Connecticut's trout anglers.

Salisbury-Canaan-Sharon-Cornwall, from the bridge at State Route 112 and U.S. Route 7 downstream to the bridge at State Route 4 and U.S. Route 7: There is no closed season for trout and charr in this area, except that those portions within 100 feet of the mouths of tributary streams, as indicated by posters, are closed to all fishing during the period July 1 through August 31. Fishing in the portion of this area indicated by posters is restricted to fly fishing only. The daily creel limit for trout and charr in the entire area is zero, and all trout and charr caught must be immediately returned, without avoidable injury. Possession of trout or charr in the waters or on the shores of this area is prohibited.

—Connecticut Angler's Guide

The Housatonic River, which originates in the Berkshire Mountains north of Pittsfield, Massachusetts, is located in northwestern Connecticut. U.S. Route 7 parallels the river along much of the trout management area, and there are signs along the river warning wading anglers. Do the constantly rising currents cause problems for both trout and the angler? What could this large river have in store for the fly fisher? There are about 50 miles of good trout water in this river, with large boulders and bedrock substrate providing some habitat for trout and the insects on which they feed. But felt-soled waders and a wading staff are necessary to effectively fish this river.

The Housatonic is a tailwater fishery, but the cold water doesn't come from the impoundment at Falls Village Hydroelectric Dam. Instead, cold tributaries along the length of the river supply some cooling water to it. These areas are closed to fishing from July 1 to August 31.

Recently, smallmouth bass have been caught in areas where fly anglers are accustomed to catching trout, and this is a serious concern to those who frequent the Housy. Tom Maxwell, cofounder of Thomas and Thomas, lives five minutes from the river and has fished it for over ten years. During the past three years he has noticed a decrease in the number of trout along with increases in river temperature and water levels that are lower than normal. Tom feels that the cumulative effect of these factors has played a significant role in the decline of trout populations on the Housy.

When fishing the Housatonic during a rising or high-water period, try fishing pockets and eddies with nymphs and streamers. Fish seem to migrate to these areas to escape the increased flows.

Important hatches to meet and fish on the Housatonic include the hendrickson, blue quill, white fly, black sedge, and grannom. Some of the areas a fly angler might wish to cast patterns for trout include Split Rock, Carse, Dun Rollin, and Corner Hole pools. All of these can be easily accessed off of U.S. Route 7.

If the Housatonic is to remain a high-quality trout fishery, serious consideration will have to be given to the quality and quantity of water that is discharged into its channel.

Best Times to Fly Fish

April 1–May 15

Little Black Caddis: #18–20, afternoon and early evening

Little Blue-Winged Olive Dun: #18–20, afternoon and early evening

Tiny Dark Blue Dun *(Pseudocloeon)*: #20–26, afternoon and evening

Quill Gordon: #12, afternoon

Hendrickson/Red Quill: #12–14, afternoon and early evening

Blue Quill: #16, afternoon and early evening

Dark Blue Sedge: #12–14, afternoon and evening

Little Sister Sedge: #14–16, afternoon and evening

Spotted Sedge: #10–14, afternoon and evening

May 16–June 15
> Little Black Caddis: #18–20, afternoon and early evening
> Quill Gordon: #12, afternoon
> Hendrickson/Red Quill: #12–14, afternoon and early evening
> March Brown: #10–12, afternoon and evening
> Green Drake: #8–10, evening
> Brown Drake: #10–12, evening
> Light Cahill: #12, late afternoon and evening
> Little Sister Sedge: #14–16, afternoon and evening
> Blue-Winged Olive: #14–16, morning and evening
> Green Sedge: #14, afternoon and evening
> Zebra Caddis: #10, afternoon and evening

June 16–July 15
> Blue-Winged Olive: #14–16, morning and evening
> Zebra Caddis: #10, afternoon and evening
> Light Cahill: #12, late afternoon and evening
> Yellow Drake: #10, evening
> Slate Drake: #10, late afternoon and evening
> Little Sister Sedge: #14–16, afternoon and evening
> Spotted Sedge: #10–14, afternoon and evening

July 16–August 15
> Trico: #20–24, morning
> Purple Sedge: #18–20, afternoon and evening
> Slate Drake: #10, late afternoon and evening
> Light Cahill: #12, late afternoon and evening

August 16–September 15
> Trico: #20–24, morning
> White Fly: #12–14, evening
> Little Blue-Winged Olive Dun: #18–20, afternoon and early
>   evening
> Little Dark Blue Dun: #20–26, morning and afternoon
> Slate Drake: #10, late afternoon and evening
> Light Cahill: #12, late afternoon and evening

September 15–October 31
> White Fly: #12–14, evening
> Little Blue-Winged Olive Dun: #18–20, afternoon and early
>   evening
> Little Dark Blue Dun: #20–26, morning and afternoon
> Great Brown Sedge: #6–8, afternoon and early evening
> Slate Drake: #10, late afternoon and evening

NEW YORK

New York has always been known for its fabled trout water. Many fly fishermen have fished the trout fisheries in the Catskills such as the Willowemoc, Esopus, and Beaverkill, while others opt for a trip north to test their skills on the scenic West Branch of the Ausable. The Beaverkill and the streams of the Adirondacks will quicken your heartbeat, especially during some of the great hatches for which these rivers are known. We will examine several of New York's quality trout fisheries.

Beaverkill River

Catch-and-release areas: 1) Delaware-Sullivan County line downstream 2.5 miles; 2) 2.6 miles near Horton–1 mile above bridge and 1.6 miles below the same bridge.

–*New York State Fishing Regulations Guide,*
New York State,
Department of Environmental Conservation

What great fly-fishing personage has not set his waders in this hallowed water? What renowned angling author has not discussed this great Catskill river? I'm referring, of course, to the famous Beaverkill.

Even though its fame attracts angling hordes far in excess of the ideal, you can still successfully match one of the dozen hatches you'll encounter on this fabled water. On an average day you'll also meet fly fishermen from New Jersey, Pennsylvania, and Connecticut vying for one of the many trout in one of the Beaverkill's famous pools: Junction, Barnhart's, Hendrickson, Cairn, Schoolhouse, Mountain, Lower Mountain, Painter Bend, Cook Falls, or Cemetery. The heaviest angling crowds flock to the section from Horton to Roscoe. A sign in Roscoe proclaims that town as the "Trout Capital of the United States."

Walt Dette, one of the great anglers of trouting legend, still lives in Roscoe, and he and his wife, Winnie, operate a store devoted to fly fishing out of their home. The store and house are chock-full of Beaverkill history from the past century. You'll see photos of some of the famous early twentieth-century fly fishermen and hear plenty of stories about this great river.

Two blue-ribbon stretches of the Beaverkill remain open year-round. The first begins at the Sullivan-Delaware County line and runs downriver for 2.5 miles. The second runs from 1 mile above the Horton bridge to 1.6 miles below that same bridge. You're required to use artificial lures and return your trout immediately to the water. The fly-fishing pressure is heaviest in these two specially regulated areas.

The Beaverkill begins just east of Hardenburgh, and above Roscoe it is a midsized stream running from 30 to 60 feet wide. Much of the land above is posted, but there is an access area in Rockland just 1 mile above Roscoe.

The Willowemoc is a major tributary of the Beaverkill, entering in Roscoe at the Junction Pool and adding more than half to the flow of the main stem. From there downstream the Beaverkill widens to twice its earlier size. You'll find great hatches and heavy brown trout in the area open to public fishing. The Willowemoc upstream holds just about all the hatches you'll find on the Beaverkill itself. The 3.2-mile section from Elm Hollow Brook downstream is open year-round to catch-and-release fishing with artificial lures only.

The Beaverkill is a freestone eastern version of the insect factory found on Henry's Fork in Idaho. No, you won't find the quality or quantity of insects that you find there, but you'll find your fair share. Almost from the beginning of the season you can fish over hatches like the little blue-winged olive dun and blue quill. Many times when these and the quill gordon and hendrickson appear, the Beaverkill's waters are still too cold to encourage trout to feed on the surface.

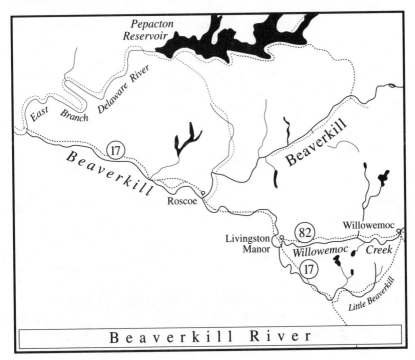

Beaverkill River

By the time May arrives and gray foxes and march browns appear, you can often enjoy great day-long fishing to these sporadic emergers. Late May and early June bring out the great hatches like the sulphur and green drake. I've hit spectacular drake hatches on the river near Cook's Falls. But the season doesn't end with the green drake; plenty of blue-winged olive duns appear in June and even later. You'll fish over yellow drakes and golden drakes in late June and July, and in late July and August tricos fall onto the river in the morning.

Fishing in the evenings on the Beaverkill in late May, June, and July can be delightfully rewarding or annoyingly difficult. Just at dusk any one of a number of spinners can start to fall onto the water and trigger a giant feeding frenzy. Rewards will come if you match the spinner fall. On the other hand, the wrong size and color spentwing will produce an evening of frustration.

Caddisflies and stoneflies have a prominent place on the Beaverkill. Walt and Winnie Dette have tied so many caddis imitations for Beaverkill anglers that they have designated them as A, B, C, D, E, F, or G, each designed to copy specific caddis hatches. One of the most common caddisflies, the green caddis, is the early *Brachycentrus* found on the water from early to mid-May. The dark blue sedge, *Psilotreta frontalis*, appears in June. You'll also find stoneflies, like the early brown stonefly, in April.

The Beaverkill contains a substrate of huge boulders, rocks, and small pebbles. It's a typical pool-riffle-pool, and many of the riffles and pockets between the pools are productive. Access areas to the stream are plentiful, and the Department of Conservation has done a great job protecting this quality water for public use. But everywhere on the river you'll see depressing signs that *Homo sapiens* has visited the pool before you: beer cans, soda cans, monofilament line, and plastic packages of all shapes and sizes.

With all the angling pressure near such a huge metropolitan area, the Beaverkill still produces remarkable hatches and heavy trout. If you're willing to forgo solitude and don't mind sharing a pool or riffle with a couple other anglers, you'll enjoy the Beaverkill, its trout, and its great hatches.

Best Times to Fly Fish

April 1–May 10
Little Blue-Winged Olive Dun: #20, morning and afternoon
Early Brown Stonefly: #12, afternoon
Blue Quill: #18, morning and afternoon
Quill Gordon: #14, afternoon

Little Black Caddis: #16, afternoon
Hendrickson and Red Quill: #14, afternoon
Black Quill: #14, afternoon (lower end)
Green Caddis: #16 or #18, morning and afternoon

May 10–June 15

Green Caddis: #16 or #18, morning and afternoon
Sulphur Dun and Spinner: #16, evening
Gray Fox: #12 or #14, morning, afternoon, and evening
March Brown: #12, morning and afternoon
Slate Drake: #12 or #14, evening
Green Drake and Coffin Fly: #10, evening
Blue-Winged Olive Dun: #14, morning; spinner – evening
Brown Drake: #12, evening (very spotty)
Blue Quill: #18, morning and afternoon
Light Cahill: #14, evening

June 15–July 15

Slate Drake: #12 or #14, evening
Dark Blue Sedge: #12 or #14, evening
Sulphur Dun and Spinner: #16, evening
Blue Quill: #18, morning and afternoon
Blue-Winged Olive Dun: #16, morning and afternoon
Yellow Drake: #12, evening
Light Cahill: #14, evening
Golden Drake: #12, evening

July 15–September 30

Trico: #24, morning
Slate Drake: #12 or #14, afternoon or evening
Little Blue-Winged Olive Dun: #20, morning and afternoon
Tan Caddis: #14, morning and afternoon
Dark Caddis: #18, morning and afternoon

The Upper Delaware River

Size regulations vary on different sections of the river. Check your latest
fishing regulations.

—New York State Fishing Regulations Guide

What you've just read about the hatches on the Beaverkill goes double
for the Upper Delaware. Thanks to some upriver impoundments and

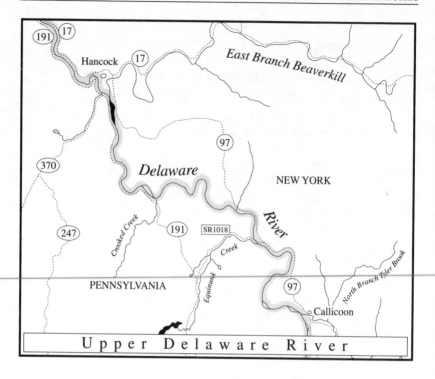

Upper Delaware River

bottom releases, this tailwater remains cool through most summer droughts.

The West Branch flows south, forming the eastern border of Pennsylvania, and just below Hancock it joins the East Branch to form the Delaware's main stem. There's great trout fishing on this river from the northern part of the West Branch down past Callicoon, New York. Many of the trout near Callicoon migrate upriver when the water in that area warms, and the two branches welcome these migrating trout to their already abundant supply.

But check the temperature before you begin fishing. The river's flow and water temperature depend on releases from the Cannonsville Reservoir on the West Branch and the Downsville Reservoir on the East Branch. Bob Sentiwany of Lehigh Tannery has fly fished the Delaware for more than twenty years, and he recalls the early 1980s when the water near Hancock was so low you could walk across the river on the exposed rocks. Long dry periods harmed the river during that period, and as long as the two dams above provide major sources of New York City water, the river periodically suffers from low volume.

Although much of the Delaware is inaccessible to waders, the section of the West Branch that borders Pennsylvania can be reached by a paved secondary road that runs north along the river. Pennsylvania State Route 370 crosses New York State Route 4014 just on the Pennsylvania side near Hancock. There's an access area designated by the Pennsylvania Fish and Boat Commission upriver a few miles at Balls Eddy, and the fishing in that vicinity is excellent. Downriver and across from Hancock, New York, Pennsylvania State Route 191 parallels the Delaware for about 10 miles to Equinunk. Just above Equinunk at Dillontown is a second access point. From that point downriver the main stem is difficult to reach until the bridge crossing the river to the town of Callicoon. Once you are on the river, however, you can move freely upriver and down.

On the east side New York State Route 97 parallels the Delaware. You'll also find a railroad track along the river on the New York side. Some anglers reach it on the east side by way of the railroad near Hankins. In this section the Delaware averages a good 100 to 150 feet wide, alternating with deep pools and productive riffles. If you cross private land, make certain to ask permission first.

Once on the Delaware you can easily wade it, but gaining access can be a major problem. Landowners jealously guard their private land along the river, the Pennsylvania Fish and Boat Commission provides only two access areas in 30 miles of water, and New York has only one. Apparently, the two states hesitate to build additional access areas because New York residents with New York licenses would use the Pennsylvania accesses and vice versa. You can fish from either side of the Delaware with either license.

It's easier to mention the hatches the Delaware doesn't offer than list the ones it has. Almost from the beginning of the season in mid-April you'll find little blue-winged olive duns, blue quills, and hendricksons. In late April you sometimes see so many hendricksons on the surface that you have no chance to match the hatch with an appropriate imitation.

Probably the best time to visit this prolific river is near the end of May. It holds generous populations of gray foxes, pink ladies, green drakes, brown drakes, and blue-winged olive duns; and since these mayflies appear around the end of May or early June, your chances of fishing over a hatch increase greatly at this time. Add to these mayflies a heavy caddisfly population and you're in for some great matching-the-hatch fishing.

State agencies add fingerlings to the native brown, rainbow, and occasional brook trout population. You'll know immediately if you hook one of the plentiful streambred rainbows from the spirited battle it puts up. If you enjoy large streambred trout that often rise to massive hatches, you'll make it a point to fish the Upper Delaware River.

Best Times to Fly Fish

April 1–May 10
 Little Blue-Winged Olive Dun: #20, morning and afternoon
 Blue Quill: #18, morning and afternoon
 Quill Gordon: #14, afternoon
 Hendrickson and Red Quill: #14, afternoon
 Grannom: #12, morning and afternoon
 Olive Caddis: #14 and #16, morning and afternoon
 Gray Caddis: #14 and #16, morning and afternoon

May 12–June 15
 Tan Caddis: #14, morning and afternoon
 Sulphur Dun and Spinner: #16 and #18, evening
 Gray Fox and Ginger Quill: #12 and #14, afternoon and evening
 March Brown: #14, morning and afternoon
 Green Drake and Coffin Fly: #10, evening
 Light Cahill: #14, evening
 Brown Drake Dun and Spinner: #12, evening
 Chocolate Dun and Spinner: #16, morning and afternoon (dun);
  evening (spinner)
 Pink Lady: #14, evening
 Slate Drake: #12 and #14, evening

June 15–July 15
 Sulphur Dun and Spinner: #16 and #18, evening
 Golden Drake: #12, evening
 Cream Cahill: #14 and #16, evening
 Slate Drake: #12 and #14, evening

July 15–September 30
 Cream Cahill: #14 and #16, evening
 Blue Quill: #18, morning and afternoon
 Trico: #24, morning
 White Mayfly: #14, evening
 Slate Drake: #12 and #14, afternoon and evening
 Little Blue-Winged Olive Dun: #20, morning and afternoon
 Blue Dun: #20 or #22, afternoon

West Branch of the Ausable River

> *In Essex County, West Branch Ausable River, from Monument Falls down-stream 2.2 miles:* artificial lures only, open all year to trout fishing. Three fish per day, minimum length 12 inches.
>
> *—New York State Fishing Regulations Guide*

As Jim Frazier, head of the entomology department at Penn State, and I approached Lake Placid on State Route 73, we came upon a site that neither of us will ever forget—the two towers of the Olympic ski jump training area. The highest tower was so tall it had to have a blinking red light on it so airplanes wouldn't collide with it, and Jim and I agreed that it would take a truly unique individual to launch himself down these ramps on skis. Little did we know that upriver from this site was the beginning of some excellent trout water on the West Branch of the Ausable River.

The West Branch of the Ausable River starts its northeastern flow

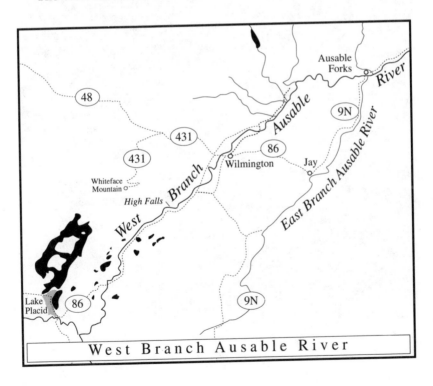

West Branch Ausable River

from the region of Mount Marcy and along the way picks up many small tributaries. From Lake Placid it flows through meadows for approximately 5 miles along State Route 86 toward the village of Wilmington. There are deep pools, fast eddies, a few waterfalls, and pocket water around large boulders that hold brown and rainbow trout. In total there are approximately 35 miles of high-quality trout water. The New York Department of Conservation stocks around eighty thousand trout in the stream each year. Additionally, hundreds of large fish in the 2- to 4-pound class are also planted in the river. Deep pools and well-oxygenated water maintain cool temperatures in the summer months.

Both Jim and I found the West Branch of the Ausable River the most difficult water we have ever waded. Felt-soled waders and a wading staff are an absolute must to effectively fish this river. You may also want to fish with a companion because of the treacherous footing associated with the large boulders in the river.

Jim Frazier fishing the West Branch of the Ausable River below Wilmington, New York. *Greg Hoover.*

Fran Betters has owned the Adirondack Sport Shop near Wilmington for twenty-six years and has been fishing the Ausable since he was nine years old. Fran is an excellent fly tyer—he was taught by Ray Bergman—and is credited with the development of the Haystack, the Usual, and the Ausable Wulff. Fran says there was a decline in the river during the 1970s, but recently he has noted more catch-and-release fishing being practiced on the river, and he has seen an increase in both aquatic insect and trout populations on the river during the 1980s. Interestingly, there are few fly fishermen in the Wilmington area. Most angling pressure comes from fishermen in the Catskills and other adjacent states.

The next morning Jim and I fished at Shadow Rock pool. The tricos were above the water at 8:20 A.M., and shortly after trout began to rise at the base of Shadow Rock. Jim cast to these fish and managed to hook several browns and rainbows. He switched to a #14 Ausable Caddis and began skating it on the surface. About midway along the rock a large trout surfaced to take Jim's presentation. After a short but exciting battle, it broke the light tippet. Both of us saw the size of that fish, and Jim's hands were shaking as he tied on another imitation. We both hooked and landed several more trout during the morning.

Later that same day we fished downriver from the impoundment in Wilmington. We observed many slate drakes emerging as we fished this boulder-strewn stretch of the river, and their nymphal cases were very apparent at the bases of many large boulders.

The following morning Jim fished at the junction of the East and West branches of the Ausable in the village of Ausable Forks. He hooked and landed several small trout on the West Branch side of this pool. Later we decided to move to a remote lower region of the West Branch locally referred to as the "Bush Country." It started to rain as we walked into this beautiful stretch of the river, but even though it rained, brook, brown, and rainbow trout were deceived by our presentations. We both enjoyed the solitude of this region of the West Branch—neither of us saw another fisherman all day.

The West Branch of the Ausable provides some excellent fishing in pools with names such as Frustration, Phillips, Bergman, Flume, Better's, and Shadow Rock, which was recently featured on the cover of *Mid Atlantic Fly Fishing Guide*. Fran Betters says the West Branch offers excellent hendrickson, gray fox, and slate drake hatches from early to late season, respectively. Be sure to contact Fran at his fly shop before you fish this picturesque river. There is no one more knowledgeable than he on the West Branch of the Ausable.

Best Times to Fly Fish

April 1–May 15
   Early Brown Stonefly: #14, afternoon
   Giant Black Stonefly: #6, morning and evening

May 16–June 15
   Hendrickson/Red Quill: #12–14, afternoon and early evening
   Grannom: #14, afternoon and evening
   Gray Fox: #12, afternoon and evening
   Light Cahill: #12–14, late afternoon and evening
   Dusty Caddis: #14, afternoon and evening
   Little Black Caddis: #18, afternoon and early evening
   Tan Caddis: #14–16, afternoon and evening

June 16–July 15
   Light Cahill: #12–14, late afternoon and evening
   Green Drake: #8–10, evening
   Golden Drake: #12, evening
   Golden Stonefly: #8, evening

July 16–August 15
   Sulphur: #16–18, evening
   Trico: #22–24, morning
   Little Blue-Winged Olive Dun: #18, afternoon and early evening
   Flying Ant: #12–16, afternoon

August 16–September 15
   Slate Drake: #10–12, afternoon and evening
   Flying Ant: #12–16, afternoon

September 16–October 15
   Slate Drake: #10–12, afternoon and evening

PENNSYLVANIA

What an endless variety of trout streams and rivers available to the fly fisherman! In the central, south-central, and southeastern sections of the state you can hop from freestone to limestone waters in minutes. You can travel from the Yellow Breeches to the Letort to the freestone Clark Creek within an hour. Many of the limestone streams hold great trico hatches from mid-July through September and a sulphur hatch from mid-May through June.

And you still haven't witnessed the great trout streams of the northern area of the Keystone State. You'll find great early and mid-season hatches on First Fork, and Kettle, Pine, and Oil creeks. All four hold fantastic blue quill hatches in April and brown drake hatches in late May or early June. Of the four, all but Oil Creek hold respectable green drake hatches, which occur at about the same time the brown drake appears. But many of these great freestone waters suffer—to a greater or lesser degree—from thermal problems in June, July, and August.

Pennsylvania boasts a considerable number of fertile trout streams within a short distance of many of its metropolitan areas. Within minutes of Philadelphia anglers can fly fish over prolific hatches on Valley Creek at Valley Forge. Just 5 miles west of Reading anglers annually match great trico hatches on the Tulpehocken Creek. Allentown area anglers also have a variety of limestone streams within reach. And the Little Lehigh, Cedar Run, and the Monocacy in nearby Bethlehem offer great hatches and matching-the-hatch opportunities.

There are more than 10,000 miles of trout streams in the Commonwealth. Which of these have the best hatches? It's difficult to choose, but among the best are Penns, Spring, Yellow Breeches, and Fishing creeks and the Little Juniata and Youghiogheny rivers. All but the Youghiogheny River are limestone waters.

Fishing Creek

Trophy Trout Project: 5 miles—from the bridge at Tylersville Fish Hatchery downstream to Fleming's Bridge at Lamar Fish Hatchery.

—*Pennsylvania Summary of Fishing Regulations and Laws,*
Pennsylvania Fish and Boat Commission

The summer of 1988 presented many problems for eastern and mid-western trout waters. By early August the water temperature on Loyalsock Creek in north-central Pennsylvania was above 80 degrees, and the normally cool Au Sable River near Grayling, Michigan, rose into the low seventies. Anglers had difficulty locating cold water to fish. However, one productive limestone stream in central Pennsylvania remained consistently cool—Fishing Creek.

Cold springs near its headwaters in Loganton provide plenty of cool water all summer long. Add to this other springs in the narrows below Tylersville and a couple large, cool, limestone tributaries—

Cedar and Long runs – just south of Mill Hall, and you get an idea why this water provides great habitat for trout all season long.

Fishing Creek holds a great population of several species of blue quills (Paraleptophlebia). The first (P. adoptiva) appears in mid-April, followed by a second major hatch (P. guttata) in June and July. I remember heading up to the narrows just above Lamar one late-June morning in 1988 to look for an early-morning blue quill emergence. A heavy fog completely filled the narrow valley. When I reached the area I planned to fly fish, I immediately stuck a thermometer into the water and found the temperature to be a nice cool 59 degrees. Shortly after dawn blue quills appeared, and a half dozen trout fed on the laggards in the pool. This cold limestone stream didn't let me down: on Fishing Creek in late June I hit a heavy blue quill hatch that I'm certain few other anglers ever witness.

What makes Fishing Creek one of the top streams in the East? It has diverse, dense hatches and predictable cold water throughout the season in a stream filled with deep pools, pockets, and heavy riffles. Fishing Creek is truly a top-notch trout stream – not just in the East but in the United States.

You don't have to wait long to greet the first hatch of the season, either. On a recent mid-April trip Jay Kapolka, Mike Marinelli, and I fished for more than three hours over four different hatches and plenty of rising trout. By 10:00 A.M. the first hatch, little blue-winged olive duns, appeared, followed shortly by blue quills, quill gordons, and hendricksons. The two heaviest hatches turned out to be the blue quill and the hendrickson. Even if you miss these four mayflies, April produces a heavy grannom caddisfly hatch. And no sooner have the April four ended than you'll see sulphurs and march browns appearing.

The stream's qualities make it a fantastic cold limestone stream with hatches and rising trout throughout the entire summer, but the heavy and long-anticipated hatch on Fishing Creek – as well as Penns Creek – is the green drake, which emerges on the narrows section a few days after the hatch has ended on Penns Creek. Since the drake appears in more limited numbers, trout are often easier to catch with a match of the green drake.

Fishing Creek has two distinct areas and some hatches seem to prefer one of the two. The upper end, the narrows, just above Lamar and below Tylersville is 4 miles long. Above Tylersville the flow becomes intermittent during the summer. In the heavily wooded narrows you'll find the green drake, blue quill, hendrickson, quill gordon, pink lady, little blue-winged olive dun, sulphur, and slate drake. In this upper section you'll catch streambred brown and brook trout. You'll also find the "trophy trout" section in this area.

Fishing Creek in the narrows holds a great green drake hatch in early June.
Charles Meck.

From Lamar downstream to Mill Hall the limestone water flows through 10 miles of farmland. In this lower end you'll see a decent hatch of sulphurs in May and early June and a fishable trico hatch from July through September. Here also you'll see several blue-winged olive dun hatches from late May until early September. Match these morning emergers with a #14 or #16 pattern, and you can have some excellent late-season matching-the-hatch excitement.

The state stocks the lower part of the stream near Mill Hall. County Route 2002 parallels the creek in the narrows section, County Route 2004 down to Mackeyville, and State Route 64 from Mackeyville to Mill Hall. Just above Mackeyville the stream flows underground in July and August. Fishing Creek enters Bald Eagle Creek just north of Mill Hall.

Fishing Creek has some productive tributaries: Little Fishing Creek enters the main stem at Lamar; Cherry Run, a freestone stream, enters 3 miles above; and Cedar and Long runs, both respectable limestone streams, enter the main stem below Mackeyville.

Best Times to Fly Fish

March 15–April 15
Little Blue-Winged Olive Dun: #20, morning and afternoon

April 15–May 5
Little Blue-Winged Olive Dun: #20, morning and afternoon
Blue Quill: #18, morning and afternoon
Quill Gordon: #14, afternoon
Hendrickson: #14, afternoon
Black Caddis: #14, morning and afternoon

May 12–June 5
Sulphur Dun and Spinner: #16, evening
March Brown: #14, morning and afternoon
Dark Green Drake: #8, afternoon and evening (spotty)
Green Drake and Coffin Fly: #10, evening
Slate Drake: #14, evening
Light Cahill: #14, evening
Pink Lady: #14, evening
Green Caddis: #14, afternoon and evening

June 5–July 20
Little Blue-Winged Olive Dun: #20, afternoon and evening
Blue Quill: #18, morning
Blue-Winged Olive Dun: #14, morning
Sulphur Dun and Spinner: #16, evening

July 15–September 30
Trico: #24, morning (lower section only)
Blue-Winged Olive Dun: #14, morning
Blue Quill: #18, morning
Little Blue-Winged Olive Dun: #20, morning and afternoon
Blue Dun: #20, afternoon

Little Juniata River

> *Miscellaneous Waters Special Regulations – from mouth of Bald Eagle Creek (near Tyrone) downstream to the confluence of the Little Juniata River and the Frankstown Branch, Juniata River, near Petersburg:* No closed season on trout. Daily limit opening day of trout season to Labor Day: eight trout; day after Labor Day to succeeding day of trout season: three trout.
>
> *—Pennsylvania Summary of Fishing Regulations and Laws*

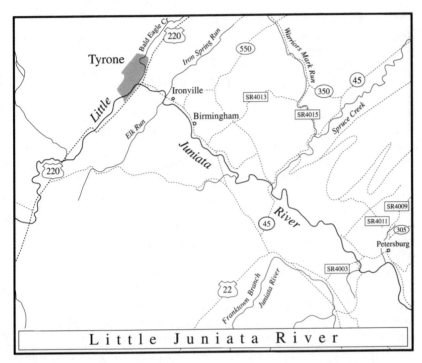

Little   Juniata   River

What a terrible excuse for a river the Little Juniata was! For decades tannic acid roiled in its dark brown water. But hatches persisted and rumors of huge trout surfaced annually; however, whatever trout the Little J held were not fit to eat. And the river had another aesthetic problem: it stank. Raw sewage poured in from upriver towns, and few anglers had the stomach to wade in it.

That was the 1960s. This is the 1990s, and things have changed dramatically for the better. Now hatches cover the surface almost every month of the year, and the Little J flows with a chalky clarity that we associate with limestone waters. You'll even find some stream-bred brown trout to accompany the thousands of small stockers the Pennsylvania Fish and Boat Commission adds each year. What a difference twenty years and environmental awareness have made in the health of the Little Juniata!

During its years of severe pollution the river still produced a few sulphurs and light cahills. Now, with the cleanup, more than a dozen mayflies emerge in numbers heavy enough to constitute a hatch. Within just the last five years the river has added to its inventory great hatches like the green drake, gray fox, and the white fly.

The green drake appears on the Little Juniata about a week before it appears on Penns Creek. Until 1985 the river had few green drakes.

That year an excited Dave Landis of Lancaster, Pennsylvania, called me after spending a night on the river and reported a terrific coffin fly spinner fall on the river between Spruce Creek and Barree.

The next year I had a chance to guide Bob Kendig, of Aurora, Colorado, during the green drake hatch on the Little J, and that evening we saw thousands of coffin flies over the water. Mating began much earlier than I had seen on Penns Creek. The spinners fell intermittently for more than two hours that night. Bob first matched the emerging duns, then switched to an imitation of the spinner. He ended the successful evening by landing a bright, full-bodied 18-inch brown trout. What a day on the Little J!

Little Juniata hatches do not appear early. The matching-the-hatch season formally begins abruptly with a downwing, the green caddis, in early May. If you meet this frustrating downwing, try using an emerger pattern. Sink the wet fly just under the surface and prepare yourself for some excitement.

Within a week of the caddis's appearance you're in for a spectacular sulphur hatch. Hatches continue off and on until late September and early October and feature the little blue dun and the slate drake. Even on those January and February days when the air temperature reaches the high forties or fifties, you'll often see pods of trout feeding in the slower pools. If you hit the water in winter, bring some #24 dark gray midges to copy the emergers.

The white fly has been coming on strong on the lower 10 miles of the Little Juniata in the past eight years. The average date for this #14 or #16 mayfly is August 23. Once the hatch begins, it normally appears on the same stretch of the river for twelve or thirteen nights. The best area to meet this hatch is from Barree to Petersburg. Review chapter 3 for more information on the white fly.

The Little Juniata River flows south from Tyrone to Petersburg in central Pennsylvania. Upstream from Tyrone the water is only marginal, except in sections where the main stem picks up productive tributaries like Bells Gap and Tipton runs and a large tributary, the Bald Eagle. A few hundred yards below Tyrone the river passes through high limestone cliffs and becomes a limestone river. For the next 10 miles, to the town of Spruce Creek, it collects a dozen limestone springs of various sizes, which provide a moderate season-long flow and help to keep its summer temperature low.

You can reach the Little J easily from Tyrone south for 6 miles via State Route 350. From that point paved secondary roads parallel the stream into Spruce Creek. From Spruce Creek to Barree the only access is by foot. This latter section, about 4 miles long, contains 15-foot-deep pools, productive riffles, heavy hatches, and plenty of wild trout.

From Barree to Petersburg, about 5 miles, a paved secondary road again parallels the river. In this area the river expands and contains fewer small trout, but it yields up some lunkers over 20 inches. Its pools are deep, and wading is dangerous in this lower end. State Route 305 crosses the river near Petersburg, and 300 yards below the Little Juniata joins the Frankstown Branch to form the Juniata River. Here the two rivers flow into the upper end of Warriors Ridge Dam, a hydroelectric project. You'll find trout below the dam near one of the many cool springs that enter the river. Trout fishing on the river is open year-round with a three-trout limit in effect from Labor Day until opening day.

The river ranges from 40 to 100 feet wide with a moderate drop of about 15 feet per mile. It contains, as I said, many large pools, some of them more than 100 yards long. Riffles and moderate water abound, and these sections teem with trout. Wading the river is treacherous, and many veteran fly casters have taken a plunge. The water hides countless medium-sized boulders covered with a slippery film, and some fast-water sections are simply impossible to cross or wade.

Before entering the Little Juniata, check with Allan Bright of Spruce Creek Outfitters in the town of Spruce Creek. Al knows the river and its hatches well and shares his information graciously.

Best Times to Fly Fish

March 1–April 1
Little Blue-Winged Olive Dun: #20, morning and afternoon
Little Black Stonefly: #16, afternoon
Early Brown Stonefly: #14, afternoon

April 1–May 1
Little Blue-Winged Olive Dun: #20, morning and afternoon
Early Brown Stonefly: #12, afternoon
Little Black Caddis: #16, afternoon (lower area of the river)
Blue Quill: #18, morning and afternoon (spotty)

May 5–May 12
Green Caddis: #14, afternoon and evening
Yellow Caddis: #14, afternoon and evening
Yellow Crane Fly: #20, afternoon and evening

May 12–June 15
Green Caddis: #14 and #16, afternoon and evening
Sulphur Dun and Spinner: #16, evening
Light Cahill Dun and Spinner: #14, evening

Gray Fox and Ginger Quill: #12, afternoon and evening
Green Drake and Shad Fly: #10, evening (from Spruce Creek
  downriver)
Dark Blue Quill: #20, early evening
Cream Cahill: #14, evening
Blue-Winged Olive Dun: #14 or #16, morning; spinner: evening
Slate Drake: #12, evening
Blue Quill: #18, morning and afternoon

June 20–July 5
Yellow Drake Dun and Spinner: #12, evening
Sulphur Dun and Spinner: #16 or #18, evening
Tan Caddis: #16, evening
Blue-Winged Olive Dun: #14, morning; spinner: evening
Slate Drake: #12, evening
Blue Quill: #18, morning and afternoon

July 15–September 30
Trico: #24, morning (spotty)
Little White Mayfly: #28, evening
Tan Caddis: #16, evening

August 22–September 1
White Mayfly: #16, evening
Winged Ant: #20, afternoon and evening
Tan Caddis: #16, evening

September 20–October 10
Slate Drake: #12, afternoon
Blue Dun: #20, afternoon
Little Blue-Winged Olive Dun: #20, morning and afternoon

Penns Creek

Catch-and-release area: 3.9 miles, from Swift Run downstream to
J. J. Soper property line.

— Pennsylvania Summary of Fishing Regulations and Laws

What hatch first comes to mind when you think of Penns Creek?
Everybody who's seen the throng of fly fishers around Memorial Day
on this famous limestone stream considers the green drake synony-

mous with Penns, and if you happen to be on hand when the huge
coffin flies reappear to lay their eggs, I promise you will never forget it.
You'll see hundreds – no, thousands – of anglers trying to coax one of
the stream's heavy browns to take their patterns. You'll see anglers
using tannish gray nymphs, emergers just under the surface, and of
course copies of the dun and spinner.

Many fly fishermen suffer extreme frustration during the green
drake hatch. They match the nymph, dun, or spinner and still come up
empty-handed. There's so much food available that the trout become
incredibly choosy. Therefore, the best time to fish the drake hatch
often is when only stragglers appear during the day. Then you can
pinpoint rising trout and catch them more readily than in the evening
when the hatch or spinner fall proceeds in full force. If you learn that
the green drake hatch has already appeared or will not emerge for a
few days, take heart. You'll certainly see gray foxes, sulphurs, march
browns, and light cahills.

Penns Creek is hardly a one-hatch stream, and it definitely produces heavy hatches much more often than just near the end of May.
Visit Penns in mid-April and you'll see the regular assortment of gray

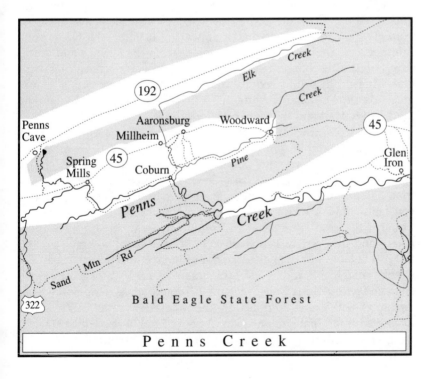

Penns Creek

colored mayflies and one of the heaviest and largest of the grannom hatches. This grannom *(Brachycentrus solomoni)* can be copied with a #10 dark brownish black caddis with dark brown wings. But as with many caddis hatches, the grannom on Penns can be frustrating: you might see thousands of caddisflies in the air and not one rising trout.

Often the best time to fish Penns Creek is just after the green drake hatch has ended. In the latter part of June and early July some great hatches cover the stream. If you happen to be on the water on one of those productive, overcast days, you might just get to enjoy a once-in-a-lifetime matching-the-hatch experience. Let me illustrate.

In 1979 on the Fourth of July at about 10:00 A.M. Andy Leitzinger and I separately appeared on Penns Creek. Andy fished several miles above me on the Broadwater section of the catch-and-release stretch; I fly fished 3 miles below on the catch-and-release section at the winter cabin. We each thought we had the entire stream to ourselves on that drizzly holiday, and both of us hooked more than forty fish each. Each of us experienced one of the best days of matching the hatch imaginable on this famous eastern limestoner.

Both of us fished a hatch not too familiar in the East. This fly, the blue-winged olive dun *(Drunella lata)*, endears itself to fly fishers because it comes on so late in the season. If you fish Michigan rivers, for example, you can see this hatch appearing in late July. On normal summer days these duns take off rapidly from the surface and give a rising trout little time to take them. But on a cool, overcast day these blue-winged olive duns require more time to dry their wings before their takeoff. Andy Leitzinger and I fished one of those days when the duns had to wait and the trout rose for hours.

Penns Creek begins a few miles north of Spring Mills at Penns Cave. The cool limestone water flows south 4 miles through Spring Mills, then through farming country southeast for 6 miles to Coburn. Some of the open meadows from Spring Mills to Coburn hold heavy trico hatches and several blue-winged olive dun species. In this area you'll also find a lot of posted land. By the time Penns arrives at Coburn, the cold spring waters from 10 miles upstream have dissipated, and for a while Penns exists only as a marginal trout stream. But just below Coburn another cold, productive limestone stream, Elk Creek, enters. Elk adds a refreshing shot of cool water to the main stem and helps Penns Creek reclaim its reputation as a top-notch trout stream over the next 20 miles. By the time Penns reaches Weikert it becomes a marginal stream again. A shot of much-needed cold water from Weikert Run enters the stream at this small town.

You can reach the stream off State Route 45. In recent years the lower end of Penns Creek near Cherry Run has suffered from several fish kills. Recent extremely hot, dry summers have taken their toll on this great limestone stream. Some anglers have reported experiencing water temperatures in the high seventies for days on the lower end of this stream.

Best Times to Fly Fish

April 10-May 1
Grannom: #10 or #12, morning and afternoon
Blue Quill: #18, morning and afternoon
Hendrickson: #14, afternoon (lower end)
Quill Gordon: #14, afternoon (spotty)
Little Black Caddis: #16, morning and afternoon

May 20-June 10
Gray Fox: #12, afternoon and evening
Ginger Quill Spinner: #12, evening
Light Cahill: #14, evening
Sulphur and Sulphur Spinner: #16, evening
Green Drake and Coffin Fly: #10, evening

June 20-July 8
Blue-Winged Olive Dun: #16, morning and afternoon
Yellow Drake Dun and Spinner: #12, evening
Great Stonefly: #10, afternoon and evening

July 15-September 1
Trico Spinner: #24, morning (spotty)
Blue Quill: #18, morning
Caenis: #26, evening
Slate Drake: #12 and #14, evening

August 15-August 30
Dark Slate Drake and Rusty Spinner: #8, evening
White Mayfly: #14 and #16, evening (lower end)

September 15-October 15
Slate Drake: #14, afternoon and evening
Dark Olive Caddis: #14, afternoon
Dark Brown Caddis: #16, afternoon

Spring Creek

Fisherman's Paradise: No-harvest fly fishing only – 1 mile, lower boundary of Spring Creek Hatchery grounds to the upper boundary of the Paradise. (No fish may be killed or had in possession.)

Miscellaneous Waters Special Regulations – from bridge at Oak Hall above Neidig Brother's Limestone Co. to the mouth: No-kill zone – unlawful to kill or possess any fish. All fish caught must be immediately returned.

– *Pennsylvania Summary of Fishing Regulations and Laws*

What a great limestone stream Spring Creek once was! What great hatches this stream once held! Back in the 1940s and 1950s you could find a green drake hatch second to none. This famous stream also held brown drakes and a couple dozen other great hatches, each vying for top spot. George Harvey, the dean of American fly fishermen, has fished the stream since 1932. He saw the impressive hatches on Spring Creek, and he matched many a green drake hatch and coffin fly spinner fall on the stream before its demise.

Enter progress to "Happy Valley," the term locals call the area through which Spring Creek flows. Soon various accidental spills into the stream from chemical plants, sewage facilities, and university sites threatened the very life of this historic trout stream. Spring Creek lost many of its hatches in the late 1950s, and now it has no more green drakes, no brown drakes, and no yellow drakes.

Responding to the pollutants that persist in the water, the Pennsylvania Fish and Boat Commission decided to stop stocking the stream and to prohibit anglers from keeping any of the affected trout. They designated the entire stream a catch-and-release project in 1982. Shortly after, anglers discovered a surprising number of streambred fingerlings, and Spring Creek now boasts a good brown trout reproduction record.

Spring Creek is staging a gallant fight back from decades of being a polluted, lifeless stream, and many of its recent aquatic insect hatches are once again impressive. Light cahills, sulphurs, tricos, and several other mayfly species now produce healthy hatches on much of the water.

Recently a State College, Pennsylvania, newspaper dedicated a week of feature articles to Spring Creek. It examined questions like how can we reconcile all the demands we make of this water source and what's the future for this stream?

Posted land already clouds the Spring Creek picture. Land above Neidig's Quarry east of Lemont has been posted by individuals and angling clubs for years. Recently a prime mile of water just a few miles below Fisherman's Paradise was fenced off. What possesses someone to post his land so others can't enjoy the water flowing through it? Why can't anglers join together like other pressure groups and boycott the interests of landowners who prohibit fishing?

In spite of the persistent problems of posted land and pollution that beset it, Spring Creek boasts some superb water with great hatches. Trico hatches and spinner falls are extremely predictable on Spring Creek. Its middle section is almost devoid of this species, but the upper and lower sections produce dependable hatches. The tricos fall in heavy numbers by the second week in July and continue to do so well into September. Spinner falls of this species occur between 7:00 and 9:00 A.M. on the hottest days and from 9:00 A.M. to noon in September. On warm, muggy mornings the spinner fall may last less than a half hour.

There are three distinct sections of Spring Creek, distinguished by the different hatches and type of water in each. The upper section, from the source above Linden Hall downstream to Houserville, is a

Walt Young fishing one of his favorite nymphs on Spring Creek near Fisherman's Paradise. *Greg Hoover.*

small meadowland limestone stream. It has a different makeup of hatches than the rest of the stream. It harbors a good number of sulphurs and a healthy trico hatch, but it also has others not present farther down. Several species of blue-winged olives (*Drunella cornuta* and others) appear daily in June and July, along with blue quills and little blue-winged olive duns. Little blue-winged olives appear as early as March and April and as late as September and October on Spring Creek.

The middle section of Spring Creek, from Houserville downstream to the upper end of Fisherman's Paradise, had lost almost all its hatches, since it was this section that received the brunt of the chemical and sewage spills. Within the last couple years, however, several mayflies have feebly repopulated this area. The trico now appears, but not in the numbers it attains above or below, and the sulphur and light cahill have also reappeared in limited quantities.

The lower section of Spring Creek, from Fisherman's Paradise downstream 6 miles to the creek's junction with Bald Eagle Creek, is larger, more productive water. It also includes a mile of posted land. Hatches like the sulphur, trico, and green caddis have become important again. Fisherman's Paradise, once a well-maintained and heavily stocked no-harvest, fly-fishing-only stretch, has lost much of its previous attraction but remains an enjoyable locale for fly-fishing enthusiasts.

Most of Spring Creek is readily accessible by car – much of the creek runs within less than 100 yards of paved road. The stream flows under State Route 26 at Lemont, and State Routes 550 and 150 bring you close to the stream near Bellefonte and Milesburg.

Spring Creek has a relatively moderate flow with plenty of productive pocket water. The stream ranges from 30 to 40 feet from bank to bank and is fairly easy to wade, although thick aquatic growth makes wading difficult in some areas. Several excellent tributaries enter Spring Creek, and most of them contain streambred brown trout. Cedar Run, a pastoral limestone stream enters Spring Creek at Oak Hall. Downstream, just below Lemont, Slab Cabin Run enters. This also has native trout, but it was also the source of much of the pollution: a minor tributary of Slab Cabin Run carried effluents from the State College sewage plant. Two other important tributaries enter near Bellefonte: Logan Branch holds plenty of large trout and joins Spring Creek just west of downtown Bellefonte, and Buffalo Run, another important native brown trout stream, joins Spring Creek at the lower (east) end of Bellefonte. All of the major tributaries of Spring Creek are productive limestone streams. Spring Creek enters Bald Eagle Creek at

Milesburg, and for the next 4 or 5 miles Bald Eagle Creek holds some heavy brown and rainbow trout in some of its deep pools.

Steve Sywensky, Dan Shields, and Walt Young of Flyfisher's Paradise can keep you posted on the conditions and the hatches on Spring Creek. You'll find the store in Lemont, near the headwaters of Spring Creek.

Will Spring Creek survive as a trout fishery into the twenty-first century? Troublesome spills and urbanization have reduced Spring Creek to a shadow of what once was one of the greatest trout streams in the nation. Its painful attempt to regain its former stature presents a test case that all fly fishermen should be watching with concern.

Best Times to Fly Fish

March 10–April 3
   Little Blue-Winged Olive Dun: #20, morning and afternoon

April 15–May 1
   Blue Quill: #18, morning and afternoon

May 5–May 20
   Green Caddis: #14, afternoon and evening

May 15–June 10
   Sulphur Dun and Spinner: #16, evening
   Light Cahill: #14, evening

June 25–July 15
   Blue-Winged Olive Dun: #14, morning and afternoon
      (upper section)

July 15–September 30
   Trico: #24, morning
   Blue Quill: #18, morning
   Caenis: #26, evening
   Pale Morning Dun: #22, morning

Yellow Breeches Creek

Catch-and-release area: 1 mile, from Boiling Springs downstream to vicinity of Allenberry.

—*Pennsylvania Summary of Fishing Regulations and Laws*

If Penns Creek and Fishing Creek are noted for their spectacular green drake hatches, the Yellow Breeches wins fame for its white fly hatch *(Ephoron leukon)*. The white fly appears on the Breeches long after many anglers have called it a year and put away their gear. For many diehards this is the last great hatch of the season.

Once the white fly appears, it continues to do so for a couple weeks. During the height of the hatch in late August you'll find hundreds of anglers fishing the late-evening hatch around Allenberry. If you didn't know better, you'd think you were fishing on the opening day of the season with anglers almost elbow to elbow.

For years many anglers felt that the Yellow Breeches held the only white fly hatch found on a viable trout stream. Many anglers found the same hatch on the Susquehanna, Potomac, Youghiogheny rivers, and on these large waters smallmouth bass rose freely to the hatch. More recently, fly fishermen have found the same hatch on the Housatonic in Connecticut. I'm certain the list of those trout waters containing the white fly is still incomplete.

But the Yellow Breeches is more than a one-fly stream. It holds plenty of other hatches, including a few hendricksons early in the season and big slate drakes *(Hexagenia atrocaudata)* in August. From July through October you'll see tricos on the stream every morning. The hatch doesn't compete with Falling Spring Branch or Spruce creeks in numbers, but it does bring trout to the surface.

You'll find most of the fishing pressure and the largest trout in the specially regulated area near Boiling Springs. You can fish this section throughout the summer with good success. Boiling Spring Run pours extremely cold water into the Yellow Breeches near Allenberry.

This fertile limestone stream begins just east of Shippensburg and flows east through Mount Holly Springs. Thirty miles farther downstream, near New Cumberland, the Yellow Breeches enters the Susquehanna River. Above Mount Holly Springs the stream flows about 20 to 30 feet wide. West of Allenberry, Mountain Creek empties into the Breeches and widens to 50 feet. Several miles below Allenberry the Breeches holds more smallmouth bass than trout. State Route 174 parallels much of the stream.

Best Times to Fly Fish

March 1–March 30
 Little Black Stonefly: #16, morning and afternoon
 Little Blue-Winged Olive Dun: #20, morning and afternoon

April 15–May 1

Little Blue-Winged Olive Dun: #20, morning and afternoon
Blue Quill: #18, morning and afternoon
Hendrickson and Red Quill: #14, afternoon

May 12–June 15

Sulphur Dun and Spinner: #16, evening
Gray Fox and Ginger Quill: #12 and #14, afternoon and evening
Blue-Winged Olive Dun: #14, morning
Slate Drake: #12 and #14, afternoon and evening

June 15–July 14

Cream Cahill: #14 and #16, evening
Yellow Drake: #12, evening

July 15–September 30

Trico: #24, morning
Big Slate and Rusty Spinner: #8, evening
White Mayfly: #14 and #16, evening
Slate Drake: #12 or #14, afternoon and evening
Little Blue-Winged Olive Dun: #20, morning and afternoon

Youghiogheny River

> *Miscellaneous Waters Special Regulations—from reservoir to mouth of river:*
> No closed season on trout. Daily limit opening day of trout season to
> Labor Day, eight trout; day after Labor Day to succeeding opening day
> of trout season, three trout.
>
> *—Pennsylvania Summary of Fishing Regulations and Laws*

Why include in the list of great rivers of the United States a river that's
still recovering from the onslaught of man's indifference to his environment? Because this river, both in Maryland and Pennsylvania, holds
the potential for becoming one of the top rivers in the nation, and
because of the foresight of some concerned conservationists the
Youghiogheny contains a bottom release gate at Confluence, Pennsylvania, that provides a tremendous tailwater fishery for more than
20 miles below.

For many years the Youghiogheny held a few trout and some fairly
good caddisfly hatches, but one of its major tributaries, the Casselman

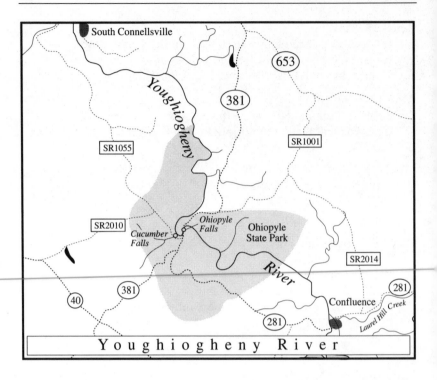

River, emptied a heavy slug of mine acid into the main stem. Even the upper end of the Youghiogheny River in Maryland and West Virginia experienced severe doses of mine acid. On the Casselman environmentalists added lime to this acid, which neutralized much of the detrimental effects, and now you'll even find trout in the river. In Maryland it holds a good supply of trout.

Upgrading the Casselman has improved the quality of the Youghiogheny below. Mayflies such as the slate drake, sulphur, blue-winged olive, yellow drake, and others, are now more common. Art Gusbar of Somerset, Pennsylvania, an avid fly fisherman on the Youghiogheny, reports that even a few green drakes have reappeared in the tailwater below Confluence. If conditions improve and mine acid runoff is contained or decreased, this fine eastern tailwater should continue to get better – but it will take time.

Probably the best time to hit this large river is early July. You'll find plenty of caddisflies, a good selection of mayflies, such as slate drakes and blue-winged olive duns, and some stoneflies. Select one of the impressive riffles on the 9-mile stretch from Confluence to Ohiopyle for your daytime fly fishing – you'll find caddisflies active on many afternoons on this fast water. Then move to one of the slower areas or glides when evening arrives, and you'll see sporadic hatches of may-flies appearing. Two of the best slow-water stretches are just below Confluence and at Bidwell Station, downriver from Confluence a few miles.

On the western side of the river the Western Pennsylvania Con-servancy maintains a bicycle-hiking path that parallels the river from Confluence to Ohiopyle, and thanks to the foresight of the Conserv-ancy, that stretch of the Youghiogheny will remain open for fishing forever. And since the only way to reach the river between these two towns is by bicycle or walking, you'll not find much fishing pressure.

Pat Docherty is the resource manager for the Corps of Engineers at the Youghiogheny Dam above the tailwater. He's a devoted fly fisher-man and fishes the water below the dam many times each season. Pat often refers to the tailwater as the "Madison of the East." The river is wide, averaging about 50 to 75 yards at Confluence. Because it's a tailwater, the river runs high well into the summer. One day Art Gusbar and I fished the river in air temperatures near 100 degrees. At the same time, the water temperature registered 63 degrees 3 miles below the release site.

Wading on the entire stretch from Confluence to Ohiopyle can be a trying experience, and at best it is treacherous even when the flow is normal. The rocks on the river's floor are uneven and difficult to cross. Add more water to the flow and wading can become downright dangerous.

You can reach the tailwater section in Pennsylvania on State Route 281 at Confluence. In Maryland State Route 495 crosses the Casselman near Grantsville, and State Route 42 crosses it near Friendsville.

Best Times to Fly Fish

April 25–May 10
   Black Caddis: #16, afternoon

May 10–June 1
   Green Drake and Coffin Fly: #10, evening (very spotty)

May 20–June 30
   Olive Caddis: #14 or #16, afternoon and evening*
   Blue Dun: #20 or #22, afternoon*
   Sulphur Dun and Spinner: #18, evening*
   Light Cahill: #14, evening*
   Blue-Winged Olive Dun: #14, morning and evening*
   Chocolate Dun: #16, afternoon and evening*
   Gray Caddis: #16, afternoon and evening

July 1–August 15
Slate Drake: #12, afternoon and evening
Yellow Drake: #12, evening
Cinnamon Caddis: #14, afternoon and evening
Perla Stonefly: #12, morning

August 1–September 30
Blue Quill: #18, morning and afternoon
Dark Gray Caddis: #18, afternoon and evening

*Hatches continue well after the ending date listed.

MARYLAND

Why have we included the small state of Maryland in our list of some of the top rivers and hatches in the United States? Once you've seen some of the rivers and streams this state has to offer, you won't question our reasons for placing them in this book. A lot has happened in Maryland in recent years that has enhanced this state's trout waters. Trout Unlimited and the Federation of Fly Fishers chapters in Maryland deserve much of the credit. Some other farsighted individuals within the state deserve kudos also. Bob Bachman, director of Freshwater Fisheries in Maryland, and his staff have accomplished much in recent years to promulgate trout fishing, and the city of Baltimore and its leaders deserve commendation for their cooperation with the Maryland Chapter of Trout Unlimited to produce the tremendous trout fishing on the Gunpowder Falls River.

Fish the likes of the Youghiogheny near Friendsville or the Casselman near Grantsville, and you can find an adequate number of trout and some good hatches. A newcomer to the scene in the past two years is the Potomac River below Bloomington Lake. This bottom release should come on strong as a cold-water fishery in the future. All three rivers have some acid mine drainage problems, but in spite of it they contain a good number of trout.

But the best is yet to come. Just 60 miles east of Morgantown, West Virginia, on the Savage River you can fish over great hatches of the green drake and sulphur, and you can fish all summer long in a tailwater that might reach 60 degrees – a tailwater that holds one of the best populations of brook trout I've ever seen. Yes, the Savage River, with its 5-mile tailwater, is a sight to behold.

Let's examine three of Maryland's trout waters: Big Hunting Creek and Gunpowder Falls River in the eastern sector near some of the large metropolitan areas and the Savage River in the west.

Big Hunting Creek

Catch-and-return fishing only.

> — *Maryland Freshwater Sportfishing Guide,*
> State of Maryland,
> Department of Natural Resources

Rob Gilford crouched low, hiding behind a huge exposed boulder in the middle of the half-empty stream. He had to. The brook, brown, and rainbow trout in this extremely low water scared easily—even the fly line innocently slapped on the surface revealed wakes from escaping trout. Two casts up to a deep, narrow riffle at the head, and a heavy streambred brown hit the Bob Brown Beetle pattern. Rob then headed up to the next pool. Here he hooked a half dozen trout. At the head of this same pool Rob had several heavy fish swirl at the terrestrial and hooked another fish.

In less than two hours of fly fishing on a hot August afternoon, in the middle of a drought, Rob Gilford and I hooked or missed more than forty trout, some of which weighed 2 pounds and measured up to 15 inches. You say there's nothing spectacular about that type of fly fishing? What if I said that all this sensational fishing took place within 55 miles of our nation's capitol? This action took place on Big Hunting Creek just north of Frederick, Maryland, off U.S. Route 15.

Why does this 30- to 50-foot-wide tumbling mountain stream hold so many trout? Rob Gilford owns the Rod Rack in Frederick, Maryland, and knows Big Hunting Creek well. He can tell you how this stream rates with him. His dad, Jim Gilford, instructs anglers on Big Hunting Creek. Jim and others in the area have formed a group called the Friends of Big Hunting Creek. This organization, along with the cooperation of Maryland Fly Anglers, Potomac Valley Fly Fishermen, Antietam Fly Anglers, Free State Fly Fishers, and the Northern Virginia Chapter of Trout Unlimited, has combined with federal and state agencies to provide better habitat on Big Hunting Creek. Friends of Big Hunting Creek has done an outstanding job in its vast stream-improvement program for the creek. Walk downstream from the Brooks Memorial area and you'll see the hundreds of man-hours these interested groups have contributed to make Big Hunting Creek a tremendous resource so close to a huge metropolitan area. Through the combined efforts of all the groups, hatch intensity has increased. Below Hunting Creek Lake you'll find streambred browns and rainbows and native brook trout, and even in low water conditions, with the stream-improvement devices presently placed in the stream, the trout have plenty of hiding places.

Big Hunting Creek holds an outstanding share of hatches. Throughout the winter months you'll find little black stoneflies appearing around midday. Around late March and early April blue quills and quill gordons appear on Big Hunting Creek's surface. By mid-May march browns appear, and a little later you'll even find a sparse hatch of green drakes.

Downwings provide plenty of food for the trout in Big Hunting Creek. On any warm winter afternoon you'll see little black stoneflies emerging on the creek. In late March and early April you can match the early brown stonefly. Caddis patterns with bodies of tan, green, and yellow also match some of the downwings present in the stream.

What hatches will you see in late summer? "Late summer is terrestrial time on the stream," said Rob Gilford as he landed a heavy stream-bred brown trout. Rob caught his biggest trout on the creek with an ant imitation. You won't find him on the stream in July and August without a good supply of ants and beetles.

There are about 2.5 miles of water open to fishing below the dam because it flows through park service and state park land. You'll also find some good fishing above the dam on Big Hunting Creek and its major tributary, Hauver Branch. State authorities built the dam in 1971 on one of the best stretches of the stream. The 40-acre impoundment, Hunting Creek Lake, contains three ports to release water. At the breast the lake runs 80 feet deep and releases water from the middle or bottom port, making the stream below a limited tailwater.

Big Hunting Creek contains heavy pocket water, some short pools, and a heavy canopy to protect it during the summer. State Route 77 parallels the stream from Thurmont upstream.

Stop in at the Rod Rack in Frederick and check with Rob Gilford on the hatches and stream conditions. If you're interested in its preservation, you can join the Friends of the Big Hunting Creek.

Best Times to Fly Fish

November 1–March 31
　　Little Black Stonefly: #18 and #20, afternoon

February 1–March 31
　　Little Black Stonefly: #14, afternoon
　　Early Brown Stonefly: #14, afternoon

March 15–April 30
　　Little Blue-Winged Olive Dun: #20, morning and afternoon

Blue Quill: #18, morning and afternoon
Quill Gordon: #14, afternoon
Hendrickson: #14, afternoon

May 10–June 10
Big Brown Stonefly: #10, afternoon and evening
Tan Caddis: #14 to #18, afternoon and evening
Green Caddis: #14, afternoon
Gray Fox: #12, afternoon and evening
March Brown: #12, morning and afternoon
Green Drake: #10, evening
Light Cahill: #14, evening
Yellow Sally: #16, evening
Yellow Caddis: #14 to #18, evening
Big Black Stonefly *(Pteronarcys dorsata)*: #6, evening

June 11–July 30
Yellow Drake: #12, evening (spotty)

August 1–September 30
Blue Quill: #18, morning and afternoon
Light Cahill: #14, afternoon and evening
Trico: #24, morning (spotty)
Little Blue-Winged Olive Dun: #20, morning and afternoon

Gunpowder Falls River

Catch-and-return trout-fishing areas (limited to use of artificial lures only):

a) Gunpowder Falls, Baltimore County, main stem from Prettyboy Reservoir Dam downstream to Falls Road (approximately 1.5 miles) and from York Road downstream to Bluemont Road.

b) A person may fish only with artificial lures, including artificial flies and streamers.

c) The open season is January 1 through December 31, inclusive.

—Maryland Freshwater Sportfishing Guide

For a week air temperatures hovered in the middle to high nineties. Radio stations in the area warned people about the hazards of hard exercise in this heated atmosphere and recommended that most people stay inside. I selected this hot week to test the qualities of a Maryland river situated just 20 miles north of Baltimore. Yes, just 20 miles

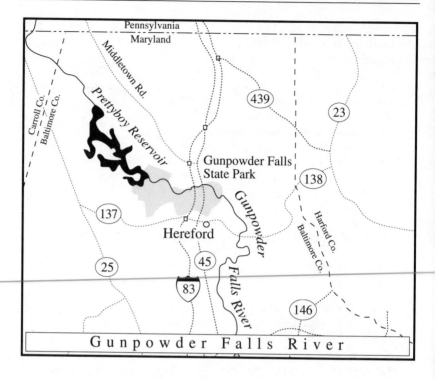

Gunpowder Falls River

from that sprawling metropolitan area. Steve Snyder of York, Pennsylvania, urged me to look at this river and suggested that it was one of the top rivers in the East. The Gunpowder Falls River certainly wouldn't be under the extraordinary heat wave we were experiencing.

Wally Vait and I entered the river where it crosses York Road. Wally operates the On the Fly shop in Monkton, Maryland, just a long stone's throw from where we parked, and has guided dozens of anglers on the Gunpowder for the past several years. When we reached the 30- to 50-foot-wide river, I noticed a thick layer of fog next to the surface. No wonder the river held a covering of fog – the river temperature registered 55 degrees.

Wally Vait caught a couple of 12-inch browns in the section rising for an assortment of cahills and terrestrials. Swimmers, trying to escape the intense heat, tested the cold water in front of us. Wally said that on weekends on this urban river hundreds of people invade the river and make it difficult for anglers.

We decided to head upriver a half mile below the bottom-release Prettyboy Dam. This 133-foot-deep reservoir, built in 1933, releases cold water from its bottom to the river below and keeps the entire section from the reservoir downriver to the holding dam, Lock Raven, cold enough to hold a good supply of streambred browns, native brook trout, and stocked and possibly streambred rainbows.

We parked at the upper catch-and-release area in the Fall Road section and hiked down a half-mile trail to the upper river. This section of the river holds an extensive variety of water types. Within a few hundred yards you'll find beaver dams, pocket water, some 3- to 5-foot-deep pools, and fishable riffles. Here, also, you'll see huge boulders scattered throughout the streambed. Add to this a heavy canopy of oaks, tulip poplars, an ample supply of mountain laurel, and other trees and you'd swear you're in some isolated mountain region far from any civilization.

Wally and I bypassed midging trout in the beaver dams for faster water below. No trout rose in this spectacular section so I tied on an attractor pattern, the Patriot, nearest the rod and a green inchworm tied by Steve Snyder of York on the tippet. Some locals call the inchworm the Green Weenie. This pattern copies many of the caterpillars you'll find in the area. The Patriot acted not only as an attractor pattern but also as a strike indicator. When the dry fly sank, I knew that a trout had struck the sinking inchworm pattern. I attached the two in the manner that I describe in the discussion on fishing the cycle in chapter 8. Then I attached a 2-foot piece of tippet material to the Patriot and tied in the improved clinch knot at the bend of the hook of the attractor dry fly. I then tied the green inchworm onto the tippet.

On the second cast with the twosome, a trout struck the attractor. I released a beautiful 12-inch Gunpowder streambred brown. Maybe five casts later the Patriot sank in midstream and I set the hook. The fish wouldn't budge, but stayed deep near branches dislodged from a beaver dam upriver. Wally urged me to put pressure on the heavy fish and keep it from tangling my line in the debris. A few minutes later I landed an 18-inch rainbow, unhooked the sinking green inchworm, and released the fish.

What an afternoon in the heat! Wally and I figure that we had hooked or missed at least forty trout on that unbearable summer afternoon. What a river! The Gunpowder showed its true colors on that August day.

The Gunpowder holds its share of hatches. Because it experienced severe fluctuation in flow until recently, hatch intensity and variety are still in a state of transition. Within the past couple years the river has experienced a good hatch of sulphurs. Wally Vait says that many of these mayflies appear from 11:00 A.M. to 3:00 P.M., followed by a sulphur spinner fall at dusk. Sulphur hatches can occur from mid-May

Wally Vait battles a trout on Gunpowder Falls River. *Charles Meck.*

until early July. You'll also see light cahills, brown drakes, little blue-winged olive duns, and much more.

Downwings on the Gunpowder provide plenty of food for trout. From early January until late May you'll see little black stoneflies on the water. In midsummer you'll find tan and gray caddisflies. Chironomids provide Gunpowder trout with a good share of their food. Make certain you carry midge patterns with you, especially #18–24 dark gray and black patterns.

A steady rather than fluctuating flow from Prettyboy Reservoir has helped to make the Gunpowder great. Until several years ago the city of Baltimore opened the gates at the reservoir to supply water to the Lock Raven holding dam. City authorities had little concern for the damage they created in the river below when they opened these gates and scoured the river. But the Maryland Chapter of Trout Unlimited, with Jim Gracie and the Department of Natural Resources, Freshwater Division, worked with the city to provide more stable releases.

You'll find the Gunpowder holds a good supply of clear, cold water all year long. Even after a heavy rain, because of the bottom release of the tailwater fishery above, you'll often find clear water to fly fish. In the upper section you'll find water temperatures from the high forties to low fifties all summer long and the bottom covered with algae. In the lower half water temperatures range from the low fifties to the low sixties. Here you'll find aquatic plants growing on the bottom. Much of the upper river flows through state park land and will remain open for all to enjoy forever. Below Falls Road you'll see some private property.

Roads intersect the river in certain areas. From the dam downriver you'll find the following roads and distances:

Gunpowder Falls
Measured Distances in Miles

Masemore Road to Bunker Hill Road	1.36
Bunker Hill Road to I-83 (York Road)	0.74
I-83 to Big Falls Road	2.37
Big Falls Road to Blue Mount Road	0.93
Blue Mount Road to Monkton Road	2.55
Monkton Road to Corbett Road	1.70
Corbett Road to Glencoe Road	2.52
Glencoe Road to Sparks Road	0.85
Sparks Road to Phoenix Road	1.53

You'll find the best fishing from the dam downriver to Corbett Road.

You can reach the river off exit 27 of Interstate 83. If you turn left at the exit, you'll reach the lower catch-and-release area. If you turn right, you're on your way to the upper end.

Stop in at Wally Vait's On the Fly in Monkton for the latest information on hatches on the river. Pennsylvania residents can check with Steve Snyder at Chet Patterson's Sporting Goods in York for reports on the river.

Best Times to Fly Fish

January 1–May 31
Little Black Stonefly: #14 and #18, midday

April 1–May 31
Little Blue-Winged Olive Dun: #20, morning and afternoon
Blue Quill: #18, morning and afternoon
Hendrickson: #14, afternoon
March Brown: #12, morning and afternoon (spotty)

May 15–July 15
Blue-Winged Olive Dun: #14 and #16, morning and afternoon
Sulphur: #16 and #18, afternoon and evening
Light Cahill: #14, evening
Yellow Drake: #12, evening (spotty)
Gray Caddis: #16, afternoon and evening
Slate Drake: #12, evening (spotty on lower end)
Green Caddis: #16, afternoon and evening

July 15–August 31
Slate Drake: #12, evening (spotty on lower end)
Tan Caddis: #16, afternoon and evening
Olive Caddis: #16, afternoon and evening
Little Blue-Winged Olive Dun: #20, morning and afternoon
Tiny Blue-Winged Olive Dun *(Pseudocloeon)*: #20 to #24, afternoon

September 1–September 30
Little Blue-Winged Olive Dun: #20, morning and afternoon
Tiny Blue-Winged Olive Dun *(Pseudocloeon)*: #20 to #24, afternoon

Savage River

> *Savage Reservoir to second suspension bridge:* catch and release, artificials only.
>
> *Second suspension bridge to Potomac River:* catch and release, artificials only, trophy trout. One trout (brown over 18 inches, brook over 12 inches, or rainbow [no size]).
>
> —*Maryland Freshwater Sportfishing Guide*

Paul Kurincak and I headed down the steep, narrow blacktop road toward a river I had heard about before but had never fished. On the trip from Morgantown, West Virginia, Paul boasted about the great fly fishing and brook trout that this river possessed. Paul should know the river—he owns the Upstream Fly Shop in Morgantown, which was the first shop in the state dedicated to the fly fisherman. We crossed several almost dry tributaries and paralleled a drought-stricken lake to reach the river. After several months of practically no rain and day upon day of temperatures in the nineties, what would the river below the lake look like? A tailwater appeared from the bottom of the deep reservoir and the cold, almost bank-full Savage River reappeared—much healthier than the one that had entered the reservoir 10 miles above. This was Maryland's answer to the so-called blue-ribbon waters of the West.

There are 5 miles of tailwater below the reservoir. Paul suggested that we go downriver 3 miles and fish for a couple hours. As soon as we geared up, I waded into the 50-foot-wide river to check the temperature.

"Fifty-seven degrees," I yelled to Paul.

Why so cold? The bottom release from the deep reservoir above made this a true cold-water fishery.

Paul selected a Pheasant Tail Nymph, and on the second or third cast he hooked a heavy brook trout. I headed downriver, searching the surface for insects. I connected with a 10-inch brook trout on a dry fly.

Two years ago the state stopped stocking the tailwater. It took courage and foresight on the part of the fisheries' managers of Maryland to make this a truly wild trout fishery, and they have succeeded.

"There's a 14-inch brown trout behind that boulder," Paul yelled to me as I cast in some heavy pocket water. The trout didn't rise to the dry fly. "There's a 15-inch rainbow in that riffle," Paul said as he pointed to a fast section near the far shore. Why did Paul know where all these

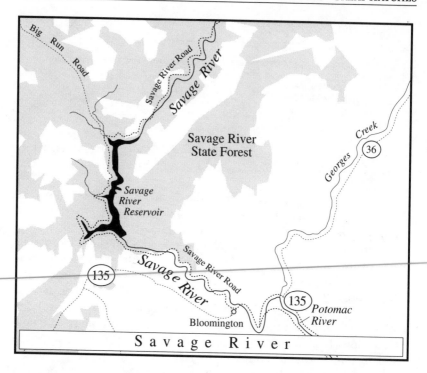

Savage River

trout lay? He's fished the river for more than seven years and has caught and released his share of them.

Three hours and a dozen heavy brook trout later we quit, satisfied that we had just spent an enjoyable midsummer afternoon and evening on the Savage River. The river fared well in spite of the extreme summer heat and drought.

You'll find an abundant supply of native brook trout in the tailwater below the reservoir, some brown trout, and a few large rainbow trout. Browns don't seem to develop as well as the brookies in this cold water. You'll have plenty of variety in water types on the river. You'll find some 10-foot-deep pools, plenty of heavy productive pocket water, and some worthwhile riffles on this 30- to 50-foot-wide river. Huge boulders dot the bank and river bed and provide plenty of cover for the trout in the 5 miles of managed area. You'll find several small canyons in the valley from the reservoir to the Potomac River at Bloomfield.

The Savage holds some excellent hatches both in the 3 miles of open water above the reservoir and in the 6 miles of tailwater below. As early as late March, mayflies appear. One of the earliest is the blue quill. In late May green drakes and sulphurs cover the surface. All summer long light cahills and pale evening duns appear during the evening.

Downwings provide plenty of food for the streambred trout. In late February and early March early black stoneflies appear daily around midday. Jack King and Brad Murdock of Oakland, Maryland, fish the river weekly throughout the summer. Jack prefers using caddis patterns in July and August and catches a lot of trout on #14–16 dark-bodied caddis patterns.

A shot of mine acid enters the Savage River just before it enters the Potomac River near Bloomington. Paul Kurincak has fished this lower area and even with the acid has still caught trout.

A blacktop road parallels the Savage River from Luke upriver along the tailwater, the lake, and the river above. Three miles of the Savage is open to public fishing above the reservoir. You'll find the water warmer in this upper area in midsummer. The green drake hatch seems to be a bit heavier in the area above the reservoir.

The river has some poaching problems, and several landowners have posted their sections of the river. The state would do well to work with these landowners to open the land adjacent to the water.

Although the Savage is rather small as tailwaters go, it is a good one. If you enjoy fly fishing over native brook trout that average 9 to 12 inches long, you'll appreciate the river. If authorities would make the entire section below the reservoir a catch-and-release area, it would enhance the stature of the trout fishery.

Check with Paul Kurincak in Morgantown at the Upstream Fly Shop regarding the hatches on the river. Paul can also help you with conditions and hatches on the Casselman, Youghiogheny, and Potomac rivers.

Best Times to Fly Fish

February 15–March 20
   Little Black Stonefly: #16, midday

March 20–April 30
   Little Blue-Winged Olive Dun: #20, morning and afternoon
   Early Brown Stonefly: #14, afternoon
   Blue Quill: #18, morning and afternoon

May 1–June 5
   Sulphur: #16, evening
   Gray Fox: #14, afternoon and evening

March Brown: #12, morning and afternoon
Green Drake: #10 and #12, evening
Light Cahill: #14, evening
Blue-Winged Olive Dun: #14 and #16, morning
Green Caddis: #14, afternoon
Cream Caddis: #14, afternoon

June 6–June 30

Blue-Winged Olive Dun: #14 and #16, morning
Blue Quill: #18, morning and afternoon
Little Green Stonefly (Lime Sally): #16 or #18, afternoon and
   evening
Yellow Stonefly (Yellow Sally): #16, afternoon and evening

July 1–August 31

Pale Evening Dun (*Heptagenia* species): #16 and #18, evening
Dark Slate Caddis: #18, evening

September 1–October 31

Little Blue-Winged Olive Dun: #20, morning and afternoon

VIRGINIA

Virginia doesn't have any viable trout streams or rivers, does it? Isn't it too far south to have any waters that hold trout? Not true. The state has some great water with plenty of good brook and brown trout from three sources: high mountain streams and rivers, springs, and tailwaters. You'll find some great trout waters associated with bottom releases from the likes of the Smith and Jackson rivers. Although the latter has been stocked with fingerlings, the state has not yet declared it an official trout water, and there remains a question of access to the river that has to be worked out.

There are several creeks like those you find in south-central Pennsylvania – such as the Mossy near Bridgewater and Smith near Harrisonburg. The most common type of trout waters you'll see in Virginia are those flowing from the Shenandoah National Park. The national park system authorities have kept these waters fairly primitive, protected the native brook trout in the streams and rivers, and set up special regulations. They deserve all anglers' thanks for a job well done.

We'll examine three of the high-mountain rivers flowing off the Shenandoah National Park – Mossy Creek and the Rapidan, Rose, and North Fork of the Moormans rivers, and a spring creek, Mossy.

Mossy Creek

Mossy Creek (Augusta County): Fly fishing only. That portion of stream upstream from the Augusta/Rockingham County line to a sign at the mouth of Joseph's Spring.

   a) Only single-hook artificial lures may be used.

   b) All fish must be immediately returned to the water unharmed. No fish may be in possession while fishing in these waters.

   c) No bait may be in possession while fishing these waters.

   d) Fishing is permitted year-round in these waters.

   e) Free permit required to fish.

— Virginia Fishing Regulations,
Virginia Department of Inland Fisheries

It looks like a chalky Letort or Big Spring near Carlisle, Pennsylvania, and it holds plenty of brown trout, many of which have remained in this limestone stream for several years. But this fine limestone is out of place—it's not situated in Pennsylvania's Cumberland Valley but near Harrisonburg, Virginia. It's Mossy Creek, a fine trout stream of the South. Robert Cramer claims that each year Mossy produces several fish in the 20- to 24-inch class, but you'll find that most of the trout run from 10 to 16 inches long. This meadowland stream provides good cold temperatures for the trout it holds until it enters the North River near Bridgewater, about 15 miles from its source.

Recently this productive trout stream has received a lot of press. Bruce Ingram wrote about the merits of this stream in the September 1989 issue of *Fly Fisherman.* He, too, felt the stream should more naturally be located in south-central Pennsylvania. *Outdoor Life* also ran an article about the merits of this trout stream.

That's the good news for Virginia anglers. Now for the bad news. These brown trout, planted in Mossy Creek as fingerlings, challenge even the most adept dry-fly fisher. The Mossy gives up its trout very sparingly. I said surface because it's almost impossible to use wet flies, except in the winter when the vegetation dies back. Somebody certainly gave Mossy a good name—with any sinking pattern you'll take weeds off the artificial on every cast. The best time to hit this difficult water is when a hatch appears on the surface—you can at least know where these tough brown trout have taken up feeding positions. Then you can match the hatch with an appropriate dry fly.

The Mossy has only a few hatches. Bob Cramer of nearby Dayton guides on the river and schedules his trips around the hatches. One of the most prolific on the Mossy is the trico. You'll have to scout the water, since trout rise to this diminutive hatch in some stretches and not others. Once you find several risers, you can concentrate on reaching them – and that's not easy. Mossy has tricky currents and it's extremely difficult to get any lengthy drag-free drift. Bob Cramer uses a variety of the slack leader cast to get all the S curves he can get in the leader to help him get a longer float.

You'll need a permit to fish the 3.5-mile open stretch. You can get one of these at Murray's Fly Shop in Edinburg; from Mossy Creek Outfitters, Route 3, Box 238-A, Dayton, VA, 22821; or from the Division of Game and Inland Fisheries. If you want a permit by mail, use a self-addressed, stamped envelope.

Parts of Mossy and Smith creeks remain open because of the hard work of many dedicated area anglers. The Thomas Jefferson Chapter of Trout Unlimited in Charlottesville deserves your financial and spiritual support to keep Mossy open to public fishing. This chapter, plus the Northern Virginia Chapter, has spent endless hours working on access. The Massanutten Chapter of Trout Unlimited out of Harrisonburg continues its work on nearby Smith Creek, another limestone stream. Kudos to all these hard-working chapters and the private landowners who allow anglers to fish on their property.

The trico appears on Mossy in unbelievable numbers. According to Bob Cramer this hatch and the other two major hatches – the sulphur and the little blue-winged olive dun – vary in intensity from year to year. You can witness some sulphur activity in April, but the heaviest hatches appear the first weeks in May. Once the sulphur hatch begins, you can expect to see it for a couple weeks. Don't overlook the dark maroon spinners of the slate drake. You'll find these dark mayflies near dusk hovering just a few feet from the surface in July and August. Trout sometimes come completely out of the water for these large mayflies.

What can you do when you don't find a hatch on Mossy? Do what Bob Cramer does. In July and August, especially, he uses beetle, cricket, and grasshopper patterns. Walk through one of the meadows along the creek and you'll see why grasshopper imitations are effective. Bob ties a Mossy Hopper made entirely of woodchuck. He greases this well and it produces some heavy brown trout. Another creation of Bob's is the Disco Cricket. He uses black crystal chenille for the body and black deer hair for the head and wings. The cricket works well on those July and August afternoons and evenings when no hatch appears on the stream.

You'll find the 3.5 miles of open water near the upper end of the stream. All of the open part is within Augusta County. That part of Mossy that flows through Rockingham County is posted. Mossy begins with several large springs near Mount Solon off State Route 42. The stream flows northeast along State routes 756 and 747. You'll find two access sites along the upper open section. Remember, before you fish the open area, you must obtain a free permit, which allows you to fish the open area for a year.

Best Times to Fly Fish

March 1–April 1
Little Blue-Winged Olive Dun: #20, morning and afternoon
Little Black Caddis: #18 and #20, afternoon

April 1–May 4
Sulphur: #16 and #18, evening

May 5–June 15
Sulphur: #16 and #18, evening
Olive Caddis: #14, afternoon and evening

June 16–July 10
Hexagenia species: #8, evening

July 1–September 30
Slate Drake: #12, evening
Trico: #24, morning
Little Blue-Winged Olive Dun: #20, morning and afternoon

October 1–October 30
Little Blue-Winged Olive Dun: #20, morning and afternoon

North Fork Moormans River

North Fork Moormans River (Albemarle County): That portion of the stream within the Shenandoah National Park.

a) Only single-hook artificial lures may be used.

b) All fish must be immediately returned to the water unharmed. No fish may be in possession while fishing in these waters.

c) No bait may be in possession while fishing these waters.

d) Fishing is permitted year-round in these waters.

— Virginia Fishing Regulations

Robert Cramer lives in Dayton and conducts guided fly-fishing trips on Virginia's spring creeks. He also teaches anglers to fly cast on rivers in the Shenandoah National Park. One of Bob's favorite rivers to fly fish for brook trout, whether he's guiding or fishing with friends, is the North Fork Moormans River. Bob will readily tell you that he catches larger trout on the Moormans River than almost any other in the park. The biggest trout Bob caught on the North Fork of Moormans was a 13-inch brook. What a beauty.

Recently I spent a half day on this productive river. I parked the car just above the Charlottesville Reservoir and hiked up the road that parallels the river. Walk for a half mile and you'll hit park land and the catch-and-release area. I entered the river just above the park boundary.

Harry Murray said that July and August are terrestrial months on the rivers of the Shenandoah National Park. Ant and beetle imitations work well all day long in middle and late summer. Use a 9-foot leader tapered to 6X for terrestrials. If you don't believe it, just scan some of the larger rocks and boulders along the river and you'll see plenty of these terrestrials moving about. Many of these get blown into the water and provide a great deal of food for trout. Paul Needham, in his book *Trout Streams*, reports on an interesting study he conducted on the food consumed by 250 brook trout for an entire year. He found

The North Fork of the Moormans River shows the effects of a long summer drought. *Charles Meck*.

that beetles constituted 6.6 percent of the brook trout's diet for a year. Add to that 3.0 percent for bees, ants, and wasps and you can see the importance of terrestrials for Shenandoah National Park brook trout.

Trout hit my beetle pattern in almost every pocket and riffle that looked like it held trout. Beautiful brook trout readily hit the terrestrial pattern. I saw none any longer than 7 inches, but Bob Cramer assures me that they're in there.

I worked my way upriver for a mile impressed with this spectacular river just a few miles from Charlottesville. At most places the boulder-strewn river flowed from 30 to 50 feet wide. The water seems to run a little warmer than the Rose and Rapidan rivers. I tested the three at the same time of day on three consecutive August days and found the Rapidan at 64 degrees, the Rose at 66 degrees, and the Moormans at 67 degrees.

The river contains many of the hatches found on most other area rivers. If you enjoy nymph fishing, in early spring try patterns copying the blue quill, quill gordon, and march brown.

To reach the North Fork Moormans River, take County Route 810 or State Route 240 to White Hall. Then take County Route 614 to the Charlottesville Reservoir (Sugar Hollow). There are 3.2 miles of improved dirt road. Once the road hits national park land, just above the lake, it becomes rutted and rocky. Park your car at the lot at the upper end of the lake and you can hike up the road that parallels the river for more than 4 miles.

Best Times to Fly Fish

March 15–April 30
Blue Quill: #18, morning and afternoon
Quill Gordon: #14, afternoon
Grannom: #16, afternoon

May 1–June 15
March Brown: #12, morning and afternoon
Pale Evening Dun: #18, evening
Light Cahill: #14, evening
Green Caddis: #14, afternoon and evening
Giant Black Stonefly: #6, evening
Yellow Sally: #16, evening

June 16–July 15
Yellow Sally: #16, evening
Slate Drake: #12, evening
Little Gray Stonefly: #18 and #20, morning and afternoon

July 16–August 31
> Slate Drake: #12, evening
> Little Gray Stonefly: #18 and #20, morning and afternoon

September 1–September 30
> Brown Sedge: #14, afternoon and evening

Rapidan River

Rapidan River (Madison County): That portion of stream and its tributaries (including Staunton River) upstream from a sign at the lower Shenandoah National Park boundary:

  a) Only single-hook artificial lures may be used.
  b) All fish must be immediately returned to the water unharmed. No fish may be in possession while fishing these waters.
  c) No bait may be in possession while fishing these waters.
  d) Fishing is permitted year-round in these waters.

> — *Virginia Fishing Regulations*

We drove up the dirt road that someone had marked "Route 649." Suddenly we came upon another small sign: "End of State Maintenance." Was that ever an understatement! For the next 2.5 miles my wife and I drove gingerly over some of the poorest excuse for a dirt road this side of the Canadian wilderness. We drove our new Toyota slowly so we wouldn't lose a muffler or other underpart. Harry Murray told me that he once had to be towed driving to this river. I feared the same.

Finally, after a half hour of careful driving we arrived at one of the most spectacular rivers I have ever seen in my more than forty years of fly fishing. I was about to set foot on the Rapidan River in central Virginia. I immediately checked the water temperature on this early August evening and the 64-degree reading and the good volume of water pleasantly surprised me.

The next morning I approached the river from the Wolftown Road. This route, State 662, gets you to the lower end of the river with much less damage to your car. There's a parking lot near the beginning of the park land, and you can then hike up along the unimproved road. As I hiked up the road a half mile, I was dismayed by the beer cans and trash that visitors had deposited in the park.

I entered the river a half mile upriver from the park boundary. I stood and gazed for what seemed like a half hour at the river ahead of me. The scenic splendor of this river mesmerized me. This scenic, boulder-strewn water held productive pockets, riffles, and pools everywhere I looked. Soon a large dark mayfly emerged in front of me on this foggy morning, then another and another. I finally caught one and identified it as a slate drake. I then looked at the rocks near my feet and saw dozens of slate drake nymphal shucks on the rocks from recently emerged mayflies. I tied on a #14 Slate Drake to copy these *Isonychia* duns and cast the fly from one pocket to another testing the pattern's effectiveness. On the second or third cast a 6-inch brook trout hit the pattern. Four more casts and another trout hit the Slate Drake. Trout hit that dark gray pattern all morning long on this overcast day.

You'll find some deep pools on the Rapidan—some over 5 feet deep. In the upper section you'll also see plenty of huge boulders scattered along the valley floor. In fact, at some areas of the river you'll

Isonychia **shucks on the Rapidan River indicate recent slate drake emergences.** *Charles Meck.*

The scenic **Rapidan River holds some hatches even in late August.** *Charles Meck.*

encounter so many boulders that it makes fly fishing difficult. There's plenty of water to fish on the Rapidan – productive pools, rapids, and abundant pocket water throughout. Much of this pocket water holds trout.

The Rapidan flows with two times the volume of the Rose and North Fork of the Moormans rivers. Even in midsummer you'll find good water and trout eager to take almost any pattern. But the best time to hit the Rapidan is in early spring, when the hatches take on prominence. Fish early April and you'll find a spectacular hatch of blue quills and quill gordons on the water. Brook trout readily feed on these mayflies all afternoon long. Hatches continue through June with march browns and light cahills. Even in July and August you'll find some slate drakes and blue quills *(Paraleptophlebia guttata)* on the surface.

You'll find 2.5 miles of terrible road that takes you to the upper part of the river. Watch out for this road, called the Rapidan-Criglersville Road. The lower road, State Route 662, has about 2 miles of improved dirt road that takes you to the national park land. Most of the water outside the park is posted.

Camp Hoover, the president's hideaway from 1928 to 1932, still stands in the upper area, near Big Rock Falls. Just a half mile upriver from the lower access on Route 662 you'll see the Staunton River flowing in from the left. This small tributary adds to the main stem.

Don't miss this fantastic river, its great hatches, and beautiful brook trout. It flows less than 100 miles from Washington, D.C., and is less than a two-hour drive from there.

Best Times to Fly Fish

March 15–April 15
Blue Quill: #18, morning and afternoon
Quill Gordon: #14, afternoon
Grannom: #16, afternoon

May 1–June 15
March Brown: #12, morning and afternoon
Pale Evening Dun: #18, evening
Light Cahill: #14, evening
Green Caddis: #14, afternoon and evening
Giant Black Stonefly: #6, evening
Yellow Sally: #16, evening

June 16–July 15
Yellow Sally: #16, evening
Slate Drake: #12, evening

July 16–August 31
Slate Drake: #12, evening
Blue Quill: #18, morning and afternoon
Little Gray Stonefly: #20, morning and afternoon

September 1–September 30
Brown Sedge: #14, afternoon and evening

Rose River

Civil War history fills the valley through which this river flows. On November 25, 1862, just a few miles east of the river, Stonewall Jackson and his troops camped for the night. The next morning they

headed out to join Lee's troops at Fredericksburg 50 miles away. Little
did Jackson realize that in eighteen days, on December 13, 1862, he
would play an important part in the major defeat of Burnside's Union
Army at the Battle of Fredericksburg.

Virginia Route 670 ends abruptly at a narrow, rocky parking lot.
I hiked up the park ranger trail along the river. In the late afternoon all
I heard up the valley was the roar of the river off about 200 yards to
my right. The well-canopied terrain hid the river from my view until
I hiked upriver a half mile. Then in front of me just a few feet I first
spotted this gem of a mountain stream—Rose River.

It was mid-August when I first appeared on the river, so when I
first entered the clear water, I checked the temperature. Summer had
been difficult for the rivers of Virginia—extremely hot daytime temperatures and a severe drought tested the quality of these mountain
streams. After a couple minutes I checked the thermometer and recorded a reading of 65 degrees. Can you believe that temperature?
Sixty-five degrees in late afternoon in mid-August.

As I headed upriver on this boulder-strewn river, trout darted
from the right and the left. Even at its lowest point I found trout in

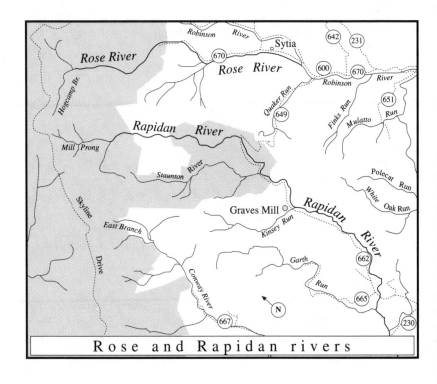

Rose   and   Rapidan   rivers

almost every pocket and deep riffle, and I still found some pools on the river several feet deep.

Only a few cream midges appeared above the pool where I decided to start fishing. It had been almost two months since the last heavy hatch appeared on the river. At that time trout even spotted a few green drakes on the Rose. I decided to try a terrestrial, which always seems to work well on these Virginia waters in July and August.

Rob Gilford of Frederick, Maryland, had given me a Bob Brown Beetle a couple days earlier, and I decided to try this pattern. It wasn't long before I landed my first Rose River brook trout. It didn't measure more than 7 inches long, but it was a beauty to behold. I don't care how big these native brook trout grow – I enjoy fly fishing for them. I picked another brookie out of the riffle at the head of the pool before I headed upriver a few feet to some deep productive-looking pocket water. I picked up another small brook trout in a 3-foot pocket behind a large boulder on the right and another one on the left side of the river. Darkness approaches quickly on the Rose River, and with the heavy canopy it's difficult to follow the fly and your footing in the evening.

Hatches begin early on the Rose. As early as late March you'll find blue quills and quill gordons appearing on the river. Three of the heaviest hatches are the blue quill, quill gordon, and the march brown. Most of the mayfly hatches have ended by mid-June.

Downwings like the grannom and green caddis can bring trout to the surface. You'll find the grannom on the river when the blue quill and quill gordon emerge.

The Rose River runs from 20 to 30 feet wide. It reminds me more of a high, rocky-mountain stream than it does a river. You'll find a heavy canopy through the watershed. At first glance you might think that someone unloaded a huge pile of rocks and boulders up and down the river. A ranger road parallels much of the lower end. If you find too many anglers on the lower end, you can hike upriver where angling pressure slackens considerably. To reach the Rose River, take State Route 231 north of Madison to Banco. From Banco take State Route 670, which parallels the river.

Harry Murray, owner of Murray's Fly Shop in Edinburg, Virginia, knows the Rose River well. In fact, he knows all of the waters in the Shenandoah National Park. He recently wrote a book entitled *Trout Fishing in the Shenandoah National Park*. Stop in at his shop for the latest information on the hatches and conditions of all the waters in the area.

Best Times to Fly Fish

March 15–April 15
Blue Quill: #18, morning and afternoon
Quill Gordon: #14, afternoon
Grannom: #16, afternoon

May 1–June 15
March Brown: #12, morning and afternoon
Pale Evening Dun: #18, evening
Light Cahill: #14, evening
Green Caddis: #14, afternoon and evening
Giant Black Stonefly: #6, evening
Yellow Sally: #16, evening

June 16–July 15
Yellow Sally: #16, evening
Slate Drake: #12, evening

July 16–August 31
Slate Drake: #12, evening
Little Gray Stonefly: #18 and #20, morning and afternoon

September 1–September 30
Brown Sedge: #14, afternoon and evening

WEST VIRGINIA

What does wild, wonderful West Virginia have in store for the fly fisherman? You'll find some great small-stream fly fishing throughout the state, and many of the tributary streams hold good populations of brook trout. Some streams hold good supplies of streambred browns and a few hold wild rainbows. But West Virginia has some tremendous problems with its trout fisheries. Look at Muddy Creek in Preston County in the northern part of the state. In its headwaters this small mountain stream holds a good number of brook trout, but go downstream a few miles and you'll find several slugs of hot mine acid flowing into this scenic watershed. The creek below reflects this surge of acid with the typical light brown stain of iron on the rocks near the shore. No trout live here.

West Virginia has problems with its large rivers, too. Examine the upper Youghiogheny River above Crellin, Maryland. Just below Crellin the Youghiogheny flows into West Virginia. Heavy slugs of mine acid pour into the main stem to pollute the river and make it barren for miles.

Mining was a way of life in West Virginia. The aftereffects of poorly planned mining will seriously affect the state's trout fishing for generations to come. Can anything be done? Authorities have placed liming devices throughout the state to abate the effects of both mine acid and acid rain. Cranberry River, Otter Creek, Holly River, and others presently offer habitat to trout because they house liming devices. And some organizations in the state have finally stood up and said that enough is enough. Recently the P. Pendleton Kennedy Chapter of Trout Unlimited, through Larry Harris in Morgantown, opposed a mining permit on Muddy Creek. Guess what? They won their battle.

West Virginia has other problems, too. Heavy siltation from a flood of recent lumbering ventures has added silt to many of the riverbeds. Add to this problems with acid rain and thermal stress from a combination of drought and high summer temperatures, and you can see the extent of the impact on this state's trout population.

Enter another complication—the Corridor H Project. Corridor H is a proposed highway from east to west in the state. One problem is that the state has recommended that the highway closely parallel much of Seneca Creek. To do this would virtually kill another productive trout stream in the state. Is there no end to what certain authorities will do?

With all these negatives you'd think that West Virginia has nothing to offer. But it has plenty to offer: you can enjoy a true wilderness experience when you fish, many of the streams in the state compare favorably to any other eastern state, and you can experience wild trout fishing and great hatches like the green drake and sulphur.

West Virginia has some good streams and rivers. The Williams, South Branch of the Potomac, and the Smoke Hole rivers all contain delayed-harvest areas. You'll also find adequate hatches and trout on the Cheat and Elk river systems. We'll take a closer look at the last two.

Cheat River System

How do the better streams in West Virginia compare to others in the East? How do they fare in July and August?

"The elevation and trees save us," Gary Lang of Elkins said as we crossed a 4,000-foot ridge on our way to the Cheat River system. Gary knows the streams and rivers of the state extremely well—he has guided anglers on them for several years and has spent many days on tributaries to the Cheat River. Gary knows that by the time the Black Fork and Shavers Fork rivers combine to form the Cheat, the main

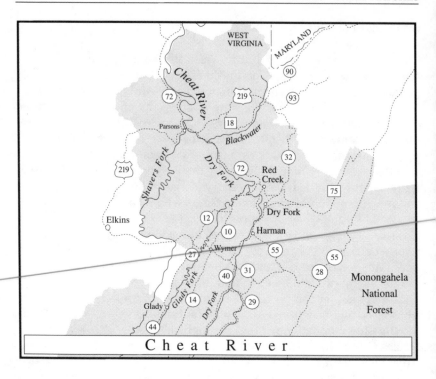

stem no longer holds trout, so he fly fishes on many of the tributaries entering the Cheat River. Gary's automobile license plate, DRYFLY, reflects his love for the sport. On the eastern part of the system Gandy Creek flows from Spruce Lake and provides the bulk of the flow for Dry Fork. Gandy Creek gets a heavy planting of trout and has a fair carryover. Spruce Lake, by the way, at 3,500 feet has some great stillwater fly fishing, with some caddis and scenes reminiscent of Canada and Maine. Laurel Fork empties into Dry Fork just north of the town of Red Creek. Five miles downriver Dry Fork adds the flow from Glady Fork. Dry Fork continues to flow towards Parsons and adds another large tributary, the Blackwater River, at Hendricks. The Blackwater holds a good number of brown trout and runs through a series of bogs before it enters Dry Fork. When the Blackwater combines with Dry Fork, they call the river the Black Fork.

On the western half waters from the 5,000-foot-high Snowshoe Mountain form Shavers Fork, which flows north for 30 miles, then joins the Black Fork to form the Cheat River. Thomas Edison, Henry Ford, and Harvey Firestone all hunted nearby and fished on Shavers Fork sixty years ago.

Most of the tributaries range from 30 to 60 feet wide, with a good flow until early July. Most of them contain some deep ledge pools and riffles that hold trout. As summer progresses, you'll find a better supply of trout in the upper reaches of the tributaries, where you'll find cool water temperatures. Near Rowlesburg mine acid empties into the main stem of the Cheat.

The system holds its share of great hatches. If you're fortunate enough to hit one of the tributaries when the blue quill appears near the end of March or early April, you're in for a real matching-the-hatch treat. Two of the most dependable to emerge are the green drake and sulphur. But you'll find plenty of other hatches on the rivers even through July and August. Throughout the summer these feeder streams hold good numbers of slate drakes. Into July you'll also see large yellow stoneflies on many of the rivers in the system.

With the mountainous terrain you'd expect the tributary streams to flow rapidly into the Cheat River, but for the most part they don't. You'll find some fairly fast water, but you'll also find some very slow pooled water.

Each of the tributaries holds an abundant supply of native brook trout. In addition, a good supply of fingerlings, legal brown, and rainbow trout is added.

It's difficult to reach parts of Shavers Fork but you can access the river at Cheat Bridge on U.S. Route 250. Forest Route 14 parallels Laurel Fork, and State Route 27 runs beside Glady and the upper end of the Blackwater River.

Both Gary Lang of Elkins and Paul Kurincak of the Upstream Fly Shop in Morgantown can help you find plenty of trout on the Cheat River system.

Best Times to Fly Fish

March 15–April 30
Little Blue-Winged Olive Dun: #20, morning and afternoon
Blue Quill: #18, morning and afternoon
Early Brown Stonefly: #12, afternoon
Hendrickson/Red Quill: #14, afternoon

May 1–June 15
Grannom: #16, afternoon
Sulphur: #16, evening
March Brown: #12, afternoon
Green Drake: #10, evening
Slate Drake: #14, evening
Blue-Winged Olive Dun: #14, morning

Tan Caddis: #16, evening
Golden Stonefly (Yellow Sally): #16, afternoon and evening

June 15–July 30

Slate Drake: #14, evening
Yellow Stonefly: #8, afternoon and evening
Blue Quill: #18, morning and afternoon
Slate Drake: #12, evening

August 1–August 31

Blue Quill: #18, morning and afternoon
Slate Drake: #12, evening

September 1–October 30

Little Blue-Winged Olive Dun: #20, morning and afternoon
Slate Drake: #14, afternoon and evening

Elk River System

> *Back Fork of Elk River in Webster County:* Catch-and-release beginning 2 miles upstream from Webster Springs, extending upstream 4 miles. This section can be reached from State secondary routes 29 and 24/3.
>
> — *West Virginia Fishing Regulations,*
> Wildlife Resources Section

Will the real Elk River come forward? Will it be the one that flows bank-full in April and May and displays a tremendous hatch of green drakes and sulphurs? Or will it be the one you experience on hot July and August days when all you see for 5 or more miles in the upper section is a dry creek bed. Recently, Gary Lang of Elkins, Paul Kurincak of the Upstream Fly Shop in Morgantown, and I traveled along the river above Bergoo. When we first saw the river, Gary pointed to it and said, "See that dry river bed? It goes underground a mile or two above here and reappears downriver several miles."

Above the area where the river disappears, the river holds some brook, brown, and rainbow trout. Paul believes that some rainbows spawn in some of the upriver tributaries.

The three of us drove for several miles down the dirt road that parallels the river and past the commercial fish hatchery before Elk River reemerged.

The main stem of Elk River appeared so low through Bergoo that Gary suggested we fly fish on the Back Fork of the Elk River just above Webster Springs. There are 5 miles of catch-and-release water on this productive tributary. I checked the water temperature when I entered the drought-stricken river. After a hot, dry summer the river just above Webster Springs showed a 73-degree water temperature. Probably not much action would happen under these conditions.

Paul and Gary decided to fish for a couple hours anyway, and not long after they began, Paul hooked a heavy rainbow trout on a dry. Upriver Gary caught a heavy brown trout. In two hours of fishing Gary and Paul had landed several trout. Does the Back Fork hold trout all year long? You bet it does.

While we fished that late July, I saw signs that thousands of slate drakes had emerged from the river in the past week or two. You'll see many other hatches on the Elk and the Back Fork—most of them earlier in the season. Both rivers hold good numbers of hendricksons and blue quills early in the season. But the best time to fly fish the Elk system is late May, when the sulphurs and green drakes appear. Hit the river at that time, and you're in for some great matching the hatch.

Downwings appear frequently on the Elk system. Grannoms and dark olive caddis appear along with stoneflies such as the yellow sally and the large yellow stonefly. The latter appears in limited numbers throughout much of the summer.

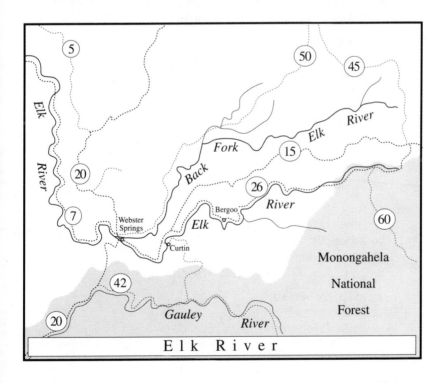

When I think of a river, I normally expect to see a fairly wide body of water. The Elk and Back Fork rivers range from 40 to 60 feet wide. Elk holds some pools more than 10 feet deep, and the Back Fork holds shallower pools and rapids flowing over ledges. You'll find plenty of bedrock on both rivers. Watch your step wading these rivers – footing is often precarious. You can reach the Elk River system at Webster Springs on State routes 15 and 20. You can reach the upper end of the Elk River on a dirt road, County 26.

The state stocks a heavy number of rainbow and brown trout to both Elk and Back Fork. If you plan to fish the Elk River, try to hit it when the green drake appears and the river flows aboveground throughout its entire length. Then you'll find the real Elk River teeming with trout and great hatches. And don't overlook the Back Fork or the Elk upriver from where it disappears. Both sections hold trout the entire year.

Best Times to Fly Fish

March 15–April 30
Blue Quill: #18, morning and afternoon
Quill Gordon: #14, afternoon
Hendrickson/Red Quill: #14, afternoon

May 1–June 15
Grannom: #16, afternoon
Sulphur: #16, evening
Gray Fox: #14, afternoon
March Brown: #12, afternoon
Green Drake: #10, evening
Blue-Winged Olive Dun: #14, morning
Light Cahill: #14, evening
Slate Drake: #14, evening
Little Yellow Stonefly (Yellow Sally): #16, afternoon and evening

June 15–July 30
Slate Drake: #14, evening
Yellow Stonefly: #8, afternoon and evening
Dark Olive Caddis: #18, evening
Blue Quill: #18, morning and afternoon

August 1–September 30
Slate Drake: #12, evening
Blue Quill: #18, morning and afternoon

NORTH CAROLINA

In the mountains of western North Carolina lie some of the best trout streams in the eastern United States. Some are very productive, while others are sensitive to slight changes in their surroundings. When you fly fish this region, be sure to stop and enjoy the many wildflowers that grow along the streambanks.

South Toe River

> Certain designated mountain trout waters are managed under very restrictive regulations in order to meet specific management objectives. These waters are marked with signs that are posted conspicuously along the watercourses.
>
> *Catch and release / fly fishing only:* Trout waters and their tributaries, except as noted, may be fished with artificial flies having one single hook. No fish may be harvested or possessed while fishing these streams.
>
> South Toe River (portion from the concrete bridge above Black Mountain Campground downstream to the game land boundary, excluding Camp Creek and Neals Creek, Yancey County).
>
> —*North Carolina Inland Fishing, Hunting, & Trapping Regulations Digest*

As I flew from Charlotte to Asheville, North Carolina, I sensed that this state may have more to offer to a fly fisherman than one would imagine. The Appalachian Mountains in western North Carolina are breathtaking. Mount Mitchell is located here, which is the highest mountain peak east of the Rockies. The locals refer to this region as "High Country."

Al Hines, owner of High Country Fly Fishing near Boone, is very familiar with streams at these high elevations. He should be—his fly shop is located at a 3,000-foot elevation. Al has been fly fishing this region for eighteen years and he and his employees guide on many trout rivers in the region. When I contacted him to arrange to fly fish this region, he was surprised to hear of someone with interest in this area. It seems there are few fly fishermen who take advantage of these pristine rivers in this part of North Carolina.

We met at the shop early one morning and traveled to fly fish the South Toe River. We drove on County Route 80 toward the town of Spruce Pine. We turned right on South Toe Road and followed the river in the Pisgah National Forest to our destination, the special-regulations area. Al prefers to use various Elkhair Caddis patterns to fish the South Toe. On his first cast in a pool on the river he hooked and released a wild rainbow. During the morning we both landed and released several beautiful fish.

The South Toe is 20 to 40 feet wide and contains some large boulders and beautiful deep runs. The river starts in the Appalachian Mountains of the Pisgah National Forest. It is a very scenic and rugged river, surrounded by large lush groves of rhododendron, with hemlock and yellow birch trees adding their own beauty. The water is gin clear and is very difficult to wade. Felt soles and a wading staff are very helpful when fishing the South Toe.

One of the interesting features on the river is a fish barrier that is located near Black Mountain Campground. It's designed to prevent fish such as white suckers from entering the upper reaches of this high-quality trout fishery. The South Toe contains wild rainbow and brown trout. Brook trout are taken on flies more frequently on the upper reaches of the river.

Important hatches to meet and fish include the quill gordon, blue

Al Hines, owner of High Country Fly Fishing, works a deep run on the South Toe River in North Carolina. *Greg Hoover.*

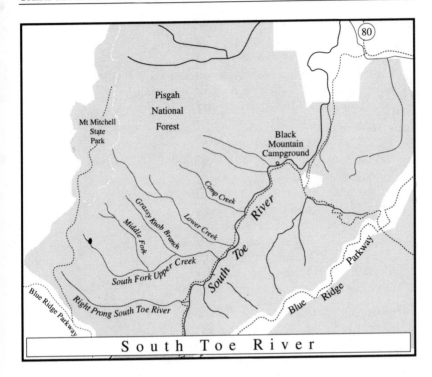

Pisgah
National
Forest

Mt Mitchell
State
Park

Black
Mountain
Campground

Comp Creek

Grassy Knob Branch

Lower Creek

Middle Fork

South Toe River

Upper Creek

South Fork

Blue Ridge Parkway

Right Prong South Toe River

Blue Ridge

Blue Ridge Parkway

80

South   Toe   River

quill, and march brown. Yellow sally stoneflies provide some excellent dry-fly fishing from June through mid-July. Crayfish are abundant as well.

The South Toe River surrounds the fly fisherman with the scenic beauty of a wilderness stream. When you fly fish this river, plan on committing a day to the river—it's the best way to enjoy all that the South Toe has to offer.

Best Times to Fly Fish

March 1–May 15
    Quill Gordon: #12, afternoon and evening
    Little Blue-Winged Olive Dun: #18, afternoon and early evening
    Grannom: #12–14, afternoon and evening
    Blue Quill: #16–18, afternoon and early evening
    Hendrickson/Red Quill: #12–14, afternoon
    March Brown: #12, afternoon and evening
    Gray Fox: #12–14, afternoon and evening
    Little Black Caddis: #18, afternoon and early evening

May 16–June 15
 Yellow Sally Stonefly: #16–18, evening
 Sulphurs: #14–16, evening
 Little Black Caddis: #18, afternoon and early evening
 Olive Caddis: #12–20, afternoon and evening
 Tan Caddis: #12–16, afternoon and evening

June 16–July 15
 Light Cahill: #12–18, evening
 Yellow Sally Stonefly: #16–18, evening
 Sulphurs: #16–18, evening
 Chartreuse Caddis: #16–18, afternoon and evening
 Lime Sally Stonefly: #16, evening
 Crickets: #12–16, morning and afternoon
 Hoppers: #10–12, morning and afternoon
 Ants: #14–18, morning and afternoon
 Beetles: #12–14, morning and afternoon
 Inchworms: #14, morning and afternoon

July 16–August 15
 Light Cahill: #12–18, evening
 Yellow Sally Stonefly: #16–18, evening
 Lime Sally Stonefly: #16, evening
 Crickets: #12–16, morning and afternoon
 Hoppers: #10–12, morning and afternoon
 Ants: #14–18, morning and afternoon
 Beetles: #12–14, morning and afternoon
 Inchworms: #14, morning and afternoon

August 16–September 15
 Light Cahill: #12–18, evening
 Crickets: #12–16, morning and afternoon
 Hoppers: #10–12, morning and afternoon
 Ants: #14–18, morning and afternoon
 Beetles: #12–14, morning and afternoon
 Inchworms: #14, morning and afternoon

September 16–November 15
 Crickets: #12–16, morning and afternoon
 Hoppers: #10–12, morning and afternoon
 Ants: #14–18, morning and afternoon
 Beetles: #12–14, morning and afternoon
 Inchworms: #14, morning and afternoon

Wilson Creek

Certain designated mountain trout waters are managed under very restrictive regulations in order to meet specific management objectives.
These waters are marked with signs that are posted conspicuously along
the watercourses.

Catch and release / artificial lures only: Trout waters may be fished only
with artificial lures having one single hook and all fish must be released.
No fish may be harvested or possessed while fishing these streams.

Wilson Creek (headwaters to game land boundary above Edgemont,
including tributaries, Avery County).

   —*North Carolina Inland Fishing, Hunting, & Trapping Regulations Digest*

Wilson Creek is a very steep gradient trout stream. An elevation
change of several hundred feet over a very short distance makes one
wonder if you should take rock-climbing gear along in order to effectively fish this creek. Stuart McCormac, a guide at High Country Fly
Fishing near Boone, casually stated that you need to be a mountain
goat in order to fly fish Wilson Creek. I won't disagree with him. I
thought my calf muscles increased slightly in mass after spending a
day fly fishing this creek.

In the Wilson you will find huge boulders and bedrock-lined pools,
which harbor brown and rainbow trout. It will test your fly-casting
skills. Short drag-free floats are the order of the day when fishing the
Wilson.

Stuart McCormac and I fly fished together on the Wilson one late-
August day. We walked in for approximately 2 miles to the river on a
U.S. Forest Service trail. The Watauga Chapter of Trout Unlimited
maintains this trail so fly fishermen can gain relatively easy access to
the river. Stuart recommends that you fish with a companion on this
wild trout water. It is rugged terrain, and I agree with his suggestion.

Pale evening duns and light cahills were emerging when we fished
this creek. Stuart has been fly fishing for eighteen years, and he decided to cast floating imitations the day we were there. I selected a
nymph pattern that works well for me in late season. We decided to
alternate fishing pools and runs while traversing this scenic trout
stream. Both of us caught some truly beautiful brown and rainbow
trout on this trip and had a trout clean us of our terminal tackle.

Many successful fly fishermen prefer to use a #14 Adams, Ausable

Wulff, or an Olive-Bodied Elkhair Caddis on the Wilson. Terrestrial imitations, such as a Black Beetle, will work well late in the season. Quill gordons and march browns are important hatches on this creek, although Stuart feels that imitating life stages of caddisflies is your best bet on the Wilson.

Wilson Creek is located in Avery County and can be accessed by traveling north on U.S. Route 221 from the town of Linville. Turn right on State Route 1514, then take the first road (State Route 192) to the right off of 1514. At this intersection State Route 192 is a hard switchback turn. When traveling on 192, look for U.S. Forest Service Trail No. 258 on the left-hand side of the road. This is the trail that will get you on the Wilson approximately 2 miles off of 192. It is highly recommended that you acquire an accurate map of this area before fishing the Wilson.

Best Times to Fly Fish

March 1–May 15
Quill Gordon: #12, afternoon and evening
Little Blue-Winged Olive Dun: #18, afternoon and early evening
Grannom: #12–14, afternoon and evening
Blue Quill: #16–18, afternoon and early evening
Hendrickson/Red Quill: #12–14, afternoon
March Brown: #12, afternoon and evening
Gray Fox: #12–14, afternoon and evening
Little Black Caddis: #18, afternoon and early evening

May 16–June 15
Yellow Sally Stonefly: #16–18, evening
Sulphurs: #14–16, evening
Little Black Caddis: #18, afternoon and early evening
Olive Caddis: #12–20, afternoon and evening
Tan Caddis: #12–16, afternoon and evening

June 16–July 15
Light Cahill: #12–18, evening
Yellow Sally Stonefly: #16–18, evening
Sulphurs: #16–18, evening
Chartreuse Caddis: #16–18, afternoon and evening
Lime Sally Stonefly: #16, evening
Crickets: #12–16, morning and afternoon
Hoppers: #10–12, morning and afternoon
Ants: #14–18, morning and afternoon

Beetles: #12–14, morning and afternoon
Inchworms: #14, morning and afternoon

July 16–August 15
Light Cahill: #12–18, evening
Yellow Sally Stonefly: #16–18, evening
Lime Sally Stonefly: #16, evening
Crickets: #12–16, morning and afternoon
Hoppers: #10–12, morning and afternoon
Ants: #14–18, morning and afternoon
Beetles: #12–14, morning and afternoon
Inchworms: #14, morning and afternoon

August 16–September 15
Light Cahill: #12–18, evening
Crickets: #12–16, morning and afternoon
Hoppers: #10–12, morning and afternoon
Ants: #14–18, morning and afternoon
Beetles: #12–14, morning and afternoon
Inchworms: #14, morning and afternoon

September 16–November 15
Crickets: #12–16, morning and afternoon
Hoppers: #10–12, morning and afternoon
Ants: #14–18, morning and afternoon
Beetles: #12–14, morning and afternoon
Inchworms: #14, morning and afternoon

TENNESSEE

This state is recently receiving additional attention about its trout program. In the scenic mountains of Tennessee you may fish to some important hatches. Let's take a look at a high-quality tailwater fishery in this state. I know you'll enjoy fly fishing the South Fork Holston River.

South Fork Holston River

Early one morning Al Hines, owner of and fly fishing guide at High Country Fly Fishing near Boone, North Carolina, Doug Suddreth of Lenoir, North Carolina, and I traveled from western North Carolina to fish the South Fork Holston River in northeastern Tennessee. Doug has been fly fishing for twenty-eight years and has been fishing the South Fork Holston for the last five. Sunrise had yet to begin as we arrived at the river, and the fog was thick along the road, which indicated to me that the river temperature would be quite cool. As the sun came up, it was still difficult to see the South Holston through the fog.

I watched Al and Doug work the river through the fog, which was still there at 7:00 A.M. I heard a yell from Doug—he was into the first trout of the day. He would land many more rainbows before we had to leave at 8:45 A.M. The successful pattern for Doug was a #14 Gold Ribbed Hares Ear nymph. He stated that you must fish a long line in this gin-clear water. The South Holston holds many heavy brown and rainbow trout, but they are very discriminating.

That late-August morning I took a water temperature at 7:10 A.M. Much to my surprise, my thermometer registered 49 degrees Fahrenheit. We were approximately 4 miles below the South Holston Dam, which releases water from a bottom discharge. That water temperature surely explained the dense fog of the morning.

The South Holston is approximately 50 to 75 feet wide. The substrate in many areas is comprised of solid bedrock, which makes felt-soled waders and a wading staff an absolute necessity on this river. There are many long, flat pools and few riffles in this high-quality trout river. You may want to fish some of the named pools—such as the Cabin, Bridge, or Ledges—when you travel to the South Holston.

I examined the aquatic life on the bottom of the river and found little blue-winged olive dun nymphs and scuds to be very abundant. Doug feels that the little blue-winged olives are an important hatch to meet and fish on this river. He witnessed a tremendous emergence of these mayflies in early March last season. The air temperature that day was 28 degrees with a snowfall. These tiny mayflies induced most trout in the river to rise to them. Fine leaders and well-presented, tiny dry flies made this particular day a very successful one. Al Hines regularly fishes small Griffith's Gnats on the South Holston. He also agrees that you must delicately present your imitations to these selective trout.

To find the South Fork Holston River travel north from Elizabethton on U.S. Route 19. Take State Route 44 north to Old Weaver Road. Turn left on Big Spring Road off of Old Weaver Road, and you will be paralleling this tremendous tailwater fishery.

There are other tailwater trout fisheries in Tennessee, and it is my impression from talking with Al Hines and Doug Suddreth that the South Fork Holston River has yet to reach its full potential. With sound management of this river by aquatic resource managers of Tennessee, it is my opinion that the South Holston could be one of the premiere trout rivers of the East.

Best Times to Fly Fish

March 1–May 15
  Little Blue-Winged Olive Duns: #18–20, afternoon and early
    evening
  Hendrickson/Red Quill: #12–14, afternoon and early evening
  Light Cahill: #16–18, late afternoon and evening
  Little Black Caddis: #18–20, afternoon and early evening

May 16–June 15
  Sulphurs: #16–20, evening
  Light Cahill: #16–18, late afternoon and evening

June 16–July 15
  Light Cahill: #16–18, late afternoon and evening

July 16–August 15
  Light Cahill: #16–18, late afternoon and evening

August 16–September 15
  Little Blue-Winged Olive Duns: #18–20, afternoon

5

Great Rivers of the Midwest and Their Hatches

The trout rivers of the midwestern United States offer a great deal of diversity for the fly fisherman and provide fly fishing to tremendous hatches of little blue-winged olive duns, march browns, gray drakes, the huge *Hexagenia limbata,* and tiny tricos. You can fly cast to some unique populations of brown, rainbow, brook, and cutthroat trout in this region of the country. Here you'll find tremendous tailwater fisheries, like the White River in Arkansas, or deep, sweeping pools and quick runs of rivers in Michigan, like the Au Sable, Manistee, and Pere Marquette. A fly fisher can also experience a western river environment while floating the North Fork of the White River in Missouri. You can also cast a fly to one of the world's few remaining populations of the McCloud River strain of rainbow on Crane Creek in Missouri.

Obviously, there are many fine trout rivers in this region. Take time to get to know the friendly stewards of the Midwest who keep a watchful eye on these truly unique, high-quality cold-water fisheries. They are conservationists armed with a wealth of knowledge that they draw on to protect these sensitive aquatic resources. After you explore the Midwest for yourself, I'm confident that you will learn to appreciate its excellent trout water. Let's examine a few of the blue-ribbon trout waters in the midwestern region of the United States.

MICHIGAN

The northern reaches of lower Michigan contain some of the finest trout water in the eastern half of the United States. With river names like the Pigeon, Sturgeon, Black, Boardman, and Rifle, one knows that quality trout fishing abounds.

The Upper Peninsula of Michigan also contains some excellent trout water for the fly fisherman. Not only do they contain fine trout populations, but they also support phenomenal insect hatches. We will examine five of Michigan's excellent trout waters.

Au Sable River

Au Sable River Main Stream (Crawford County)—from Burtons Landing to Wakeley Bridge (8.7 miles): flies only. Daily possession limit: zero (catch and release only). Trout may not be possessed in no-kill area regardless of where caught; no closed season.

Au Sable River Main Stream (Oscoda County)—Mio powerline (sec. 7 T26N, R3E) to McKinley (14.2 miles): artificial lures and flies only. Size limit 15 inches on brown trout; 12 inches on other trout, two trout per day, last Saturday in April to September 30.

—Michigan Fishing Guide,
Michigan Department of Natural Resources

I have wanted to fish the Michigan caddis, or *Hexagenia limbata*, hatch on the Au Sable River for quite some time. I've read about the hatch for over a decade. Would I ever get to fly fish to this huge burrowing mayfly, which has intrigued me for so many years? Finally I had a chance to meet and fish to this huge mayfly. One evening in late June I floated the main stem with Rusty Gates, owner of Gates Lodge and Pro Shop, located on Stephan Bridge Road, east of Grayling off of State Route 37. Dark lead-winged olives, blue-winged olive duns, and yellow sallys appeared as we started to fish. Later the trout fed on huge *Hexagenia limbata* spinners between the hours of 10:30 and 11:15 P.M. White suckers also were evident, creating their typical sucking/sipping sound underneath tight overhead cover in back eddies associated with logjams. With the quietness of this evening, it became quite apparent there was a great deal of food for trout.

I must say that it was one of the most enjoyable fly-fishing trips that I've ever been on, even though we didn't land many trout. Rusty caught and released a really good brown on a Hex Spinner imitation, and there were several heavy fish feeding as we floated during the night. Beaver were slapping their tails all along the way; sometimes it was difficult differentiating them from the hard rises of the trout. Off in the distance a barred owl called, and, to top it off, the northern lights were on display. I can see why people want to fly fish – and eventually retire – in this region of Michigan; it is truly a beautiful and relaxing environment. On the way back to the lodge we must have seen twenty to thirty whitetails.

Waters may be difficult to navigate at night, but the Au Sable riverboat, which was used by loggers around the turn of the century, is an amazing piece of watercraft. By trailing chains behind the boat, the rate of float speed is controlled. The back of the boat is fashioned with a slightly upward angle. This construction allows the water to rush alongside with very little pressure on the riverboat. Rusty handled the riverboat very competently. He put the nose of the boat wherever you suggested, lining you up magnificently with the trout's feeding lane in mind. His clients benefit from the wealth of information that he possesses regarding hatches and conditions on the Au Sable. Rusty is a conservationist and keeps the quality of the environment surrounding the Au Sable uppermost in his mind. He is unique among those people I have met in the fly-fishing world. Check with him at his pro shop if you need to discover what is currently happening on the river.

The Au Sable is without a doubt the best-known brown-trout fishery in the midwestern United States. This river once contained only grayling, but brook trout are now found in the Au Sable, and in recent years more rainbows also were being caught.

The Au Sable flows through the town of Grayling, Michigan, and flows approximately 115 miles east to Lake Huron. The river can be accessed at several points on roads that intersect with State Route 72 east of Grayling. Some of these are Louie's Landing, Stephan Bridge, Wakeley Bridge, and McMaster's Bridge roads. The flies-only water from Burtons Landing, east of Grayling, to Wakeley Bridge is sometimes referred to as the "holy water." The sites and sounds of the Au Sable are truly unforgettable. When you fish the Au Sable (French for "the river of sands"), your fly-fishing skills will be tested.

The main stem of the Au Sable has excellent overhead cover for trout. The average width of the river ranges from 35 to 100 feet, and the depth averages from 2 to 6 feet, with some deeper pools. The Au Sable has gravel and sand substrate so it maintains a diversity of aquatic life forms. Recently, fine sediments have begun to affect the quality of this world-class trout fishery. Once the sandy soil has been disturbed along this river, it becomes difficult for vegetation to grow and stabilize the damaged streambank.

I'll never forget the feeling that came over me when I peered into the Au Sable for the first time. Where else can you fish after dark and be treated to a display of northern lights that is so stirring they almost take your mind off fly fishing to an emergence of *Hexagenia limbata*? Rusty Gates told me that this river has that effect on most people who fish it. Not only can you view the "holy water" from the dining room at Rusty's, you can also eat the best food in Crawford County. As in all good fly shops, Rusty has surrounded himself with a cadre of excellent fly-fishing guides. Brothers Jim and Mike Calvin, Craig Perry, Scott Rob, and Charlie Weaver all have fly-fishing expertise and collectively have spent many years on the main stem of the Au Sable.

There are many groundwater influences along the river's main stem. You wouldn't come to this conclusion on your first visit to the Au Sable region, but when you examine aquatic insect emergence sequences on the main stem, you quickly realize that there are differences in water temperatures at key points along the Au Sable. This significantly influences the areas where you may observe an emergence, especially with the *Hexagenia limbata*. Some aquatic vegetation is evident in the Au Sable. According to George Griffith, cofounder of Trout Unlimited and who has a home along the "holy water," the abundance of aquatic plants has decreased since the treatment facility at Grayling was improved. Additionally, George has personally noted a decline in the abundance of stoneflies during the more than fifty years that he has fly fished the Au Sable. Obviously this is difficult to quantify, but stoneflies are much more important here than on most trout water in the eastern United States. Some fly fishermen at Gates Lodge and Pro Shop feel that stonefly populations have been on the increase during the past three seasons. We all hope their observations are accurate. Wouldn't it be fantastic if the water quality of the Au Sable is starting its recovery back to the days of George Griffith and George Mason?

Best Times to Fly Fish

March 1–May 15
Early Black Stonefly: #14, afternoon
Little Blue-Winged Olive Dun: #18–20, afternoon and early evening
Hendrickson/Red Quill: #12–14, afternoon and early evening

Black Willow Stonefly *(Acroneuria nigrita)*: #8–10, afternoon
and evening
Little Black Caddis: #18–20, afternoon and early evening
Great Speckled Olive Dun *(Siphloplecton basale)*: #10–12,
afternoon
Dark Blue Quill: #16–18, afternoon and early evening

May 16–June 15

Black Willow Stonefly *(Acroneuria nigrita)*: #8–10, afternoon
and evening
Little Black Caddis: #18–20, afternoon and early evening
Dark Blue Quill: #16–18, afternoon and early evening
Black Quill: #12–14, afternoon
Lime Sally Stonefly: #14–16, afternoon
American March Brown: #10–12, afternoon and evening
Grannom: #12–14, afternoon and evening
Gray Drake: #12–14, afternoon and evening
Pale Evening Dun: #14–16, afternoon and evening
Tan Caddis: #14, afternoon and evening
Sulphur/Pale Evening Dun: #16–18, evening
Brown Drake: #8–10, evening
Dark Green Stonefly: #14, evening

June 16–July 15

Dark Green Stonefly: #14, evening
Light Cahill: #14, late afternoon and evening
Slate Drake/Mahogany Dun: #12, evening
Yellow Sally Stonefly: #16, evening
Michigan Caddis/Hex *(Hexagenia limbata)*: #6–8, evening
Blue-Winged Olive Dun: #14–16, morning and evening
Tiny Blue-Winged Olive *(Pseudocloeon)*: #22, afternoon and
evening
Trico: #24, morning

July 16–August 15

Light Cahill: #14, late afternoon and evening
Yellow Drake *(Ephemera varia,* on certain stretches): #10–12,
evening
Slate Drake/Mahogany Dun: #12, evening
Yellow Sally Stonefly: #16, evening
Blue-Winged Olive Dun: #14–16, morning and evening
Tiny Blue-Winged Olive *(Pseudocloeon)*: #22, afternoon and
evening

Little Tan Caddis: #16–18, late afternoon and evening
Grasshoppers: #8–12, afternoon and early evening
Trico: #24, morning
White Mayfly (*Ephoron leukon*, on certain stretches): #12–14,
  evening

August 16–September 15
Little Tan Caddis: #16–18, late afternoon and evening
Grasshoppers: #8–12, afternoon and early evening
Trico: #24, morning
White Mayfly (*Ephoron leukon*, on certain stretches): #12–14,
  evening
Dark Olive Caddis: #16, afternoon

September 16–November 10
Dark Olive Caddis: #16, afternoon
Little Blue-Winged Olive Dun: #18, afternoon

North Branch of the Au Sable River

> *North Branch Au Sable River (Crawford County)—sheep ranch access (up-
> stream of Twin Bridges) to mouth (21 miles):* flies only; size limit 8 inches
> brook trout, 10 inches other trout; five trout per day; last Saturday in
> April to October 31.
>
> *—Michigan Fishing Guide*

What a great place to escape the angling pressure that you find on
other rivers in the Au Sable region! The North Branch contains some
of the finest brook trout populations in this area of Michigan. It is truly
a fly fisherman's dream to fish this river and to enjoy all the solitude
and enjoyment that goes with catching these colorful trout. One day I
talked with Terry Miller, who fishes this river, and he said that the
North Branch also yields some good browns. The lower 21 miles of this
36-mile-long river is designated as a quality fishing (flies-only) area
and remains open until October 31.

The river originates just south of Gaylord, then flows through the
Pigeon River Country State Forest. The bottom is sand and gravel
down to the town of Lovells. From there to the mouth it is primarily
gravel substrate. Near Lovells the river flows through the Au Sable
State Forest. It is in these stretches of the North Branch off of Twin

Bridges Road that an excellent brook trout and sizable brown trout fishery exists. One access point on the North Branch is at Kellogg Bridge at North Down River Road.

The river provides excellent cover for the growth of trout. The North Branch has a reputation for tremendous insect hatches and offers most of the common mayfly species. According to those who fish it, hendricksons, sulphurs, and brown drakes are quite abundant; mahogany duns and tricos also occur in prodigious numbers; the little black caddis is an excellent early-to-midseason hatch.

One June afternoon I fished the North Branch near Kellogg Bridge. I managed to land and release several brook and brown trout on tiny nymphs and terrestrial imitations. The habitat in this section of the river provides adequate cover for even larger trout. As I was leaving, I observed some pale evening duns emerging from the river. I didn't want to leave this pristine setting, but I was intent on meeting and fishing the *Hexagenia limbata* on the main stem of the Au Sable.

Best Times to Fly Fish

March 1–May 15

Early Black Stonefly: #14, afternoon

Little Blue-Winged Olive Dun: #18–20, afternoon and early evening

Hendrickson/Red Quill: #12–14, afternoon and early evening

Black Willow Stonefly *(Acroneuria nigrita)*: #8–10, afternoon and evening

Little Black Caddis: #18–20, afternoon and early evening

Great Speckled Olive Dun *(Siphloplecton basale)*: #10–12, afternoon

Dark Blue Quill: #16–18, afternoon and early evening

May 16–June 15

Black Willow Stonefly *(Acroneuria nigrita)*: #8–10, afternoon and evening

Little Black Caddis: #18–20, afternoon and early evening

Dark Blue Quill: #16–18, afternoon and early evening

Black Quill: #12–14, afternoon

Lime Sally Stonefly: #14–16, afternoon

American March Brown: #10–12, afternoon and evening

Grannom: #12–14, afternoon and evening

Gray Drake: #12–14, afternoon and evening

Pale Evening Dun: #14–16, afternoon and evening

Tan Caddis: #14, afternoon and evening
Sulphur/Pale Evening Dun: #16–18, evening
Brown Drake: #8–10, evening
Dark Green Stonefly: #14, evening
Light Cahill: #14, late afternoon and evening
Slate Drake/Mahogany Dun: #12, evening
Yellow Sally Stonefly: #16, evening

June 16–July 15

Sulphur/Pale Evening Dun: #16–18, evening
Little Black Caddis: #18–20, afternoon and early evening
Dark Green Stonefly: #14, evening
Light Cahill: #14, late afternoon and evening
Slate Drake/Mahogany Dun: #12, evening
Yellow Sally Stonefly: #16, evening
Michigan Caddis/Hex *(Hexagenia limbata)*: #6–8, evening
Blue-Winged Olive Dun: #14–16, morning and evening
Tiny Blue-Winged Olive *(Pseudocloeon)*: #22, afternoon and
    evening
Little Tan Caddis: #16–18, late afternoon and evening
Grasshoppers: #8–12, afternoon and early evening
Trico: #24, morning

July 16–August 15

Light Cahill: #14, late afternoon and evening
Blue-Winged Olive Dun: #14–16, morning and evening
Tiny Blue-Winged Olive *(Pseudocloeon)*: #22, afternoon and
    evening
Slate Drake/Mahogany Dun: #12, evening
Yellow Sally Stonefly: #16, evening
Little Tan Caddis: #16–18, late afternoon and evening
Grasshoppers: #8–12, afternoon and early evening
Trico: #24, morning

August 16–September 15

Slate Drake/Mahogany Dun: #12, evening
Yellow Sally Stonefly: #16, evening
Little Tan Caddis: #16–18, late afternoon and evening
Grasshoppers: #8–12, afternoon and early evening
Trico: #24, morning

September 16–November 10

Dark Olive Caddis: #16, afternoon
Little Blue-Winged Olive Dun: #18, afternoon

South Branch of the Au Sable River

> *South Branch Au Sable River (Crawford County)—down from Chase Bridge to lower high banks (4 miles):* flies only, no kill, last Saturday in April to October 31. *Note:* Trout may not be possessed in no-kill areas regardless of where caught.
>
> *South Branch Au Sable River (Crawford County)—lower high banks to mouth (11 miles):* flies only; size limit 8 inches brook trout, 10 inches other trout; five trout per day; last Saturday in April to October 31.
>
> *—Michigan Fishing Guide*

The northern lights displayed their unique beauty on that mid-June trip to the South Branch of the Au Sable. Mike Calvin, a very talented fly tyer, accompanied me to the Mason Tract in search of the great *Hexagenia limbata* hatch. We took a few minutes to search the mud-banks for nymphs and located one mature nymph with darkened wing pads. After our sampling, we fished to some rising trout. A spinner fall of mahoganies or slate drakes saved the evening. Mike and I managed to hook and release several brown trout on our patterns.

The following evening I fished with Mike, Tim Roodvoets, and Preston Mann of Lapeer, Michigan. At first there was very little surface activity, then around 8:30 P.M. slate drake spinners began to show above the water. Mike and Tim did very well that evening. Tim managed to hook and land over a dozen fish on a #16 Robert's Yellow Drake, which is a local imitation, and Mike also got a very heavy brown trout on it. This fly was originated by Clarence Roberts, a former conservation officer who lived in Grayling. Several fish broke off, and one good fish got away from Tim on the pattern.

When people discuss the Au Sable River, they more than likely are referring to the South Branch. This water contains some of the heaviest trout in the Au Sable River system. The South Branch offers a wilderness-type fly-fishing experience as the result of a most generous donation from the late George W. Mason. He provided Michigan with twelve hundred acres that envelop both banks of the river for more than 14 miles. The natural history associated with the Mason Tract is truly remarkable. Where else can you see beaver swimming by and deer browsing, hear coyotes howling and barred owls calling, all while you enjoy fly fishing the evening hatches? The South Branch is known for its tremendous hatches of brown drakes and the huge mayfly *Hexagenia limbata*, often referred to as the Michigan caddis. I was never able to discover the origin of this unique common name that has long been used to describe this mayfly.

The South Branch originates at Lake St. Helen and flows to the town of Roscommon. This region of the river is too warm to support a high-quality trout fishery and does not attain trout status until it reaches the Chase Bridge area about 6 miles below Roscommon. The South Branch from Chase Bridge to Smith Bridge is fantastic fly-fishing water and is buffered by the Mason Tract. There is a great deal of groundwater influence in this region of the South Branch, which maintains excellent water temperatures during the summer. The river is slightly alkaline, which supports a diversity of species important as trout food. One disappointment to fly fishers – canoeing pressure is extremely heavy during weekends on the South Branch, and it does detract from the fly-fishing experience of this picturesque river in Michigan.

If you enjoy fishing in a truly wilderness setting, I would highly recommend the South Branch of the Au Sable. For information on this river, contact the folks at Gates Lodge and Pro Shop near Grayling.

517-348-8462

Best Times to Fly Fish

March 1–May 15
Early Black Stonefly: #14, afternoon
Little Blue-Winged Olive Dun: #18–20, afternoon and early evening
Hendrickson/Red Quill: #12–14, afternoon and early evening
Black Willow Stonefly *(Acroneuria nigrita)*: #8–10, afternoon and evening
Little Black Caddis: #18–20, afternoon and early evening
Great Speckled Olive Dun *(Siphloplecton basale)*: #10–12, afternoon
Dark Blue Quill: #16–18, afternoon and early evening

May 16–June 15
Dark Blue Quill: #16–18, afternoon and early evening
Black Willow Stonefly *(Acroneuria nigrita)*: #8–10, afternoon and evening
Little Black Caddis: #18–20, afternoon and early evening
Black Quill: #12–14, afternoon
Lime Sally Stonefly: #14–16, afternoon
American March Brown: #10–12, afternoon and evening
Grannom: #12–14, afternoon and evening
Gray Drake: #12–14, afternoon and evening
Pale Evening Dun: #14–16, afternoon and evening

Tan Caddis: #14, afternoon and evening
Sulphur/Pale Evening Dun: #16–18, evening
Brown Drake: #8–10, evening
Dark Green Stonefly: #14, evening
Light Cahill: #14, late afternoon and evening
Slate Drake/Mahogany Dun: #12, evening
Yellow Sally Stonefly: #16, evening

June 16–July 15
Sulphur/Pale Evening Dun: #16–18, evening
Dark Green Stonefly: #14, evening
Light Cahill: #14, late afternoon and evening
Michigan Caddis/Hex *(Hexagenia limbata)*: #6–8, evening
Blue-Winged Olive Dun: #14–16, morning and evening
Tiny Blue-Winged Olive *(Pseudocloeon)*: #22, afternoon and
  evening
Little Black Caddis: #18–20, afternoon and early evening
Little Tan Caddis: #16–18, late afternoon and evening
Grasshoppers: #8–12, afternoon and early evening
Trico: #24, morning

July 16–August 15
Light Cahill: #14, late afternoon and evening
Slate Drake/Mahogany Dun: #12, evening
Yellow Sally Stonefly: #16, evening
Blue-Winged Olive Dun: #14–16, morning and evening
Tiny Blue-Winged Olive *(Pseudocloeon)*: #22, afternoon and
  evening
Little Tan Caddis: #16–18, late afternoon and evening
Grasshoppers: #8–12, afternoon and early evening
Trico: #24, morning

August 16–September 15
Slate Drake/Mahogany Dun: #12, evening
Yellow Sally Stonefly: #16, evening
Little Tan Caddis: #16–18, late afternoon and evening
Grasshoppers: #8–12, afternoon and early evening
Trico: #24, morning
Dark Olive Caddis: #16, afternoon

September 16–November 10
Dark Olive Caddis: #16, afternoon
Little Blue-Winged Olive Dun: #18, afternoon

Manistee River

Manistee River (Kalkaska County)—Yellowtrees Landing to C.C.C. Bridge (7.5 miles): flies only; size limit 8 inches brook trout, 12 inches other trout; five trout per day, last Saturday in April to October 31.

— *Michigan Fishing Guide*

The Manistee River is also one of Michigan's classic trout waters. It may not be as famous as the Au Sable, but fly-fishing guide Charlie Weaver says it provides excellent fly fishing and that later in the summer months grasshopper imitations work well. Sometimes these tactics yield some really heavy browns during daylight hours. The upper reaches of the Manistee offer more of a wilderness experience than most rivers in this region of Michigan. The upper region is primarily a sandy streambed with very little gravel. Wild brook and brown trout can be taken on a fly in this portion of the river. Like the Au Sable, the Manistee was once famous for the grayling it supported.

Both the Manistee and the Au Sable originate close to one another in sandy, glacial deposits in Antrim County. Their headwaters flow south for approximately 15 miles, then the Au Sable turns east to Lake Huron and the Manistee turns west toward Lake Michigan. These rivers were important during early days of exploration and fur trading.

One afternoon Charlie Weaver, an excellent guide on the Manistee, and I fished the headwater region of this river. Originally from Ridgeway, Pennsylvania, Charlie has spent eight seasons on the Manistee River. He, Joe Kutkuhn, a nationally recognized fisheries biologist, and other conservationists keep a watchful eye on this fishery by noting changes in the sediment load in the river. The sandy substrate provided some difficult wading, but both of us managed to take wild brook and brown trout on various dry-fly imitations. There is plenty of overhead cover in this section of the Manistee. Beaver populations in this area may be one of the most detrimental factors affecting the wild trout fishery in this section of the river because the water backed up by their dams allows it to become heated by the sun. These impoundments also reduce the flow so that fine sands accumulate, choking off the spaces between rock and gravel in the stream bottom. The lack of these spaces reduces the aquatic insect fauna in most rivers. Obviously this will have a direct impact on a trout fishery.

The Manistee supports a phenomenal *Hexagenia limbata* population. Many people prefer to fish this river over the Au Sable during the emergence of this important mayfly. Additionally, the Manistee has a fine brown drake population. In the lower reaches of this river you may catch more rainbow trout.

The Manistee receives most of its water from groundwater and surprisingly is influenced very little by runoff. The rate of flow remains fairly uniform throughout the season. Water temperature fluctuation is usually not that obvious. The best fly fishing is above State Route 72, where cover is excellent, especially above the Cameron Bridge. Cover is afforded by deep pools, logjams, and undercut banks as a result of habitat work done in the 1950s. The riverbanks are blessed with pine and hardwoods. The flies-only water starts at Yellowtrees Landing on the Manistee and extends to the C.C.C. Campground, a distance of about 7.5 miles. This river is unique, and you may want to place it on your list of rivers to fly fish.

Best Times to Fly Fish

March 1–May 15
Early Black Stonefly: #14, afternoon
Little Blue-Winged Olive Dun: #18–20, afternoon and early evening
Hendrickson/Red Quill: #12–14, afternoon and early evening
Black Willow Stonefly *(Acroneuria nigrita)*: #8–10, afternoon and evening
Little Black Caddis: #18–20, afternoon and early evening
Great Speckled Olive Dun *(Siphloplecton basale)*: #10–12, afternoon
Dark Blue Quill: #16–18, afternoon and early evening

May 16–June 15
Black Willow Stonefly *(Acroneuria nigrita)*: #8–10, afternoon and evening
Little Black Caddis: #18–20, afternoon and early evening
Dark Blue Quill: #16–18, afternoon and early evening
Black Quill: #12–14, afternoon
Lime Sally Stonefly: #14–16, afternoon
American March Brown: #10–12, afternoon and evening
Grannom: #12–14, afternoon and evening
Gray Drake: #12–14, afternoon and evening
Pale Evening Dun: #14–16, afternoon and evening
Tan Caddis: #14, afternoon and evening
Sulphur/Pale Evening Dun: #16–18, evening

Brown Drake: #8–10, evening
Dark Green Stonefly: #14, evening
Light Cahill: #14, late afternoon and evening
Slate Drake/Mahogany Dun: #12, evening
Yellow Sally Stonefly: #16, evening

June 16–July 15

Little Black Caddis: #18–20, afternoon and early evening
Sulphur/Pale Evening Dun: #16–18, evening
Dark Green Stonefly: #14, evening
Light Cahill: #14, late afternoon and evening
Slate Drake/Mahogany Dun: #12, evening
Yellow Sally Stonefly: #16, evening
Michigan Caddis/Hex *(Hexagenia limbata)*: #6–8, evening
Blue-Winged Olive Dun: #14–16, morning and evening
Tiny Blue-Winged Olive *(Pseudocloeon)*: #22, afternoon and
   evening
Little Tan Caddis: #16–18, late afternoon and evening
Grasshoppers: #8–12, afternoon and early evening
Trico: #24, morning

July 16–August 15

Light Cahill: #14, late afternoon and evening
Slate Drake/Mahogany Dun: #12, evening
Yellow Sally Stonefly: #16, evening
Blue-Winged Olive Dun: #14–16, morning and evening
Tiny Blue-Winged Olive *(Pseudocloeon)*: #22, afternoon and
   evening
Little Tan Caddis: #16–18, late afternoon and evening
Grasshoppers: #8–12, afternoon and early evening
Trico: #24, morning

August 16–September 15

Slate Drake/Mahogany Dun: #12, evening
Yellow Sally Stonefly: #16, evening
Little Tan Caddis: #16–18, late afternoon and evening
Grasshoppers: #8–12, afternoon and early evening
Trico: #24, morning
Dark Olive Caddis: #16, afternoon

September 16–November 10

Dark Olive Caddis: #16, afternoon
Little Blue-Winged Olive Dun: #18, afternoon

Pere Marquette River

> *Pere Marquette River (Lake County)—State Route 37 Bridge downstream to Gleason's Landing (7 miles):* no closed season; artificial flies only; creel limits: last Saturday in April to September 30, three trout or salmon over 10 inches, but no more than one over 16 inches; remainder of year one fish over 16 inches. No-kill on brown trout and Atlantic salmon during extended season.
>
> *—Michigan Fishing Guide*

This productive river first received brown trout in 1883; before that it boasted a good supply of grayling; later it would receive rainbow trout. It holds some of the best hatches in the Midwest. You'll find the *Hexagenia limbata* hatch, trico, hendrickson, brown drake, and much, much more. It's the Pere Marquette River.

John Kestner of Johnson's Pere Marquette Lodge in Baldwin, Michigan, and I fished the flies-only stretch of the river from the State Route 37 access to Gleason's Landing one afternoon and evening. Not only can John handle a drift boat, he also is an excellent fly fisherman. We managed to take a few fish that day, but none were of the caliber that you know are lying in the bends of the deep runs and pools of this river. We saw several species of stoneflies during our float and landed fish on imitations of these important aquatic insects. What more could this fine midwestern trout stream have to offer?

The following evening Jim Empie, an avid fly tyer and excellent rod builder at Johnson's Lodge and Fly Shop, Charles Belt, and I fished Smith's Pool. Even though this water looks like it will fish easy, one is quickly humbled by the diversity of currents that a fly fisher must overcome. Early in the evening, at 8:20 P.M., blue-winged olive dun spinners fell on the water, and small trout rose to these #16 mayflies. A few *Hexagenia limbata* spinners came down on the water late, and trout took them slowly in the eddy on the far side of the pool. Jim hooked and landed a very heavy rainbow that rose to his Hex Spinner. The air temperature cooled quickly after darkness set in, and the trout soon stopped surfacing, which signaled the time to call it an evening.

The next afternoon John Kestner and I were back on the river in a drift boat and caught a lot more trout than on the previous float. John was taking fish on a wide array of imitations, while I decided to test some bottom feeders with some nymphs. On almost every cast with a stonefly nymph imitation I encountered a bump from a fish. Several browns and rainbows were landed that afternoon and evening on my nymph patterns.

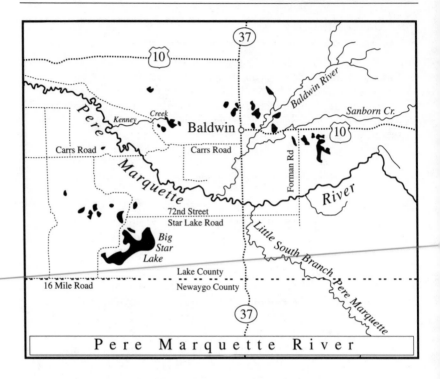

Pere   Marquette   River

The Pere Marquette River has some of the finest trout water in the Midwest. Undercut banks and clay-lined pools are common in the special-regulated area. Additional overhead cover is evident in association with the many stream-improvement devices that were constructed in the late 1950s.

The main stem of the Pere Marquette begins about .5 mile east of State Route 37. The first 8 miles of the river consists of riffle areas in sections broken up by deep, meandering pools. You can see depressions in the gravel associated with the riffles in this section. John Kestner told me that these are remnants of the spawning beds of steelhead and chinook salmon. When you fish this water, you have no doubts that it will harbor heavy brown trout. Many mature species of deciduous and coniferous trees line this picturesque section of the Pere Marquette. The pools of the river have names associated with them and are of important interest to the fly fisherman. To name just a few: Ledge Hole, Island Hole, Claybank, Springhole, Alligator Alley, Grayling Hole, and Old Reliable. All have unique characteristics that offer challenges to the fly caster.

Recently I ate breakfast with Larry Demmick. As a resident of Michigan, Larry has been fishing the Pere Marquette for twenty-four

years and has caught some heavy trout. He finds that hendricksons/
red quills, brown drakes, and gray drakes can be very productive
hatches. He prefers the gray drake over most of the other hatches that
occur on the river. In addition to these, Larry also says that the Pere
Marquette has an excellent trico hatch.

This river offers many challenges, and I hope to return sometime
soon. The urge to return to fish the Pere Marquette's beautiful pools
and deep undercut bends that hide heavy trout is one I'm sure you'll
sense after spending time fly fishing the river. For information on
current conditions on the Pere Marquette contact John Kestner, Jim,
Phyllis, or Tom Johnson at Johnson's Lodge and Fly Shop in Baldwin,
Michigan.

Best Times to Fly Fish

March 20-May 15
Little Black Stonefly: #16–18, afternoon
Little Black Caddis: #16–18, afternoon and early evening
Hendrickson/Red Quill: #12–14, afternoon and early evening
Little Blue-Winged Olive Dun: #18–22, afternoon and early
evening

May 16-June 15
Little Black Caddis: #16–18, afternoon and early evening
Hendrickson/Red Quill: #12–14, afternoon and early evening
Little Blue-Winged Olive Dun: #18–22, afternoon and early
evening
American March Brown: #12–14, afternoon and evening
Pale Evening Dun: #14–18, afternoon and evening
Black Quill: #12–14, afternoon and early evening
Green Caddis: #10–18, afternoon and evening
Tan Caddis: #14–16, afternoon and evening
Yellow Sally Stonefly: #14–16, late afternoon and evening
Mahogany Dun/Slate Drake (*Isonychia* spp.): #10–12, evening
Gray Drake: #10–14, evening
Brown Drake: #10–12, evening
Giant Stonefly: #2–8, evening

June 16-July 15
Little Black Caddis: #16–18, afternoon and early evening
Tan Caddis: #14–16, afternoon and evening
Yellow Sally Stonefly: #14–16, late afternoon and evening
Mahogany Dun/Slate Drake (*Isonychia* spp.): #10–12, evening
Gray Drake: #10–14, evening

Giant Stonefly: #2–8, evening
Michigan Caddis/Hex *(Hexagenia limbata)*: #4–8, evening
Light Cahill: #12–14, late afternoon and evening
Ants: #8–10, afternoon
Little Blue-Winged Olive Dun: #18–22, afternoon

July 16–August 15
Mahogany Dun/Slate Drake *(Isonychia* spp.): #10–12, evening
Light Cahill: #12–14, late afternoon and evening
Ants: #8–10, afternoon
Little Blue-Winged Olive Dun: #18–22, afternoon
Cream Sedge: #8–10, evening
Crickets: #8–12, afternoon
Grasshoppers: #6–14, afternoon
Trico: #22–26, morning

August 16–September 15
Crickets: #8–12, afternoon
Grasshoppers: #6–14, afternoon
Trico: #22–26, morning

WISCONSIN

Many people feel that Wisconsin is known more for its warm-water fishing than its cold-water fishing. There are many lakes in this state that do provide excellent fishing for warm-water species, but we will concern ourselves with one of several blue-ribbon trout streams that occur in this state. Over 3,000 miles of streams and rivers exist in Wisconsin, and some of the most picturesque water can be found in the northern section of the state. Wisconsin's famous trout waters include the Brule, Wolf, Iron, White, and Peshtigo rivers. The Namekagon River is one of the state's finest trout fisheries. Let's take a look at it in more detail.

Namekagon River

The Namekagon originates in Namekagon Lake in Bayfield County. It meanders for more than 60 miles through three Wisconsin counties until it meets the St. Croix River at Riverside. In 1967 the Namekagon was included in the National Wild and Scenic Rivers Act, so it should remain a high-quality fishery into the future. There are two distinct regions of the river. The upper 20 miles, from Hayward to its source, is excellent trout water. U.S. Route 63 parallels much of the Namekagon, and access to the river can be gained by several county roads that intersect it.

The Namekagon in this region is easily waded. From the lake downstream to the village of Cable the river is fast-flowing, forested trout water with very few road accesses. Here you will find brook trout. Downriver from Cable toward the village of Hayward the Namekagon widens and contains an excellent pool-and-riffle sequence. The undercut banks and alders provide plenty of overhead cover for trout in this section of the river, and brown and rainbow trout are commonly caught in this stretch. Several lakes along the upper section serve to minimize stormwater flows into the river.

According to Ron Manz, owner of Brule River Classics just south of Brule, the drought of 1988 has really had an impact on trout populations in the Namekagon. The river still maintains a diversity of aquatic insect life that supports wild brown trout in the river. The hendrickson, brown drake, Michigan caddis, white mayfly, and trico are important mayflies to meet and fish to in this river. Additionally, the Namekagon has a wide variety of caddisfly hatches. Most fly fishermen agree that the best dry-fly fishing occurs in the evenings from late May through mid-July. Crayfish and scuds provide additional food for the

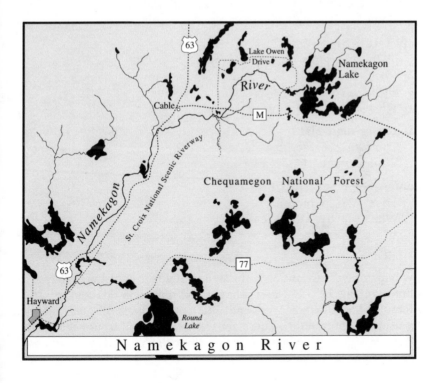

Namekagon River

trout in the Namekagon. Hellgrammites (larval stage of the dobsonfly) are common, and imitations of this insect prove very effective on this river.

For additional information on the Namekagon, contact Ron Manz at Brule River Classics near Brule. He and his son Cordell logged more than 300 hours in 1991 while guiding on trout water in northwestern Wisconsin.

Best Times to Fly Fish

May 1–May 31
    Hendrickson/Red Quill: #12–14, afternoon and early evening
    March Brown: #10–12, afternoon and evening
    Gray Fox: #12, afternoon and evening

June 1–June 30
    Hendrickson/Red Quill: #12–14, afternoon and early evening
    Brown Drake: #8–10, evening
    March Brown: #10–12, afternoon and evening
    Gray Fox: #12, afternoon and evening
    Light Cahill: #12–14, late afternoon and evening
    Giant Black Stonefly *(Pteronarcys)*: #6, evening

July 1–July 31
    Michigan Caddis/Hex: #6–8, evening
    March Brown: #10–12, afternoon and evening
    Slate Drake: #10–12, afternoon and evening
    Trico: #22–26, morning

August 1–August 31
    Trico: #22–26, morning
    White Fly: #12–14, evening

September 1–September 30
    Trico: #22–26, morning
    White Mayfly: #12–14, evening

MISSOURI

I will be forever envious of the Show-Me State's trout waters. They are unique among the cold-water fisheries that remain in this country. The Meramec and Current rivers and Blue Spring Creek all offer quality fly-fishing opportunities. There are two very special trout fisheries in Missouri – Crane Creek and North Fork of the White River – and we will examine them here.

Crane Creek

Artificial lures only, catch-and-release area on the upper 3 miles of the creek in the Wire Road Wildlife Area.

—*Missouri Department of Conservation Fishing Regulations*

Where in the world does a pure strain of California's McCloud River rainbow trout still maintain itself? It no longer resides in California, but this unique strain of rainbow trout still exists. According to Spencer Turner, a well-known fisheries biologist with the Missouri Department of Conservation, Crane Creek supports one of only five or six pure populations remaining in the world. It is one of the few remaining rivers east of the Rocky Mountains where you can fish for stream-bred rainbows.

The moment I saw this pristine little creek, I thought I had returned to a small trout stream in the East. Its gravel substrate was clean and covered with snails. There are many undercut banks with tree roots offering cover for the unique trout of this creek. And the Crane has more going for it than the unusual strain of trout that it harbors.

I traveled with Shawn Taylor of Taylormade River Treks in Tecumseh and Ray Krouscup of Crane one early day in August. Ray has spent the last several years fly fishing this little gem, and Shawn has often wanted to test his skills on these wild rainbows. Crane Creek ranges from 8 to 25 feet wide. The midday water temperature was 64 degrees Fahrenheit when the air temperature had climbed above 100 degrees. Most of the Crane has a good box elder and sycamore canopy to protect it from the heat of the sun. We took turns casting our imitations on pools and riffles of the Crane, but the overhead cover made long, drag-free floats almost impossible. Nevertheless, even though the cover was tight, the three of us managed to land some beautiful trout.

We decided to take a break from fly fishing to examine the aquatic life on the bottom of this creek. Light cahill, golden stonefly, little sister sedge, cased caddisfly, and little dark blue dun immatures were present in the kick samples we made with my D-frame aquatic net. Scuds, sowbugs, and crayfish were also very abundant in these samples. Ray hasn't observed trout feeding on small flies during his tenure on this creek and feels that fishing small flies isn't productive. Effective patterns are #14 and #16 Tan Elkhair Caddis and #12 Prince Nymph.

You can access Crane Creek by traveling south from Springfield to the town of Crane in Stone County on State Route 13/173. Walk softly when you fish this stream. Your fly-fishing skills will be tested on this small creek, but the reward of a beautiful crimson-striped rainbow will be well worth your efforts.

Best Times to Fly Fish

March 1–May 15
Little Blue-Winged Olive Dun: #18, afternoon
Little Black Caddis: #18, afternoon and early evening
Light Cahill: #12–14, late afternoon and evening
Little Dark Blue Dun: #20–26, afternoon and early evening

May 16–June 15
Little Black Caddis: #18, afternoon and early evening
Light Cahill: #12–14, late afternoon and evening
Little Sister Sedge: #12–14, afternoon and evening
Ant: #12–18, afternoon
Beetle: #12–16, afternoon
Inchworm: #12, afternoon

June 16–July 15
Light Cahill: #12–14, late afternoon and evening
Little Sister Sedge: #12–14, afternoon and evening
Ant: #12–18, afternoon
Beetle: #12–16, afternoon
Inchworm: #12, afternoon

July 16–August 15
Little Sister Sedge: #12–14, afternoon and evening
Ant: #12–18, afternoon
Beetle: #12–16, afternoon
Inchworm: #12, afternoon

North Fork of the White River

Trophy-trout fishing areas are established on the unimpounded portion of the North Fork of the White River and its tributaries in Ozark County. Within these areas the daily and possession limit is three trout of any species. All trout less than 15 inches in total length must be returned to the water unharmed immediately after being caught. No trout less than 15 inches long may be possessed in these areas. Statewide limits apply to other species.

—Missouri Department of Conservation Fishing Regulations

Recently, I fished the North Fork of the White River with Shawn Taylor, a dedicated fly fisherman who has guided for several years in Alaska and has fished many rivers in the West. He operates Taylor-made River Treks, located on the North Fork near Tecumseh, Missouri. Shawn is a true conservationist and a strong advocate of catch-and-release fly fishing. Recently, he and many other fly fishers have brought the appropriate attention to the North Fork. They personally contacted and corresponded with fishery managers regarding the unique value of the North Fork. It is a high-quality trout fishery for 13 miles downstream from the Double or Rainbow Spring, the third largest spring in Missouri.

The North Fork can be accessed off of U.S. Route 160 on County Routes H or PP, which will take you to an access point known as Blair Bridge. Most of the river is best fished by floating in a boat, and if you prefer that way, use an experienced guide like Shawn Taylor or portage at the Falls, which is downstream of McKee Bridge. This bedrock outcrop doesn't look all that bad, but many accidents have occurred on the river at this location.

The North Fork was designated a trophy-trout stream in 1978 and is the only large river in Missouri with a wild rainbow trout popula-

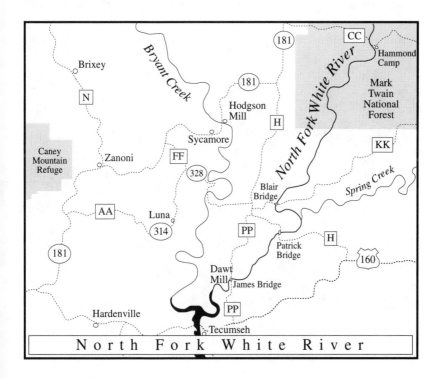

North Fork White River

tion. The trophy-trout area is gorgeous water. This high-quality river is the only remaining free-flowing section of the White River system. Here you will find an excellent wild rainbow trout population, with streambred rainbows approaching 10 pounds. Brown trout, which may attain 15 pounds in weight, are added once a year and are protected by the 15-inch minimum length limit.

When you fish the North Fork, you will have the feeling of fishing a western river. The Ozark bluffs are beautiful as you float along the trout water. While we drifted in Shawn's boat, I couldn't help but enjoy the scenic beauty of this unique aquatic resource. If additional protection were to be provided for trout in the North Fork, it could become one of the best trout fisheries in the eastern half of the United States.

The North Fork is 50 to 90 feet wide, with heavy riffles that are separated by long, deep runs and pools. Much of the bottom is coarse rock and gravel, and there are bedrock outcrops that cover the entire bottom of the river. At 4:00 P.M., when the air temperature was around 95 degrees, the water temperature in the middle of this river was 66 degrees.

According to Shawn, the nymph imitation known as the Prince is king on the North Fork. When you fish the North Fork, you surely will want to have plenty of #10 and #12 Prince nymphs in your possession.

Evidence that the Prince nymph is king of the North Fork of the White River in the Ozark region of Missouri. *Greg Hoover.*

The Long Pool of the Deerfield River in Massachusetts. *Greg Hoover.*

Jim Frazier fishes Shadow Rock Pool of the West Branch of the Ausable River in New York. *Greg Hoover.*

Fog rises off the Gunpowder Falls River in Maryland. *Charles Meck*.

Al Hines on North Carolina's South Toe River. *Greg Hoover*.

Oregon's spectacular Metolius River is difficult even with a hatch to match. *Charles Meck*.

The clear water of Crane Creek in Missouri reveals crayfish and darters on the bottom. *Greg Hoover*.

The Fryingpan River in Colorado. *Charles Meck*.

Green drake male (imago) from Penns Creek in Pennsylvania. *Greg Hoover*.

Female green drake dun from Penns Creek. *Greg Hoover*.

A swarm of caddisflies. *Greg Hoover.*

The trout's-eye view of *Tricorythodes* male duns on the North Fork of the White River in Missouri. *Greg Hoover.*

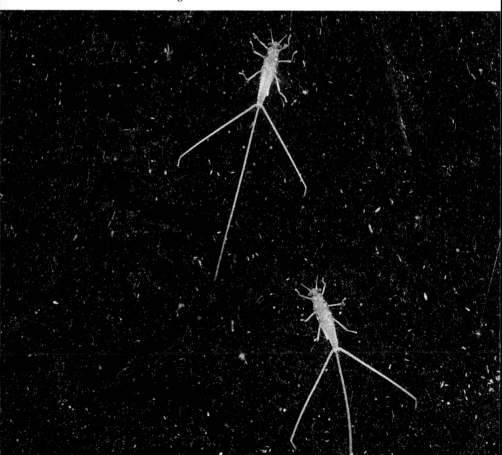

Slate drake nymphs (*Isonychia* sp.) from New York's West Branch of the Ausable River. *Greg Hoover.*

Hexagenia limbata female (subimago) from Michigan's Au Sable River. *Greg Hoover.*

Green Drake Nymph. *Greg Hoover.*

Cut Wing Sulphur. *Greg Hoover.*

I attempted to fish the river with some of my own preferred nymph patterns, but none performed as well as the Prince. We both caught many beautiful brown and rainbow trout on this imitation while fishing through deep, quick runs.

Shawn feels that imitating small forms of trout food isn't productive on the North Fork. When I conducted a few kick samples, I found two stonefly families; crawler, clinger, and swimmer-type mayflies; scuds; crayfish; hellgrammites; fishflies; free-living caddisflies; and mollusks on the bottom of the North Fork. If your fly boxes contain imitations of the adult and immature life stages of these aquatic inhabitants, you should greatly improve your chances for an unforgettable day on this picturesque river.

Best Times to Fly Fish

March 1–May 15
> Little Blue-Winged Olive Dun: #18–20, afternoon and early evening
> Hendrickson/Red Quill: #12–14, afternoon and early evening
> Light Cahill: #14, late afternoon and evening

May 16–June 15
> Light Cahill: #14, late afternoon and evening
> Pale Evening Dun: #16–18, evening
> Slate Drake: #12, late afternoon and evening
> Brown Drake: #8–10, evening

June 16–July 15
> Golden Drake: #12, evening
> Pale Speckle-Winged Dun: #16, morning

July 16–August 15
> Pale Evening Dun: #14–16, evening
> Trico: #24, morning

August 16–September 15
> Trico: #24, morning

ARKANSAS

When people discuss Arkansas, they usually are not talking about fishing for trout. Until the Norfork River yielded a world-record brown trout, few people entertained the idea of a quality trout-fishing experience in this state. Most high-quality trout water is considered a tailwater fishery. The one most often mentioned in this state is the White River downstream of Bull Shoals Lake. This river is a special one, and we hope you will get a chance to fly fish it in the near future.

White River

> *Brown Trout Restrictions on White River:* It shall be unlawful in the White River, from Bull Shoals Dam to the downstream boundary of Bull Shoals State Park, from November 1 through January 31, to retain brown trout in possession. It is also unlawful to use tackle other than artificial lures or flies with a single, barbless hook, not larger than #8, when fishing for any species in the above-described waters during the November 1– January 31 period.
>
> *—Arkansas Game and Fish Commission Regulations Guide*

The lettering on the water tower in Cotter, Arkansas, read "Trout Capital." I wondered if there were any truth to the statement. Would I get a chance to land one of the monster browns for which this river is recognized? I was really anxious to cast a fly in this famous trout river.

The White River in Arkansas is one of the most famous tailwater trout fisheries in the United States and provides excellent brown and rainbow trout fishing. Many fish exceeding 10 pounds are caught during the year.

Recently, Shawn Taylor of Taylormade River Treks in Tecumseh, Missouri, and I fished at Roundhouse Shoals on the White River. Shawn guides and fly fishes the White River regularly. We arrived on the river early in the morning and waded out to the far channel in the river. A few fish rose to small midges. Both Shawn and I tied on #14 Cress Bugs to our 6X tippets. After fishing both channels, Shawn and I hooked and released over fifty rainbow trout. Additionally, Shawn landed a beautiful cutthroat. Many times during the trip we both had fish on at the same time.

The temperature at this point on the river, approximately 18 miles downriver from the water-release site below Bull Shoals Lake, was 66 degrees while the air temperature was between 90 and 100 degrees. The discharge temperature from the release drawn from 120 feet below the surface of the lake is usually 55 degrees. The water temperature of the White River is truly remarkable when you consider its size.

It is advised to use extreme caution when wading the White. The water level fluctuates greatly during a twenty-four-hour period, and you can't rely on horns or other warnings when fishing miles below

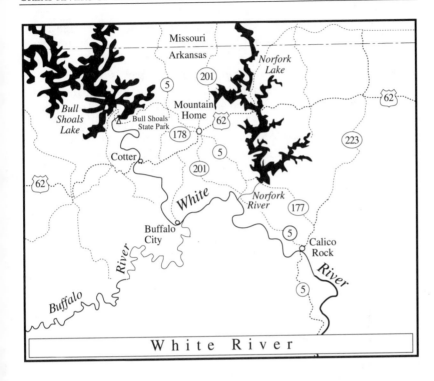

Missouri
Arkansas
Norfork Lake
(5)
(201)
(62)
Bull Shoals Lake
Mountain Home
Bull Shoals State Park
(62)
(178)
(223)
Cotter
(5)
(201)
(62)
White
Norfork River
(177)
Buffalo City
(5)
Calico Rock
River
(5)
Buffalo River

W h i t e   R i v e r

Bull Shoals Lake. When fly fishing the White, move to safe ground when the river starts to rise. And don't delay, because the water can rise rapidly.

When fishing the White, you will hear the local term, "shoal," which generally means a shallow run or riffle. Some of the favorite riffles to fly fish in the White are the Upper, Middle, Lower, Wildcat, Roundhouse, Rim, White, and Buffalo shoals. All of these are upstream of the confluence with the Norfork River. The Rim Shoal area is the best known fly-fishing area on the river. The Upper, Middle, and Lower shoals can be accessed at Bull Shoals State Park off of State Route 178. Roundhouse Shoal can be accessed by turning left off of U.S. Route 62 downriver from the town of Cotter. There is an island in the middle of the river at this site. Don't get caught in the far channel during rising water. To fish Rim Shoals turn from U.S. Route 62 onto Route 126S. Travel approximately 3 miles on 126S until you come to a well-maintained gravel road to the right. Follow this road to the river.

Hank Weir of Lakeview, Arkansas, has been guiding for eleven years on the White River and generally logs 100 to 125 trips per year. Hank is a self-taught fly tyer and a superb fly fisherman, and he knows how and where to float his fly-fishing clients on the White. He prefers fishing Red Fox Squirrel nymphs and Woolly Buggers to entice trout when he is casting a fly. According to Hank, there is steady midge activity and the most important mayfly on the river is the sulphur.

The White River offers an opportunity for a fly fisher to hook some very large trout. The river also needs to be respected for its unpredictable flows. Don't let feeding trout overcome your own sense of personal safety. You can enjoy some great fly fishing on the White, especially if you contact and fish with someone who spends time on and knows this fabulous tailwater fishery.

Best Times to Fly Fish

April 1–May 15
Light Cahill: #14–18, afternoon and evening

May 16–June 15
Light Cahill: #14–18, afternoon and evening
Sulphur: #18, evening
Sowbug: #10–16, morning and afternoon
Brown Caddis: #18–20, afternoon and evening

June 16–July 15
Light Cahill: #14–18, evening
Gray Midge: #20–22, morning and afternoon
Black Midge: #20–22, morning and afternoon
Sowbug: #10–16, morning and afternoon

July 16–August 15
Sowbug: #10–16, morning and afternoon
Gray Midge: #20–22, morning and afternoon

August 16–September 15
Sowbug: #10–16, morning and afternoon

September 16–October 15
Dark Olive Caddis: #16–20, afternoon

6

Great Rivers of the West and Their Hatches

Back in 1972 when I began research on *Meeting and Fishing the Hatches*, I contacted a prominent fly-fishing writer from Montana. I asked him to talk about the hatches found on western waters. He cursorily answered that the West contained few hatches. "You'll find the salmon fly on many waters, but not much else," he replied.

I believed him briefly—until I visited a few prolific rivers of the West like Henry's Fork in Idaho, the Metolius in Oregon, the Madison in Montana, and others. These and many other western waters hold a wide array of prominent hatches that provide exciting fishing-the-hatch events all year long. From the western march brown that appears on the McKenzie in Oregon in late February to the little blue-winged olive dun on the San Juan in New Mexico in March and April to the trico on the South Platte and North Platte rivers in late October, the West truly holds a multitude of great hatches across its mountains, deserts, and fertile valleys. Whether you're fly fishing one of the spring creeks, rushing rivers, cold tailwaters, or fertile lakes—many of them boast great hatches.

But the West has extreme diversity. You can fly fish waters in Oregon and Washington that barely flow above sea level, such as the McKenzie River at Eugene, Oregon, at 300 feet above sea level. Compare that with the Blue River in Colorado and hundreds of others where you're fly fishing at altitudes above 8,000 feet! Altitude and weather affect the hatching episode tremendously. On Oregon's Mc-Kenzie River you can fish over heavy western march brown hatches in early March, but a heavy winter mantle still envelops many of the Rocky Mountain rivers then. On near-coastal waters you'll find western green drakes and pale morning duns on the water in late May, but these same hatches don't appear for another month on Henry's Fork in Idaho and other nearby waters.

You'll find that many of the great western rivers are famous for one or more hatches. When Oregon anglers think of the *Hexagenia limbata* hatch, they think of the Williamson River. When fly fishermen think of matching a brown drake hatch in Idaho, many of them think of Henry's Fork or Silver Creek. We'll examine some of these western rivers and their important hatches.

WASHINGTON

Washington–a state of extreme contrasts. West of the Cascade Mountain Range you'll find lush, green vegetation and anadromous fisheries full of salmon and steelhead. A few rivers west of the Cascade Range do have respectable trout populations, however. Rivers and creeks like the Tilton (Lewis County), Yellow Jacket, Skate (Lewis County), and the Elwa River do hold trout. The latter brags a sea-run cutthroat population into October. However, many of the better trout waters lie east of the Cascades. You'll find arid conditions in areas that annually receive less than 10 inches of rain. You'll also find rivers and creeks like the Yakima River and Rocky Ford Creek. Additionally, you'll find a contradiction in terms: desert lakes. Some of these, like Nunnally Lake, hold a good supply of rainbows and browns over 20 inches long. We'll examine fly fishing in these lakes and rivers of eastern Washington. However, don't overlook some other possibilities.

George Cook suggests that two other rivers deserve attention. He feels the upper Columbia River near the Canadian border is a sleeper. He also recommends trying the Spokane River near the city of Spokane.

You'll find great hatches across the state. The huge salmon fly *(Pteronarcys)* inhabits the Yakima and other state rivers. You'll find mayflies like the western green drake and pale morning dun on many streams and rivers from mid-May through much of June. At the same time, the speckle-winged dun *(Callibaetis)* emerges on slower waters. In August and September many of the streams and rivers hold good hatches of the diminutive trico.

The Desert Lakes

Check local regulations. Nunnally Lake allows anglers to keep one
trout. You must use a single barbless hook.

— *Washington Department of Wildlife Game Fish Regulations,*
Washington Department of Wildlife

Recently Craig Shuman, Dick Turner, Garry Sandstrom, and I headed
for a day of fly fishing on the Yakima River. When we met our two
guides for the day, Dean Stephenson and Mike Kuffler, we all decided
to postpone our trip—the river was over its banks in many places on
this April day. All six of us decided to head to one of the nearby lakes
to fish for trout. Here we knew we didn't have to contend with high
spring runoff.

Garry led the group on the short hike to the lake. He runs a fly
shop in Tacoma, Washington, and, like an increasing number of fly-
fishing shop owners, he not only knows his tackle but also excels at
fly-fishing techniques.

As we entered from a slight hillside, we noted a dozen or more
trout taking large dark gray chironomids near the surface. Garry
couldn't wait to get started. He tied on a #14 black chironomid pupa to
match what the trout pursued. For the next two hours Garry, Dick,
and Craig caught heavy rainbows and browns on that sinking imitation. As an added bonus, these fish were strong, fighting fish. Garry
used a strike indicator made of yarn and varied the depth of the
chironomid pattern by moving the yarn indicator on his tippet. When
he saw little action near the surface, he moved his indicator 6 feet
above the fly. That's an important rule I learned watching that day:
vary the depth of your emerging pupa. If you see trout working just
under the surface, fish the imitation in the same location. If you see
naturals emerging but no trout near the surface, then set your pattern
to drift deeper. Experiment and watch for the slightest hesitation of
your indicator. Fish seem to be leader shy, so try to use a long 6X or 7X
tippet. When you go deep with the pattern, you might want to add a
micro shot.

Chironomid hatches are prominent in the spring on these eastern
Washington lakes, and trout sometimes feed all day. As the water
warms in the summer, trout move to colder, deeper water and often
feed only from dusk to dawn. Damselfly and dragonfly nymphs work
especially well in the summer.

Don't overlook speckle-winged dun hatches during the middle of the morning. You'll see these on the water from May through September. You can match the *Callibaetis* nymph underneath or the dun or spinner on the surface.

Craig and Dick used float tubes to get near the rising trout, several other fly fishermen nearby used small johnboats, and several of us waded along the shoreline. Anglers in the boats cast their imitations with their fly rods. Then they set down their fly rods and waited for the slightest movement on their strike indicators.

Nunnally Lake is only one of several productive lakes in the region. In the December 1988 issue of *Fly Fisherman* Steve Probasco wrote about Lakes Merry and Lenice, which are close to Nunnally Lake. He also mentioned huge Lake Lenore and its strain of Lahontan cutthroats. Just a couple miles north of Lake Lenore you'll find the much smaller Dry Falls Lake. All are productive eastern Washington fisheries. You can reach all of these lakes off Interstate 90. Just east of Vantage Bridge crossing the Columbia River you'll find Merry, Nunnally, and Lenice lakes south of the interstate and Lenore and Dry Falls lakes north of it.

There are still more productive public lakes in eastern Washington as well as a few private lakes that are extremely productive. On some of these private lakes there's as much as a two-year waiting period for anglers. Three of these are located on Isaak Ranch, 30 miles north of the town of Soap Lake.

George Cook guides guests on these productive Isaak Ranch lakes. In 1987 the owner of the ranch showed George a photo of some of the trout caught in these desert lakes, which was enough to cause George to make these lakes available for private fishing under his guidance. The growth rate on the trout on Isaak Ranch is phenomenal. Three-and-one-half-year-old trout on the ranch lakes can measure over 26 inches long. In June 1990 an angler landed a 30½-inch brown trout. The charge per day on these lakes is very reasonable.

Best Times to Fly Fish (A Typical Western Desert Lake)

April 10–May 1
> Chironomid (various colors and sizes, but gray and black most common in #14–24);* sporadic in May and June; on other streams, rivers, and lakes you'll find hatches all year long.

May 10–June 15
> Damselfly: #6 and #8, afternoon
> Speckle-Winged Dun: #14 and #16, morning and afternoon (sporadic into November)**

*See section on the chironomid hatch on the Cache la Poudre
in Colorado.
**Later on Rocky Mountain waters.

Rocky Ford Creek

> Fly fishing only; barbless hook; limit one trout per day; no wading.
>
> — *Washington Department of Wildlife Game Fish Regulations*

Rocky Ford Creek near Moses Lake in eastern Washington doesn't look
like one of the more productive spring creeks of the West, and at many
points it resembles a small pond rather than a fertile stream chock-full
of rainbow trout. At some sections its slow-moving water flows
through large cattail patches and two commercial trout hatcheries.

Even though Rocky Ford Creek lacks the aesthetic scenery normally associated with a wild-trout stream, it does contain an unbelievable supply of hefty rainbows, which consistently feed on minutia that
can drive you crazy if you come unprepared — minutia like the dark
gray chironomids that appear throughout the year, but especially in
the spring, and a heavy trico hatch that occurs from early June
through much of October and November. Both the chironomids and
tricos are matched with #20–24 imitations.

Walk along the heavily traveled path that closely parallels the
stream below the hatchery and you'll find a public western spring
creek full of heavy streambred and stocked rainbows. But watch out
for rattlesnakes in the summer — the Rocky Ford Creek area is full
of them.

The 7-mile-long creek is supplied from a spring. A commercial
hatchery covers the first quarter-mile section of the water. Algae float
atop much of the stream partially due to the rich effluents from the
hatchery. This growth creates a casting problem — after every other
cast you must check the fly.

Don't fly fish Rocky Ford Creek without a good supply of chironomids. Spring finds a good hatch of black or dark gray midges on the
water all day long. Both the dry-fly pattern and the CDC imitation (to
copy the emerger) work well. Rocky Ford Creek also holds a good
supply of pale morning duns in late May and June. Because much of
the water is slow running, you'll also find an impressive population of
speckle-winged duns *(Callibaetis)* from late May. Darrel Martin says
that many anglers use a pale gray Adams to copy this mayfly. Add an

extensive number of dark olive gray and pale gray scuds to all these prolific hatches, and you can readily see why trout in Rocky Ford Creek grow rapidly.

Recently Craig Shuman, Dick Turner, Garry Sandstrom, and I arrived at the Rocky Ford parking lot. Garry used to be a biologist with the Washington Department of Wildlife and now runs the Morning Hatch in Tacoma. He is an excellent fly fisherman and knows area streams well. Dick Turner is an attorney in the Tacoma area, and Craig Shuman is an entrepreneur from Washington. We had difficulty finding a parking spot – it seemed everyone had come for a day of fly fishing. Rocky Ford Creek provides Tacoma–Seattle-area fly fishermen with a quality stream within four hours travel time, and on this day more than thirty cars and maybe fifty or more anglers had flocked to the available space.

The four of us hiked downstream a mile, where the number of anglers thinned out considerably. Here we had large stretches of water to ourselves. It seems that few anglers cared to venture far from the parking lot.

In five hours of fly fishing with a Griffith's Gnat, Black Chironomid Emerger, and Blue Quill, the four of us had on more than a dozen heavy rainbows. Garry landed one heavy 2-foot rainbow.

Rocky Ford Creek does possess its share of problems in addition to its lack of aesthetics: at present there's a one-trout limit per day on the stream – the stream should be designated as a no-kill stream; because of the large number of trophy trout, there's some poaching; algae present a problem – you'll find plenty of this primitive plant material floating on the surface of many segments of the stream; and the parking lots need to be expanded and others added below to take the pressure off of one area of the creek.

If you like to see rainbows over 20 inches long feeding much of the day and you don't mind a pondlike stream, then you'll enjoy Rocky Ford Creek in eastern Washington's Grant County. You can reach the water off State Route 17. Thanks to the foresight of the Washington Department of Wildlife for making Rocky Ford Creek a fly-fishing-only project.

Best Times to Fly Fish

December 1–March 31
   Black Chironomid: #24, morning and afternoon

April 1–May 1
   Black Chironomid: #24, morning and afternoon
   Little Blue-Winged Olive Dun: #20, morning and afternoon

June 1–July 15
Pale Morning Dun: #16 and #18, morning and afternoon
Speckle-Winged Dun: #14 and #16, morning and afternoon
Blue Quill: #18, morning and afternoon
Dark Gray Caddis: #18, afternoon and evening
Tan Caddis: #16 and #18, afternoon and evening

July 15–September 1
Trico: #24, morning
Speckle-Winged Dun: #14 and #16, morning and afternoon
Blue Quill: #18, morning and afternoon

September 1–October 30
Little Blue-Winged Olive Dun: #20, morning and afternoon

Yakima River

a) From mouth of river to 400 feet below Wapato Dam, open year-round except closed April 1 to May 31 for trout and steelhead. Trout: catch limit two; minimum length 12 inches. Steelhead: catch limit one and wild steelhead must be released.

b) From Wapato Dam to 400 feet below Roza Dam, open June 1 through March 31. Trout: catch limit two; minimum length 12 inches. Steelhead: catch limit one and wild steelhead must be released.

c) From Roza Dam to 400 feet below Easton Dam, catch-and-release year-round season for trout and steelhead; barbless artificial flies or barbless single point lures only, bait prohibited. Except: whitefish fishing allowed with bait and single-point barbed hooks January 1 through end of February.

d) From Lake Easton to Keechelus Dam, open June 1 through October 31. Trout: catch limit eight, with 8-inch minimum size and no more than two of the trout may be greater than 12 inches in length.

— Washington Department of Wildlife Game Fish Regulations

George Cook is the famous casting teacher associated with Sage Rods. If you've seen Sage's huge color photo of an expert casting a fly with a tight loop, that's a photo of George. He fishes and hunts all over the West. He calls the Yakima the Madison of Washington State. The Yakima is Washington's answer to a blue-ribbon river—it holds plenty of rainbow trout, some heavy hatches, quality water, and spectacular scenery.

Mike Kuffler and Dean Stephenson are two of about twenty ex-

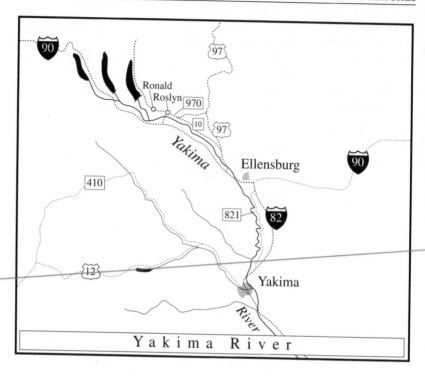

Yakima River

cellent guides you'll find on the Yakima. Both guides float the lower canyon between Ellensburg and Roza Dam. There are about 47 miles of excellent fly fishing from Elk Meadow downriver to the dam, which is several miles below Ellensburg. From June through October Mike and Dean often select the section from Teanaway Junction to Ellensburg. An effective way to fly fish the water is in a McKenzie boat, fishing as you drift, and stopping along the way to wade and fly fish some of the quality water. Mike has seen some anglers catch 24-inch rainbows.

The river ranges from 75 to 150 feet wide, and early spring rains and snowmelt can cause high-water conditions until early June. The best dry-fly fishing is from July through October – hatches still appear and the water lowers considerably at that time.

Hatches occur early on the Yakima. In April you'll find the western march brown and the little blue-winged olive dun on the water. If water conditions are low enough, you can match the hatch in spring. Stoneflies and caddisflies populate the river and create some fishable hatches. According to Darrel Martin, the Yakima River has one of the most prolific, varied stonefly hatches in the West, and around mid-

May or a little later the river holds a respectable salmon fly hatch. Best hatches of this huge stonefly occur in the middle and upper sections. Match this large *Pteronarcys* nymph, and you're in for some excellent action all day long. When the orange-bodied adults return to the river to lay eggs, it's time for the huge salmon fly imitation. From May through September you'll see large golden stoneflies on the water almost daily. Garry Sandstrom, owner of the Morning Hatch Fly Fishing Shoppe in Tacoma, recommends using a #6 Golden Stonefly simulator to match these large stoneflies.

Other downwings can create hatches on the river. In early May you'll find a #16 gray caddis. In addition to this spring caddis hatch, green, ginger, and tan caddisflies are found in September. Garry Sandstrom says fall hatches can produce some fine fishing.

Mayfly hatches continue throughout much of the summer. You'll find western green drakes and pale morning duns in late May, gray drakes in June, and even some tricos in August and September. The two-generation little blue-winged olive dun also appears in September and October.

The Yakima is not without its problems, though. Poaching bait fishermen illegally take their share of streambred rainbows, and other people readily use the river during the summer months. Rafters and innertubers can cause problems for fly fishermen casting to rising trout.

Water temperatures stay cool throughout the year. Mike Kuffler and Dean Stephenson say that the water stays in the low sixties all summer long.

Best Times to Fly Fish

April 1–May 15
Western March Brown: #14, afternoon
Little Blue-Winged Olive Dun: #20, morning and afternoon
Gray Caddis: #16, afternoon and evening

May 15–June 25
Salmon Fly: #6, afternoon and evening
Golden Stonefly: #8, afternoon and evening
Gray Caddis: #16, afternoon and evening
Speckle-Winged Dun: #14 and #16, sporadic
Western Green Drake: #10 and #12, morning and afternoon
Gray Drake: #10 and #12, afternoon
Pale Morning Dun: #16 and #18, morning and afternoon

June 15–July 20
   Golden Stonefly: #6, afternoon and evening
   Gray Drake: #10 and #12, afternoon
   Pale Morning Dun: #16 and #18, morning and afternoon
   Slate Drake (Mahogany Dun): #12, evening

July 20–September 1
   Trico: #18–22, morning
   Golden Stonefly: #8, afternoon and evening
   Slate Gray Dun: #14 and #16, afternoon and evening

September 1–October 30
   Trico: #24, morning
   Green Caddis: #14, afternoon and evening
   Trico: #18–22, morning
   October Caddis: #8, afternoon and evening
   Little Blue-Winged Olive Dun: #20, morning and afternoon
   Slate Gray Dun: #14 and #16, late afternoon and evening
   Blue Dun: #22, afternoon and evening

OREGON

If Washington is a state of contrasts, so is Oregon. But Oregon has many more great trout rivers and great hatches. Bob Zagorin, executive director of the Oregon Guides and Packers Association, feels that the best rivers west of the Cascades are the McKenzie and North Santiam rivers. East of the Cascades he feels that rivers like the Deschutes and Williamson compare favorably with any in the nation. Are Oregon rivers really that good? Bob claims that the state is second only to Idaho in the number of licensed guides.

What about great hatches in Oregon? The state has its share. If you'd like to fish over the great *Pteronarcys* stonefly, then try the Deschutes or Wood rivers. If you want to fly fish in March or April over a predictable hatch that appears every afternoon, then fish the McKenzie River when the western march brown appears. You can fly fish the western green drake hatch on Oregon's miniature answer to Henry's Fork, the Metolius River. Oregon even boasts the same huge mayfly found on Michigan rivers, the Michigan caddis, or *H. limbata* hatch. Fish the Williamson in southern Oregon at dusk in late June, and you'll find these gigantic mayflies on the river in abundance.

Great rivers and great hatches – Oregon has both. Throw in an added bonus of spectacular scenery, and you're in for a delightful surprise when fishing this state's top rivers.

Deschutes River

a) From mouth of river (I-84 bridge) up to Sherar Falls:

1) Restricted to barbless flies and lures only, except that bait may be used with single-point ⅝ inch or larger barbless hooks from Sherar Falls downstream to upper trestle (about 2 miles). Commercially canned fish may be used in the bait area.

2) Rainbow over 20 inches are steelhead.

3) Only adipose clipped steelhead may be taken; others must be released unharmed.

4) No angling from a floating device that is buoyant and supporting the angler.

b) From Sherar Falls up to Pelton Regulating Dam:

1) Restricted to barbless flies and lures only.

2) Rainbow over 20 inches are steelhead.

3) Only adipose clipped steelhead may be taken; others must be released unharmed.

4) Two trout per day, 10-inch minimum and 13-inch maximum length.

c) From Lake Billy Chinook up to Lower Bridge:

1) Two trout per day, 6-inch minimum, only one over 20 inches.

d) Lower Bridge up to North Canal Dam in Bend:

1) Two trout per day, 6-inch minimum, only one over 20 inches.

e) From North Canal Dam up to Little Lava Lake:

1) No more than two brown trout from Bend to Wickiup Dam.

2) No angling from Wickiup Dam down about ¼ mile to cable crossing September 1 to October 31.

3) No angling from Crane Prairie Dam down to marker below mouth of Browns Creek September 1 to October 31.

4) No angling from Prairie Reservoir up to Little Lava Lake, including tributaries, prior to June 1.

—Oregon Sport Fishing, Regulations Edition,
Oregon Department of Fish and Wildlife

I hate nymph fishing. I avoid it at all costs. I like to see the fly in full view on the surface and see the action take place right in front of me. But the Deschutes River in central Oregon changed my thinking on nymph fishing forever.

Craig Lacy guided Jay Kapolka and me through a series of rapids and pools on the Deschutes near Madras. The cold morning warmed only slightly, and by noon temperatures had barely reached 50 degrees–which equaled the water temperature exactly. Nothing happened for the first two hours, and I sat in the boat and watched Craig show Jay how to fish this blue-ribbon river. Jay had three trout to show for a half day's work on the river in late May. Where was this excellent trout fishing that the river supposedly held?

When we stopped for lunch at one of the many islands along the way, we began to see a few of the large salmon flies climbing up vegetation on the shore. First we saw dozens, then hundreds of the huge *Pteronarcys* adults that had emerged within the past day or two. I immediately tied on a pattern copying the adult and began casting under bushes near the far shore. An occasional native rainbow trout rose to the few adults that the strong gusting winds had blown back onto the water. Craig correctly assured us that trout had not yet keyed in on the adult, but most certainly they fed on the nymphs moving toward the shoreline. I tried a dry Salmon Fly and convinced two small trout to take the #6 long-shank pattern.

After an hour of relative inaction Craig handed me a fly rod with a nymph and told me to fish a seam of the riffle in front of me. I resisted for a minute but finally agreed to test the underwater pattern. On the Deschutes most anglers use the high-stick method of fishing stonefly nymphs. They attach a strike indicator to their lines about one and one-half times the distance of the depth of the water. They then cast upriver and out 10 to 20 feet, mend the line once or twice, lift the rod high, and follow the strike indicator downriver. This method gets the weighted nymph down near the bottom. Any slight hesitation of the indicator might mean a strike. On casts two, six, twelve, fourteen, eighteen, and twenty, trout hit the nymph. Some of these weighed close to 3 pounds and measured 15 to 16 inches.

We floated downriver a half mile, and Craig directed Jay and me to try the weighted stonefly nymphs in another productive-looking seam. After a few casts an 18-inch "red sider" took the nymph. Within minutes two more hit the pattern. Wow, was this great fly fishing! We ended up the day with a few more strikes and ended our trip at the Trout Creek launching site.

You can deduce from the previous story that the river holds an excellent salmon-fly hatch that lasts for a couple weeks. One problem with the salmon-fly hatch is the horde of anglers it brings to the river. When the word gets out that the huge stonefly has begun to emerge, thousands of fly fishermen swarm to the river to fish the hatch.

The Deschutes has many unusual features. If you're fishing it for the first time, it's best to hire a guide to show you the regimen. You have to purchase an Indian permit if you plan to fish from the left side on a 6-mile stretch of the river on the Warm Springs Reservation. You can't fish from some of the islands that are sacred to the Indians, and you can't fish from a boat, but must exit and fish by foot.

What makes the Deschutes a blue-ribbon river? Several years ago Oregon Fish and Wildlife found more than twenty-five hundred trout over 8 inches long per mile on the river. To produce this many fish, the river must hold a lot of food for trout. As Craig Lacy put it, the trout in the Deschutes are insect eaters, not piscavores. Check the bottom of the river, and you'll see why these fish are heavy and healthy. Craig Lacy sampled the bottom and we found several *Pteronarcys* nymphs, several pale morning nymphs, dozens of caddisfly species, four more stonefly species, and three more mayfly species. Of the mayflies one of the heaviest and most dependable hatches is the little blue-winged olive dun in March and April and again in September and October. This hatch can produce some great dry-fly fishing. The pale morning dun appears from late May into July. Those specimens that I've examined have a reddish tan color on their bodies.

Many anglers fish the trico hatch on the Deschutes. Jim Hare of Alexandria, Virginia, travels to the river every July and floats the river with Lynn Sawyer, an expert local guide. Jim has hit the trico on almost every trip. He feels it's one of the most challenging hatches the river holds. In contrast, Lynn feels that the little blue-winged olive falls at the same time as the trico and that the former is much more important.

Some areas of the river report a respectable western green drake hatch, which appears on the surface about the same time as the salmon fly. Caddisfly hatches also produce some great matching-the-hatch opportunities on the Deschutes. From the green caddis in early May to the huge October caddis in fall, the Deschutes holds a huge variety. Craig Lacy finds that fishing an imitation of the pupa works best when the October caddis appears. And don't overlook midges on the Deschutes. You'll find these chironomids on the water in heavy numbers from July through October.

But all is not well for the Deschutes. The river suffers from many problems, some serious enough to question its future blue-ribbon status. Rafters overuse the water, and on the lower river you'll find too many jet boaters. In one recent year more than 250,000 used the water. This resource is not prepared for that. The state is considering an allocation system to limit the number of boaters on busy weekends. On a recent Memorial Day trip guided by Alan Stewart of the Fly Box of Bend, Oregon, Jay Kapolka and I saw hundreds of other boats carrying campers and rafters down the river. It certainly wasn't the experience I wanted.

Dams in the upper Deschutes also present problems. Man-made impoundments cause a highly irregular flow in the upper end, which in turn affects the trout spawning and the aquatic insect population. Also because of this you'll find siltation problems in the upper area. These dams from top to bottom–Crane Prairie Reservoir, Wickiup Reservoir, Round Butte Dam, Pelton Dam, and the Regulating Dam– produce a lot of problems on the river.

Poaching is also a problem on the river, although minor. Some anglers don't adhere to the limit on the river, and there's little enforcement.

The Deschutes River begins south of Bend and flows north emptying into the Columbia River near Biggs. U.S. Route 97 parallels much of the river. Many of the float trips begin just below Pelton Dam near Madras. A typical one-day float begins near Warm Springs and ends at the boat-launching site at Trout Creek. Overnight trips end on the lower Deschutes near Maupin.

You can inquire about guides on the river at the Fly Box in Bend. Merril Hummer, Bill Merrill, and Alan Stewart can help you with the local hatches and locating a guide.

In spite of all of its problems, the Deschutes remains a top river with some great hatches. The Deschutes ranges from 100 to 150 feet wide at most places, and it's difficult to wade fast water. If you hit this river around the end of May when the salmon fly appears, you're in for a great hatch on a great river.

Best Times to Fly Fish

February 1–March 15
  Little Black Stonefly: #16 or #18, afternoon

March 1–April 30
  Little Blue-Winged Olive Dun: #20, morning and afternoon
  Western March Brown: #12 and #14, afternoon

May 1–May 15
  Western March Brown: #12 and #14, afternoon
  Grannom: #14, morning and afternoon
  Gray Caddis: #16, afternoon and evening

May 15–July 4

Salmon Fly: #6, afternoon and evening
Golden Stonefly: #8, afternoon and evening
Pale Morning Dun: #16 and #18, morning and afternoon
Yellow Sally Stonefly: #16, afternoon and evening
Tan Caddis: #14 and #16, afternoon and evening
Rock Worm (Green Caddis): #16, afternoon and evening
Pale Evening Dun: #14, afternoon and evening
Blue Quill: #18, morning and afternoon
Western Green Drake: #10 and #12, morning and afternoon
Brown Drake: #10 and #12, evening

July 15–July 30

Pale Morning Dun: #16 and #18, morning, afternoon, and evening
Olive Caddis: #14 and #16, morning, afternoon, and evening
Pale Evening Dun: #14, afternoon and evening
Blue Quill: #18, morning and afternoon
Trico: #20–24, morning

August 1–September 14

Trico: #24, morning

September 15–October 30

Trico: #24, morning
October Caddis: #8 or #10, afternoon and evening
Little Blue-Winged Olive Dun: #20, morning and afternoon

McKenzie River

> *McKenzie River above Oregon Department of Fish and Wildlife (ODFW) markers (200 yards below Hayden Bridge boat ramp):* No trout can be kept 14 inches or over. McKenzie from mouth upstream to ODFW markers: Barbless flies and barbless lures except bait allowed on barbless hooks during salmon and steelhead season. All nonclipped trout must be released. Trout fishing open the entire year in this section.
>
> *—Oregon Sport Fishing, Regulations Edition*

If you want to see your share of foul weather during February, March, and April, fish one of the Oregon rivers in the Willamette Valley. It seems that every time I visit the area in spring, I hit one of those foul-weather days.

April 28 was a cold, blustery, rainy day on the McKenzie River near Eugene, Oregon. Mike Manfredo boasted for years about the great hatch on the river this time of year. The hatch, the western march brown *(Rhithrogena morrisoni)*, appears on Willamette Valley rivers in late February and continues every afternoon into late May. This #14 mayfly brings scores of rainbows to the surface during the hatch.

Long before many western fly fishermen think of hatches, this mayfly appears. Why does it begin appearing in February? Because spring often comes early to the Willamette Valley – much earlier than to the Rocky Mountain area.

Ken Helfrich of nearby Springfield, Oregon, would be our guide for the 6-mile float trip down to the Willamette River. The river is difficult to access and to fish from shore, so drifting with a McKenzie-type boat is the only suitable alternative. Ken also guides on Oregon's Rogue River and Idaho's Middle Fork of the Salmon River. He not only handles the McKenzie boat well on the river, but he's also an excellent fly fisherman and knows the hatches the McKenzie holds. He's a member of the McKenzie River Guides Association and the Oregon Guides and Packers.

In late February to late April Ken often drifts the river near Eugene to meet the western march brown hatch. In May you'll find him 30 miles upriver above Vida fishing the same hatch. Just about the time the western march brown lessens, a heavy western green drake appears on the river. Ken also regards this latter hatch as a great time to meet and fish the hatch.

Annually, the state stocks 150,000 trout in the McKenzie. You're not allowed to kill any trout over 14 inches on the river. Ken says that restriction, which was placed on the McKenzie twenty years ago, has saved the river.

We entered the river that morning just across from a state park near Eugene. As I do so often when I first begin to fly fish, I took a few seconds to check the water temperature. The thermometer rose to 50 degrees. I say rose because the air temperature never got out of the high forties. But Ken, Mike, and I had adequately prepared for the inclement weather with heavy jackets and rainwear.

I hadn't done much float fishing before, so Ken had to teach me quickly the refloat method he uses for dry-fly fishing from a McKenzie boat. First, you cast your dry fly 45 degrees downriver from the boat, then lift the fly upriver the distance of your leader and let it float back downriver. We tied Ken's favorite pattern, a parachute Western March Brown dry fly, onto the tippet and a wet-fly version of the imitation onto the dropper.

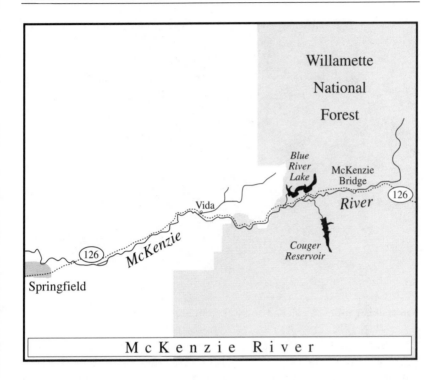

McKenzie River

Ken drifted us through several sets of rapids, possibly 2 miles down from our point of entry. Only occasionally did we see any western march browns. Then we reached a moderate but deep rapids followed by a long flat pool. As we approached the rapids from above, we suddenly saw thousands of western march browns emerge onto the surface. With the cold air and drizzle, only a small percent of the duns successfully struggled free from the water and became airborne. What seemed like hundreds of rainbows rose to this early spring bonanza throughout the upper part of the pool. With Ken's expert guidance, Mike and I caught a dozen trout before we exited the pool. Each riffle and pool downriver contained a good number of rainbows eager to surface feed. At several pools the surface action became so intense that we left the boat and fished to risers from the shore. Duns first appeared in massive numbers at 2:00 P.M. and a few were still appearing at 4:00 P.M.

Four miles downriver we entered the cloudy Willamette River where few trout rose. What a day this had been! What a spectacular hatch! Mike, Ken, and I caught more than fifty trout within a few miles of Eugene, Oregon, on that dismal, overcast day.

Ken Helfrich fishes the McKenzie River from his boat. *Charles Meck.*

Mike and Ken fish the western march brown from the end of February until late May on the McKenzie. Ken feels that the best hatches of the western march brown occur in March and April. By the time May rolls around, air and water temperatures rise and the emerging duns take flight more rapidly.

Ken grew up on the McKenzie River and for eighteen years has guided fly fishermen over trout rising to an abundant supply of western march brown duns. He's seen this same hatch on the river thousands of times, and he's had some fishermen on his boat catch as many as one hundred trout during a western march brown, western green drake, or October caddis hatch on the river. You'd think by now that he would lose some of his enthusiasm for the hatch, the river, and his success. Not Ken – he still gets excited about meeting and fishing this tremendous extended western hatch.

There are many more hatches than just the western march brown. In fact, hatches occur just about year-round. After the western march brown has waned, you'll see a great McKenzie caddis on the water. You'll need a #10 or #12 pattern in two distinct body colors to match the hatch. Copy the male with a dark reddish brown body and the female with a dark greenish gray body. The female has a distinct green to its mottled gray wings.

You'll find a respectable trico hatch on the lower end of the river in the Eugene area. It begins in middle to late July and continues well into October. I've never seen another angler fishing to this potentially productive spinner fall on the river. During the trico spinner fall I've seen pods of ten and fifteen trout feeding on the spent imagoes. While we're discussing fall hatches, don't overlook the October caddis hatch on the river. You can have some fantastic last-season fly fishing over a hatch for a week or more when this down-wing appears.

Also, don't overlook some of the smaller tributaries of the Mc-Kenzie. Around the Vida area you find some with heavy rainbow and cutthroat populations. Recently, on an early May Trip, Ken Helfrich and I found the main stem of the McKenzie several feet above normal. We hiked up a couple of the smaller tributaries and caught rainbow trout all day long.

The McKenzie begins in the same area where the Santiam River begins—in the Willamette National Forest at Clear Lake. The river flows to McKenzie Bridge, then more than 50 miles west toward Eugene. Just below McKenzie Bridge, at Blue River, the main stem picks up the South Fork. In Eugene the McKenzie flows into the Willamette River.

Ken feels that the best hatches on the river occur above McKenzie Bridge. The upper McKenzie holds a respectable western green drake population and some salmon flies. It also holds a lot of fast water. This upper section from Trail Bridge Reservoir to Clear Lake gets little fishing pressure. You'll find only native rainbows and cutthroats in the upper section, both of which appear near the end of May. A half-mile stretch near Vida, called Bylerland Flat, also holds some great hatches and good dry-fly-fishing water. If you enjoy spectacular scenery, then you must take a float trip on the upper McKenzie from Olallie Campgrounds to McKenzie Bridge. Use an experienced guide when you drift fish these treacherous waters.

The McKenzie is almost impossible to wade, and at many places the river extends more than 150 feet from bank to bank. Treacherously deep pocket water negates wading any distance on this river. The bottom is uneven, and wading on many areas is dangerous. In the Eugene area, where wading is easier, it's difficult to access the river. There are many areas set aside by the state for access to the river. State Route 126 parallels much of the river from near its source at Clear Lake downriver to Eugene. You'll see many McKenzie River boats on this water. The best way to fly fish this river is with a member of the McKenzie River Guide Association. Contact any member of the Oregon Guides and Packers and they can arrange a memorable float trip on this river.

With the more liberal laws now in effect, fly fishermen can legally enjoy the western march brown hatch in February, March, and April. The lower section of the river from near Hayden Bridge downriver to the Willamette is now open year-round.

If you want the latest information on the river, its hatches, or you just want some fishing conversation, visit the Caddis Fly Shop on Main Street in Eugene. Bob Guard, Chris Daughters, and Steve Baker can tell you about the current conditions and hatches on the McKenzie or Willamette rivers.

Best Times to Fly Fish

February 20–May 15
Western March Brown: #14 and #16, afternoon
Dark Gray Caddis: #14, afternoon
Early Brown Stonefly: #14, midday
Gray Caddis: #14, afternoon and evening

May 15–June 15
Western March Brown: #12 and #14, afternoon
Blue Quill: #18, morning and afternoon
Gray Drake: #12 and #14, afternoon
Pink Lady: #14, afternoon and evening
Pale Morning Dun and Spinner: #16, morning and afternoon
Western Green Drake: #12, morning and afternoon (spotty – most in upper end)
Green Caddis*: #10, midday and evening
Dark Brown Caddis**: #10, midday and evening
Salmon Fly: #6, afternoon and evening (spotty – most in upper end)
Little Yellow Stonefly: #16, midday
Black Ant: #20, morning, afternoon, and evening
Orange Caddis: #10 and #12, afternoon and evening
Yellow Caddis: #12, afternoon and evening

July 15–October 30
Trico: #24, morning (lower end)

September 15–October 15
October Caddis: #10, afternoon and evening

*Locals call this female the McKenzie caddis.
**Locals call this male the McKenzie caddis.

Metolius River

a) On main stem, all nonfinclipped (wild) trout, except Kokanee, must be released unharmed. No angling from a floating device that is buoyant and supporting the angler.

b) Main stem above Bridge 99 is restricted to fly angling with barbless hooks only.

c) Main stem below Bridge 99 is restricted to barbless flies and lures only (no bait), except in the area from Bridge 99 downstream approximately .5 mile to ODFW markers, where bait with barbless hooks may be used.

—Oregon Sport Fishing, Regulations Edition

The Metolius is a spectacular river. Tom Neff of Bend and Gary Kish of Portland first took me to this spectacular spring creek in 1986. The Metolius River begins in the Cascades near the 10,000-foot peak, Mount Jefferson. If you visit the source of the spring, you'll see the snow-covered mountain in the background. It's a spellbinding sight. Fishing on this extraordinary spring creek begins near Camp Sherman.

The Metolius without a hatch can be one of the most frustrating rivers in the United States. Gary Kish feels that many anglers who fish the river never learn to fish for the native trout. Gary spends much of his time educating anglers on how to fish for wild trout, especially on the Metolius. He says that the planted trout distract many people from learning how to catch wild trout, and this produces two separate schools of fishing here—one for planters and one for native trout. Gary guided out of the Camp Sherman store from 1984 to 1988. While he did, he developed a hatch chart to the aquatic insects on the water. He still knows the river and the hatches it holds well, and he can consistently catch the wily rainbows and bull trout it contains.

Even with a hatch, the river from the gorge downriver presents unusually difficult drag problems. Getting a drag-free float any distance isn't possible on much of this water, yet it is crucial to success. How can you succeed on this baffling river? Use slack line casts and good leaders and try to fly fish one of the many hatches. One of the best on the river is the western green drake *(Drunella grandis)*. You'll also find another *Drunella* species—the blue-winged olive dun, which looks like the western green drake but is much smaller. Tie some of the drakes for the Metolius in #14 if you plan to fly fish there. The pale morning dun appears in unbelievable numbers in this area. The duns

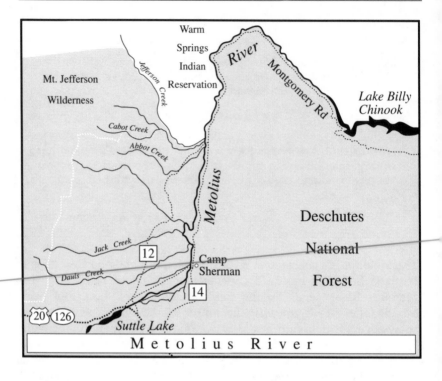

Warm
Springs
Indian
Reservation

Mt. Jefferson
Wilderness

Jefferson Creek

River

Montgomery Rd

*Lake Billy
Chinook*

Cabot Creek

Abbot Creek

Metolius

Deschutes

National

Forest

Jack Creek

12

Camp
Sherman

Dauls Creek

14

20 126

Suttle Lake

M e t o l i u s   R i v e r

have a distinct pale olive cast to their bodies. Trout seem to prefer that light olive body.

Recently Gary Kish, Dick Turner of Tacoma, Washington, Jay Kapolka of Pennsylvania, and I met to spend an afternoon on the Metolius. I invited Dick Turner to join us since he shared the frustration many anglers feel on this river. We hiked down the narrow trail at the upper end of the gorge and arrived at a series of pools around 2:00 P.M. Gary said we should wait for the western green drake, and within minutes the first one appeared. Soon a sparse hatch of these huge insects appeared on the surface, but few took flight. Native rainbows took almost every natural that failed to become airborne. The four of us took turns fishing to rising trout, and all of us caught trout on a Western Green Drake dry fly. The hatch, though not spectacular that day, proved to succeed. It's important to look at an interesting sidelight to this trip. While we all fished, not one of us caught a trout more than 30 feet from shore. Why? Any cast longer than that resulted in an immediate dragging fly. The current on the part below the meadows is almost impossible to fish with a drag-free float.

I said earlier that the Metolius is extremely difficult when there is no hatch to match. The previous incident occurred with just a meager hatch. But look what happened six days later in the identical location with a full-blown hatch under way. It was a lousy day! Jay and I had just returned to the Metolius River for a second try at the native trout. We had canceled our scheduled trip to the Blitzen River south of Burns because of recent heavy snowmelt. We arrived 1 mile downriver at the gorge section of the river where Gary Kish had taken us the previous week at 2:00 P.M. A fine, cold drizzle fell all afternoon, and the temperature remained just slightly below 50 degrees on this May 29. As we arrived we saw birds dashing out toward the center of the river to catch mayflies. At the first fishable pool Jay and I saw what we had hoped for – an extensive pale morning dun hatch had just begun on the Metolius. More than a dozen trout rose in this first pool, and I decided to fly fish for them. Jay headed downriver to seek out some other risers. Thousands and thousands of pale morning duns floated on the surface, and very few took flight because of the lousy weather. Four trout hit my #14 Pale Morning Dun. The remainder refused the pattern, so I headed upriver to an eddy to examine some of the naturals on the surface. I noted four separate heavy hatches in the eddy. In addition to the pale morning duns, little blue-winged olives, western green drakes, and blue-winged olives also rested on the surface. All four had olive bodies, so I tied on a #14 Blue-Winged Olive Dun. On the first ten casts six trout hit the pattern. Meanwhile, downriver, Jay Kapolka shared the same success. He too switched from the Pale Morning Dun to a Blue-Winged Olive Dun. What an afternoon! We quit after three hours of one of the heaviest multiple hatches either of us had ever witnessed – and all of this occurred on one of the lousiest, most inclement days I have witnessed in years.

Gary Kish feels that the best hatch on the river for the entire year is the western green drake. But you'll see more than that hatch here. The Metolius is a miniature insect factory, similar to Henry's Fork in Idaho. Almost any season you travel there you'll see insects on the surface. As early as February and March you'll encounter little winter stoneflies and western march browns emerging. In January you'll witness little blue-winged olive duns, and by late May the fantastic western green drake emerges on the river. The best little blue-winged olive dun hatches are in January and February. While we fished over the sporadic western green drake, we also saw a respectable pale morning dun appear. Even into September you'll see insects on the water and trout rising to them. Every afternoon in late summer golden stoneflies return to the surface to deposit their eggs and complete their life cycle, and an occasional rainbow rushes to take any careless insect.

Fishing pressure gets heavy on this spectacular river during the summer months. You'll see plenty of campers and anglers up and down the river.

The Metolius is easy to reach off U.S. Route 20 about halfway between Sweet Home and Bend, Oregon. You reach the river by following the road to Camp Sherman. The river enters Lake Billy Chinook, which is formed by Round Butte Dam, which dammed the Metolius, Deschutes, and Crooked rivers.

Gary Kish divides the river into four sections. The slow meadow section around and below Camp Sherman is the "upper river"; the area from just below Jack Creek to Wizzard Falls anglers call the "gorge"; the section from Wizzard Falls to Bridge 99, residents term the "mid-river"; and the water below that is the "lower river."

John Judy, a local guide who also guides anglers on the Deschutes, knows the Metolius well and has written a booklet on the river. Harry Teel of the Fly Fishers Place in nearby Sisters, Oregon, lists the hatches currently appearing on the Metolius and other nearby rivers at his store, and he and Jeff Perrin can help you decide what to use and where to go. They also provide a guide service on the nearby Deschutes River.

Best Times to Fly Fish

January 1–February 28
Little Blue-Winged Olive Dun: #18 and #20, 12:00 noon to 2:00 P.M.

February 25–April 15
Little Winter Stonefly: #16 and #18, late morning and early afternoon
Western March Brown: #14, afternoon
Gray Caddis: #16, afternoon
Amber Caddis: #14, afternoon

April 15–May 30
Western March Brown: #14, afternoon
Little Blue-Winged Olive Dun: #20, morning and afternoon
Western Green Drake: #12 and #14, morning and afternoon
Pale Morning Dun: #16 and 18, morning and afternoon
Blue-Winged Olive Dun: #14, afternoon

June 1–June 30
Little Blue-Winged Olive Dun: #20, morning and afternoon
Western Green Drake: #12 and #14, morning and afternoon

Pale Morning Dun: #16 and #18, morning and afternoon
Golden Stonefly: #8, afternoon
Blue-Winged Olive Dun: #14, afternoon

July 1–July 31
Golden Stonefly: #8, afternoon
Pale Morning Dun: #16 and #18, morning and afternoon

September 1–October 15
Little Blue-Winged Olive Dun: #20, morning and afternoon
October Caddis: #10, afternoon and evening
Little Cinnamon Stonefly: #16, afternoon
Autumn Green Drake: #12, afternoon

Williamson River

a) *Mouth of river up to bridge on Agency Lake Road (#427):* Two trout per day, 20-inch minimum length.

b) *Agency Lake Road up to Chiloquin Bridge:* Restricted to use of artificial flies or lures.

c) *Chiloquin Bridge up to Kirk Bridge:* Trout, catch and release only with barbless flies and lures September 1 to October 31.

—Oregon Sport Fishing, Regulations Edition

What's a "Michigan river" doing in south-central Oregon? It even boasts a heavy Michigan caddis, or as the locals call it, the big yellow may, hatch. Oregon's Williamson River certainly looks out of place. It's a slow, meandering, large spring creek that carries cold water all summer long.

What about the great hatches on the Williamson? It holds them from the beginning of the season until late October. Even before the season opens on the last Saturday in May, you'll find little blue-winged olive duns, pale morning duns, and a huge stonefly *(Pteronarcys californica)*, the salmon fly, emerging. If you're fortunate enough, the salmon fly will hold off until the season opens so you can match the hatch. But the great hatch on the river appears in middle to late June and early July. The big yellow may, *Hexagenia limbata*, hatch brings heavy trout to the surface. Contrasting to the heavy hatch on midwestern rivers, the one on the Williamson can appear sporadically all day long with a burst at dusk.

The gray drake, or as the locals call it, the black drake, appears in incredible numbers on the Williamson. It truly is one of the heaviest hatches on the upper river. Nymphs crawl out of the water on submerged vegetation.

Even in midsummer you'll find insects on the water. Late July brings some tricos to the Williamson, and in August you'll see hoppers all over the surface. Good hopper patterns can cause some heavy rainbows in the 3- to 6-pound class to rise.

Because the Williamson flows at a slow pace, you'll find a good *Callibaetis* hatch. Clyde Keller of Bend, Oregon, looks forward to this hatch each year on the river.

September means it's caddis time. Sure, the tricos continue and a second generation of little blue-winged olives appears, but in late September and early October you'll find the October caddis present. The #8 pattern can also encourage heavy trout to come to the surface.

You'll find chironomids on the Williamson and Klamath Lake much of the season. Dark gray chironomids from #14 to #24 are especially heavy in May and June.

With all these chances to fish over great hatches, you'd think catching trout on the Williamson would be easy. It isn't. Paul Pursell of Chiloquin lives next to the river. He's fly fished on the Williamson for years and thinks it's one of the most frustrating and difficult rivers in the West. Until a couple years ago he had no trouble catching heavy Williamson River trout on a Peacock and Black Palmer or a Woolly Worm. Those patterns haven't worked for him the past couple years, but he's heard reports that California anglers have had success with a Gold Ribbed Hare's Ear.

Ed Miranda recently took Jay Kapolka and me on a 10-mile float trip down the Williamson. Ed's been a full-time guide for the past five years on the river. He recently took former President Jimmy Carter on the same float trip. It's an unusual one – the first one where I've seen a motor used on a drift boat. We floated mile after mile of slow, deep pools and shallow, slow riffles. In the 10 miles we saw no more than four trout. That's the enigma of the Williamson. The water in the two large tributaries seems to hold large rainbows only when the lake warms appreciably or when they run upriver to spawn. Ed said that at this May date most of the trout were still in Klamath Lake downriver 10 miles. When the impoundment below warms appreciably, the fish move up the Wood and Williamson rivers. I doubt that the Williamson holds a viable resident rainbow trout population. It does hold some heavy brown trout that remain in the river, but most of the rainbows move downriver to the lake. When the trout in Klamath Lake decide to move up the Williamson, you're in for some fantastic matching-the-hatch opportunities. In many cases you're fly fishing over 3- to 5-pound rising trout.

Normally the Williamson runs gin clear. After a heavy rain or snowmelt the Sprague River, a large downriver tributary, throws muddy water into the main stem. High water also produces a tannic brown color on the main stem from the Klamath Marsh upriver. A large tributary, Spring Creek, flows in from the west. Spring Creek runs cold and clear and comes out of the side of a mountain just north of Spring, Oregon. A totally different strain of rainbows runs up Spring Creek than those going farther up the Williamson River.

Because the river is extremely clear most of the time, Ed Miranda uses a 15- to 18-foot leader on the Williamson. When he's using a nymph, he uses the long-distance nymphing technique. He uses an intermediate weight-forward line and casts across or downstream, mending four times or more. When the nymph swings into its arc, he uses a twitching technique by placing the fly line over the middle right finger and moving that finger back and forth but not retrieving the line. After the fly has completed its arc, Ed uses an irregular short retrieve all the time, with the tip of the fly rod under the water.

On a recent float trip on the Williamson Jay Kapolka said that a good river needs all the friends it can get. This river really needs friends! Although it has gained distinction just recently, it has count-less problems. Some of them seem severe enough to jeopardize the very future of this public stream. On the float trip I was amazed to find both sides of the river dotted with "No Trespassing" signs. The Williamson River Club leases a 1-mile stretch of the lower river on the east side (the Long Ranch), and the only access to this is by boat. The first 20 miles of the river that flows through Yamsi, Sand Creek, and Deep Creek ranches are also private. Oregon Fish and Wildlife needs to provide more access for the wading fisherman. Unlike the McKenzie, the Williamson has very few boat-launching sites and needs additional ones.

Water quality on the Williamson River and Klamath Lake have declined noticeably in the past few years. Water use, erosion, grazing, and other impacts have deteriorated the water quality. Algae have become a critical problem with the lake, and in midsummer you'll encounter algal blooms on the impoundment. Paul Pursell worries about the hatches on the lower end of the river; he's seen a reduction in the number of caddisflies appearing on the Williamson.

Too many trout are killed in the lake and the Williamson. The state should make the entire river a catch-and-release site. When doing that, they could expand the fishing dates to make it available all year.

The river meanders slowly from its source for more than 50 miles before it enters Klamath Lake near the town of Klamath Falls. The river drops only about 1,000 feet from its source to its mouth. U.S. Route 97 and State routes 49 and 46 parallel the river to its source. In the upper end the river runs 30 to 60 feet wide, and in the lower end 60 to 150 feet wide.

Steve and Judy Carothers of Williamson River Anglers at the junction of U.S. 97 and State Route 62 can tell you what is happening on the river and will provide guide services. Denny Rickards of Rocky Point Resort, 25 miles from the river, knows the hatches on both the Williamson and Wood rivers well. Rocky Point provides excellent accommodations for anglers planning to fish the Wood and Williamson rivers. Denny and Steve and Judy Carothers are all amiable and willing to help any angler.

Don't overlook the Wood River about 10 miles to the west of the Williamson. This smaller river also holds some heavy rainbows. It also contains a good western green drake and a heavier salmon fly hatch than the Williamson. Like the Williamson, the Wood also suffers from the lack of many access spots.

Will the Williamson continue to provide anglers with quality fishing throughout the 1990s? As we said earlier, the river has many problems that seem almost insurmountable unless those who enjoy the river and its wild trout band together and save it. How to get ranchers, landowners, the Klamath Tribe, and anglers to combine in a joint effort for the betterment of the river seems like a herculean task.

Best Times to Fly Fish

May 25–June 15
    Little Blue-Winged Olive Dun: #20, morning and afternoon
    Western Green Drake: #10 and #12, morning and afternoon
    Blue Quill: #18, morning and afternoon
    Pale Morning Dun: #16 and #18, morning and afternoon
    Salmon Fly: #6, afternoon and evening
    Speckle-Winged Dun: #14 and #16, morning and afternoon
    Golden Stonefly: #8, afternoon and evening
    Black Caddis: #14, afternoon
    Green Caddis: #16, afternoon
    Dark Gray Caddis: #18, afternoon
    Speckle-Winged Dun: #14 and #16, morning and afternoon

June 15–July 30
    Big Yellow May *(Hexagenia limbata)*: #8, dusk

Dark Tan Caddis: #12 and #14, afternoon and evening
Speckle-Winged Dun: #14 and #16, morning and afternoon
Black Drake (Gray Drake): #12, morning, afternoon, and night
Orange Caddis: #12 or #14, afternoon and evening
Green Caddis: #12, afternoon and evening

July 30–September 1
Trico: #24, morning
Black Drake (Gray Drake): #12, morning, afternoon, and night

September 1–October 30
Trico: #24, morning
Little Blue-Winged Olive Dun: #20, morning and afternoon
October Caddis: #8, afternoon and evening
Tan Caddis: #14, afternoon and evening

CALIFORNIA

You might not consider California as a state for great trout fishing. With its huge population increase in the past fifty years, you would think that California would lack great rivers and great hatches. But the Golden State, especially the northern half, does boast a number of great trout waters, and we will discuss two of them – Fall River and Hat Creek.

Fall River

> Daily bag and possession limit: two. Maximum size limit: 14 inches total length. Only artificial lures with barbless hooks may be used. These regulations pertain to Fall River from its origin at Thousand Springs downstream to the mouth of the Tule River and include Spring Creek but exclude all other tributaries.
>
> — *1990–1991 California Fishing Regulations,*
> Department of Fish and Game

"It holds one of the best pale morning dun hatches in the state. It's the best hatch of pale morning duns I've ever seen," said Andy Burk, who works at the Fly Shop on Churn Creek Road in Redding, California. And Andy should know – he's guided anglers on Fall River for three years and has fished the river for many more.

Hatches on this river near Fall River Mills are heavy and long-

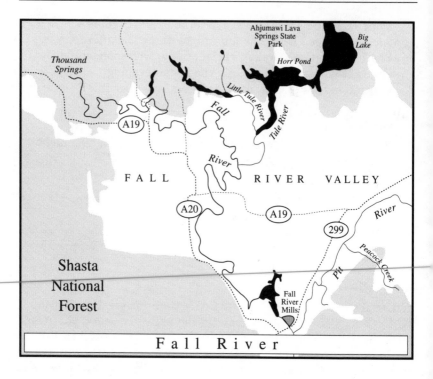

Fall River

lasting. For example, the pale morning dun appears on the river from April until November, and the spinner fall for this species provides some dynamite matching-the-hatch opportunities. Anglers on July mornings can fly fish to hatches of tricos and pale morning spinners. The trico hatch also continues throughout the summer and fall and into November. Little blue-winged olive duns appear much of September and October.

But this 75- to 100-foot-wide river holds many other great hatches. Like Williamson River in Oregon, its counterpart to the north, Fall River holds plenty of gin-clear flat water for the *Hexagenia limbata*, which emerges from mid-June through July. Add to all these hatches some downwings, and you see why many area anglers like fly fishing on Fall River.

There are plenty of 14- to 17-inch streambred rainbows and brown trout in the river, with rainbows in the majority.

The river is difficult to wade because of aquatic growth and limited access. There are wooded areas in the upper half and rice fields in the lower 17 miles. You'll find two public access spots – one maintained by California Trout and the other by the state. Because of access and wading difficulty, the best method for the river is a flat or johnboat. Duane Willeman services anglers through his guide service at the Fly Shop in Redding, California, and he guides dozens of anglers on Hat Creek and Fall River annually.

You can reach the river on State Route 299 near Fall River Mills.

Best Times to Fly Fish

March 1–May 31
Little Blue-Winged Olive Dun: #20, morning and afternoon
Pale Morning Dun: #16 and #18, morning, afternoon, and evening
Western Green Drake: #10 and #12, morning and afternoon

June 1–July 31
Gray Drake: #12, afternoon (spotty)
Dark Brown Caddis: #16, afternoon and evening
Hex (Hexagenia limbata): #6, evening
Trico: #24, morning

August 1–September 30
Trico: #24, morning
Little Blue-Winged Olive Dun: #20, morning and afternoon
Western Green Drake: #10 and #12, morning and afternoon

Hat Creek

Daily bag and possession limit: two. Minimum size limit: 18 inches total length. Only artificial lures with barbless hooks may be used. Aquatic invertebrates of the orders Plecoptera (stoneflies), Ephemeroptera (mayflies), and Trichoptera (caddisflies) may not be taken or possessed. These regulations pertain to Hat Creek from Lake Britton upstream to Baum Lake, exclusive of the concrete Hat No. 2 intake canal between Baum Lake and the Hat No. 2 powerhouse.

—1990–1991 California Fishing Regulations

Near Burney, just 20 miles away from Fall River in northern California, you'll find another top western stream. Hat Creek flows out of Lassen National Forest and provides western anglers with plenty of great hatches.

Talk about fantastic downwing hatches—you'll see many of them

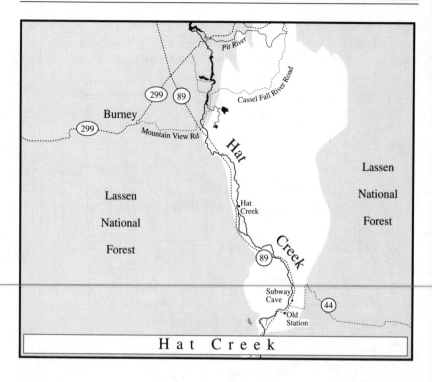

Hat Creek

on Hat Creek. Would you like to see a salmon fly hatch? Hat Creek holds one. How about the huge October caddis? You'll also find that downwing on the stream. All summer long you'll hit terrific caddisfly hatches in the evening. Carry plenty of caddis patterns with bodies of tan, gray, olive, and brown. Andy Burk of the Fly Shop in Redding says that caddis and microcaddis appear in droves throughout the season on Hat Creek. Add to the downwings a generous supply of pale morning duns, tricos, and several *Baetis* species, and you'll see why anglers enjoy fly fishing on the stream.

Hat Creek comes out of a powerhouse. You'll find riffles for the first 200 yards below the dam. For 2 miles below the riffle you'll fish a flat meadow stream. Below the meadow Hat Creek forms another riffle before it flows into another unnamed dam.

The past few decades haven't been kind to the stream, however, and in recent years a siltation problem has reduced the numbers of browns and rainbows considerably. The stream flows from 75 to 100 feet wide and holds a good variety of water types. State Route 299 near Burney gets you to the river, and much of the stream is accessible to anglers.

Best Times to Fly Fish

March 1–May 31
Little Blue-Winged Olive Dun: #20, morning and afternoon
Pale Morning Dun: #16 and #18, morning, afternoon, and evening
Salmon Fly: #6, afternoon and evening
Western Green Drake: #10 and #12, morning and afternoon

June 1–July 31
Western Green Drake: #10 and #12, morning and afternoon
Golden Stonefly: #8, afternoon and evening
Little Yellow Stonefly: #16, afternoon
Pale Morning Dun: #16 and #18, morning, afternoon, and evening
Little Blue-Winged Olive Dun: #20, morning and afternoon
Trico: #24, morning

August 1–September 30
Trico: #24, morning
Tiny Blue-Winged Olive *(Pseudocloeon)*: #20–24, afternoon
Little Blue-Winged Olive Dun: #20, morning and afternoon
October Caddis: #8, afternoon and evening

October 1–October 31
October Caddis: #8, afternoon and evening
Little Blue-Winged Olive Dun: #20, morning and afternoon
Tiny Blue-Winged Olive *(Pseudocloeon)*: #20–24, afternoon

MONTANA

Montana – Big Sky Country. Home of some of the greatest rivers in the United States, this state boasts a wide array of trout and great hatches. Like many other western states, Montana suffers from water and land-use problems. Unlike many other western states, some sportsmen's groups have allied with farmers and ranchers in a joint effort to overcome water problems and their associated obstacles to better trout management. In 1987 more than a mile of the Ruby River went dry. Many blamed this on poor irrigation planning. Ranchers who use the water agreed to work with the Montana Fish and Wildlife Department to monitor the flow so it wouldn't happen again. Here's an example of where two groups, rather than battling, agreed to work together. Another example is the nearby Big Hole. For years trout migrated up the irrigation channels only to be stranded later and die. The ranchers' co-op realized what was happening and agreed to shut down the water supply in three stages, one-third at a time. They found that trout left the ditches after the water began to lower at the first stage. These and other matters have been worked out in a civilized manner by the joint efforts of Montana Trout Unlimited, the Environmental Quality Office in Helena, local sports groups, and the Fishing Outfitters Association of Montana. Together these groups have formed the Alliance for Montana Waters, which works with the state and agriculture to maintain Montana fishing. Jack D. Hutchison, until recently president of the Fishing Outfitters Association of Montana and former owner of Hutchison's Fly Shop in Sheridan, seems to think that the state has a unique approach to water problems.

What about hatches in Montana? You'll find great ones in almost every stream and river in the state. Hatch dates vary considerably, however, from year to year depending on spring air temperatures and snow pack. Jack Hutchison said that on a normal year the salmon fly appears on the Big Hole from June 8 to June 20. The earliest hatch he saw occurred in mid-May.

Bighorn River

> Special trout-management section catch and release for rainbow trout from Afterbay fishing access site to Bighorn fishing access site.
>
> —*Montana Fishing Regulations,*
> Montana Department of Fish, Wildlife, and Parks

Mike Manfredo has boasted about this great south-central Montana river for more than two years and has raved about the heavy browns and rainbows the river held and the great hatches that emerged, so I was very excited on this first trip to the Bighorn River. That night I had a difficult time sleeping, dreaming of catching heavy trout the next morning.

We awoke around 8:00 A.M. to a dreary day that first morning in October, and the higher hills around our Fort Smith motel had a fresh coating of snow. The temperature at 9:00 A.M. still hovered around 40 degrees. That was too cold for me—I prefer warm, sunny days to fly fish. I detest fly fishing on cold, rainy days when my hands become numbed by the cold wind. To make matters worse, local fishermen told us that the lake was turning over and the river below the lake displayed a cloudy color, unusual for this blue-ribbon stream.

In two days of fly fishing Mike and I caught nothing more than a couple dozen trout. What had happened to this blue-ribbon water? Would I ever return to the Bighorn to fish again? With the bad experience in my mind – probably not.

But we tend to forget unfavorable events quickly and remember the successful days much longer. So I decided to make a return trip to the Bighorn to give it one more chance to live up to its superb reputation.

Bryan Meck accompanied me on our float trip down the river this second time. Richie Montella guided us on the 13.5-mile trip from the Afterbay to the Bighorn access. Richie has floated this blue-ribbon trout stream more than sixteen hundred times and knows where just about every trout feeds on the upper river.

The three of us floated a mile or more before Richie suggested that we get out and look for rising trout in some shallow water near the shore. As we walked along the river bank, Richie shouted for Bryan and me to bring our fly rods. We counted more than a dozen fish feeding in the shallows right in front of us.

I tied on a Pale Morning Compara-dun and cast to the nearest cruising trout. No strikes, so I quickly tied on a Pale Morning Spinner. Finally, on the fourth try, I covered a heavy riser. The hefty fish slowly rose to the tan-bodied spinner, I set the hook, and the fight was on. It headed to midriver, taking me well into my backing. There it stayed motionless for a minute or more, then it moved downriver, where I netted the 4-pound brown trout. I moved back up to the pod of feeding fish and made a delicate cast to the next rising trout. It, too, sucked in the spinner imitation without hesitation. The next two trout also took the Pale Morning Spinner. Each of the four trout weighed about 4 pounds and measured 20 inches long.

This was too much! I handed the fly rod to Bryan, wanting him to experience the same success with the Pale Morning Spinner. After landing four more trout, we saw still more trout taking spinners near the shore. Bryan cast to another heavy rising trout that slowly porpoised. A strike, a miss. Another strike and another miss. Bryan set the hook too quickly for these deliberate risers. When a third trout rose to his spinner, he took his time and felt the heavy trout take his line out rapidly. He landed the 4-pound brown and moved up to the next rising fish. Bryan landed three more risers in the pod before he handed the rod back to me.

We left that hot spot two hours and fifteen trout later. What a hatch! What a river! What beautiful rising trout!

We floated downriver several miles more before Bryan and I once again exited the boat. Richie spotted another pod of heavy risers. Two of these trout took the Pale Morning Spinner, but several others refused the #16 pattern. I scanned the surface and saw thousands of rusty spinners spent on the surface. I looked above the surface and saw clouds of these spinners *(Pseudocloeon)* near bushes along the shore.

The three of us continued on our float to the Bighorn exit. We left the boat a couple hundred yards above the Bighorn access around 8:00 P.M. for a last fling at the river and its heavy trout. A moderate hatch of black caddisflies appeared over the surface. I examined the body of this downwing closely and saw that the body had an olive cast to the black abdomen. Bryan tied on an emerging pupa, twitched it on its swing, and caught or lost ten trout with the pattern. I used an adult caddis pattern with a trailing shuck and caught two trout.

We ended the eleven-hour day exhausted, arms tired, but happy and assured that we had just fished one of the finest fisheries in the lower forty-eight states – confident that we had matched two hatches satisfactorily. The Bighorn had redeemed itself from my earlier disappointing experience.

What makes the Bighorn River in southern Montana so great? Ask Don Daugenbaugh. He works at the National Park Service's Visitors' Center at Fort Smith and has fly fished the river for almost ten years. He first taught President Jimmy Carter to fly fish. Don will tell you that at some spots Bighorn Lake is 500 feet deep and 22 miles wide. He also says that the bottom release from the lake and an average pH of 8.2 recorded in July make the river behave like a giant spring creek chock-full of scuds, aquatic worms, caddisflies, chironomids, and mayflies. Even 4-pound trout continue to feed on insects. Water temperatures average from 58 to 62 degrees on the upper end of the river. Don would also tell you that the river produces heavy fish because of the catch-and-release philosophy of most of the fly fishers who float the river. Last year a survey conducted by authorities found that of 15,000 trout caught only 309 browns were killed. That's a 98 percent release rate.

You'll witness hatches almost daily on the Bighorn. In late April, May, and early June you can fly fish over heavy little blue-winged olive and chironomid hatches daily. Visit this river in mid-July and you'll see pale morning duns and spinners on the water daily, and they last until the end of August. The pale morning dun disappeared almost completely a few years ago, but it reappeared and has been heavy and predictable for the past four years. The Bighorn pale morning dun has a pale tannish yellow body.

Even with the approach of late summer and early fall you'll encounter great hatches and spinner falls on the Bighorn. In late August and September tricos appear. In September you'll again fish over little blue-wings and tiny blue-wings (Pseudocloeon). This latter species appears in heavy numbers in May, July, and again in September. Add to the smorgasbord a generous supply of caddisflies, and you can see how important hatches are to the trout of the Bighorn River.

The Bighorn was opened to the public for fishing in August 1981 after the courts finally resolved the problem of access. There are 65 miles of trout water, although most anglers agree that the upper 13 miles contain the most trout. In that area, during a recent survey of 7-inch or larger trout, authorities found seven thousand browns and two thousand rainbows. You'll find a fair number of access points along the river. Starting at the Yellowtail Dam you'll find Afterbay, Lind (3 miles below Afterbay), Bighorn (13.5 miles), Mallard's Landing (29 miles), Two Leggins (35 miles), Arapooish (42 miles), and Custer (51 miles).

Most of the guides and local anglers have affectionately named the pools and rapids on the river. From the dam downriver to the Bighorn access you'll find the Meat Hole, Aquarium, Glory Hole, Dag's Run, Carl Hole, Gravel Hole (35 feet deep at spots), Snag Hole (because of the huge trees that fall into the river there), Corral Hole, Twenty Dollar Hole, Bighorn Rapids, Little Bighorn Rapids, and Richie's Run.

You can obtain information on the hatches and water conditions or pick up gear at one of three Fort Smith fly-fishing shops. Stop at the Quill Gordon (operated by Gordon and June Rose), Big Horn Angler (operated by Mike Craig and Holly Brooks), or the Big Horn Trout Shop (operated by Steve Hilbers and Hale Harris)—all three will give you the latest information on hatches and river conditions.

County Route 313 parallels the river from Hardin to Fort Smith.

Best Times to Fly Fish

April 1–June 30
Gray Midge: #24, morning and afternoon
Little Blue-Winged Olive Dun: #16–20, morning and afternoon
Tiny Blue-Winged Olive (Pseudocloeon): #20–24, afternoon

July 1–July 31
Pale Morning Dun: #16 and #18, morning, afternoon, and evening
Black (Olive) Caddis: #16, evening
Tan Caddis: #16, evening

Ginger Caddis: #14, evening
Golden Stonefly: #8, morning and afternoon
Tiny Blue-Winged Olive *(Pseudocloeon)*: #20–24, afternoon and
    evening

August 1–September 30

Trico: #24, morning
Pale Morning Dun: #16 and #18, morning, afternoon, and evening
Black Caddis: #16, evening
Ginger Caddis: #14, evening
Tiny Blue-Winged Olive *(Pseudocloeon)*: #20–24, afternoon and
    evening
Little Blue-Winged Olive Dun: #20, morning and afternoon
Tan Caddis: #14, evening

Bitterroot

Main stem and West Fork upstream to Painted Rocks Reservoir:
  a) Cutthroat trout catch and release only.

*From Stevensville Bridge to Florence Bridge and 1 mile downstream from
Darby Bridge to Como Bridge:*
  a) Limit A: five trout per day under 12 inches or four trout under 12
     inches and one over 20 inches; cutthroat trout catch and release
     only. Artificial lures only.

Main stem and East and West Forks:
  a) Extended whitefish season and catch and release for trout open
     December 1 to the third Saturday in May with maggots and/or
     artificial lures only.
  b) Open to catching of whitefish for commercial sale.

— Montana Fishing Regulations

I vividly remember the first time I fly fished this mighty river. I arrived
on the water on an early-July morning. It was unusually high from
snowmelt from the Bitterroot Range off to the west. I approached the
river alone with no one to show me where to fish. Would I find any
hatches? Would trout rise in this high water? I didn't have to wait long
to find out. By 11:00 A.M. a sporadic but productive hatch of western
green drakes futilely attempted to take off from the high water. Occasionally I saw a rainbow or brown trout surface after these huge

mayflies. Each quick cast of the Western Green Drake pattern over the riser brought another rise to the artificial. The sporadic hatch lasted for two hours and produced ten heavy browns and rainbows.

I returned the next morning to the same spot—about 10 miles from Victor, Montana. I arrived by 10:00 A.M. and was greeted by a hatch of pale morning duns. Several trout fed on these #16 and #18 insects until noon. At that time more western green drakes appeared.

I returned to the river near Florence several times in the evening. Spinner falls take on importance in July and August in the evening. Many of the *Rhithrogena* spinners you find on the Bitterroot can be copied by #12 and #14 Quill Gordons. Even a #14 Light Cahill, which effectively copies *Cinygma dimicki*, works well on many July evenings. Make sure you carry a light and dark pattern to match these two important evening hatches on the Bitterroot.

Even with the advent of August the river holds great hatches. Waters begin to lower in mid-July, and, along with a much lower volume, you'll see plenty of tricos on this excellent water. On August afternoons you'll see some gray drakes appear on the river. Also don't forget the fall brown drake, *Timpanoga hecuba*. This huge mayfly appears sporadically at midday from late August into early September. Chuck Stranahan, owner of the River Bend Fly-fisher in Hamilton, Montana, says that this hatch is one of the greatest on the river.

Chuck lists the other two prominent hatches on the river. One is the olive stonefly in a #10. This hatch appears in good numbers in late April and early May, when the river is in prerunoff condition. He lists the western green drake as another top hatch.

If you prefer fishing before July, you'll have to cope with high runoff from snowmelt. Prior to early July the Bitterroot is a raging torrent. After mid-July it lowers to a dry-fly fisher's dream.

Recently, Jerry Meck and I took a float trip on the upper section of the river above Hamilton. Even with the high snowmelt waters in late June, we saw a few pale morning duns emerge, but only a few trout rose to these mayflies. Our guide for the day, Brian Nelson, had guided on the river for five years. He has experienced other quiet days on the river, but also more than his share of productive ones. Brian guides on the Clark Fork, Rock Creek (wading only), and several other waters.

The Bitterroot is easy to reach from Missoula. The West and East forks join near Conner in southwestern Montana. U.S. Route 93 parallels the main stem and the East Fork for more than 50 miles. County Route 473 parallels the West Fork.

You'll find plenty of well-marked access areas along the river. From Missoula upriver you'll see Lolo, Chief Looking Glass, Poker Joe,

Florence, Bass Creek, Stevensville, Bell Crossing, Tucker Crossing, Woodside (not marked), Hannon Memorial, and Wally Crawford at the forks. From the forks to Missoula the Bitterroot flows for about 75 miles.

The Bitterroot River looks like three different rivers. In the upper end from the forks to Hamilton it looks like a small stream and ranges from 50 to 75 feet wide with fast water and more boulders. From Hamilton to Stevensville you'll find braided channels. At some point the river runs in four and five separate channels. From Stevensville to the mouth you'll find a broader tailwater-type river. Fish tend to pod up more in this section. The river enters the Clark Fork in Missoula.

The Bitterroot follows four or five channels in its flow north through Hamilton to Missoula. Some of these channels dry up in late July and August. I've seen many blue quills emerging from water holes now cut off from the main flow. Because the river follows several channels, it's difficult to judge the width. It averages 50 to 150 feet, depending on the location and the time of year, and it is easy to wade late in the year. It contains brown, rainbow, and cutthroat trout. The water remains relatively cool throughout the year because of the snowmelt from the Bitterroot Range to the west. Some of the tributaries flowing off the Bitterroot Range hold excellent populations of cutthroats.

You'll find several access sites maintained by the state along U.S. Route 93. Most of the river is private, so get permission before you cross private land.

Doug Brewer, who operates the Streamside Angler in Missoula, fishes the river weekly. Check with him on the latest information on the river and its hatches.

Best Times to Fly Fish

March 15–April 15
   Early Black Stonefly: #16, afternoon

April 15–May 15
   Little Blue-Winged Olive Dun: #20, morning and afternoon
   Olive Stonefly: #10, afternoon
   Grannom: #16, afternoon and evening
   Black Stonefly: #14, afternoon

June 1–July 15
   Salmon Fly: #6, afternoon and evening
   Golden Stonefly: #8, afternoon and evening

Blue Quill: #18, morning and afternoon
Pale Morning Dun: #16 and #18, morning and afternoon
Western Green Drake: #12, morning and afternoon
Light Cahill *(Cinygma dimicki)*: #14, evening
Quill Gordon: #14, evening
Red Quill: #12, afternoon
Common Sedge (Tan): #14, evening
Green Rock Worm: #14, afternoon
Yellow Sally: #14, afternoon

July 15–August 15

Light Cahill: #14, evening
Gray Drake: #12, afternoon
Pale Morning Dun: #16, #18, and #20, morning and afternoon
Trico: #24, morning
Blue Quill: #18, morning and afternoon
Quill Gordon: #12, afternoon; Red Quill (spinner): #12, evening
    (Rhithrogena undulata)
Dark Brown Dun and Spinner *(Ameletus cooki)*: #18, morning and
    afternoon

August 15–September 30

Gray Drake: #12, afternoon
Trico: #24, morning
Little Blue-Winged Olive Dun: #20, morning and afternoon
Fall Brown Drake *(Timpanoga hecuba)*: #10, midday

Kootenai River

Vince Gigliotti, Al Gretz, and I first fly fished the Kootenai River in
1987. We fished on a section just below the dam and another section
5 miles below Libby, Montana. In the evenings we hit productive
hatches of olive-bodied pale morning duns above Libby and great
caddisfly hatches below the town. Tan caddis by the thousands decided to lay their eggs one evening when Al Gretz and I hit the lower
river. Rainbows took our downwing copies all evening long.

That was my only experience with the Kootenai River—until recently, when Dave Blackburn invited me to fly fish it again. He guides
on the river under the guise of the Kootenai Angler out of Libby,
Montana. We entered the section of the river Dave calls the Home Pool
because it's right behind his house and floated the section from his
home 13 miles downriver to Libby.

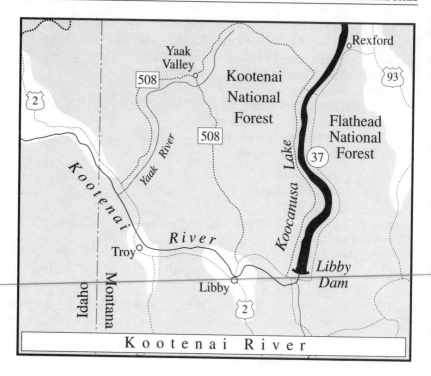

For June 24 the day turned into a downright miserable one. Leaden gray skies began pouring a fine mist on us. The temperature that morning never reached 60 degrees. Dave drifted us through a series of pools, riffles, and glides in the morning. An osprey and an eagle fought above the river for a white fish that the former had caught, and several deer fed along the bank of the river. Jerry Meck and I experienced only minimal success using weighted Woolly Buggers, but even though we had experienced less than a successful trip, there's more to fly fishing than just fishing.

Shortly after noon we stopped just above the Haul Bridge for lunch. I checked a nearby eddy to see if any mayflies had emerged. In the eddy hundreds of blue-winged olives and western march browns interspersed with a few western green drakes and pale morning duns floated aimlessly in the backwater. Little did we realize that in less than a few hours we would experience one of the heaviest hatches and the most rising trout that any of us have witnessed in recent years.

At 5:00 P.M. we drifted through yet another heavy riffle, and Dave suggested that we try a floating pattern. Here we saw our first two trout rising to an ample supply of dazed pale morning duns on the surface. By the time we had drifted a hundred more yards, a full-blown hatch of duns appeared on the surface. As we entered a heavy glide, we saw over fifty heavy rainbows feeding on the surface. Jerry and I proceeded to pick out risers closest to the boat. A drag-free drift over a riser with the Pale Morning Compara-dun and a trailing shuck induced a strike. Five trout hit the compara-duns at the first stop. We then drifted downriver a couple hundred feet to more risers. There a dozen more rainbows rose freely to the duns. We picked up a half dozen fish at the second stop and proceeded downriver to our next pod.

The action continued for more than two hours. We probably drifted over more than two hundred rising trout and hooked maybe a third of them. What a fantastic float trip. We still had 6 miles to drift to our takeout point. We arrived in Libby cold but confident that we had just enjoyed and succeeded at one of the most memorable matching-the-hatch episodes we had ever experienced. Certainly one of the best I had experienced in the West.

The Kootenai also has other great hatches. You'll find plenty of little blue-winged olives in the spring and fall. The olive stonefly (Skwala parallela) appears near the middle or end of May, and it can also bring trout to a feeding frenzy. You'll find this downwing species on many western Montana rivers in April before snowmelt begins.

You'll find caddisflies on the Kootenai River from early May into September and October. The river holds a great grannom hatch in May and some October caddis in late September. Interspersed between those two are some tan and brown caddis.

The Kootenai River is not without its problems, however. Drastically fluctuating water levels from Libby Dam seem to have caused a decline in the number of insects in the river. Rates can range from 28,000 to as low as 4,000 cfs (cubic feet per second). The water level varies by as much as 3 feet from day to day. Before the dam and tailwater below were finished, the Kootenai had a population of salmon flies. The locals called them periwinkles. Now they are few and far between.

Because of the fluctuations in water level, Dave Blackburn feels that fishing the Kootenai is like fishing ten different rivers. As waters recede or rise, trout relocate. Riffles in shallow water become heavy runs, and backwater becomes pools.

Too many of the trout in the river are presently being harvested. As you travel along the river, you'll see anglers with five-gallon buckets that they brought with them to take trout home. Regulations on the water must be more limited to keep this a blue-ribbon river.

Thanks must go to the Kootenai Fly Fishers, who have worked diligently for better regulations for the river. They're hoping for a slot limit from the David Thompson Bridge downriver several miles to the Haul Bridge.

From upriver you'll find several sections. Just below the Libby Dam, which can release water from depths that assure a cold supply of water downriver all year long, you'll find the David Thompson Bridge. Below the bridge you'll find Guano Land, Dunn Creek Flats, Moonshine Island, Blackwell Flats, Mouth of the Fisher River, Home Pool, Jennings Rapids, Riverside Pool, Mike's Run, Fantasy Island, Log Jam, Haul Bridge, Ripley, Elk Horn Lodge, Zonolite Pool, Orchard Pool, Boothman Pool, Holy Water, and Silver Creek in Libby. It's best to float the river above Libby. In the town and below you can access the river and wade at some spots.

You'll find more than 30 miles of blue-ribbon trout water on the Kootenai. You can reach the river by flying into Kalispell, Montana, or Spokane, Washington. U.S. Route 2 parallels the river below Libby and State Route 37 above that town.

Don't overlook this top-notch trout river. It's worth a trip to fly fish this 150- to 200-foot-wide river in northwestern Montana.

Best Times to Fly Fish

March 1–April 30
Little Blue-Winged Olive Dun: #20, morning and afternoon

April 1–April 30
Olive Stonefly: #10, afternoon

May 1–June 15
Western March Brown: #14, afternoon
Grannom: #14 and #16, afternoon
Blue Quill: #18, morning and afternoon

June 15–July 15
Pale Morning Dun: #16 and #18, morning, afternoon, and
    evening*
Western Green Drake: #10 and #12, morning and afternoon
    (spotty)
Salmon Fly: #6, afternoon and evening (very spotty)
Blue-Winged Olive Dun: #14, evening
Blue Quill: #18, morning and afternoon
Tan Caddis: #14 and #16, evening
Pink Lady: #14 and #16, evening (spotty)

Dark Brown Dun *(Rhithrogena hageni)*: #14, morning and
   afternoon
Brown Caddis: #14 and #16, afternoon and evening

September 1–October 31
Little Blue-Winged Olive Dun: #20, morning and afternoon
Tiny Blue-Winged Olive *(Pseudocloeon)*: #20–24, afternoon
Cinnamon Sedge: #8, afternoon and evening

*Some species on this river have a distinct pale olive body; others
   have tannish orange, wine, and olive yellow bodies.

Madison River

> *Yellowstone Park:* Fly fishing only
>
> — *Yellowstone National Park, Fishing Regulations*
>
> *Special Limit Area — Reynolds Pass Bridge downriver to Varney Bridge:*
> a) Artificial flies and lures only.
> b) Trout, catch-and-release fishing only.
> c) Whitefish, limit 100.
>
> — *Montana Fishing Regulations*

The Madison River is a river for all seasons. That's what expert guide
Nick Nicklas calls it, and he should know – he's guided thousands of
fly fishermen from all over the country on this blue-ribbon river for
more than fourteen years. He's fished just about every one of the 100
miles this fantastic fertile river covers. He's fly fished it from its beginning at the junction of the Gibbons and Firehole rivers in Yellowstone
Park to Bear Trap Canyon. If you're going to succeed at fly fishing on
the Madison, Nick feels strongly that you have to be flexible – you
have to use a variety of techniques and patterns.

Nick also feels that the river changes character eight times in its
100-mile journey to form the Missouri River. In the upper end in
Yellowstone National Park you'll find a meadow river 50 to 100 feet
wide. The lower section of the park downriver to Hebgen Lake consti-
tutes a second zone on the river, which contains wide runs, riffles, and
pools. The next zone is Hebgen Lake. In the fall you'll find heavy
brown trout migrating upriver out of the lake. You'll also find a good

Nick Nicklas lands a rainbow taken with a *Pteronarcys* nymph on the Madison River. *Charles Meck*.

trico hatch on the lake. Zone four is the top 8 to 10 miles just below Quake Lake. This part of the river contains heavy pocket water. Zone five, the next 8 miles down to McAtee, is a transition zone of very wide riffles. From McAtee to Channels you'll encounter Towerands Flats, a series of shallow glides. From Varney to Ennis Lake you'll find deep pools, deep runs, and side channels. The final zone is Bear Trap Canyon, which contains white water.

I said earlier that this is a river for all seasons. Let's look at the hot spots for each season. You can take trout even in the winter season, especially the top 8 miles just below Hebgen Lake. A top producer this season is one of many chironomid patterns. Prerunoff spring season produces hatches and trout at Channels, in the park, and the area just below Hebgen Lake. Three hatches you'll hit at this time are the pale morning duns, little blue-winged olives, and chironomids. Spring runoff occurs in late May, all of June, and early July. During runoff the two best areas to fly fish are in the park, fishing over a pale morning dun hatch, and the area just below Hebgen Lake, with a *Pteronarcys* nymph. Salmon flies usually appear on the river near the end of June. The whole river outside of the park comes alive with hoppers, stone-flies, and caddisflies. Even in fall the river holds great hatches, such as the little blue-winged olives. Fall fly fishing just above Hebgen Lake can be superb with the fall brown trout spawning.

One of the greatest hatches on the river comes near the end of June. The salmon fly brings big trout to the surface and hordes of anglers to the river to try their luck with their favorite pattern. You'll find almost as many patterns for the nymph and adult *Pteronarcys* as there are anglers on the river. By far the most distinctive salmon fly pattern copying the adult is Simple Salmon. This pattern, tied by Nick Nicklas, is tied on a #6 hook with a body of orange poly. But there the similarity between the Simple Salmon and others parts company. It's tied like you'd tie six small caddisflies – all tied on the same hook. This down-wing has an exceptionally low profile and is a top producer during the salmon fly hatch.

Don't fish the Madison without an ample supply of caddisfly patterns. You'll find these downwings on the river from late April through October. Stop in at Blue Ribbon Flies in West Yellowstone, Montana, and Craig Mathews, the owner, and Nick Nicklas, guide and fly tyer, will show you not only well-tied patterns but also some really innovative ones.

U.S. Route 87 parallels much of the river below the park, and the main highway from West Yellowstone follows the river inside Yellowstone Park. Throughout the 100 miles of the river, you'll find plenty of 16- to 18-inch rainbows and browns.

Best Times to Fly Fish

April 10–May 30
   Grannom: #12 and #14, afternoon*
   Little Blue-Winged Olive Dun: #20, morning and afternoon

May 1–June 1
   Little Blue-Winged Olive Dun: #20, morning and afternoon
   Gray-Brown Caddis: #14 or #16, morning and afternoon

May 25–July 20
   Western Black Quill: #12, morning and afternoon
   Pale Morning Dun: #16 and #18, morning and afternoon
   Brown Drake: #12, evening
   Western Green Drake: #12, morning and afternoon
   Blue Quill: #18, morning and afternoon
   Pink Lady: #12, morning and afternoon
   Blue-Winged Olive Dun: #14, morning; spinner: evening
   Pale Brown Dun: #14, morning and afternoon
   Green Sedge: #12 and #14, afternoon and evening
   Little Sister Sedge: #14 and #16, afternoon and evening
   Salmon Fly: #6, afternoon and evening

Golden Stonefly: #8, afternoon and evening
Spotted Sedge: #12 and #14, afternoon and evening*
Sulphur (*Centroptilum* species): #20, evening*
Green Sedge: #12–16, afternoon and evening

July 20–September 1

Pale Brown Dun (*Rhithrogena hageni*): #14, morning and
  afternoon
Pale Morning Dun: #16 and #18, morning and afternoon
Blue-Winged Olive Dun: #14, morning; spinner: evening
Red Quill: #14, morning and afternoon
Gray Drake: #12, morning and afternoon
Trico: #24, morning
Little Yellow Stonefly: #14 and #16, afternoon*
Little Olive Stonefly: #14 and #16, afternoon*

September 1–October 30

Trico: #24, morning
Tiny Blue-Winged Olive (*Pseudocloeon*): #20–24, afternoon
Purple-Breasted Sedge: #16–20, afternoon
Little Blue-Winged Olive Dun: #20, morning and afternoon

*Found only on lower Madison.

Missouri River

> *Holter Dam to Cascade:* Limit A: may include only one brown trout,
> minimum length 22 inches.
>
> *—Montana Fishing Regulations*

Bryan Meck and I headed eagerly down the access road from Wolf Creek to Craig, Montana, anticipating a great day of fly fishing on the Missouri River with our guides Pat Elam and Mike Bay. Both men guide almost daily on the Missouri River. As we turned a curve in the road just outside Craig, I pointed to an early-morning dust devil forming over the blacktop a few hundred yards in front of us. The vortex seemed to extend a couple hundred feet into the air. As we approached, the dust devil evolved into an unbelievable number of trico spinners appearing over the highway. Our excitement grew as we pulled into Craig. We were about to fish the "mother of all hatches"–the trico on the Missouri River.

The Missouri trico hatch begins around July 15 and continues well into September. Many who fish this hatch complain that the diminutive mayfly emerges in such enormous numbers that it's difficult to take trout on an imitation. Trout often take several spinners on each rise. Pat Elam, Mike Bay, and other guides often suggest that their anglers use a trico pattern imitating a cluster of the small spinners.

Bryan, Pat, Mike, and I entered the McKenzie boat at the Craig boat-launching site around 9:00 A.M. Thousands and thousands of trico spinners already blanketed the river, and pods of trout had already taken up positions to feed on the spent spinners. Add to the trico spinners some trico duns, tan caddis, pale morning duns and spinners, pale olive duns, pale evening duns *(Heptagenia solitaria)*, and you'll see that the Missouri River set the four of us up for an unbelievable fly-fishing smorgasbord.

A mile downriver Mike stopped the boat and had Bryan wade to a pod of a half dozen trout rising to tricos. After five perfect casts over the closest trout, it struck the #20 pattern and Bryan missed the fish. We floated downriver another mile and anchored out from another pod of a half dozen trout rising within inches of the shore. Because of the cold tailwater from Holder Dam located upriver, trout often feed in very shallow water. Mike and Bryan decided to test these rising trout. Mike had a strike on a Tan Caddis pattern. He set the hook and the heavy fish broke his 5X tippet. I tied on a Tan Caddis with a trailing shuck for Bryan. On about the fifth float over a riser it took the down-wing. Now the fight was on. The lunker brown leaped completely out of the water once, then went deep and stayed almost motionless for a few minutes. Pat, Mike, and I yelled words of encouragement to Bryan; and after a fifteen- to twenty-minute battle, Mike lowered the net into the water and landed the fish. Mike quickly weighed the magnificently colored brown trout. He recorded the 4½ pounds and 22 inches, and after a few photos returned the trout to the river.

The four of us floated downriver, more confident now that one of us had broken the ice and landed a lunker. Mike anchored the boat at a riffle and suggested that the four of us wade to some rising trout. All four of us scored in the riffle with more than a dozen hooked rainbows up to 15 inches long. What a fitting end to a magnificent, hatch-filled day on the Missouri.

Pat runs the Missouri Trout River Shop in Craig and Mike owns the High Plains Outfitters in Helena. Pat said that anglers he takes on the river seldom get shut out. He carries plenty of patterns of his own creation – the Candy Cane – and uses them when fishing gets tough. But don't think fly fishing on the Missouri River is a piece of cake. You earn every fish you catch on the river. You've got to constantly out-

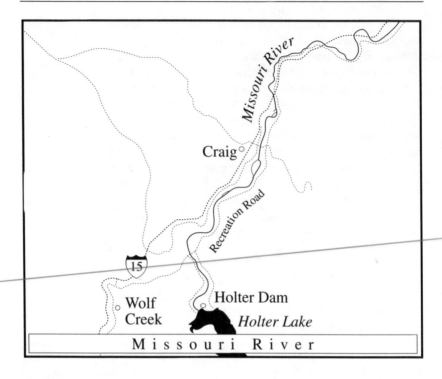

think every rising trout. If you succeed, you'll experience a great day—
even a spectacular one. Often, however, you don't succeed and you go
away frustrated.

The river holds hatches other than the trico. You'll find pale morning duns on the surface for almost six weeks. In April and again in
September the surface fills with little blue-winged olives. Mike Bay
feels that one of the best times to fly fish the river occurs in September
and October, when the angling crowds have thinned out and the little
blue-winged olives still hatch. Paul and Pat Antolosky of Bellefonte,
Pennsylvania, agree. They prefer the river after Labor Day, when most
of the fly fishermen quit for the year.

Don't go near the river without a good supply of caddis patterns in
black, tan, olive, and brown. You'll even find the prolific orange-bodied
October caddis on the water in late September and October. A #8
pattern copying the downwing brings lunkers to the surface.

There are 31 miles of blue-ribbon fishing on the Missouri from
Holter Dam downriver to Cascade. The best section is the 16 miles
from Holter Dam downriver to the Dearborn River. You'll find plenty
of access points all along the river. In fact, it is one of the most accessible rivers in the West. Wading on this 100- to 200-foot-wide tailwater

is extremely easy, with few rapids except for the one under the Hardy Creek bridge. Water temperatures through much of the summer remain in the low sixties because of the bottom release upriver. The marked access points from the dam downriver are Dam, Wolf Creek Bridge, Craig, Stickney Creek, Spite Hill, Mouth of the Dearborn, Mid Canyon, Mountain Palm, Prewitt Creek, Pelican Point, and Cascades.

Often when you see rising trout on the river, you'll see pods of a dozen or more. It's important to think that your first cast over a riser might be your last. The trout are often leader shy and spook easily. If you see a pod of risers, cast to the one farthest downriver first. Don't let the fly drag in front of the fish. Cast a few feet upriver from the rising trout. Pick out the most consistent rising trout and try to time your cast to a rhythmic feeder.

The Missouri has some problems. Motor boats on the river cause wakes for the anglers, and some regulations should be enacted to restrict their use. The limit on the river at present is too liberal, and bait fishermen often kill their limit of five trout per day. Fluctuating water levels affect the fish, insect activity, and fishing success also. Thanks to organizations like the Pat Barnes Memorial Chapter of Trout Unlimited in Helena, many of the problems on the Missouri are being addressed.

The Jefferson, Madison, and Gallatin rivers join near Three Forks, Montana, to form the Missouri River. The Missouri then flows north toward Great Falls. Interstate 15 and Recreation Road, an access road, parallel the river from Holter Dam to Cascade.

Stop by the Missouri River Trout Shop in Craig, where they have the latest information on the hatches and floating conditions. Pat Elam, Jerry Lappier, and Allan Ranes are always willing to help you.

Best Times to Fly Fish

April 1–April 30
Little Blue-Winged Olive Dun: #20, morning and afternoon
Tiny Blue-Winged Olive (Pseudocloeon): #20–24, afternoon

May 1–May 25
Tiny Blue-Winged Olive (Pseudocloeon): #20–24, afternoon

May 25–July 1
Pale Morning Dun: #16 and #18, morning and afternoon
Pale Olive Dun (Baetis bicaudatus): #20, afternoon
Speckle-Winged Dun: #14 and #16, morning and afternoon
Brown Drake: #10 and #12, evening (spotty)
Black Caddis: #16, evening

July 1–September 30
Olive Caddis: #16, evening
Brown Caddis: #16, evening
Pale Evening Dun: #14, afternoon and evening
Tan Caddis: #16, afternoon and evening
Blue Dun (Western Olive): #20 or #22, afternoon
Trico: #24, morning
Pale Morning Dun: #16 and #18, morning, afternoon, and evening
Pale Olive Dun: #20, afternoon and evening
Pale Evening Dun: #14, afternoon and evening
Tiny Blue-Winged Olive *(Pseudocloeon)*: #20–24, afternoon
October Caddis: #8, afternoon and evening

Yellowstone River

No fishing in Yellowstone Park before July 15.

> *— Yellowstone National Park, Fishing Regulations*

Special limit area — from Emigrant Bridge downriver to Pine Creek Bridge:
a) Artificial flies and lures only. Maggots allowed for whitefish between December 1 and third Saturday in May. All trout caught on
   maggots must be released.
b) Cutthroat trout, catch-and-release fishing only.
c) Rainbow and brown trout, five-fish limit, four under 13 inches, one
   over 22 inches.
d) Whitefish, limit 100.

> *— Montana Fishing Regulations*

Nick Nicklas has guided anglers from all over the United States on the
Yellowstone River from the lake in the park downriver to Livingston,
Montana. On his days off you'll find him on the river looking for
hatches and rising trout and tying flies commercially. He annually ties
more than two thousand dozen for resale. His patterns are some of the
most creative, well-thought-out patterns I have ever seen. He's originally from Pennsylvania, but you wouldn't know it. He's as knowledgeable about Yellowstone Park area streams and rivers as anyone in the
nation. Most of all, Nick enjoys fishing the hatches on the Yellowstone.
"On a nonhatch situation you're going to have a low catch rate on the
Yellowstone," Nick said. "Ninety percent of the time you're fishing a
hatch on the river." With a hatch, Nick says, the cutthroats are rela-

tively easy to catch. Without a hatch it can be very, very slow. Nick has caught trout up to 22 inches above the falls and 24 inches below.

If the Yellowstone is difficult without a hatch, then when is the best time and what are the best hatches to fish? Nick's two favorite hatches appear on the river after the hordes of tourists leave the park. His favorite hatch is also one of the smallest. It's the diminutive, but important, little blue-winged olive. "If the hatch appears on a cloudy day, trout will feed for hours on the hatch." Nick prefers to use an emerger pattern fished on the surface while the hatch appears.

A second great hatch on the upper Yellowstone also appears in September. It often appears along with the little blue-winged olive. This hatch, a *Paraleptophlebia* species, which occurs for two weeks in September, is called the mahogany dun by the locals. Spinners of the species fall in the morning and duns emerge in the afternoon and evening. Duns have bodies with an olive-gray cast.

Hatches on the river below Gardiner that appear before runoff can create some great matching-the-hatch experiences. The little blue-winged olive and the black caddis appear in early May and produce rising trout on the lower river. The caddis is often called the Mother's Day caddis because of the time of year it appears.

The Yellowstone River contains a good supply of trout from above the lake downriver to Livingston, Montana. At most places the river averages 200 to 400 feet wide. However, wading is not recommended on much of the river from the canyon in the park downriver to the end of Yankee Jim Canyon. The Park Service allows wading from the lake downriver to the canyon. There's an area around Hayden Valley where you're not allowed to fish because of spawning beds – and bears.

You can fly fish above the lake by reaching it with a canoe or a pack horse, but it takes a full day to get to the area called Thoroughfare. From the upper falls upriver to the headwaters you'll find only one fish in the water – the Yellowstone cutthroat. Below the falls you'll find cutthroats, rainbows, hybrids, and browns.

There are places in the canyon in the park where you can enter and fish, but after you hike to the area, you might have only 100 feet to fish. If by chance someone is also in the same area, you've got to hike back uphill without even wetting a line. You'll find access points in the canyon area at Towers Falls, Black Canyon, Hellroaring Creek Trail, and Gardiner.

Below Gardiner and out of the park you'll find many access points along the river. Congratulations to the Montana Division of Fish, Wildlife, and Parks for providing well-marked access signs to the river.

The lower end of the Yellowstone from Gardiner holds fewer explosive hatches and not as many trout when compared to the Madison

River. You will find an excellent salmon fly hatch on this part of the river in early to mid-July.

Fishing in the park opens on July 15. Snowmelt causes high runoff annually from late May until mid-July. Water levels in August and September are often ideal for fishing the hatches. Thunderstorms in the park often muddy the water quickly. U.S. Route 89 and County Road 540 parallel the river to Livingston.

You'll find four outfitters in West Yellowstone – all of them offer quality guide services for the Yellowstone area.

Best Times to Fly Fish

April 20–June 10
   Little Blue-Winged Olive Dun: #20, morning and afternoon
   Grannom: #12–14, afternoon*

June 15–July 15
   Salmon Fly: #6, morning, afternoon, and evening
   Golden Stonefly: #8, afternoon and evening
   Pale Morning Dun: #16 and #18, morning and afternoon
   Tan Caddis: #12–16, afternoon and evening
   Black Caddis: #12 and #14, afternoon and evening
   Little Olive Stonefly (Yellow Sally): #12–16, afternoon
   Western Green Drake: #10 and #12, morning and afternoon
   Pink Lady: #14 and #16, evening
   Western Quill Gordon (Epeorus longimanus): #12 and #14,
      afternoon
   Western Black Quill (Rhithrogena undulata): #12, afternoon*
   Spotted Sedge: #12–14, afternoon and evening*
   Little Yellow Stonefly: #14 and #16, afternoon*
   Little Sister Sedge (Dark Olive): #14 and #16, afternoon and
      evening*

July 10–August 15
   Western Green Drake: #10 and #12, morning and afternoon
   Blue-Winged Olive Dun: #14, evening
   Gray Drake: #10 and #12, afternoon
   Trico: #20–24, morning
   Speckle-Winged Dun: #14 and #16, morning and afternoon
   Little Sister Sedge: #14 and #16, afternoon and evening*
   Cream Caddis: #16, evening

August 15–September 30
   Trico: #20–24, morning

Blue Quill (Mahogany Dun): #16 and #18, morning and afternoon
Blue Dun (Tiny Blue-Winged Olive) *(Pseudocloeon edmundsi)*: #22
and #24, afternoon and evening
Little Blue-Winged Olive Dun: #20, morning and afternoon
White Mayfly: #14, evening*

*Found mainly from Gardiner to Reed Point.

IDAHO

We've moved inland from the Pacific Coast more than 400 miles, and you'll find little modifying effect from the Pacific Ocean in the southern half of the state. You'll find hard winters and hot, dry summers. You'll also find two types of rivers predominating in Idaho. First you'll see some of the greatest spring creeks in the world in this state. The hatches on Henry's Fork and Silver Creek can be spectacular, and here you'll find your typical dry-fly water. The second type of water is the fairly large river whose existence depends on snowmelt. Many of these are difficult to fly fish until mid-July, when the snowmelt abates. Underfished rivers like the Lochsa and Coeur d'Alene in the northern half of the state are waiting for the fly fisherman to test.

Big Wood River

> *Big Wood River, Main Stem:*
>
> a) Upstream from its confluence with the Little Wood River to the Richfield Canal Diversion Dam—open all year.
> b) From the Richfield Canal Diversion Dam upstream to Magic Dam.
> c) From the Glendale Diversion, approximately 3 miles below Bellevue, upstream to Highway 75 Bridge at milepost 122.2: Trout limit two—single-barbless hooks only; none between 12 inches and 16 inches.
> d) From Highway 75 Bridge at milepost 122.2 (first bridge north of Hailey) upstream to the mouth of the North Fork: catch and release.
>
> —*Idaho General Fishing Seasons & Regulations,*
> Idaho Fish and Game

The Big Wood River. It sounds like one of those big western rivers, but, you're in for a surprise—this river, flowing south through Sun Valley, is diminutive as some western rivers go, but it's chock-full of rainbow trout. At any of the more than dozen access areas provided on the river, you'll not find the Big Wood any wider than 100 feet, and in many places it's 40 to 70 feet wide. If the high mountains experience a normal snowfall, the Big Wood will run high through much of May and continue into late June. When the water level lowers on this productive river, you're in for some great fishing over generous hatches.

Even as the water lowers, you'll encounter some western green drakes. Todd Van Bramer of Sun Valley Outfitters says that "the neatest hatch of the season is the western green drake. It's quite spectacular because it's large and it's the first great hatch of the season on the Wood River." Todd should know – he guides many anglers on Ketchum-area rivers.

Hatching continues well into September and October with little blue-wings and tricos. The Wood is a sleeper during the trico hatch – you'll find trout rising to this hatch almost every morning from late July until late September.

The Big Wood has a lot going for it, but it has some problems that tear at the very fiber of this river. Enter a concerned citizens group called Friends of the Big Wood River. Within a few years this conservation group has initiated many valuable changes, and they have worked diligently on trout habitat/stabilization in the river. The group can use your help.

You'll find more than twenty access points to the river from Galena to Bellevue. Many of these are poorly marked and difficult for the outsider to locate. State Route 75 parallels much of the river.

Best Times to Fly Fish

April 1–May 31
    Little Blue-Winged Olive Dun: #20, morning and afternoon

June 1–July 15
    Red Quill (Quill Gordon): #14 and #16, afternoon
    Western Black Quill (Dark Brown Dun): #16, afternoon
    Western Green Drake: #10 and #12, morning and afternoon
    Dark Brown Dun *(Baetis hageni)*: #20, afternoon
    Golden Stonefly: #8, afternoon and evening
    Salmon Fly: #6, afternoon and evening (spotty)

July 15–August 31
    Trico: #24, morning
    Pink Lady: #14 and #16, evening
    Dark Brown Dun: #20, afternoon

Dark Olive Caddis: #16, evening
Dark Brown Caddis: #16, evening

September 1–October 31
Gray Drake: #10 and #12, afternoon
Little Blue-Winged Olive Dun: #20, morning and afternoon
Blue Quill (Slate-Winged Mahogany Dun): #18, morning and
afternoon
Trico: #24, morning

Henry's Fork of the Snake River

Snake River, North (Henry's) Fork:

a) From the posted boundary above Riverside Campground upstream
to Harriman State Park: catch and release.

b) Harriman Ranch State Park (including East Harriman) EXCEPT the
bird sanctuary: June 15 to October 15, fly fishing only, catch and
release.

   1) Harriman bird sanctuary (Osborn Bridge upstream to the ranch
bridge): June 15 to September 30, fly fishing only, catch and
release.

c) From Harriman Ranch State Park upstream to Island Park Dam:
catch and release.

d) From Henry's Lake outlet to and including the head of Big Springs:
closed to fishing.

—Idaho General Fishing Seasons & Regulations

The Fourth of July on Henry's Fork began with a heavy frost on this
6,200-foot-high river. Al Gretz and I barely had time to assemble our
rods before a heavy pale morning dun hatch greeted us. By 11:00 A.M.
a much darker, larger insect appeared on the surface and rested for
several seconds before attempting to become airborne. Dozens of trout
took up feeding positions for these large mayflies. Al and I caught
trout for more than three hours on the sporadic hatch of western green
drakes. This species is one of my favorite hatches to fish on Henry's
Fork. The drakes can emerge from mid-June to mid-July, depending on
weather conditions. If you hit the hatch, you'll have to contend with
not only plenty of other anglers nearby but also some heavy surface-
feeding rainbows.

Henry's Fork is one of those truly special streams where hatches
appear almost daily at almost any hour during the day throughout the

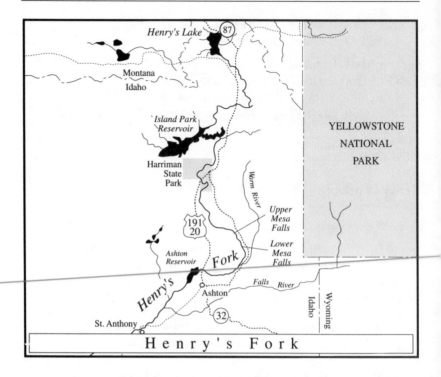

Henry's Fork

fishing season. There are only a handful of streams and rivers in the
United States like it. The Delaware and Beaverkill fall into this category, but they don't come even close to the hatches that Henry's Fork
presents. On any given day in June or July you might be confronted
with three, four, or five hatches and spinner falls, each taking a place
of prominence for a couple hours.

But the above event occurred more than seventeen years ago. I
had heard rumors that the angling fraternity on this huge spring had
grown unbelievably large, so I had avoided the water for a long time.
But now I was about to hit Henry's Fork again with Jerry Meck and
Mike Lawson, our host. Mike owns Henry's Fork Anglers Shop at
Island Park, Idaho. He has fly fished the water most of his life and has
caught many rainbows over 20 inches long on the fork.

No sooner had the three of us entered the water than an explosive
hatch of pale morning duns appeared. These duns appear in two distinct color phases – one with a pale mahogany body and the other with
an olive gray body. Tie copies of both *Ephemerella inermis* phases because trout key in on both. On the second cast Mike hooked a heavy
Henry's Fork rainbow. As the season progresses, the size of the pale

morning dun diminishes. In July and August carry plenty of patterns in a #18. Mike Lawson's favorite pattern for the Henry's Fork is a Pale Morning Emerger.

For the next two hours the three of us looked at the heavy hatch of little blue-wings and pale morning duns with a few western green drakes thrown in for good measure, and we all wondered why no more trout rose. Later that afternoon Jerry and I hit a spectacular blue quill hatch. The two of us, in two hours of fishing to risers to this hatch, saw less than a couple dozen trout feeding. After a seventeen-year hiatus, Henry's Fork still deserved its reputation as an insect factory. However, the trout population appears to have dwindled.

Hatches appear early and continue through much of October. Even in May you'll encounter little blue-winged olives, black caddis, and western march browns. Hatches continue through June, with the best time to fish the hatches being the last week of that month and the first week in July.

In June and July you'll see #20 little blue-winged olive duns *(Baetis bicaudatus)*, thousands of blue-winged olive duns, and a heavy brown drake spinner fall.

You'll find many types of stoneflies on Henry's Fork. Around the beginning of June salmon flies appear in the Box Canyon area. No sooner have these huge downwings ended their mating cycle for the year than the golden stonefly begins to appear. Add to this several other stoneflies, like the yellow sally and the mormon girl, and you can see why downwings are important on the water.

Caddisflies also deserve mention. Carry patterns in body colors of black and green to match many of the caddisflies on Henry's Fork. Microcaddis, especially the dark gray caddis, in a #20 can be important in June.

Al Gretz and I hit Henry's Fork at just the right time. We fly fished the Railroad Ranch the last week in June and the first week in July. This is also the time that throngs of other anglers frequent the area. If you don't like crowds and you don't mind missing some of the great hatches, try to come earlier – in late May or early June – or in August or September. If you hit Henry's Fork in August and early September, make certain you carry a good supply of terrestrials with you. In addition to the great mayfly, stonefly, and caddisfly hatches, you'll see plenty of grasshoppers in the fields around the ranch. Imitations of this terrestrial work especially well in late summer and early fall.

Henry's Fork begins at Henry's Lake in southeastern Idaho. The spring-fed waters flow south to the Island Park Reservoir at Island Park Village where Buffalo River enters. The Buffalo holds some heavy trout. Just below the Island Park Reservoir the river enters a series of swift waters called the Box Canyon. Here's where you'll find a good supply of salmon flies around the first of June. Just below Box Canyon you'll find slower, more placid waters in the Railroad Ranch section, now called Harriman Ranch State Park. I've watched thousands of mayflies emerge there and wondered where the duns rested before they changed to spinners, and I've watched these duns blown a mile or two back from the river by strong winds. In this section there are places where trees are few and far between.

You'll find great fly fishing on Henry's Fork from the Box Canyon area downstream to the confluence of Fall River just north of St. Anthony. Many anglers flock to the Railroad Ranch or Harriman Ranch State Park, where you'll find spectacular western green and brown drake hatches.

Several miles below the ranch you'll see Sheep Falls, Upper Mesa Falls, and Lower Mesa Falls. Just below the last fall Warm River enters the Henry's Fork. U.S. Route 20 parallels the river.

Henry's Fork ranges from 100 to 150 feet wide at most places and 2 to 4 feet deep, and the bottom is covered with aquatic plants. The velocity of Henry's Fork is deceiving – it looks much slower than it really is.

Henry's Fork has some problems. The water has suffered from several years of below-average rainfall, and an extremely cold spell in December 1990 created a fish-kill in Henry's Lake. The concerned citizens formed the Henry's Fork Foundation to address some of the concerns of this national resource.

Check in with Mike or Sheralee Lawson at Henry's Fork Anglers at Island Park, Idaho, for the latest information on the hatches and river conditions. Mike also offers float trips on several nearby rivers. They have a great map that shows some of the hatches and the major areas on the fork.

Best Times to Fly Fish

April 10–May 15

Little Blue-Winged Olive Dun: #16 and #18, morning and
   afternoon
Western March Brown: #12 and #14, afternoon
Black Caddis: #14 and #16, afternoon and evening

May 20–June 15

Western March Brown: #12 and #14, afternoon

Salmon Fly: #6, evening (Box Canyon)
Little Blue-Winged Olive Dun: #20–24, morning and afternoon
Green Caddis: #16, evening
Pale Morning Dun: #16 and #18, morning and afternoon
Speckle-Winged Dun: #14 and #16, morning and afternoon
Golden Stonefly: #8, afternoon and evening

June 15–July 15

Pale Morning Dun: #16 and #18, morning, afternoon, and
    evening*
Blue-Winged Olive Dun: #14, morning and evening
Western Green Drake: #12, morning and afternoon
Little Blue-Winged Olive Dun: #20–24, morning and afternoon
Brown Drake: #12, evening
Blue Quill: #18 and #20, morning and afternoon
Dark Brown Dun *(Baetis hageni)*: #20, afternoon
Pink Lady: #14, evening
Speckle-Winged Dun: #14 or #16, morning and afternoon
Little Blue Dun *(Pseudocloeon edmundsi)*: #20, morning and
    afternoon
Golden Stonefly: #8, afternoon
Yellow Sally: #12 and #14, afternoon
Mormon Girl: #16, afternoon

July 15–August 15

Pale Morning Dun: #16 and #18, morning, afternoon, and
    evening*
Pink Lady: #14, evening
Blue-Winged Olive Dun: #14, morning and evening
Dark Brown Dun: #20, afternoon
Little Blue-Winged Olive Dun: #20, morning and afternoon
Trico: #24, morning
Gray Drake: #10, afternoon
Blue Quill: #18, morning and afternoon
Speckle-Winged Dun: #14 and #16, late morning
Gray Fox *(Heptagenia solitaria)*: #14 and #16, evening
Green Caddis: #16, afternoon and evening
Black Caddis: #16, afternoon and evening

August 15–September 15

Trico: #24, morning
Little Blue Dun *(Pseudocloeon* species): #20 or #22, afternoon and
    evening
Little Blue-Winged Olive Dun: #20, morning and afternoon

October 1–October 30
   Little Blue-Winged Olive Dun: #16 and #18, morning and
   afternoon

   *You'll find some members of the species with reddish brown
   bodies.

Silver Creek

Nature Conservancy Silver Creek Preserve: catch and release, barbless
hooks, fly fishing only.

Point of Rocks—Fish and Game Public Access Area—Slot Limit: two fish
over 16 inches or under 12 inches.

Silver Creek:

   a) Downstream from Highway 93: January 1 to October 15.

   b) From Highway 93 upstream to a posted boundary at Point of Rocks
      on the Fish and Game access area: no fishing from rafts or boats.
      Float tubes permissible.

   c) From a posted boundary of Point of Rocks on the Fish and Game
      access area upstream to the right-of-way fence on the west side of
      Kilpatrick Bridge: catch and release. No fishing from rafts or boats.
      Float tubes permissible.

   d) From the road right-of-way fence on the west side of Kilpatrick
      Bridge upstream to the confluence of Grove and Stalker creeks,
      including all tributaries and Sullivan Lake within the Nature Con-
      servancy property: fly fishing only. Catch and release. No fishing
      from rafts or boats. Float tubes permissible.

                                          —*Idaho General Fishing Seasons & Regulations*

Brett Drummond and other local anglers call it a smaller version of
Henry's Fork. It even looks like Henry's Fork. It has cool spring water
all summer long just like Henry's Fork and a pH that hovers around 8.7
in late June. It also has a succession of great mayfly hatches from the
little blue-winged olive dun to one of the heaviest brown drake
hatches in the West. What is this smaller version of Henry's Fork? It's
Silver Creek, just southeast of Hailey, Idaho.

   Silver Creek had access problems, but thanks to the Nature Conservancy's purchase of 480 acres in 1975, this problem has lessened
somewhat. This conservation-minded organization had the foresight

to purchase the former Sun Valley Ranch. Silver Creek runs through much of the Conservancy property, and any fly fisher can fish this property. All they have to do is to register at the Preserve headquarters. Thanks to the Conservancy for keeping this fantastic fishery open to anglers.

Hatches on Silver Creek continue throughout the summer. After the little blue-winged olives have waned in May, you'll find speckle-wings and pale morning duns on the water all day long. But possibly the two best hatches on Silver Creek are the brown drake and the trico. You'll find brown drakes on the surface around the middle of June, and they often continue to emerge and lay eggs for about a week. The brown drake appears on Silver Creek from an area just north of U.S. Route 20 downstream to near Picabo. Brett Drummond says that he finds few drakes on the Conservancy property.

Tricos appear in unbelievable numbers on this spring creek. They begin around the end of July and continue into late September and October. You can meet duns around daybreak and continue to fish over female, then male, spinners for several hours.

Grasshoppers work well on Silver Creek in August and September,

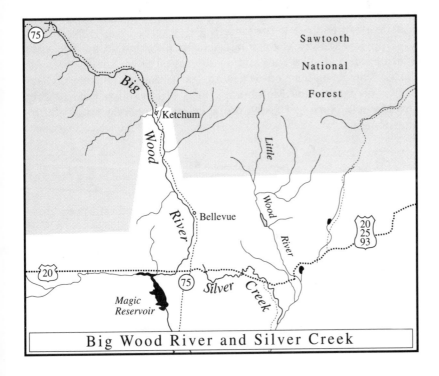

Big Wood River and Silver Creek

and patterns like Dave's Hopper produce some big rainbows and browns.

Trout are definitely not easy to catch on Silver Creek. You'll find a 30- to 90-foot-wide meandering, serpentine stream that flows at a very slow velocity with many different currents. Getting a drag-free float on this fertile spring creek presents a challenge even to the best fly fisherman. Further, if you plan to use any submerged fly, you'll find that algae floating in Silver Creek present a severe problem. You'll have to clean your fly after just about every cast, so your best approach is to use a dry fly, and even then you'll get algae caught on the floating pattern.

In addition to the stream you'll find two sloughs, or springs, flowing into Silver Creek on the Conservancy property. If you like stillwater fly fishing, you'll love these sections. You'll find plenty of trout 18 to 22 inches long cruising in these pondlike areas feeding on chironomids, speckle-winged duns, and a few gray drakes.

Recently Brett Drummond took Jerry Meck of Massillon, Ohio, and me to fly fish on the Conservancy land. We spent an hour fly fishing one of the sloughs. Brett caught two heavy rainbows on a speckle-winged emerger. When fishing these sloughs, you cast near a rising trout, then let the fly sit on the surface for some time, hoping a cruising trout will rise to the pattern.

Stop in at Silver Creek Outfitters in Ketchum to get the latest information on the hatches and conditions on Silver Creek or the Big Wood River. Whether you deal with Terry Ring, the owner, or Peter Crow, Jerry Eder, Joe McKinnon, Doug Breary, Nick Cox, or Brett Drummond, you'll get truly professional help on your fly-fishing questions.

Best Times to Fly Fish

May 1–June 1
Little Blue-Winged Olive Dun: #20, morning and afternoon

June 1–June 30
Brown Drake: #10 and #12, evening (Point of Rocks area)
Pale Morning Dun: #16 and #18, morning and afternoon
Dark Brown Dun: #20, afternoon
Speckle-Winged Dun: #14 and #16, morning and afternoon
Gray Drake: #10 and #12, afternoon
Tan Caddis: #12, afternoon and evening

July 15–August 31
   Trico: #24, morning
   Speckle-Winged Dun: #14 and #16, morning and afternoon
   Gray Drake: #10 and #12, afternoon
   Dark Brown Dun: #20, afternoon

September 1–October 31
   Little Blue-Winged Olive Dun: #20, morning and afternoon
   Trico: #24, morning
   Gray Drake: #10 and #12, afternoon
   Blue Quill: #18, morning and afternoon
   Blue Dun (Western Olive): #20 or #22, afternoon
   Dark Brown Dun: #20, afternoon

WYOMING

Wide open Wyoming–few roads, few towns, few people! You have to drive miles between trout waters, but Wyoming has its share of good ones. The Wind, Tongue, North Platte, and Bighorn rivers provide great fly fishing for both the residents and tourists.

Wyoming rivers contain some great hatches. Probably the three most common in the state are the little blue-winged olive dun, the trico, and the pale morning dun. You'll find tremendous trico hatches on the North Platte, the Bighorn, and many other rivers.

The state has several problems when you look at its streams and rivers and their future as great trout waters. Land use, irrigation, water rights, and four years of extreme drought have diminished some of the once-great rivers. This past September I had a chance to fly fish on the North Platte River at the Six Mile access and I was amazed at the exceedingly low water conditions in the area at that time.

In Wyoming ownership of the riverbed is vested in the owner of the land. As I understand it, an angler can't legally wade, throw out an anchor, or touch the bottom of private water. What nonsense! In 1988, 115,136 resident and 267,185 nonresident anglers purchased Wyoming fishing licenses. That's over 375,000 total licenses–more than the total population of the state. And yet a few large landowners dictate policy to the anglers. It's time lawmakers recognize the number of anglers and make the waters of this great western state available to all, not just a privileged few. And Wyoming could do much more to prominently display access to its better rivers, especially for nonresident anglers.

We'll look at three of Wyoming's finest rivers–the North Platte;

Wind, called the Bighorn in the lower reaches; and the Firehole. Even though the latter is completely within Yellowstone Park, we've included it here.

Bighorn River

> *From Kirby Diversion Headgate downstream (7.9 miles) to Black Mountain Road bridge:* limit three trout per day; only one may exceed 18 inches; trout 13 to 18 inches must be released; fishing with artificial flies or lures only.
>
> —*Wyoming Fishing Regulations,*
> Wyoming Game and Fish Commission

How can the same river be called the Wind above and the Bighorn below? Because cartographers couldn't believe that the Wind River, which flows southeast, could be the same as the Bighorn River, which flows north.

Travel along U.S. Route 26, then U.S. Route 20 from Riverton to Thermopolis, and you'll find first a huge lake – the Boysen Reservoir – then a river flowing through a steep canyon – the Wind River Canyon. This river, the Wind, becomes the Bighorn River at the end of the canyon at a section called the "wedding of the waters." Above Riverton you'll find a river 60 to 100 feet wide that holds rainbows, browns, cutthroats, and some brook trout. Phil Phillips, who runs the Wind River Fly Shop in DuBois, says that the upper Wind River, from the Wind River Indian Reservation to the headwaters, holds plenty of trout, some great hatches, and good access. There are nearly 21 miles of public access in the upper river.

In the lower river – the Bighorn – near Kirby you'll find a medium-sized river about 100 to 200 feet wide, with browns and rainbows in residence.

A shot of hot water from a hot spring enters the main stem at Thermopolis. In this vicinity you'll find a heavy concentration of tricos on the water from mid-July until late September. Get there early for the spinner fall, because the tricos often fall to the surface before 9:00 A.M. From late June through much of July you'll also find a good supply of pale morning duns on the surface. Add to this some little blue-wings, tiny blue-wings, and a generous inventory of caddisflies, and you can see that the Bighorn in Wyoming has some good match-the-hatch opportunities. Phil Phillips suggests that you carry #12–20 caddis patterns in tan and brown.

The Bighorn has many problems. Because of clay particles suspended in the bottom, you'll find the river off-color on occasion. It's difficult to fish with wet flies because on almost every cast your hook collects moss, chunks of which you'll find floating in the river. Water temperatures downriver from Thermopolis warm considerably in midsummer. I've encountered temperatures in the low to middle seventies in late July. Heavy downpours in Red and Buffalo creek headwaters often cause the main stem to become discolored quickly.

If you'd like to fish the section around Riverton, you'll need an Indian permit.

U.S. Route 20 parallels the Bighorn River from below Thermopolis to Worland. U.S. Route 26 follows the Wind upriver from Riverton. Stop in at the Wind River Fly Shop in DuBois, and Phil Phillips will give you information on the latest conditions and hatches on the river. If you plan to float the Bighorn below the canyon, you can contact Dan Miller at the Wind River Outfitters in Thermopolis. Dan floats 25 miles of the river.

Best Times to Fly Fish

April 15–May 15
Little Blue-Winged Olive Dun: #20, morning and afternoon
Tiny Blue-Winged Olive *(Pseudocloeon)*: #20–24, afternoon
Western March Brown: #14, afternoon

May 15–June 15
Western March Brown: #14, afternoon
Grannom: #16, evening

June 15–July 15
Pale Morning Dun: #16 and #18, morning, afternoon, and evening
Blue-Winged Olive Dun: #14, evening

July 15–August 31
Blue-Winged Olive Dun: #14, evening
Pale Morning Dun: #16 and #18, morning, afternoon, and evening
Trico: #20–24, morning
Tiny Blue-Winged Olive *(Pseudocloeon)*: #20–24, afternoon
Pale Evening Dun: #14–18, evening
Tan Caddis: #16, evening

September 1–October 15
Trico: #20–24, morning

Firehole River

> Fly fishing only.
>
> — *Yellowstone National Park, Fishing Regulations*

It looks like what you'd expect to see in Hades—boiling cauldrons pouring steaming water into the river. Just upriver from where you stand you'll find the Midway Geyser Basin and the dependable one, Old Faithful. These plus dozens of other geysers form tributaries to the river by spilling in lukewarm, warm, and hot water into the main stem. Watch your footing as you get closer to the river—with each step nearer you'll feel the ground shake for several yards around you. Enter the water to fish and you'll encounter a combination of soft mud and jagged rocks and ledges. Welcome to fly fishing on the Firehole River. Water temperatures might surprise you; check the temperature in late June and you might find yourself fishing to rising trout with water temperatures in the high seventies.

Jerry Meck had never seen the Firehole River before. In fact, he

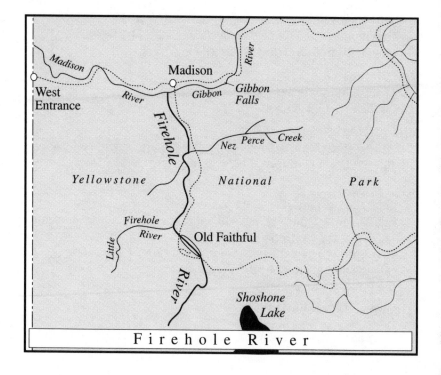

Firehole River

had never seen anything like it before. Nick Nicklas, one of the best guides in the Yellowstone area, agreed to take the two of us to a section of the Firehole River just below the Midway Geyser Basin area. When the three of us entered the water, I commented on how warm the river felt. I checked the water temperature immediately and took a second look at the 78-degree reading. Just the past two days the Madison and Yellowstone rivers registered temperatures in the low fifties and the Firehole in the high seventies. Would we find active trout under these warm water conditions? It didn't take us very long to find out. Nick gave Jerry and me a dark gray-bodied soft hackle to copy the down-wing caddis emerging that evening, and before I had my pattern tied on, Nick had hooked and released a couple small brown trout. Within minutes he had two more hooked on the soft hackle pattern. I watched Nick cast his emerger pattern across the stream, make a couple exaggerated mends in the line so it would drift drag free, then wait for the action. He didn't have to wait very long—he caught several more trout before I began fishing.

Jerry and I entered the river 100 yards below where the Firehole forms a deep riffle with a productive glide below. In a 100-yard section of the river the three of us landed and released more than twenty trout that evening—an evening when the wind at times blew more than thirty miles per hour, when few caddisflies emerged, and when the water temperature approached 80 degrees. The Firehole certainly showed the three of us its true character.

Great hatches? The Firehole River holds its share. You'll find two dependable mayfly hatches on the river—the pale morning dun and the little blue-winged olive dun. If you fish the river in June and early July, you'll find pale morning duns appearing daily. Don't overlook the olive spinner of this species. A spinner fall in midmorning can be frustrating without a match for it. You'll even find a few brown drakes and western green drakes on the Firehole. The best time to hit the little blue-winged olive is in early September. After the tourists have vacated the park, you'll have fly fishing pretty much to yourself. The lower canyon area of the Firehole River holds a fairly eventful hatch of salmon flies in mid-June. If you use a pattern like Nick Nicklas's own Simple Salmon, you should do well during and after the hatch.

Caddisflies abound on the Firehole, so don't go near the river without a generous supply of #14–18 caddis emergers and dry flies in tan, gray, brown, black, and olive. The patterns will often save the day for you.

You'll find at least six areas on the river. The lower area, before it joins the Gibbons to form the Madison, is called the Firehole Canyon. Drive on the blacktop road that parallels much of the river, and you'll see at the upper end of the canyon the Firehole Cascade. Above the canyon area you'll find the picnic area. This section has a good supply of pale morning duns. Above the picnic area you'll see the Fountain Freight Road, Midway Geyser Basin, Mule Shoe, Woods, and Biscuit Basin.

Stop in at Blue Ribbon Flies in West Yellowstone, Montana, to get the latest information on the hatches and the conditions on the Firehole as well as all the other Yellowstone-area waters. Jackie and Craig Mathews, Dale Fulton, and Nick Nicklas can help you have a successful trip.

Fishing pressure is heavy until Labor Day, but in late September you can experience some of the best matching-the-hatch episodes. You'll find browns and rainbows in the Firehole. You can reach the Firehole River from the West Entrance at West Yellowstone. Obtain a free fishing permit at the park entrance. Travel east along the Madison River about 14 miles to Madison. Turn right towards Old Faithful. This road parallels the Firehole River.

Best Times to Fly Fish

April 1–May 1
Little Blue-Winged Olive Dun: #20, morning and afternoon

May 25–June 30
Western Green Drake: #10 and #12, morning, afternoon, and evening
Salmon Fly: #6, afternoon and evening
Brown Drake: #10 and #12, evening (spotty)
Western Green Drake: #10 and #12, morning and afternoon (spotty)
Gray Drake: #10 and #12, afternoon (spotty)
Dark Gray Caddis: #16, evening
Dark Brown Caddis: #16, evening
Green Caddis: #16, evening
Black Caddis: #16, evening

July 1–August 31
Tan Caddis: #16, evening
Little Sister Sedge: #16, evening

September 1–October 30
Little Blue-Winged Olive Dun: #20, morning and afternoon
Tiny Blue-Winged Olive (Pseudocloeon): #20–24, afternoon
Dark Gray Caddis: #16, evening

North Platte River

> *From Pick Bridge 5 miles downstream to the downstream end of the old Frazier place public fishing area:* limit six trout; only one may exceed 20 inches; all trout 10 to 20 inches must be released; fishing with artificial flies and lures only.
>
> *From the Saratoga Inn bridge upstream to the Wyoming-Colorado state line:* limit six trout per day; only one may exceed 16 inches; all trout 10 to 16 inches long must be released; fishing with artificial flies and lures only.
>
> *— Wyoming Fishing Regulations*

Bryan Meck, Rod Walinchus, and I headed down the steep, rutted, winding road to the North Platte River an hour out of Rawlins, Wyoming. Anglers call the area we planned to fly fish the "miracle mile" because of the good quantity of trout it holds.

"See that dent in the guard rail?" Rod asked. "That's where my car slid into it several winters ago." We made a sharp left at the bottom of a steep decline and Rod commented, "See those trees there? My car slid into them several times." Rod gets extremely excited each and every time he fly fishes the North Platte. He should—he's caught plenty of trophy-sized trout on this blue-ribbon fishery in south-central Wyoming. At one time, for five years, he even guided anglers on the North Platte. Rod's an accomplished outdoor artist and illustrates frequently for *Fly Fisherman*. Recently he opened a gallery in Livingston, Montana. He often writes about fly fishing and the North Platte River in *Wyoming Wildlife*, and in his latest article he wrote about midge fishing. Rod, along with Steve Hays and Fred Stabler, recently published a book called the *Flies of Southern Wyoming* in conjunction with the Great Divide Flyfishers Chapter of Trout Unlimited.

Rod fly fishes the North Platte River in Wyoming and lists several regions in the 150-mile-long trout fishery. Anglers rank the 60-mile section from the Colorado state line to Rawlins as blue ribbon. From Rawlins to Seminole Reservoir they rank it as a red-ribbon fishery.

The type of fishery varies greatly from one area of the river to another. You'll see at least five. From state line to Saratoga you'll find a mountainous river with huge boulders holding mainly brown trout. In the Saratoga area you'll find ranch bottom land and a river holding almost equal numbers of browns and rainbows. From Rawlins to Seminole Reservoir you'll see high-plains desert. In the miracle-mile section you'll see desert, and from Alcova to Casper, high plains. Much of the upper section is posted, but there are a fair number of access spots.

The North Platte River has its share of great hatches. I hit the trico one September morning at the Six Mile access and saw brown trout taking spinners until noon. These trout averaged in the 3-pound class. Hit the river in late June and early July, and you'll probably see the pale morning dun and spinner on the water. One of the most unusual hatches to appear on the river is the white mayfly in late August. Fish in the evening near the Dunway access, and you'll probably see rising trout and mayflies just above the surface.

Downwings take on importance in midsummer, with tan caddis and olive caddis appearing in the evening. You'll also find salmon flies on the North Platte in late May.

The river volume varies tremendously, which affects hatches and trout. The water often becomes discolored because of the mineral malachite. Sage Creek also discolors quickly after a storm.

Thanks go to three Trout Unlimited chapters in the area who are watchdogs for better water quality and less fluctuation from the dams above, and who constantly work on more restrictive limits on the river. All three–the Saratoga Chapter, the Curt Gowdy Chapter in Cheyenne, and the Great Divide Flyfishers–deserve your support. The Great Divide Chapter out of Rawlins is presently placing signs on the river to show anglers where public access is. The state needs to sign more than 100 miles of the river.

You can reach the upper river near the state line on State routes 230 and 130. North of Interstate 80 you can reach the river via a dirt road from Sinclair to Kortes Dam. From Alcova to Casper, State Route 220 parallels the river.

Best Times to Fly Fish

April 15–May 15
Little Blue-Winged Olive Dun: #20, morning and afternoon
Grannom: #16, afternoon
Tiny Blue-Winged Olive (*Pseudocloeon*): #20–24, afternoon

May 15–June 15
Grannom: #16, afternoon
Green Caddis: #16, afternoon and evening
Little Green Stonefly: #16, evening
Little Yellow Stonefly: #16, evening
Western Green Drake: #10 and #12, morning and afternoon
    (spotty)
Salmon Fly: #6, afternoon and evening
Golden Stonefly: #8, afternoon and evening

June 15–July 15

Green Caddis: #16, afternoon and evening
Pale Morning Dun: #16 and #18, morning, afternoon, and evening
Blue-Winged Olive Dun: #14, evening

July 15–August 15

Trico: #20–24, morning
Tan Caddis: #16, evening
Olive Caddis: #16, evening
Black Caddis: #16, evening
Pale Evening Dun *(Heptagenia elegantula)*: #14 and #16, evening
White Mayfly: #14 and #16, evening

August 15–September 30

Trico: #20–24, morning
Little Blue-Winged Olive Dun: #20, morning and afternoon
Tiny Blue-Winged Olive *(Pseudocloeon)*: #20–24, afternoon
October Caddis: #6, afternoon and evening
Orange Caddis: #12 and #14, afternoon and evening
Gray Drake: #12, afternoon
Gray Fox: #14, evening
Blue Quill: #18, morning and afternoon

UTAH

Few anglers think of Utah when they think of great places to fly fish. They may mention the Green River in Flaming Gorge, but almost no one I've met can think of another productive Utah river. Those who have fly fished the Provo River, however, know that, like the Green, this water can also prove to be very productive, especially in the winter and spring.

In our examination of Utah fly fishing we'll take a closer look at the Green River in the northeastern corner of the state.

Green River

From Colorado state line in Brown's Park upstream to Flaming Gorge Dam: artificial flies and lures only.

—*State of Utah Fishing Rules Summary,*
State of Utah,
Division of Wildlife Resources

Somebody out there owes Farrell Hirst a milkshake! Last year an out-door writer from New Jersey floated the Green River. As she entered her drift boat at the spillway ramp, she complained to Farrell Hirst, the campground operator, about her lack of success in the past few fishing trips. It seems that she ran into a long string of bad luck, and she was certain that she was jinxed. At the spillway ramp she bet Farrell a milkshake that she wouldn't catch a single trout on her 7-mile trip from the spillway to the takeout at Little Hole. Guess what? Farrell is still waiting for his milkshake. The guide told Farrell a couple days later that the lady angler caught more than thirty-five trout on her float trip, and two of the browns measured over 20 inches long. When the Green is hot, even a jinxed visitor can catch trout.

But in 1991 hard times came to the Flaming Gorge where the Green River flows. The Bureau of Reclamation had altered the river's flow the past spring, and this tampering seems to have affected the fishing on the river. That, along with two years of drought in the drainage, has definitely reduced the trout population. The guides I interviewed feel that anyone, even raw neophytes, could catch trout prior to this year. Now, although the fishing is great compared to other United States rivers, anglers work for each fish they catch.

I had to experience this great river on a float trip from the dam to Little Hole. My guide for the day was Hank Boehm from Park City. Hank works for Utah's largest fishing store–Angler's Inn–out of Salt Lake City and for Chris Kunkel, owner of the Fly Shop in Park City. Hank has guided on the Green River for the past four years, and a friend of his, Mark Forslund of Western Rivers Flyfishers, developed a pattern called the Mamba specifically for the Green River. The Mamba resembles a big timber ant and has proven to be extremely effective on the river.

I tied on a large attractor pattern to act as a strike indicator and tied a #18 Black Midge Pupa onto the bend of the hook of the attractor. I've said before that western anglers are among the most innovative in the world. By tying a 30-inch dropper directly onto the bend of the pattern nearest your rod, the forward pattern won't twist with the rear pattern.

We hadn't drifted out of sight of the spillway access when I had my first strike on the midge pattern. But I missed that trout and the next three. I incorrectly rationalized that I had to get acclimated to this newfangled setup. The fifth trout wasn't so lucky–a heavy 18-inch rainbow hit the pupa. For the next three hours trout struck that pat-tern. In almost every pool and pocket I had a strike with the black midge. The brown, rainbow, and cutthroat averaged 19 to 20 inches long and fought as well as any trout I've caught in any western river.

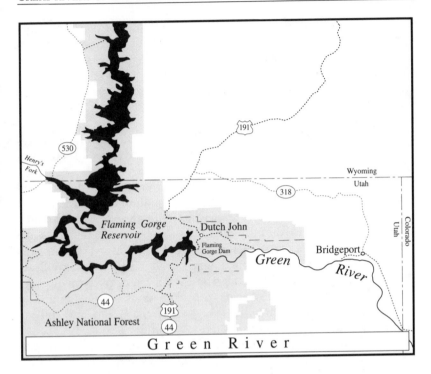

A heavy thunderstorm chased Hank and me onto the shore and underneath an overhanging ledge, where we waited for more than an hour before the storm passed.

By the time Hank and I arrived at the area called "can of worms" by the locals, we noticed a few tiny blue-winged olives *(Pseudocloeon)* emerging, and a half hour later the hatch turned into a fishable one, with huge trout sipping in dozens of these 4–5 millimeter (#22) mayflies. I tied on a #20 Blue Dun to match the hatch. I should have used a #22, but because of the overcast skies I had difficulty picking out which imitation to use among all the naturals. In front of us maybe a dozen heavy trout fed methodically on the lazy duns. On the tenth cast a 19-inch rainbow sucked in the imitation, and I set the hook. Trout kept sipping in little blue duns all the way to the takeout at Little Hole.

Hit the Green River when there's a hatch in progress, and you'll be amazed at the matching-the-hatch episodes you'll experience. Kenton Williams, area manager at Little Hole, fishes the trico hatch in his area. He looks forward to the spinner fall every morning in August. Kenton also looks forward to the little blue-wing hatch that appears in April and September. He recently caught a 9-pound, 29-inch trout matching the little blue-wing on the Green River.

When you think of the Green, you often think of the cicada that appears on the trees in the gorge from the middle of May through much of June. These cicadas didn't appear in the numbers in 1991 that they have in previous years because of the cool, wet spring the area experienced. But Mormon crickets made up for the small number of cicadas. Kenton said that trout gorged themselves on the crickets around the end of June.

Midges and scuds make up the bulk of the diet. Hank Boehm says that midges appear on the water all year long. He sees them with black, olive, and red body colors.

The Green River is a tailwater with several baffles to mix and bring the water out at 56 degrees. If you're unfamiliar with the river, I recommend you float it for at least a day with an experienced guide. There are ten permitted outfitters on the river, some in the Salt Lake City area. There are three sections to float. The upper section runs from the spillway at the dam downriver to Little Hole and flows through a deep spectacular gorge. Here you'll see every type of water imaginable – from riffles to rapids to pocket water to pools to almost still water. The water is unbelievably clear on the Green, and you can see to the bottom of many of the 10- to 20-foot-deep pools. It's about a 7.5-mile float trip in the upper section. You'll find all the rapids and some of the sections named here. From top to bottom you'll see Lunker Flat, Anticipation Rapids, Little Steamboat Rapids, Bridge Rapids, Roller Coaster Rapids, Secret Riffle, Diving Board Rapids, Skinny Dip Rapids, Mother-in-Law, Honey Hole, Lunker Lane, Dead Man Rapids, Rock Garden, Dripping Springs, Can of Worms Shoal, Black Lagoon, Cat Walk Shoals, and Little Hole. You'll hit the best little blue-wing hatches on Secret Riffle, the best caddisfly hatches from Dead Man Rapids to Dripping Springs. The Rock Garden holds productive pocket water.

In the middle section, from Little Hole to Indian Crossing, or section B, you'll hit shallower water that broadens out and contains more brown trout. The float trip on this section is 9 miles long.

The lower section, from Indian Crossing to Swallow Canyon, is almost totally flat and shallow, and long casts are required. Here you're fishing almost exclusively to brown trout. Steve Robinson of Pittsburgh and Lysle Sherwin of Ligonier, Pennsylvania, prefer this section. "If conditions are right, it's a superb brown trout fishery," Steve said. This float is also 9 miles long.

With such spectacular scenery and a great trout river, you'd expect to see few problems. There are some, however. The river has become too popular, and anglers in boats compete with rafters for room on the river. Many of the rafters are lacking in etiquette, and on weekends you'll find water battles by the rafters upsetting anglers up and down the river. Someone must start limiting the number of rafters on the river. You'll also see float tubes used on the river. These look dangerous.

After heavy thunderstorms Red Creek, below Little Hole, pours silt into the Green River. For days the area below this tributary flows dark brown. The state needs a siltation dam on the creek to prevent this, and an earlier study of the siltation problem recommended it.

Radical fluctuations from the Flaming Gorge Dam have adversely impacted upon the insect and trout populations. A consistent water flow would be more appropriate for a healthy and stable trout population.

Has the trout fishing on the Green River declined in the past year? It might have, but the Green River still stands as one of the top ten in the nation.

Best Times to Fly Fish

April 1–May 15
   Little Blue-Winged Olive Dun: #18 and #20, morning and
      afternoon

May 15–June 25
   Cicadas: #8–10, morning and afternoon
   Pale Morning Dun*: #16 and #18, morning and afternoon
   Golden Stonefly: #12, afternoon and evening

June 26–July 31
   Pale Morning Dun*: #16 and #18, morning and afternoon
   Golden Stonefly: #14, afternoon and evening
   Trico: #20 and #24, morning

August 1–August 31
   Trico: #20–22, morning
   Tan Caddis: #14 and #16, afternoon and evening
   Tiny Blue-Winged Olive *(Pseudocloeon)*: #20–24, afternoon
   Little Gray Caddis: #20 and #22, afternoon and evening

September 1–October 10
   Little Blue-Winged Olive Dun: #18 and #20, morning and
      afternoon
   Tiny Blue-Winged Olive *(Pseudocloeon)*: #20–24, afternoon

   *Body is pale olive.

COLORADO

Colorful Colorado – high mountains, pristine setting, and tremendous trout rivers. Who hasn't heard of great rivers like the South Platte or the Fryingpan. But Colorado has other great rivers with much less notoriety. Fish the likes of the Gunnison, Rio Grande, Roaring Fork, or the Arkansas and you're in for some great fishing. Colorado Division of Wildlife classifies the first three of these as gold-medal rivers.

Colorado also holds its share of great hatches. You'll find a fantastic trico hatch on the South Platte and a respectable one on the lower part of the Cache la Poudre near Fort Collins. You'll hit great western green drakes on the Roaring Fork and the Fryingpan rivers. Few Colorado rivers don't hold a pale morning dun hatch – these mayflies flourish in the rivers throughout the state.

We'll examine two rivers familiar to many anglers – the South Platte and the Fryingpan. We'll also look at two rivers not quite as well known – the Roaring Fork and the Arkansas.

Arkansas River

Arkansas River (Chaffee and Freemont counties):

a) From the Stockyard Bridge below Salida downstream to the confluence with Badger Creek (7.5 miles).

1) Fishing by artificial flies or artificial lures only.

b) From the Mugford lease at Big Bend downstream to the Chaffee County Road 166 bridge (above Salida).

1) Fishing by artificial flies or artificial lures only.

– Colorado Fishing Season Information,
Colorado Division of Wildlife

"If I had only one river to fish the rest of my life, it would be the Arkansas. This river is one of the best-kept secrets in the West." So says Don Puterbaugh of Salida, Colorado. Don has conducted the Columbine School of Flyfishing for fifteen years on the Arkansas, South Platte, and on rivers in Alaska. He coauthored several books on fly tying and for the past ten years has drawn lifelike insects and flies for magazines and books. Don's truly one of a kind and a fantastic fisherman. Furthermore, he knows the Arkansas as well as he knows the back of his hand.

Recently Phil Camera, maker of Larva Lace; Bill McMillen of Salida; and I spent a day on the Arkansas with Don Puterbaugh, who wanted to show us the river's true value as a top-notch fishery.

"Fish the pockets along the shore. Too many anglers fish the middle of the river when they should be fishing the pockets near the shore. They're wading where they should be fishing!" Don said emphatically.

About 10:00 A.M. we hiked down a path to the river just below Salida in the specially regulated area. Don had assured us that we didn't need to hit the river earlier. The river holds a few tricos, but the hatch at most places is very sparse, and few trout rise for the meager spinner fall.

"The best action on the Arkansas often takes place between 10:00 A.M. and 3:00 P.M.," Don said. We were about to find out why.

As we entered the water, Don pointed to a half dozen pale morning duns already emerging. These #18 duns had a tan to tannish cream body color. Don suggested that I tie on one of his Pale Morning Dun patterns on the tippet and a larger, #12, dry fly on the dropper. Like many of the guides do on the Green River, Don suggested that I tie a 30-inch piece of leader to the bend of the hook of the larger fly. Tie in the tippet with an improved clinch knot. The large fly helps you locate the smaller Pale Morning Dun on the rough water in the Arkansas.

Don and Bill decided to stand back on the bank and direct Phil and me. With each trout that rose to the dry fly, they yelled in unison, "Strike." Almost every time they shouted, we missed the riser. Up and down the river anglers and campers heard "strike" dozens of times.

Phil Camera broke the ice first, landing a heavy Arkansas brown about 13 inches long. I missed the first ten trout that struck the Pale Morning Dun pattern. Trout rise readily to dry flies on the Arkansas, but to hook and land them is another matter. It is a delicate balance between drag and a proper tight line in this fast pocket water. When they do strike, you have to set the hook quickly because they spit out the fly as quickly as they take it. Finally, I landed a heavy 12-inch Arkansas brown after a courageous fight.

For four hours we fished various sections below Salida and caught trout. The four of us estimated that we had well over fifty strikes in that time, but we landed only a small percent of them. The Arkansas in that four-hour trip had proven its worth.

The river holds some great hatches. Even as early as mid-March you'll find some good hatches of little blue-winged olives and blue quills on the surface. By mid-May snowmelt from nearby Collegiate Peaks muddies and raises the level of the water. You'll find some snowmelt on the river until mid-July; after that time pale morning duns, blue quills, and an assortment of stoneflies appear on the surface and encourage trout to rise. In September little blue-winged olives appear for a second time and can create some great matching-the-hatch episodes.

What about downwings on this river? "You can't breathe – it's like fly fishing in a snowstorm," Don says about the prolific grannom hatch that appears around May 1. This is the time to hit the river – you'll see the grannom by the millions. Don copies the caddisfly by tying an olive body, then he colors the front half of the body with a black Pantone marker.

The 60- to 100-foot-wide Arkansas provides more than 70 miles of quality fishing from Canyon City upriver above Buena Vista. U.S. Route 50 parallels the river most of the way and access at most points is no problem. Watch the water if you plan to fish the lower end of the river. Any quick summer thunderstorm muddies Badger Creek quickly, so you might want to fish further upriver.

The Arkansas has several critical problems. Heavy metals from California Gulch and Yak Tunnel near Leadville have affected the quality of the fishery. Planned settlement ponds should help alleviate this problem. Rafters and rafting on the river present a serious difficulty to fly fishers. In addition, the Bureau of Reclamation provides a minimum flow from July 1 to August 15 for rafters, and these flows affect the fish and the insect population. If this river were better managed for fly fishing, it would be a boon to the upper Arkansas River valley. This management would include a catch-and-release area and better regulation of the fluctuations in flow.

Thanks to the Collegiate Peaks Chapter of Trout Unlimited in Salida, Colorado, for fighting for a more viable fishery on the Arkansas. Its members help with riparian repairs on the tributaries and many other projects to improve the quality of fishing on the river. They need and deserve your support.

Wading on much of the river can be treacherous, and several rafters drown annually. A section between Salida and Buena Vista, called Brown's Canyon, is especially dangerous. Watch your step, and don't go out too far. If you enjoy fishing pocket water, then the Arkansas is for you. Throw in some productive riffles and a few deep pools and you'll readily see why the Arkansas is a great trout river. You'll find mostly brown trout with some heavy rainbows in the river.

Was Don Puterbaugh correct in saying that the Arkansas is the best-kept secret? Try it and find out for yourself.

Best Times to Fly Fish

March 15–April 30
Little Blue-Winged Olive Dun: #20, morning and afternoon
Blue Quill: #18, morning and afternoon

May 1–May 31
Grannom: #16, morning and afternoon

July 1–August 31
Pale Morning Dun: #18, morning and afternoon
Blue Quill: #18, morning and afternoon
Yellow Sally: #16, afternoon
Dark Gray Caddis: #20, afternoon and evening
Trico: #24, morning (very spotty)

September 1–October 15
Little Blue-Winged Olive Dun: #20, morning and afternoon
Blue Quill: #18, morning and afternoon

Fryingpan River

Fryingpan River (Eagle and Pitkin counties):

a) From Ruedi Dam downstream to the upper boundary of the Cap K Ranch, approximately 4 miles – Gold-Medal Water: Fishing by artificial flies or artificial lures only; and all fish caught must be returned to the water immediately.

b) From the upper boundary of the Cap K Ranch to its confluence with the Roaring Fork River – Gold-Medal Water: Fishing by artificial flies or artificial lures only; and all rainbow trout caught must be returned to the water immediately.

– Colorado Fishing Season Information

It had been a long time since my last visit to the Fryingpan River – thirteen years almost to the date. Had the river changed? Did it still hold those great hatches that I remembered from the past? What about the heavy trout the river once held – did it still hold them?

Roy Palm would be my guide for the day, and he assured me that the Fryingpan deserved the recent gold-medal status awarded it by the

Colorado Division of Wildlife. Roy should know—he has fished the Fryingpan for thirty years, has guided clients on the river for the past twenty years, and opened the Frying Pan Anglers seven years ago. He's devoted much of his adult life to fishing the Fryingpan River.

No need to start early on this river. Hatches usually don't begin until after 10:00 A.M. on this unusually cold water. Roy and I entered a section locals call "the Flats," just a couple hundred feet below Ruedi Reservoir. I stuck my thermometer into the icy water and took a second look at the 46-degree reading. Water comes from the bottom of the 250-foot lake above and keeps the river unusually cold all summer long.

Within a few minutes we experienced an incredibly prolific chironomid hatch. Not one trout rose in the Flats, so Roy and I moved downstream, where Roy hooked a 3- or 4-pound rainbow on a crane fly larva imitation. Roy spotted the heavy rainbow feeding just in front of a big boulder. He tells all anglers to spot trout and fish to them when there's no activity on the surface. He also suggests that anglers fish some of the extremely fast water on the river and look for the slower pockets. Few anglers fish these sections.

Still no insects on the water! Still no rising trout! Roy looked at his watch and decided it was time to head a few miles downriver for the expected hatch.

"We'll see the western green drake here this afternoon," Roy said, as we waded into a long, 1- to 2-foot-deep riffle. Western green drakes appear for an extended period on the Roaring Fork and the Fryingpan rivers, first appearing on the Roaring Fork downriver near Glenwood Springs around late June. The hatch moves upriver on the Fork, then up the Fryingpan to Ruedi Reservoir, where they might appear as late as mid-September. That's eight to ten weeks of matching drake hatches if you know exactly where the hatch is on the two rivers.

We had no sooner entered the water a second time than we saw western green drakes already appearing. These large mayflies struggled to become airborne, and a half dozen browns and rainbows just upstream from us eagerly surface-fed on the stragglers. Roy and I took turns fishing to the rises and hooked or missed a dozen heavy trout. Within two hours the hatch diminished and surface activity ended.

Roy and I took a break and discussed the hatch, the effective hairwing pattern we both used, our success, and the beauty of the Fryingpan trout. These discussions are a natural ending to a successful fly-fishing event.

We headed downriver another few miles for the late-afternoon hatch on the Fryingpan. Roy said #22 little blue duns (*Pseudocloeon* species) and #16 or #18 blue-winged olive duns (*Drunella* species) would appear shortly. As we headed toward a productive riffle, we already saw a half dozen trout taking a mixture of blue and olive duns.

The water temperature in this section had risen to 52 degrees. Roy tied on a #20 Crippled Blue Dun Emerger and fished it on the surface. On the second or third cast he hooked up with a heavy rainbow. I soon landed a heavy brown taken on a #18 Blue Dun dry. Often these Fryingpan River trout don't just take in a dry fly – they attack it. During the hour-long hatch we caught a dozen or more trout. Then we headed back to Roy's van and again talked about the great hatches and responsive trout we had experienced all afternoon.

You'll find hatches on the river much of the year. Winter is Roy's favorite time to fly fish. Then the crowds have thinned out, and Roy has trout rising to chironomids all afternoon long. Some anglers even take a skiing-fishing vacation.

You'll find many other great hatches on the river. Pinkish tan pale morning duns fill the surface in July on the Fryingpan, and trout rise readily to an imitation of these. Almost every evening you'll find a healthy spinner fall followed by caddis activity at dusk.

Below Ruedi Reservoir you'll find about 14 miles of tailwater fishing. Posted property dots the shoreline below the dam, with about a third of the land below the dam being posted. Rocky Fork Creek, found about 5 miles above Basalt, turns the river muddy after a heavy thunderstorm. Roy divides the tailwater into the upper, middle, and lower rivers. You'll find mainly fast water in the upper section, slow water in the middle, and fast pocket water in the lower area. The lower section contains a canyonlike area just above Basalt that Roy says few people ever fish.

The Fryingpan ranges from 50 to 100 feet wide. In a few gorgelike areas the river constricts to 20 or 30 feet wide. The river holds many of the same characteristics that the Roaring Fork does. You'll find a lot of productive pocket water throughout. In the upper tailwater, just below Ruedi, there are some slow glides and pools. You'll find browns and rainbows in the tailwater, with a few brooks and cutthroats near the reservoir. The Fryingpan enters the Roaring Fork River in the town of Basalt. There's a blacktop road that parallels the river from Basalt upriver.

Fishing pressure gets heavy during the western green drake hatch. On any given day you might find fifty to one hundred anglers fishing the tailwater.

Like so many rivers, the Fryingpan is not without its problems. The dam should have multiple gates so a mix of top and bottom releases could warm the river below. We found 46-degree temperatures just below the bottom release in mid-August. Public access to the river should be better marked, and Colorado also has to strive to get more access to all this tailwater resource. Anglers must respect private property on the river and also strive for proper fishing etiquette. Recently the Division of Wildlife raised the flow to 1,100 cfs from 125 cfs in five or six hours. This can't be beneficial to the river, especially to the hatches and the trout.

Stop in at the Frying Pan Anglers in Basalt, Colorado, for the latest hatching information and river conditions. Roy and his congenial staff – Mike Costello, Jeff Solis, Scott Henry, and Rob Baxter – are happy to answer any questions. Mike, Jeff, Rob, and John Van Ingen guide anglers on both the Roaring Fork and Fryingpan rivers. Since some of their clientele are novices, part of their assignment is to provide instruction in the finer details of fly fishing.

Did the Fryingpan River live up to my expectations? Yes, it still ranks among the top twenty in my list of favorite waters in the United States.

Best Times to Fly Fish

April 1–May 31
Little Blue-Winged Olive Dun: #20, morning and afternoon
Tiny Blue-Winged Olive (Pseudocloeon): #20–24, afternoon

June 15–August 15
Pale Morning Dun: #16 and #18, morning and afternoon
Pink Lady: #14 and #16, evening
Red Quill: #10, afternoon
Blue-Winged Olive Dun: #14, evening
Yellow Sally: #16, afternoon
Brown Drake (Ephemera compar): #10 and #12, evening
Red Quill (Timpanoga hecuba): #10, morning and afternoon

July 16–August 31
Speckle-Winged Dun: #14 and #16, morning and afternoon
Western Green Drake: #10 and #12, morning and afternoon
Pale Morning Dun: #16 and #18, morning, afternoon, and evening
Tan Caddis: #16 and #18, evening

Little Olive Dun: #20, late afternoon
Quill Gordon *(Rhithrogena futilis)*: #14, afternoon
Olive Caddis: #10–14, afternoon and evening
Orange Caddis: #10, afternoon and evening
Blue-Winged Olive Dun: #16, afternoon

September 1–October 15

Orange Caddis: #10, afternoon and evening
Little Blue-Winged Olive Dun: #20, morning and afternoon
Tiny Blue-Winged Olive *(Pseudocloeon)*: #20–24, afternoon
Blue Quill: #18, morning and afternoon

Roaring Fork River

Roaring Fork River (Pitkin and Garfield counties):

a) From McFarlane Creek downstream to the upper Woody Creek bridge: fishing by artificial flies only; and all fish caught must be returned to the water immediately.

b) From the upper Woody Creek bridge to the Colorado River: fishing by artificial flies or artificial lures only. The bag possession and size limit for trout is two fish, 16 inches or longer.

c) Gold-medal water, from the Crystal River downstream to the Colorado River.

—Colorado Fishing Season Information

Like Rodney Dangerfield, it gets no respect. According to Roy Palm and others who fish it frequently, it receives little press, but it's one of the top trout rivers in the West. Other than a few anglers fishing the river just below Basalt, you'll find little angling pressure on the river. The Division of Wildlife knows its true value—they've classified it as a gold-medal stream. You'll find trophy trout on this 40 miles of productive water. Last year an angler released a 14-pound brown trout on the river. It's one of a decreasing number of western freestone rivers that has no dam in its headwaters. It's a fast-flowing river from Aspen to Basalt, and it deserves its name—Roaring Fork River.

One of the best ways to sample this gold-medal river is by McKenzie boat. Many anglers and guides put in at Carbondale and take out at West Bank or put in at West Bank and take out at Glenwood Springs.

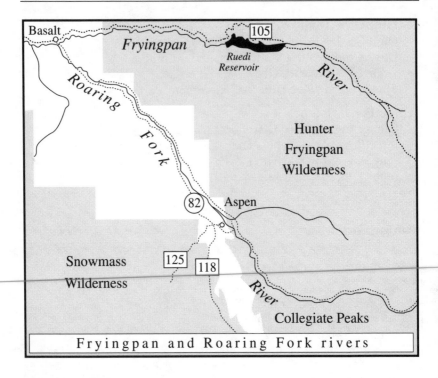

Fryingpan and Roaring Fork rivers

You're not allowed to set foot on some of the river bottom in this area, so the only way to fish it is by boat. The best time to float is from March to early July. The Frying Pan Anglers usually float the Roaring Fork more than two hundred times each year. Try to float it when it displays one of its many great hatches.

The river holds some great hatches. The western green drake usually first appears near Glenwood Springs near the end of June and continues to move up the river a few miles each week. If you know where the hatch is, you can have some fantastic midday matching the hatch for several weeks.

The Roaring Fork holds a respectable salmon fly hatch. This stonefly, however, appears on the river during the height of spring snowmelt, and because of extremely high water at that time, provides few matching-the-hatch opportunities.

You'll find plenty of pocket water on the upper river from Aspen to Basalt. Here the river runs about 50 to 100 feet wide. Below Basalt the river widens to 100 feet and more and you'll find heavier water with huge productive pools and riffles.

Although I've only ever caught rainbows on the river, Roy Palm assures me that it holds rainbows and browns in almost equal portions.

State Route 82 follows the river from Aspen downriver for 40 miles to Glenwood Springs, where it enters the Colorado River. There's some posted land around the Carbondale area.

Colorado needs to do a better job of designating public land on the river so out-of-town anglers know where they can fish. If you have any questions about open stretches, river conditions, or hatches, stop in at the Frying Pan Anglers. This fly shop has imitations of each and every hatch you'll ever encounter on the Roaring Fork.

Does the river deserve its gold-medal rating? Try fishing this great river when one of its many hatches appears. Once you give it a fair try, you will see the true character of this fantastic water, and Roaring Fork River will become one of your favorites.

Best Times to Fly Fish

April 1–April 30
Little Blue-Winged Olive Dun: #20, morning and afternoon

May 15–June 30
Salmon Fly: #6, afternoon and evening
Golden Stonefly: #8, afternoon and evening
Western Green Drake: #10 and #12, morning and afternoon

July 1–July 31
Pale Morning Dun: #16 and #18, morning, afternoon, and evening
Western Green Drake: #10 and #12, morning and afternoon
Yellow Sally: #16, afternoon

August 1–August 31
Pale Morning Dun: #16 and #18, morning, afternoon, and evening
Western Green Drake: #10 and #12, morning and afternoon
Tan Caddis: #16 and #18, evening
Tiny Blue-Winged Olive (Pseudocloeon): #20–24, afternoon
Olive Caddis: #14, afternoon and evening

September 1–September 30
Little Blue-Winged Olive Dun: #20, morning and afternoon
Tiny Blue-Winged Olive (Pseudocloeon): #20–24, afternoon

South Platte River

South Platte River (Douglas, Jefferson, Park, and Teller counties):

a) The Middle Fork of the South Platte River downstream from the Highway 9 bridge (4.9 miles north of Garo) and the South Fork of the South Platte River downstream from the lower boundary of the Denver Water Department property line, and from the confluence of the Middle and South forks of the South Platte downstream to the inlet of Spinney Mountain Reservoir – Gold-medal water:

   1) Fishing by artificial flies or artificial lures only.

   2) The bag and size limit for trout is one fish 20 inches or longer.

b) From the outlet of Spinney Mountain Reservoir downstream to the County Road 59 bridge – Gold-medal water:

   1) Fishing by artificial flies or artificial lures only.

   2) All fish caught must be returned to the water immediately.

c) From the County Road 59 bridge to the buoy line at the inlet of Elevenmile Reservoir – Gold-medal water:

   1) Fishing by artificial flies or artificial lures only.

   2) All fish caught must be returned to the water immediately except that anglers in possession of a Trophy Trout Permit and Tag may take one trout.

d) South Platte River from Cheesman Dam downstream to the upper Wigwam property line – Gold-medal water:

   1) Fishing by artificial flies or artificial lures only.

   2) All fish caught must be returned to the water immediately.

e) South Platte River from the lower boundary of the Wigwam Club to Scraggy View Picnic Ground – Gold-medal water:

   1) Fishing is by artificial flies or artificial lures only.

f) South Platte River from Strontia Springs Dam downstream to 300 yards upstream from the Denver Water Board's Diversion structure:

   1) Fishing by artificial flies or artificial lures, except that only naturally occurring aquatic nymphs and/or larvae in the South Platte River are permitted as bait.

—Colorado Fishing Season Information

The South Platte, along with its sister river the North Platte, has a spectacular dependable trico hatch from mid-July into September. With good weather you can hit the hatch some years into late October.

Ken Walters and Ed Exum of Denver showed me how productive this river can become with this spinner fall. We hiked in for several miles on the South Platte near Deckers and just several miles below Cheesman Reservoir. We arrived at the river just as the last of the female trico duns emerged. Already a heavy mating swarm of male tricos had formed 20 feet above my head.

Soon the first female spinners mated and fell onto the pocket water I was fishing. Huge brown trout fed on the first spinners to hit the water. I noticed that these spinners were much larger than those in the East and Midwest. What a break! On this late-July morning I matched the spinner fall with a #20 Trico – not a #24. The spinner fall lasted for more than an hour, and I hooked ten trout on the spent-wing imitation. The trico fall on the South Platte is very predictable and lengthy. If you don't hit an extremely cold autumn, you can fish the spinner until late October.

But that trip occurred more than twenty years ago. I returned to the South Platte River for a second try at the challenging trico.

Phil Camera woke me at 5:45 A.M., and we had a long ride down to the Middle Fork of the South Platte River. Phil wanted us to arrive just below Spinney Reservoir when the trico duns began to appear. Phil knows the river well – he's guided on the South Platte for years and lives only forty-five minutes away. Phil, an innovative fly tyer, recently marketed Larva Lace, a fantastic new synthetic product used in making all types of bodies.

When we arrived at the upper parking lot just below Spinney Reservoir, there were already a half dozen cars with anglers preparing their lines and leaders for the big challenge – the trico hatch on the South Platte River. Phil and I hiked upriver and began casting to more than two dozen risers. For the next two hours trout fed on emergers and duns under a heavy cloud cover. During that time Phil and I picked up a few heavy rainbows on Crystal Trico Compara-duns.

Spinners began falling under the leaden, cold mid-August skies around 10:00 A.M. Trout stayed near the surface scooping in a dozen or more imagoes at a time. Phil and I changed to Trico spinners. Only after three or four perfect drifts over a rising trout would it take the Trico. Of the takes, we landed only one of five trout. Yes, the South Platte River gives up its heavy trout very miserly.

But the South Platte is not a one-hatch river – it holds many of the noted western hatches, such as mayflies, caddisflies, and stoneflies. As early as April you can witness some afternoon little blue-winged olive duns on the surface. Probably the best time to match the hatches, however, is from early June through July. In quick succession you'll hit

A heavy South Platte rainbow. *Charles Meck*.

hatches like the pale morning dun, western green drake, blue-winged olive dun, blue quill, and more.

The South Platte looks like three or four different rivers, depending on where you're fishing. Below Spinney Reservoir it resembles a slow spring creek. At spots in the Elevenmile Canyon and below Cheesman Reservoir the river gathers speed. Since the character of the river changes so much, it's reasonable to expect hatches on certain parts of the river and not on others.

Phil Camera, however, feels that the best times to head to the river are in April and September. In September you'll often find the little blue-winged olive duns along with tricos. And the tourists have vacated the river, so you won't find the huge crowds of July and August.

But caddisflies and stoneflies also provide plenty of matching-the-hatch opportunities. You'll find tan caddis and gray caddis on the river.

There are several reservoirs on the South Platte. Below Antero Reservoir there is private water. Just above the second dam, Spinney Reservoir, there are 5 miles of public fishing. Some of the best fishing and most pressure on the river occur just below Spinney Reservoir. You'll find three accesses to this 3-mile stretch between Spinney and Elevenmile reservoirs. In this area, called South Park, the river ranges from 50 to 80 feet wide. It serpentines slowly in its 3-mile trip to the Elevenmile Reservoir. If you select the one just below Spinney, you have to pay a three-dollar fee, but you don't have to pay in the two lower accesses. Below Elevenmile Reservoir you'll find Elevenmile Canyon. Here are 9 miles of tumbling river interrupted every so often with placid pools and slow riffles. A dirt road parallels this entire canyon. When the river emerges from the canyon, you'll find Lake George. Three miles below Lake George, at Happy Meadows Campground, there's another section of open fishing. Here you'll find productive pocket water full of trout.

Below the next dam, Cheesman Reservoir, there are 3.5 miles of open water. You have to hike into this canyon-type water. You will find trout and good fishing well below Deckers.

Rainbow trout seem to outnumber browns by about three to one. You'll also catch cutthroats, cutbows, and some salmon, especially below Spinney Reservoir.

The Middle Fork of the river flows through Fairplay, Colorado, and picks up the South Fork a few miles below Antero Reservoir, near Hartsel. Most of the South Fork remains private water. The river picks up the North Fork at the town of South Platte, several miles below Deckers, then enters the Waterton Canyon.

Brad Befus at the Front Range Angler in Boulder, Colorado, once asked me why the tricos on the South Platte vary in size from the beginning to the end of the hatch. I explained that the species had two generations per year and that the first generation, or cohort, live much longer than the second and, therefore, was often larger. It was almost like a light went on in his brain. He had been curious about this phenomenon for years – now he understood it. Review the trico emergence in chapter 3. It's important that you understand this event.

If you fish the area around Spinney Reservoir, you'll see the need for some trees in the area. If you park your car in one of the lots, you'll note that the tricos shed their subimagal skin on the parked cars. Dave Fawcett of Lake George, Colorado, guides on Spinney Reservoir and the South Platte River.

Is the South Platte as good as it was twenty years ago? Except for the increased fishing pressure – you bet it is!

Best Times to Fly Fish

April 15–May 10
Little Blue-Winged Olive Dun: #20, morning and afternoon

May 11–July 15
Gray Caddis: #16, afternoon and evening
Salmon Fly: #6, evening
Tan Caddis: #16, afternoon and evening
Pale Morning Dun: #16 and #18, morning, afternoon, and evening
Blue-Winged Olive Dun: #16, morning and evening
Western Green Drake: #12, morning and afternoon
Blue Quill: #18, morning and afternoon
Quill Gordon: #14, afternoon
Speckle-Winged Dun: #14 and #16, morning and afternoon
Gray Drake: #10 and #12, afternoon

July 15–September 30
Gray Drake: #10 and #12, afternoon
Trico: #20–24, morning
Olive Sedge: #8, evening
Little Blue-Winged Olive Dun: #20, morning and afternoon
Speckle-Winged Dun: #14 and #16, morning and afternoon
Blue Quill: #18, morning and afternoon

NEW MEXICO

When anglers think of great trout fishing states, they normally don't think of New Mexico. With the advent of tailwater fisheries, however, New Mexico has come to the forefront with the San Juan River. Many fly fishermen who fish this New Mexico water frequently rate it as one of the tops in the nation.

San Juan River

Special Trout Water from Navajo Dam downstream 3.75 miles to the east side of Section 16: In the first quarter of a mile from Navajo Dam to the cable crossing, all fish caught must be returned immediately to the water, and no fish may be in possession. From the cable crossing 3.5 miles to the east side of Section 16, bag limit is one trout 20 inches or longer per day, two in possession. No trout under 20 inches long may be in possession while fishing this section. Only artificial flies and lures with barbless, single hooks are permitted.

—New Mexico Fishing Proclamation,
State of New Mexico,
Department of Fish and Game

"It's the best rainbow stream in the United States." That's what Tim Chavez of nearby Navajo Dam, New Mexico, says about the San Juan River. Tim should know—he's fished the river for years. And for the past five years Tim has guided hundreds of anglers on this excellent 120- to 150-foot-wide tailwater fishery in northwestern New Mexico. Tim's outfitting company, Born and Raised on the San Juan, Inc., reflects his long presence on the river. On many occasions Tim told customers at his father's store—Abe's Store and Motel in Navajo Dam— what pattern to use and where to fish the river. "Several of them have come back after their fishing trip with 7- to 9-pound browns and rainbows," Tim said.

Tim's not alone in his praise of the San Juan. "It's one of the top ten trout rivers in the United States. No, it's one of the top five," Phil Camera of Woodland Park, Colorado, says about one of his favorite western rivers. You'll find Phil making the five-hour trip to this river from his home at least three or four times a year.

Even in the dead of winter anglers can catch trout on this highly productive river. For example, in late February you'll find feeding trout and moderate fishing pressure on the San Juan. You'll also see insects emerging. Temperatures at this time of year often rise to the high fifties.

When many anglers think of the San Juan, they often think of wet-fly fishing at its finest. Patterns like WD40, Pheasant Tail Nymph, RS2, and Hare's Ear work extremely well all year long. All patterns copy the predominant *Baetis* mayfly hatch on the river, which appears from early March until late October. Tim suggests that you use patterns in #16–20 to copy the *Baetis* nymph. The WD40 pattern works extremely well on the river. The fly has a tail of mallard flank, a body made from olive chocolate thread, and dark gray dubbing under a mallard flank wing case.

Other productive patterns for the San Juan include Woolly Bug-gers, Brassies, Gray and Black Midge Pupa – and, of course, the fa-mous San Juan Worm.

Midges make up an important part of the trout's diet on the San Juan River, and you'll find them on the water all year long. Tie chirono-mid patterns in #20–24 in dark gray and black. Anglers often use strike indicators with their midge patterns and fish them with a dead drift. If you prefer to use dry flies, try a #14 or #16 Adams to copy clusters of dead midge adults.

If you enjoy fishing terrestrials, then August is the time for you to hit the river. Trout readily take hoppers, ants, and beetles in late summer and early autumn.

The San Juan River holds several respectable hatches. "When these hatches appear, it's a great river to match the hatch with a dry fly," Tim Chavez says. If you hit the little blue-winged olive dun, pale morning duns, or one of the caddisfly hatches, you'll see 2- to 4-pound trout feeding freely on the surface.

You'll find the best water on the San Juan just below the dam. The state has rated the first 3.75 miles as quality water. The first quarter mile of this water is catch and release only. There are about 10 miles of excellent trout water downriver from the Navajo Dam.

The upper 3.75 miles contain about 98 percent rainbow trout. The lower half has limited access, and you'll find more brown trout there. Use your neoprenes if you plan to wade this river. Water temperatures just below the dam range from 42 to 50 degrees.

The water flow in the San Juan could be managed to better support the trout and insect populations in the river. During the past few years the water flow has averaged below 1,000 cfs. If authorities kept the flow between 1,000 and 1,500 cfs, it would become even a better trout river than it presently is.

You can reach the river from Farmington, New Mexico. State Route 173 crosses the river near Abe's Store. U.S. Route 550 parallels much of the upper river, including the upper 3.75 miles designated as quality water. U.S. Route 64 crosses the lower half. Wading on some of the river is extremely hazardous, so take a wading staff with you. If you enjoy fishing slower water, you'll find plenty of long, productive pools on the river.

For the latest information on guides, hatches, and river flow, check with Abe's Store and Motel, Rizuto's Fly Shop, or Duranglers, all in Navajo Dam.

Are Tim Chavez and Phil Camera correct in their lavish praise of the San Juan River? Is it one of the top rivers in the nation? Once you've fly fished this great tailwater in the Southwest, I think you'll also be one of its supporters.

Best Times to Fly Fish

March 1–October 31
Little Blue-Winged Olive Dun: #20, morning and afternoon

May 1–June 30
Gray Caddis: #16, afternoon and evening

July 10–September 15
Pale Morning Dun: #16 and #18, morning, afternoon, and evening
Grasshoppers: #6 and #8, afternoon
Little Blue-Winged Olive Dun: #20, morning and afternoon

September 16–October 31
Little Blue-Winged Olive Dun: #20, morning and afternoon

7

Great Hatches on
Lousy Days

In this chapter Charles Meck describes firsthand how weather affects the hatches and how to enjoy excellent fishing during inclement weather.

It's mid-April and the fishing season began just a couple of days ago. For a week now the weather has been unbelievably hot for early spring, and the warm air temperatures have warmed the water to 55 degrees. A cold front arrived just this morning and air temperatures are expected to stay in the forties and the sky overcast. Should you still go to your favorite stream, or should you wait for a warmer day? Go. This could be one of those fortuitous lousy days you've been waiting for. Why?

First, you feel confident that a hendrickson hatch will appear today shortly after noon. It has emerged on this stretch of your stream for the past two days but has escaped rapidly from the surface in the 75-degree temperatures. Now you have the slowdown factor on your side – cold weather.

Hendricksons begin emerging about the same time they did yesterday, shortly before 1:00 P.M., with one big change – these #14 duns are resting on the entire length of the 200-foot-long pool. The 40-degree temperature is delaying, or even preventing, the mayflies from ever escaping. The water temperature holds in the low fifties, and trout begin to feed on the dazed, stunned, cold duns. For more than an hour a dozen trout feed on mayflies in a pool that before seemed devoid of trout. Even after the last dun attempts to emerge in the pool, stunned duns from several pools float past you and trout feed on them.

The previous example of a lousy day converted an average hatch into an incredible one. Recall for a moment your encounters with truly great hatches like the green drake, the white mayfly, the hendrickson, the western march brown, the western green drake, or the Michigan caddis. What elements help make these hatches spectacular?

The density of the hatch has to be one important factor. I've seen hatches where the emerging insect mass wasn't really heavy enough to entice trout to rise to the surface. On the other hand, I've seen the hendrickson, white mayfly, green drake, and Michigan caddis appear all at once on the water in unbelievable numbers. I have quit in disgust when green drakes, hendricksons, and tricos covered the surface in such great numbers that the trout became more selective than the most finicky gourmet.

To some extent, size is another element, although numbers can overcome the size of the species, as it does with the trico. Few of us ever pay attention to the *Caenis* hatches so prevalent on waters in midsummer. Few trout surface to feed on them, and besides, who wants to match a hatch with a #28 pattern? Most of us would much rather match a larger fly like the march brown or western green drake.

The length of time the dun rests on the surface after it emerges is another important criterion for the dry-fly fisherman. I've fished many a pale evening dun hatch (*Heptagenia* species) in midsummer without a single trout rising to them. Why? These mayflies tend to take off rapidly from the surface and don't give trout a chance to react to them. But weather changes can alter their departure and turn minor hatches into major ones. Foul weather can, in fact, suddenly change a mediocre hatch into a great one.

Al Caucci and Bob Nastasi in *Hatches II* also talk about gloomy-day hatches. Writing about *Pseudocloeon*, they say: "Primarily, the emergence [of *Pseudocloeon*] takes place a few hours before dark (7:00 P.M.), but on overcast days, when the water temperature remains low, hatching may start as early as 11:00 A.M. and continue sporadically throughout the day."

I have seen little blue-winged olive duns (*Baetis*), blue duns (*Pseudocloeon*), and many others emerge early and often on misty days. Let's look at a few memorable stories about these lousy days.

Ken Helfrich guided Mike Manfredo and me through some hazardous rapids on the McKenzie River near Eugene, Oregon. For the first half hour of the float we hardly fly fished at all. All three of us wore heavy coats under raincoats. It was the end of April, and the coastal areas of Oregon were predictably unpredictable. A heavy mist made the air feel much cooler than the 50 degrees that my thermometer registered. Around 2:00 P.M. we drifted into a shallow rapids at the head of a long, slow pool, and Ken guided us over to a slow section of the river. The wait was brief. Within minutes large, dark brown mayflies emerged all over the surface of that river. Many appeared stunned, unable to take flight. Rainbows soon took advantage of the laggards, and more than fifty trout rose in the rapids above the pool in front of us. Mike and I fly fished for more than two hours that day over trout rising to a heavy western march brown hatch. What a memorable day!

A couple years ago on May 21, Bryan Meck, Vince Gigliotti, and I fly fished Elk Creek in central Pennsylvania. Our companions included a cool breeze and a fine, annoying mist that lasted most of the day. That day Bryan landed two trout more than 17 inches long, and he didn't stop there. More than twenty trout took his #16 Sulphur. Sulphur duns appeared all day long under the cloudy skies, and the trout fed on them as long as they lasted. Vince, fishing nearby, experienced similarly spectacular action.

You've already read about the day Jay Kapolka and I experienced on the Metolius River in the Oregon Cascades one May 29. By 2:00 P.M. the air temperature hovered near 50 degrees, and a drizzle fell all afternoon. Four separate, heavy hatches appeared on the surface that afternoon, and a handful of mayflies took flight. Trout fed for three hours on the dazed duns. First they took the pale morning dun, then the western green drake, then the blue-winged olive dun. They never did rise to the fourth hatch, the little blue-winged olive dun. Where just five days before only a handful of trout rose to a sporadic hatch of western green drakes, now dozens had easy pickings at the thousands of duns unable to escape the surface.

In my recent book, *Pennsylvania Trout Streams and Their Hatches*, I described a memorable day with blue-winged olive duns on Penns Creek. That spectacular hatch on that chilly, drizzly day wasn't an illusion. Two miles upstream from me on Penns Creek that Fourth of July afternoon, Andrew Leitzinger of Collegeville, Pennsylvania, also experienced the same hatch. On an early July day, when the temperature never rose above 60 degrees, the two of us experienced one of the greatest fly-fishing days in our many years of fishing the hatches.

A mid-September morning a few years ago found me on the North Branch of the Au Sable River near Grayling, Michigan, even though Rusty Gates told me that I was too late to meet a sizable trico hatch. I came to the river just after 9:00 A.M. and was greeted by a bone-numbing 39 degrees. Not for an hour did I begin to see a few trico duns on the surface. With temperatures so chilly, the duns rode the surface from 50 to 100 feet before taking flight. Trout rose only now and then to the duns, evidently waiting for the trico spinner fall. The tiny spinners waited until almost noon to fall back onto the water, and the eager trout fed on the spent food for more than two hours.

A similar incident occurred, this time in early October, on the Little Juniata River in central Pennsylvania. Mike Camera of Amherst, Ohio, accompanied me on a cold Saturday afternoon. Hatches on the river start in April with little blue-winged olive duns and the green caddis and continue through late October, when slate drakes, little blue-winged olive duns, and blue duns appear before the onset of winter. As Mike and I approached the water, we saw thousands of duns riding the surface. Trout gorged themselves on these stunned insects, taking two or three with every rise. The duns were emerging from still-warm 55-degree water into air that never rose above 48 degrees. Mike took more than twenty fine trout in the chill of that October afternoon.

You've just read six examples of fantastic fly fishing for trout. All those spectacular, memorable trips occurred on days when you would ordinarily expect nothing. Moreover, those fishing trips covered the entire season: one happened in late April, two in May, another in July, one in September, and one in October. You've also noticed that these productive trips occurred in (more or less) different areas of the country. Each day of fishing over a hatch on an overcast day produced a memorable event, and each one resulted in a generous number of trout caught during a hatch. What threads do these six adventures have in common? How can you enjoy the same type of memorable trout fishing adventure?

The fishing trips on inclement days to streams in the East, Midwest, and West that turned into memorable trips did, in fact, have several common elements that made them all productive. Let's closely examine these common threads.

1) *All the memorable trips occurred during a hatch.* In April on the McKenzie River I fly fished during the western march brown hatch; on Elk Creek during a sulphur hatch; on Penns Creek when blue-winged olive duns rested on the surface; on the North Branch of the Au Sable River during a trico hatch; on the Metolius in Oregon when the little blue-winged olive dun, blue-winged olive dun, pale morning dun, and western green drake emerged; and on the Little Juniata River while the slate drake and blue dun appeared. Chapter 3 includes a list of

mayflies, caddisflies, and stoneflies that tend to produce memorable events. These may not be the heaviest hatches you'll encounter, but many of them produce unforgettable fishing trips.

I recently interviewed two experienced fly-fishing guides on the McKenzie River near Eugene, Oregon. I asked Ken Helfrich and Bob Houghton to tell me about their best trips on the river. The two combine more than thirty years of drifting anglers over hatches in their McKenzie boats, and three elements appeared in their most memorable experiences: a great hatch, a miserable day, and rising trout. (Bob Houghton does remember a couple spectacular days when the weather was reasonably warm and clear.)

Roy Palm of Frying Pan Anglers in Basalt, Colorado, likes those dreary days. "You have the river to yourself on those days. Nobody believes how great the fishing can be when a hatch appears on the surface."

In *Meeting and Fishing the Hatches*, I rated hatches according to the length of time they spend on the surface before taking flight. I also suggested that the takeoff time tends to vary with the weather. It's an important element.

2) *You'll often experience a spectacular fly-fishing event on an unusually cold day.* Most hatches appear on the surface, rest there for a split second, then take flight for a nearby bush or tree. But cold air greeting mayflies, stoneflies, and caddisflies slows their takeoff. When water temperatures drop below 45 degrees, you'll find few insects taking flight, and air temperatures below 50 degrees slow down the takeoff. The more the temperature falls below that point, the longer it takes for the insect to take flight.

3) *The water temperature should be above 50 degrees.* Terrific hatches often occur between 50 and 60 degrees. If the water temperature is much below 50 degrees, you'll find fewer and fewer insects appearing.

4) *On all these memorable occasions the day was overcast.* I'm convinced that trout come to the surface to feed much more readily on cloudy days than on sunny days. In each of these paradigm events I fly fished under overcast skies. Bright, sunlit skies keep trout deep during the day. Bring on a full-fledged major hatch under cloudy skies, and you're almost certain to see a lot of rising trout.

5) *During four of the six trips a light rain fell.* On the Metolius River, McKenzie River, Penns Creek, and Elk Creek a light drizzle fell during much of the fly-fishing trip. Drizzle joined with the cold air to help slow the insects' liftoff. Even mayflies like the slate drake, which normally take off rapidly, escape in slow motion on cold, damp days.

6) *On all of these occasions I happened to be on productive water.*
What would have happened had I fished a marginal stream or river
rather than the class-A waters I visited during these six memorable
trips? If the water contains few hatches, you'll see few rising trout no
matter how ideal the conditions may be. The Au Sable, McKenzie,
Little Juniata, and Metolius rivers all have one thing in common: great
hatches in good quantities. Elk Creek and Penns Creek also boast a
good number of aquatic insects.

7) *The water level had not noticeably risen.* What a great trip I once
had to the Bitterroot River near Missoula, Montana – great, but not
productive. I arrived just in time for a sporadic hatch of western green
drakes. These huge mayflies began fluttering on the surface a couple
hours before noon. Ten of them struggled to take off in front of me. A
single 15-inch rainbow fed on the duns. Where were the other fish in
this productive river? A snowmelt in early July had produced high,
rolling water on the Bitterroot, keeping most of the trout from rising to
the few stragglers on the surface.

You say you've never enjoyed one of those forty-plus-fish fly-
fishing days? Have you thought seriously of planning your trips to
coincide with cold weather and drizzly, overcast days? Probably not.
Have you planned your trips for those streams or rivers where you can
count on a good hatch? You probably have. Now think about planning
a trip when these two elements occur together. It may very well be a
memorable one.

8

Patterns for the Hatches

"By far the most innovative fly tyers in the United States are those found in the West." So says John Randolph, editor of *Fly Fisherman* magazine. Why have western fly tyers far outdistanced many of their counterparts in the East and Midwest? Some of the newer patterns—like Crystal Compara-duns, trailing shucks on caddis, Larva Lace, and dozens of recent creations—have come from western anglers. Why? I feel these anglers aren't under the restraint of years of tradition that anglers in the East and Midwest find themselves. Do these innovative patterns really work? Look at my experiences.

Recently on the Kootenai River near Libby, Montana, an explosive hatch of pale morning duns (PMD) appeared. I first cast a conventionally tied pale olive yellow over a pod of three risers without any success. By "conventionally tied" I refer to a typical pattern with a tail of cream hackle fibers, body of dubbed poly, pale gray hen hackle for wings, and two cream hackles for the legs. The size of the pattern was correct, but not the color. I quickly tore off the olive-body PMD for an orange-tinted one. This proved to be a little more successful, but still many of the trout refused the pattern. In desperation I turned to a pattern tied by Nick Nicklas and created by Craig Mathews of Blue Ribbon Flies in West Yellowstone, Montana. It was a Pale Morning

A Sulphur Crystal Compara-dun. *Charles Meck.*

Compara-dun with a twist: it had as part of the tail a brown piece of brown Z-lon, which imitated the trailing shuck of the emerger. It's called a Crystal Compara-dun. Almost from the instant I tried that pattern trout struck it freely. In fact, it became so commonplace for rising trout to take the pattern that Dave Blackburn, our guide, would count, "one, two, three, strike," and I'd invariably have a trout on the end of the line. So many trout took the compara-dun with a trailing shuck that I quit and gave the rod to Dave.

What a great pattern! Here's one that copies an emerger right on the surface in full view of the angler. But the pattern doesn't seem to work too well for those mayflies that are quick emergers. Robert Budd of Altoona, Pennsylvania, has used the pattern when the white mayfly *(Ephoron leukon)* appears on the Little Juniata River in central Pennsylvania. He had no more success with this pattern than with a conventional one. Both Bob and I have had much more success with a tan-bodied down-wing emerger fished during the white mayfly hatch. The white mayfly emerges rapidly – so rapidly that you'll often see trout chasing the nymph on its rise toward the surface and directly into the air above the surface after the adult has emerged.

Patterns with trailing shucks do work, but a lot of their success depends on the emergence type of the species you're copying. You'll often see many crippled pale morning dun *(Ephemerella inermis)* emergers. The same goes for the closely related eastern and midwestern mayfly, the sulphur *(Ephemerella rotunda)*. A pattern with a trailing shuck works well for both. The trailing shuck pattern should work well with just about all ephemerellids.

In Figures 3 to 5 you'll see emerger stages for mayflies and caddisflies. Let's look at mayflies first. For years writers have referred to emergers as if all were similar. They aren't, and fly fishermen have been confused as to exactly what is an emerger. Look at the quill gordon, *Epeorus pleuralis* (Figure 3). Duns break out of their nymphal shuck on the bottom of streams and rivers. The dun then moves to the surface. You'll see that type of emerger classed as Stage 3. All *Epeorus* species emerge in this manner. For the quill gordon and other closely related species you would use a wet fly to imitate all but the nymphal stage on the bottom and the dun on the surface. In other words, species like the quill gordon would go from Stage 1 to Stage 3 to Stage 5 on the surface, skipping Stages 2 and 4.

A Sulphur parachute with a trailing shuck. *Charles Meck.*

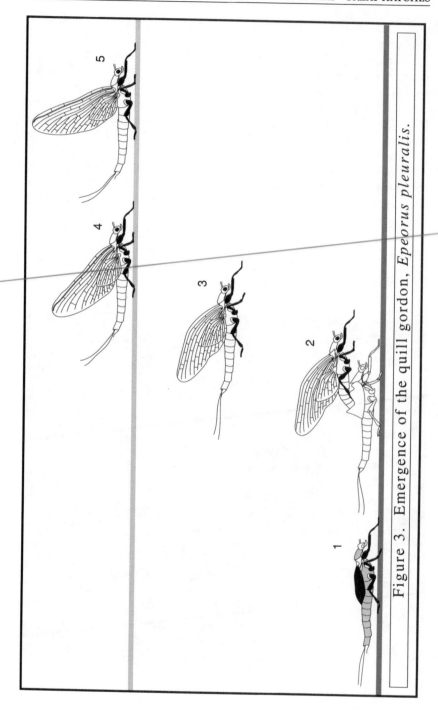

Figure 3. Emergence of the quill gordon, *Epeorus pleuralis*.

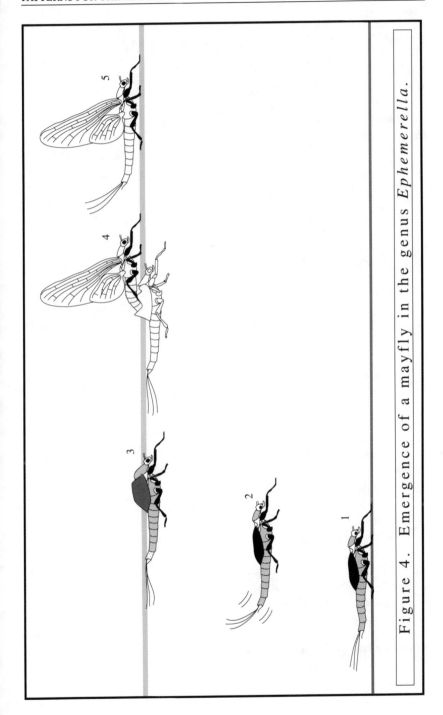

Figure 4. Emergence of a mayfly in the genus *Ephemerella*.

Look at other mayflies as examples (Figure 4). The nymph moves toward the surface (Stage 2), then breaks its nymphal skin dorsally (Stage 3). The dun appears gradually from the nymphal case (Stage 4). Finally the dun appears on the surface – some of these still have the nymphal shuck attached (Stage 4). The emerged mayfly dun now rests on the surface (Stage 5). This emerging activity for Stages 3 and 4 for most species (other than *Epeorus*) occurs near the surface, most often in the surface film.

Look at the tying descriptions for the Sulphur as an example.

Stage 1 Emerger (nymph)

Thread: grayish brown
Tail: brown pheasant tail fibers (short)
Body: brown (ground color) fur
Wings: dark gray mallard quill section, tied down over thorax
Hackle: cree hackle
Hook: 3906B, #14 or #16

Stage 2 Emerger

Thread: grayish brown
Tail: brown pheasant tail fibers (short)
Body: brown (ground color) fur
Wings: pale gray poly or other material (like Z-lon) tied in a
    small loop; or you can tie a short post of pale gray deer hair
    and tie hackle around it.
Hackle: cree hackle
Hook: 94840, #14 or #16

Stage 3 Emerger

Thread: grayish brown
Tail: brown pheasant tail fibers (short)
Body: brown (ground color) fur; front top dub a small section
    of yellowish orange poly.
Wings: pale gray loop (larger than Stage 2); or deer hair, dyed
    pale, longer than Stage 2
Hackle: cree hackle
Hook: 94840, #14 or #16

Stage 4 Emerger (trailing shuck)

Thread: yellow

A Sulphur emerger with a trailing shuck. *Charles Meck.*

Tail: cream hackle fibers; place a piece of dark brown Z-lon the length of the shank of the hook over top of the tail extending as far as the tail
Body: usually pale yellow poly with an orange (and sometimes olive orange) cast
Wings: pale gray hackle tips
Hackle: cream hackle
Hook: 94840, #14 and #16

Stage 5 Emerger (dun)

Thread: yellow
Tail: cream hackle fibers
Body: usually pale yellow poly with an orange (and sometimes olive orange) cast
Wings: pale gray hackle tips
Hackle: cream hackle
Hook: 94840, #14 and #16

Rather than use the conventional tie that we suggest above, you can tie Stages 4 and 5 as compara-duns or with a parachute-style tie. The longer I fly fish, the more I recognize the need for the body of patterns to lie flat and prone on the surface. With a conventionally tied fly with the hackle at the front, the body of the pattern often doesn't touch the surface. The same pattern tied as a compara-dun or parachute allows the body to lie flat on the surface. Try tying Stages 3 through 5 as compara-duns or parachutes. I prefer tying parachutes over compara-duns because I feel these flies hold up better.

Look at the five stages tied parachute.

Stage 1 Emerger (nymph)

Thread: grayish brown
Tail: brown pheasant tail fibers (short)
Body: brown (ground color) fur
Wings: dark gray mallard quill section, tied down over thorax
Hackle: cree hackle
Hook: 3906B, #14 or #16

Stage 2 Emerger

Thread: grayish brown
Tail: brown pheasant tail fibers (short)
Body: brown (ground color) fur
Wings: pale gray deer hair or caribou tied as a very short post
Hackle: cree or brown hackle wound around the post
Hook: 94840, #14 or #16

Stage 3 Emerger

Thread: grayish brown
Tail: brown pheasant tail fibers (short)
Body: brown (ground color) fur; make three or four turns of
    orange poly dubbed onto tying thread around the post
Wings: pale gray deer hair or caribou tied as a post (longer than
    Stage 2)
Hackle: cree hackle or brown hackle wound around the post
Hook: 94840, #14 or #16

Stage 4 Emerger (trailing shuck)

Thread: yellow
Tail: cream hackle fibers; place a piece of dark brown Z-lon the

length of the shank of the hook over top of the tail extending as far as the tail

Body: usually orange poly, dubbed (and sometimes olive orange)

Wings: pale gray deer hair or caribou tied in as a post and longer than Stage 3

Hackle: cream hackle

Hook: 94840, #14 and #16

Stage 5 Emerger (dun)

Thread: yellow

Tail: cream hackle fibers

Body: orange poly, dubbed

Wings: pale gray deer hair or caribou, tied in as a post and as wing in Stage 4

Hackle: cream hackle

Hook: 94840, #14 and #16

The secret to tying Stage 3 is to dub some orange poly and wind it around the deer or caribou post before you wind the hackle parachute style. Make three or four winds of the dubbed orange poly around the base of the hair wing to suggest the color of the dun emerging from the nymphal shuck. Then wind some of the orange poly around the head and come back to the wing. Tie in a hackle or two and wind them around the base.

Caddisflies have a complete life cycle because their development includes a pupal stage. Some species, like those in the genus *Rhyacophila*, have no case for protection of the larvae. Others, like *Brachycentrus*, encase themselves in small pieces of plant material. Still other caddisflies build cases of stones, pine needles, or other material. Caddisflies go into a resting, or pupal, stage before they emerge on the surface as adults. When they're ready to emerge, the pupa moves toward the surface and appears on the surface as an adult. The larval, pupal, and adult life stages of a caddisfly are important to copy.

Look at the emergence of the typical caddisfly (Figure 5). The pupa rides toward the surface within its external pupal skin (Stage 2). At the surface the pupa emerges out of the case and the shuck trails behind it (Stage 4). The adult rests on the surface only for a split second (Stage 5) before it escapes. Try tying some of your caddis patterns with the trailing shuck. This pattern works well during a hatch of these downwings.

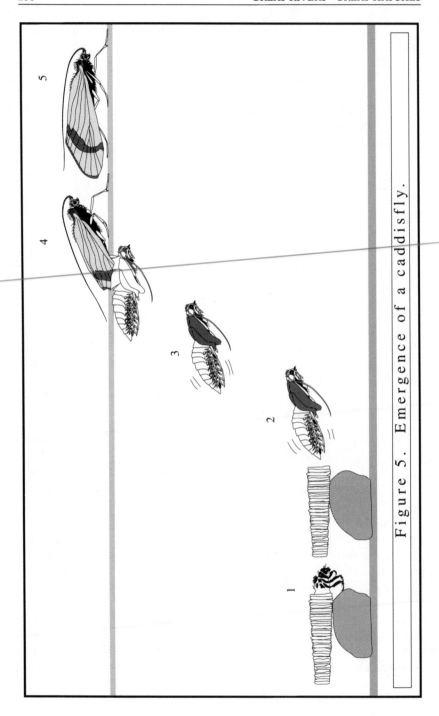

Figure 5. Emergence of a caddisfly.

Green Caddis, TS (trailing shuck)

Tail: a light tan piece of Z-lon about as long as the body
Body: green poly, dubbed
Wings: elk hair
Hackle: ginger (optional)
Hook: 94840, #14 or #16

Also try tying trailing shucks when you're copying chironomids. If you look closely at an emerging midge, you'll often see the shuck trailing behind the adult on the surface. Examine the shuck carefully and you'll see it is ribbed. Take a piece of white Z-lon and with a permanent marker with a fine tip make a ribbing effect. Tie the shuck on where the tail would normally be.

Dark Gray Midge, TS (trailing shuck)

Tail: white Z-lon marked with a fine black marking pen (mark stripes about every $1/32$ inch)
Body: herl from peacock eye, stripped
Hackle: grizzly
Hook: 94840, #24

A caddis with a trailing shuck works well during caddis hatches. *Charles Meck.*

FISHING THE CYCLE

Fred Templin and I headed for a night of fly fishing on the Little Juniata River. For more than five years I bragged to Fred about this intriguing white mayfly hatch. When we arrived, a dozen or more trout were already feeding on a good supply of winged ants that found their way onto the surface. Fred tied on a #22 ant while I stood back and watched. I looked forward to the white mayfly that might appear an hour or two later. I had already tied the two patterns onto my leader and didn't want to change them. Two patterns you say? Yes, I tied a #16 White Fly onto the 5X tippet. I then tied a 30-inch piece of ⁵X tippet onto the bend of the hook of the White Fly and secured it with an improved clinch knot. Onto this extension I tied a tan nymph to copy the emerging natural.

By 7:30 P.M. white mayflies appeared a foot above the riffle at the head of the pool. These adults moved upstream, then downstream, tantalizing every trout in that section of the pool. Several heavy trout came completely out of the water after emerging adults. I grew eager to try my new technique – which I call fishing the cycle because I had a nymph on the end and 30 inches above that I had an imitation of the adult. When I floated the tandem drag free, the dry fly acted as a strike indicator. When I dragged the dry fly in front of rising trout, they had a choice of striking the nymph or the dry fly. I cast the two patterns over a heavy trout that splashed at the white fly nymph or adult and dragged the pattern in front of the fish. Soon there was a violent splash at one of the patterns, and the fish was on. I soon landed and released the small trout from the nymph pattern. Nearby another trout chased an emerging nymph. I lifted the rod and the two patterns came in front of this second riser. It also took the nymph rather than the dry fly. A third rising trout took the dry fly. Action continued all night long, with trout eagerly taking one or the other of the two patterns I had attached.

Try this effective method for other hatches. Tie an imitation of the nymph on the end tippet and a dry fly imitation of the dun 30 inches above. I call these two flies attached the "bi-cycle." This way you'll catch trout whether they're taking the emerger or the dun. The tandem is tangle free and relatively easy to cast. In fact, most of the time you don't even realize you're casting two flies.

If the law allows it and you want to try three patterns at the same time, you can tie on a crippled emerger or emerger 18 inches behind the dry fly, then add a nymph pattern 18 inches behind the emerger. I call this the "tri-cycle." This gives feeding trout a real selection.

You can use the bi-cycle for caddisflies. Tie an emerging pupa on the end and an adult caddis on the tippet nearer your fly rod.

Why tie your own flies? If you want to match the hatches more accurately, then you definitely should tie your own flies. Try to buy that Pale Morning Dun in a pale olive, wine, or tannish orange that matches the hatch on the Kootenai River. Try matching the western green drake hatch on the Bitterroot River with a commercial pattern. On the Kootenai near Libby, Montana, you'll find a great pale morning dun hatch. However, it often appears in the evening, and it exhibits a light olive body rather than the more common yellowish one. On Henry's Fork the pale morning dun appears as an olive gray or maroon insect. Compare the western green drake on Henry's Fork with the one I found on the Fryingpan in Colorado or the one found on the Bitterroot in Montana. The specimens found on Henry's Fork are much lighter, with a greenish olive body. Those drakes found on the Bitterroot and Fryingpan rivers have a much darker olive body.

You'll find tying descriptions for the nymph, dun, and spinner below. From the description above you'll be able to tie those emergers that you find important on rivers you fish. In each case the hook numbers refer to Mustad hooks. Although you'll find hackle listed for spinner patterns, you might want to omit this material.

Patterns for Eastern and Midwestern Hatches
Order Ephemeroptera: mayflies

Blue Dun or Little Blue-Winged Olive Dun
Copies *Baetis tricaudatus* and some *Pseudocloeon* species

> Thread: dark gray
> Tail: medium to dark gray hackle fibers
> Body: gray muskrat or medium gray poly, dubbed; for the Little Blue-Winged Olive use olive gray poly
> Wings: on smaller sizes (#20) use dark gray mallard quills; on larger sizes use dark gray hackle tips
> Hackle: blue dun
> Hook: 94840, #18 and #20

Rusty Spinner
> Thread: dark brown
> Tail: dark grayish brown hackle fibers
> Body: grayish brown poly, dubbed and ribbed with fine tan thread

Wings: pale gray poly yarn, tied spent
Hook: 94840, #18 and #20

Nymph

Thread: dark olive
Tail: wood duck fibers, dyed dark olive
Body: dark olive brown opossum
Wings: dark gray mallard quill section
Hackle: cree or ginger-variant hackle, dyed dark olive
Hook: 3906B, #18

Speckle-Winged Dun

Copies species like *Callibaetis skokianis*

Thread: gray
Tail: tan
Body: medium to dark gray poly (with olive reflections)
Wings: dark gray mallard flank
Hackle: tan with a turn of grizzly
Hook: 94840, #14 and #16

Speckle-Winged Spinner

Thread: gray
Tail: blue dun
Body: slate gray poly
Wings: pale gray poly yarn, tied spent
Hook: 94840, #14 and #16

Blue Quill

Copies most *Paraleptophlebia* species

Thread: dark gray
Tail: medium to dark gray hackle fibers
Body: eyed peacock herl, stripped, or dark gray poly, dubbed
Wings: dark gray hackle tips
Hackle: light to medium blue dun
Hook: 94840, #18 or #20

Dark Brown Spinner

Thread: dark brown
Tail: dark brown hackle fibers
Body: dark brown poly, dubbed

Wings: pale gray poly yarn, tied spent
Hook: 94840, #18 or #20

Nymph

Thread: dark brown
Tail: mallard flank feather, dyed dark brown
Body: dark brown angora, dubbed
Wings: one dark gray mallard quill tied down
Hackle: dark gray
Hook: 3906B, #16 and #18

Quill Gordon
Copies species like *Epeorus pleuralis*

Thread: dark gray
Tail: dark gray hackle fibers
Body: eyed peacock herl, stripped and lacquered
Wings: wood duck or imitation wood duck, divided; or dark
   gray hackle tips
Hackle: dark gray hackle
Hook: 94840, #14

Red Quill Spinner
Use same pattern as spinner listed under Hendrickson

Nymph

Thread: dark brown
Tail: fibers from a mallard flank feather, dyed dark amber
Body: dark brown fur or angora, mixed with a bit of lighter
   brown or amber
Wings: mottled brown turkey, tied down over thorax
Hackle: cree or ginger-variant hackle (dark and amber mixed)
Hook: 3906B, #14

Red Quill and Hendrickson
Red Quill copies the male and the Hendrickson copies the female
   of *Ephemerella subvaria* and several closely related subspecies. In
   addition, the Red Quill effectively imitates many spinners like
   E. subvaria, Epeorus pleuralis, and the male spinner of *Ephemerella
   invaria* and *E. rotunda.*

Thread: brown

Tail: medium gray hackle fibers
Body (Red Quill): reddish brown hackle fiber stripped of its
   barbules and wound from the bend of the hook to the wings.
   (Hendrickson): tan poly, dubbed.
Wings: wood duck, divided. Optional on Hendrickson are gray
   hackle tips
Hackle: medium gray hackle
Hook: 94840, #14 and #16

Red Quill Spinner

Thread: brown
Tail: bronze dun hackle fibers
Body: dark tannish brown poly, dubbed and ribbed finely with
   tan thread.
Wings: pale gray poly yarn, tied spent
Hook: 94840, #14 and #16

Nymph

Thread: dark brown
Tail: fibers for a mallard flank feather, dyed dark brown
Body: dark angora, mixed with a bit of amber
Wings: dark brown turkey
Hackle: cree
Hook: 3906B, #14

Great Speckled Olive Dun

Copies mayflies like *Siphloplecton basale*

Thread: pale gray
Tail: medium blue dun fibers
Body: pale gray poly, dubbed
Wings: mallard flank
Hackle: medium blue dun
Hook: 94840, #12

Great Speckled Spinner

Thread: gray
Tail: bronze dun variant fibers
Body: pale gray poly, dubbed
Wings: pale tan poly yarn
Hackle: bronze dun variant
Hook: 94840, #12

Nymph

> Thread: gray
> Tail: blue dun hackle tips
> Body: light gray angora
> Wings: dark gray mallard quill section
> Hackle: gray partridge
> Hook: 3906B, #12

Black Quill

Copies *Leptophlebia cupida*

> Thread: dark brown
> Tail: dark bronze dun hackle fibers
> Body: eyed peacock herl, stripped
> Wings: dark gray hackle tips
> Hackle: dark brown hackle with a turn or two of tan hackle
>   in the rear
> Hook: 94840, #14

Early Brown Spinner

> Thread: dark brown
> Tail: dark brown hackle fibers
> Body: dark reddish brown poly ribbed with pale yellow thread
> Wings: pale tan poly
> Hackle: dark brown hackle
> Hook: 94840, #14

Nymph

> Thread: dark brown
> Tail: dark brown hackle fibers
> Body: chocolate brown angora, loosely dubbed
> Wings: dark mallard section
> Hackle: dark brown hackle
> Hook: 3906B, #12 or #14

Sulphur Dun

Copies *Ephemerella rotunda, E. invaria, E. septentrionalis,* and to a
lesser degree *E. dorothea*

> Thread: yellow
> Tail: cream hackle fibers
> Body: usually pale yellow poly with an orange (and sometimes
>   olive orange) cast

Wings: pale gray hackle tips
Hackle: cream hackle
Hook: 94840, #16 and #18

Sulphur Spinner

Thread: tan
Tail: tan deer hair
Body: female with eggs – yellowish tan poly; female without
eggs – tan poly; male – bright red hackle stem, stripped and
wound around hook
Wings: pale gray poly yarn, tied spent (also tie some upright)
Hook: 94840, #16 and #18

Nymph

Thread: grayish brown
Tail: brown pheasant tail fibers
Body: brown (ground color) fur
Wings: dark gray mallard quill section, tied down over thorax
Hackle: cree or brown partridge hackle
Hook: 3906B, #14, #16, and #18

Pale Evening Dun

Copies species like *Leucrocuta (Heptagenia) aphrodite* and *L. hebe*
Thread: yellow
Tail: creamish yellow hackle fibers
Body: creamish yellow poly with olive cast (*L. hebe* has no
olive cast)
Wings: pale gray mallard flank
Hackle: yellowish cream hackle
Hook: 94840, 3906, #14–18

Pale Evening Spinner

Thread: yellow
Tail: cream hackle fibers
Body: pale yellow poly
Wings: white poly tied spent
Hackle: pale yellow hackle
Hook: 94840, #14–18

Nymph

Thread: brown
Tail: tan fibers

Body: dark brown angora
Wings: dark mallard
Hackle: tan hackle
Hook: 3906B, #14–18

Light Cahill

Copies *Stenacron interpunctatum* subspecies

Thread: cream or tan
Tail: cream hackle fibers
Body: cream poly, fox fur, or angora, dubbed
Wings: mallard flank feather, dyed pale yellow, divided
Hackle: cream hackle
Hook: 94840, #14

Light Cahill Spinner

Same as dun except omit hackle and add pale yellow poly yarn for
wings. Tie them spent.

Nymph

Thread: brown
Tail: fibers from a mallard flank feather, dyed brown
Body: dark brown angora yarn on top and pale amber belly,
dubbed
Wings: dark brown turkey
Hackle: dark cree
Hook: 3906B, #12

Slate Drake

Copies many *Isonychia* species

Thread: black
Tail: dark gray hackle fibers
Body: peacock herl (not from eye), stripped; or dark gray poly,
or muskrat, dubbed
Wings: dark gray hackle tips
Hackle: one cream hackle tied in behind and one dark brown
hackle tied in front
Hook: 94840, #12 or #14

White-Gloved Howdy

Thread: dark brown or maroon
Tail: medium gray hackle fibers
Body: dark mahogany poly, dubbed

Wings: pale gray poly yarn
Hook: 94840, #12 or #14

Nymph

Thread: dark brown
Tail: three dark brown hackles with one side cut off
Body: very dark brown angora or opossum
Wings: dark gray mallard quill section, tied down over thorax
Hackle: cree hackle, dyed pale olive
Hook: 3906B, #12 or #14

Brown Drake

Copies mayflies like *Ephemera simulans*

Thread: brown
Tail: dark brown deer hair
Body: grayish tan poly
Wings: grayish tan flank feather
Hackle: dark brown hackle with a few turns of ginger
Hook: 94840, #10 or #12

Brown Drake Spinner

Thread: brown
Tail: same as dun
Body: dark tannish yellow poly, dark brown markings
Wings: pale tan poly yarn with dark brown fibers tied upright
    or spent
Hackle: Same as dun
Hook: 94840, #10 or #12

Nymph

Thread: brown
Tail: three light brown hackles, trimmed and tied in
Body: tan angora or opossum
Wings: brown turkey, tied down and over thorax
Hackle: dark cree
Hook: 3906B, #10 or #12

Pink Lady or Pink Cahill

Copies the female of *Epeorus vitreus*

Thread: cream
Tail: dark blue dun hackle fibers
Body: male – pale yellow; female – pinkish cream poly

Wings: pale yellow mallard flank
Hackle: creamish yellow hackle
Hook: 94840, #14

Salmon Spinner

Thread: salmon
Tail: cream ginger hackle fibers
Body: coral poly
Wings: pale gray poly
Hackle: cream ginger hackle
Hook: 94840, #14

Nymph

Thread: tan
Tail: dark brown fibers from a pheasant tail
Body: dub amber on the entire shank, tie in a dark brown yarn
  at the bend of the hook and bring up and over and tie in at
  where you tie in the wings
Wings: brown turkey section
Hackle: several turns of a ginger hackle
Hook: 3906B, #14

Blue-Winged Olive Dun

Copies many *Drunella (Ephemerella)* species and *Dannella* like
  D. cornuta, D. longicornus, and *D. lata*

Thread: olive
Tail: grayish olive hackle fibers
Body: light to medium olive poly, dubbed
Wings: dark gray hackle tips
Hackle: medium creamish olive
Hook: 94840, #14 to #20

Dark Olive Spinner

Thread: dark olive or black
Tail: moose mane (dark brown)
Body: dark olive poly (almost black with an olive cast)
Wings: pale gray poly yarn, tied spent
Hook: 94840, #14 to #20

Nymph

Thread: olive
Tail: wood duck

Body: dark brown angora tied over dubbed-in olive opossum
Wings: brown turkey
Hackle: ginger variant, dyed olive
Hook: 3906B, #14 to #18

Green Drake

Copies *Ephemera guttulata*

Thread: cream
Tail: moose mane
Body: cream poly, dubbed
Wings: mallard flank dyed yellowish green, divided
Hackle: rear – cream hackle; front – dark brown hackle
Hook: 94831, #8 and #10

Coffin Fly

Thread: white
Tail: light tan deer hair
Body: white poly, dubbed
Wings: grayish yellow poly yarn, tied spent
Hook: 94831, #8 and #10

Nymph

Thread: tan
Tail: three medium brown hackles, trimmed and tied in
Body: pale tan angora
Wings: dark brown turkey, tied down and over thorax
Hackle: cree
Hook: 3906B or 9672, #8 to #12

March Brown

Copies *Stenonema vicarium*

Thread: yellow
Tail: dark brown hackle fibers
Body: tan poly, dubbed and ribbed with dark brown thread
Wings: mallard flank feather, dyed yellowish brown and
divided
Hackle: one cream and one dark brown, mixed
Hook: 94840, #12

Great Red Spinner

Thread: dark brown
Tail: dark brown hackle fibers

Body: dark reddish brown poly, dubbed
Wings: pale gray poly yarn, tied spent
Hackle: dark brown with a turn or two of pale ginger mixed
Hook: 94840, #12

Nymph

Thread: brown
Tail: fibers from a mallard flank feather, dyed brown
Body: cream poly, dubbed
Wings: dark brown turkey, tied down over thorax
Hackle: dark cree
Hook: 3906B, #12

Gray Fox

Copies *Stenonema fuscum*

Thread: cream
Tail: tan deer hair
Body: cream poly, dubbed
Wings: mallard flank feather, dyed pale yellowish tan, divided
Hackle: cree hackle or one brown and one cream mixed
Hook: 94840, #12 or #14

Ginger Quill Spinner

Thread: brown
Tail: dark brown hackle fibers
Body: eyed peacock herl, dyed tan and stripped, or grayish
   brown poly, ribbed with brown thread
Wings: gray hackle tips (conventional); or pale gray poly yarn,
   tied spent
Hackle: dark ginger (conventional); or none with poly yarn
   wings
Hook: 94840, #12 or #14

Nymph

Thread: brown
Tail: fibers from a mallard flank feather, dyed brown
Body: brown angora yarn, tied on top over cream. Tie in brown
   at tail and dub in cream so that top *(tergites)* of body is brown
   and the belly *(sternites)* is cream
Wings: dark brown turkey, tied down over thorax
Hackle: dark cree
Hook: 3906B, #12

Chocolate Dun

Copies species like *Eurylophella bicolor* and *Ephemerella needhami*

Thread: brown
Tail: medium gray
Body: chocolate brown poly finely ribbed with lighter brown thread
Wings: dark gray hackle tips
Hackle: tan hackle
Hook: 94840, #16

Chocolate Spinner

Thread: dark brown
Tail: tannish gray hackle fibers
Body: dark rusty brown poly, dubbed
Wings: pale gray poly yarn, tied spent
Hook: 94840, #16

Nymph

Thread: brown
Tail: light brown mallard flank feather fibers
Body: light brown poly nymph dubbing
Wings: dark gray mallard quill
Hackle: brown hackle
Hook: 3906B, #16

Dark Green Drake

Copies small-stream species like *Litobrancha recurvata*

Thread: dark gray
Tail: dark brown moose mane
Body: very dark slate poly, dubbed and ribbed with yellow thread
Wings: mallard flank, heavily barred and dyed dark green
Hackle: rear – tannish brown hackle; front – dark brown hackle
Hook: 94831, #8 or #10

Brown Drake Spinner

Thread: brown
Tail: brown hackle fibers
Body: reddish brown poly, dubbed and ribbed with yellow thread
Wings: pale gray poly yarn, tied spent

Hackle: dark brown
Hook: 94831, #8

Nymph

Thread: light brown
Tail: three dark bronze hackles, trimmed and tied in
Body: tan with a grayish cast angora, or opossum
Wings: dark brown turkey
Hackle: dark cree
Hook: 9672, #8 or #10

Cream Cahill

Copies species like *Stenonema pulchellum*

Thread: cream
Tail: tan hackle fibers
Body: white or pale cream polypropylene
Wings: very pale cream mallard flank feather
Hackle: cream hackle
Hook: 94840, #14 or #16

Cream Cahill Spinner

Tail: pale tan hackle fibers
Body: white poly, pale cream body
Wings: use dun imitation and substitute pale gray poly yarn for
the wings
Hackle: pale cream hackle
Hook: 94840, #14 or #16

Nymph

Thread: olive brown
Tail: light brown hackle fibers
Body: dub pale creamish gray on hook, then tie pale brownish
olive yarn in at bend and bring over top to wing case and tie
in
Wings: dark brown turkey
Hackle: dark olive brown
Hook: 3906B, #14 or #16

Light Cahill

Copies species like *Heptagenia marginalis*

Thread: cream
Tail: dark brown hackle fibers

Body: yellowish cream poly
Wings: yellow mallard flank
Hackle: one cream and one blue dun hackle
Hook: 94840, #12

Olive Cahill Spinner

Thread: cream
Tail: dark brown hackle fibers
Body: fox belly fur dubbed
Wings: pale gray hackle tips or cream poly yarn tied spent
Hackle: front – dark brown hackle; rear – cream hackle
Hook: 94840, #12

Nymph

Thread: brown
Tail: tan mallard flank fibers
Body: light brown angora
Wings: brown mottled turkey
Hackle: tan hackle
Hook: 3906B, #12

Dark Slatewinged Olive

Copies *Dannella (Ephemerella) simplex*

Thread: brown
Tail: brown hackle fibers
Body: dark brown fur
Wings: blue dun hackle tips
Hackle: ginger
Hook: 94840, #16 or #18

Spinner

Thread: brown
Tail: light brown hackle fibers
Body: light brown poly
Wings: pale gray poly tied spent
Hackle: light ginger
Hook: 94840, #16 or #18

Nymph

Thread: brown
Tail: blue dun hackle fibers
Body: brown rabbit

Wings: brown turkey
Hackle: dark brown
Hook: 3906B, #16 or #18

Michigan Caddis
Copies *Hexagenia limbata*

Thread: brown
Tail: brown hackle fibers
Body: yellowish brown poly
Wings: teal flank feather, dyed smoky gray and with an olive
  cast
Hackle: cream ginger hackle with a couple turns of brown
Hook: 94831, #6

Michigan or Hex Spinner

Thread: brown
Tail: cream ginger hackle fibers
Body: brownish yellow poly
Wings: mallard flank feather (front area)
Hackle: one dark brown and two cream ginger hackles
Hook: 94831, #6

Nymph

Thread: brown
Tail: gray hackle fibers
Body: pale tan angora, dubbed
Wings: dark gray goose quill section
Hackle: sandy dun hackle
Hook: 3906B, #6

Yellow Drake
Copies species like *Ephemera varia*

Thread: pale yellow
Tail: pale deer hair
Body: pale yellow poly (primrose)
Wings: pale yellow mallard flank
Hackle: creamish yellow with a turn of grizzly in front
Hook: 94840, #10 or #12

Yellow Drake Spinner

Thread: pale yellow
Tail: dark deer hair

Body: pale creamish yellow poly
Wings: mallard flank or pale poly, tied spent
Hackle: Dun variant
Hook: 94840, #10 or #12

Nymph

Thread: tan
Tail: pale gray, trimmed
Body: amber colored angora or opossum
Wings: medium to light brown turkey
Hackle: ginger
Hook: 3906B, #10 or #12

Big Slate Drake

Copies large mayflies like *Hexagenia atrocaudata*

Thread: dark gray
Tail: dark gray hackle fibers
Body: peacock, stripped (take from bottom of herl)
Wings: dark gray calf tail
Hackle: dark brown hackle
Hook: 94831, #8

Dark Rusty Spinner

Tail: dark brown hackle fibers
Body: tannish yellow poly ribbed with dark brown thread
Wings: brown mallard flank feathers or tan poly
Hackle: one dark brown hackle in front and a tannish yellow
    one in the rear
Hook: 94840, #6

Nymph

Thread: amber
Tail: olive brown hackle fibers
Body: tan angora, dubbed
Wings: dark mallard quill
Hackle: grouse
Hook: 3906B, #6

Trico

Copies all *Tricorythodes* species

Thread: pale olive
Tail: cream hackle fibers

Body: pale olive green poly, dubbed; male dun – dark brown
poly
Wings: pale gray hackle tips
Hackle: cream hackle
Hook: 94840, #20–24

Trico Spinner

Thread: dark brown
Tail: female – short cream hackle fibers; male – long dark brown
moose mane
Body: female – rear one-third is cream poly, dubbed, and front
two-thirds is dark brown poly, dubbed; male – dark brown
poly, dubbed and ribbed with a very fine light tan thread
Wings: white poly yarn, tied spent
Hook: 94840, #20–24

Nymph

Thread: black
Tail: dark brown hackle fibers
Body: dark brownish black fur
Wings: dark gray mallard quill section
Hackle: dark reddish brown
Hook: 3906B, #18–24

White Fly or White Mayfly

Copies mayflies like *Ephoron leukon* and *E. album*

Thread: white or cream
Tail: pale blue dun hackle fibers
Body: pale cream or white poly
Wings: pale gray hackle tips or pale gray poly, upright
Hackle: white hackle with a turn of dark brown in front
Hook: 94840, #14 and #16

Spinner (male only)

Tail: pale gray
Body: white (rear two brown)
Wings: clear
Hackle: front – dark brown; rear – white
Hook: 94840, #14 and #16

Nymph

Thread: tan

Tail: brown hackle fibers
Body: pale tan
Wings: mottled brown turkey
Hackle: ginger hackle
Hook: 3906B, #12

Patterns for Western Hatches
Order Ephemeroptera: mayflies

Western March Brown
Copies *Rhithrogena morrisoni* and *R. hageni*

Thread: brown
Tail: medium brown
Body: medium brown poly, dubbed
Wings: medium gray hackle wings
Hackle: dark brown hackle
Hook: 94840, #14

Dark Tan Spinner
Thread: tan
Tail: dark brown hackle fibers
Body: dark brown poly, dubbed
Wings: pale gray poly yarn
Hook: 94840, #14

Nymph
Thread: dark brown
Tail: imitation wood duck fibers
Body: dark brown rabbit fur with brown hackle rib, clipped at
   bottom
Wings: dark brown turkey
Hackle: very dark cree hackle
Hook: 3906B, #14

Blue Quill
Copies *Paraleptophlebia* species including *P. debilis, P. heteronea,
P. memorialis, P. gregalis,* and *P. bicornuta*

Thread: dark gray
Tail: medium gray hackle fibers
Body: eyed peacock herl, stripped
Wings: dark gray hackle tips
Hackle: medium gray or dun
Hook: 94840, #18

Dark Brown Spinner

Thread: dark brown
Tail: dark brown hackle fibers
Body: dark brown poly, dubbed
Wings: pale gray poly yarn, tied spent
Hook: 94840, #18

Nymph

Thread: dark brown
Tail: mallard flank feather, dyed dark brown
Body: dark brown angora, dubbed
Wings: one dark gray mallard quill
Hackle: dark gray
Hook: 3906B, #16 and #18

Blue Dun or Little Blue-Winged Olive Dun

Copies *Baetis bicaudatus, B. tricaudatus, B. intermedius,* and others
and some *Pseudocloeon* species

Thread: dark gray
Tail: medium to dark gray hackle fibers
Body: gray muskrat or medium gray poly with a slight olive
cast, dubbed (the body of *Baetis bicaudatus* is more olive than
the others)
Wings: on smaller sizes (#20) use dark gray mallard quills; on
larger sizes use dark gray hackle tips
Hackle: blue dun
Hook: 94840, #18 and #20

Rusty Spinner

Thread: dark brown
Tail: dark grayish brown hackle fibers
Body: grayish brown poly, dubbed and ribbed with fine tan
thread
Wings: pale gray poly yarn, tied spent
Hook: 94840, #18 and #20

Nymph

Thread: dark olive
Tail: wood duck fibers, dyed dark olive
Body: dark olive brown opossum
Wings: dark gray mallard quill section

Hackle: cree hackle, dyed dark olive
Hook: 3906B, #18

Dark Red Quill

Copies *Cinygmula ramaleyi*

Thread: brown
Tail: medium dun hackle fibers
Body: dark reddish brown hackle stem, stripped
Wings: dark mallard quills, dark gray calf tail, or hackle tips
Hackle: bronze dun hackle
Hook: 94840, #16 or #18

Red Quill Spinner

Thread: brown
Tail: pale dun hackle fibers
Body: reddish brown hackle stem
Wings: very pale tan poly tied spent
Hackle: brown hackle
Hook: 94840, #16 or #18

Nymph

Thread: dark brown
Tail: mallard flank, dyed amber
Body: dark grayish brown furry foam over top of amber angora
Wings: dark mallard quill
Hackle: dark grouse or partridge hackle
Hook: 3906B, #16

Quill Gordon

Copies *Epeorus longimanus*

Thread: gray
Tail: medium dun hackle
Body: pale to medium gray poly or muskrat fur dubbed
Wings: dark mallard quills, dark gray calf tail, or dark gray
   hackle tips
Hackle: pale tannish gray hackle
Hook: 94840, #12 or #14

Red Quill Spinner

Thread: tan
Tail: moose mane
Body: pale yellowish brown poly

Wings: pale tan poly
Hackle: ginger hackle with a turn of brown
Hook: 94840, #12 or #14

Nymph

Thread: dark brown
Tail: mallard flank dyed amber
Body: dark brown furry foam over top
Wings: dark mallard quill
Hackle: dark grouse or partridge
Hook: 3906B, #14

Red Quill

Copies *Serratella (Ephemerella) tibialis*

Thread: brown
Tail: pale gray hackle fibers
Body: dark reddish brown poly
Wings: pale gray hackle tips
Hackle: creamish yellow hackle
Hook: 94840, #16 or #18

White-Gloved Howdy

Thread: dark brown
Tail: gray hackle fibers
Body: dark purplish brown poly
Wings: pale gray poly
Hackle: pale yellow hackle
Hook: 94840, #16 or #18

Dark Brown Dun

Copies *Baetis hageni (parvus)*

Thread: dark brown
Tail: ginger cream hackle fibers
Body: dark brown poly
Wings: gray mallard quills
Hackle: ginger cream hackle
Hook: 94840, #20

Dark Brown Spinner

Thread: brown
Tail: pale dun hackle fibers
Body: dark brown poly

Wings: pale gray poly
Hackle: ginger cream hackle
Hook: 94840, #20

Nymph

Thread: dark olive
Tail: dark olive mallard flank
Body: dark olive angora
Wings: dark mallard quill
Hackle: dark olive fibers
Hook: 3906B, #20

Hexagenia limbata
(See tying description under Eastern and Midwestern section)

Speckle-Winged Dun

Callibaetis coloradensis and *C. nigritus* (both are now considered
C. americanus)

Thread: tan
Tail: cream ginger hackle fibers
Body: grayish tan poly
Wings: dark gray mallard flank
Hackle: pale bronze dun hackle
Hook: 94840, #14 and #16

Speckle-Winged Spinner

Thread: gray
Tail: cream ginger hackle fibers
Body: pale gray poly
Wings: mallard flank feather
Hackle: pale bronze dun hackle
Hook: 94840, #14 and #16

Nymph

Thread: brown
Tail: pheasant tail fibers
Body: medium brown angora, loosely dubbed
Wings: dark mallard quill section
Hackle: dark brown grouse or partridge
Hook: 3906B, #14

Blue-Winged Olive Dun
Copies *Drunella (Ephemerella) flavilinea*

Thread: olive
Tail: dark brown moose mane
Body: olive green (dark on many) poly
Wings: dark gray mallard quills or dark gray hackle tips
Hackle: dark olive brown hackle
Hook: 94840, #14

Dark Olive Spinner

Thread: brown
Tail: dark olive hackle fibers
Body: dark olive brown poly
Wings: pale gray poly
Hackle: dark olive hackle
Hook: 94840, #14

Nymph

Thread: dark brown
Tail: mallard flank, dyed brown
Body: dubbed cream angora, dark brown furry foam on top
Wings: dark mottled turkey
Hackle: grouse or partridge
Hook: 3906B, #14

Western Green Drake
Drunella (Ephemerella) grandis

Thread: dark olive
Tail: moose mane
Body: olive black poly, ribbed with pale yellow thread
Wings: impala, dyed dark gray, or deer hair
Hackle: grayish black hackle
Hook: 94840, #10 or #12

Great Red Spinner

Thread: black
Tail: moose mane
Body: same as dun
Wings: white poly, tied spent
Hackle: brownish black hackle
Hook: 94840, #10 or #12

Nymph

Thread: dark brown
Tail: mallard flank dyed amber
Body: dark olive angora with a piece of dark brown furry foam
over top
Wings: mottled brown
Hackle: turkey cree, dyed olive
Hook: 3906B, #12

Light Cahill

Copies *Cinygma dimicki*

Thread: yellow
Tail: ginger hackle fibers
Body: pale creamish yellow poly
Wings: wood duck or imitation flank feather
Hackle: ginger cream hackle
Hook: 94840, #12

Light Cahill

Thread: yellow
Tail: ginger hackle fibers
Body: yellowish cream poly
Wings: pale gray poly
Hackle: yellowish cream hackle
Hook: 94840, #12

Pale Brown Dun

Copies *Cinygmula reticulata*

Thread: tan
Tail: ginger cream hackle fibers
Body: pale brown poly
Wings: yellow mallard flank
Hackle: ginger cream hackle
Hook: 94840, #12 or #14

Dark Rusty Spinner

Thread: brown
Tail: dark brown hackle fibers
Body: dark brown poly
Wings: pale yellow poly
Hackle: dark brown hackle
Hook: 94840, #12 or #14

Pink Lady
Copies *Epeorus albertae*
Thread: cream
Tail: cream ginger hackle fibers
Body: grayish cream poly
Wings: gray mallard quills or dark gray hackle tips
Hackle: cream or badger hackle
Hook: 94840, #12

Salmon Spinner
Thread: cream
Tail: dark brown moose mane
Body: female – pinkish red poly; male – cream gray poly
Wings: pale gray poly
Hackle: pale blue dun hackle
Hook: 94840, #12

Nymph
Thread: brown
Tail: brown mallard flank
Body: medium brown furry foam over tan angora
Wings: light mottled turkey
Hackle: sandy dun hackle
Hook: 3906B, #12

Gray Drake
Copies *Siphlonurus occidentalis*
Thread: dark brown
Tail: medium dun hackle fibers
Body: brownish black poly (sometimes with an olive cast) with
    tan thread for ribbing
Wings: dark gray mallard flank
Hackle: pale bronze dun hackle
Hook: 94840, 3906, #12

Brown Quill Spinner
Thread: dark brown
Tail: dark brown moose mane
Body: dark reddish brown poly ribbed with tan thread
Wings: pale gray poly
Hackle: dark brown hackle
Hook: 94840, #12

Nymph
Thread: dark brown
Tail: light dun fibers
Body: light dun angora fur, dubbed and dark ground colored
furry foam on top
Wings: mallard quill
Hackle: sandy dun hackle
Hook: 3906B, #10

Gray Fox
Copies many species like *Heptagenia solitaria* dun
Thread: tan
Tail: bronze dun hackle fibers
Body: yellowish tan poly
Wings: pale gray hackle tips
Hackle: bronze dun hackle
Hook: 94840, #12

Ginger Quill Spinner
Thread: tan
Tail: ginger hackle fibers
Body: eyed peacock herl, dyed tan and stripped
Wings: pale gray poly
Hackle: ginger hackle
Hook: 94840, #12

Nymph
Thread: brown
Tail: brown mallard flank
Body: dark brown furry foam over pale yellow
Wings: dark mottled turkey
Hackle: grouse or partridge
Hook: 3906B, #14

Pale Brown Dun
Copies *Rhithrogena hageni*
Thread: olive
Tail: cream hackle fibers
Body: tannish olive poly
Wings: gray mallard quills or dark gray hackle tips

Hackle: cream ginger hackle
Hook: 94840, #12

Dark Tan Spinner

Thread: tan
Tail: gray hackle fibers
Body: pale olive tan poly
Wings: pale gray poly
Hackle: cream, mixed with dark tan hackle
Hook: 94840, #12

Nymph

Thread: dark brown
Tail: wood duck (few fibers)
Body: greenish brown rabbit with claret hackle
Wings: dark brown turkey
Hackle: dark brown
Hook: 3906B, #12

Dark Brown Dun

Copies *Ameletus cooki*

Thread: dark brown
Tail: dark brown hackle fibers
Body: dark brown poly
Wings: teal flank feather
Hackle: dark brown hackle
Hook: 94840, #12 or #14

Dark Brown Spinner

Thread: dark brown
Tail: dark brown hackle fibers
Body: dark brown poly
Wings: teal flank feather, dyed yellow
Hackle: dark brown hackle
Hook: 94840, #12 or #14

Quill Gordon

Copies *Rhithrogena futilis*

Thread: gray
Tail: rusty dun hackle fibers
Body: tannish gray poly

Wings: gray mallard quills or dark gray hackle tips
Hackle: rusty dun hackle
Hook: 94840, #12

Quill Gordon Spinner

Thread: black
Tail: dark dun hackle fibers
Body: peacock herl, eyed, stripped
Wings: pale gray poly
Hackle: dark dun hackle
Hook: 94840, #12

Dark Red Quill

Copies many species like *Rhithrogena undulata*

Thread: dark brown
Tail: dark blue dun hackle fibers
Body: dark brown hackle stem
Wings: gray mallard quills or dark gray hackle tips
Legs: dark brown hackle
Hook: 94840, #12

Red Quill Spinner

Thread: dark brown
Tail: ginger to dark brown hackle fibers
Body: red to dark brown hackle stems
Wings: white or pale gray poly yarn
Hackle: ginger to dark brown hackle
Hook: 94840, #12

Great Red Quill

Copies *Timpanoga (Ephemerella) hecuba*

Thread: brown
Tail: moose mane
Body: large reddish brown hackle stem, stripped
Wings: dark gray impala
Hackle: dark brown hackle
Hook: 94840, #10 or #12

Great Red Spinner

Thread: dark brown
Tail: moose mane
Body: dark brown hackle stems, stripped

Wings: pale gray hackle tips
Hackle: dark brown hackle
Hook: 94840, #10 or #12

Nymph

Thread: brown
Tail: brown mallard flank
Body: dark brown furry foam over pale gray angora
Wings: dark mottled turkey
Hackle: grouse or partridge
Hook: 3906B, #10

Dark Olive Dun

Copies *Drunella (Ephemerella) coloradensis*

Thread: dark brown
Tail: gray hackle fibers
Body: dark olive brown poly
Wings: gray mallard quills or dark gray hackle tips
Hackle: ginger hackle
Hook: 94840, #12

Dark Brown Spinner

Thread: dark brown
Tail: dark brown moose mane
Body: dark brown poly
Wings: pale tan poly
Hackle: dark brown hackle
Hook: 94840, #12

Nymph

Thread: brown
Tail: amber mallard flank
Body: brown furry foam over tan angora
Wings: mallard quill
Hackle: sandy dun hackle
Hook: 3906B, #14

Trico

Copies *Tricorythodes minutus*

Thread: pale olive
Tail: cream hackle fibers
Body: pale olive poly, dubbed

Wings: pale gray hackle tips
Hackle: cream hackle
Hook: 94840, #20–24

Trico Spinner

Thread: dark brown
Tail: female – short cream hackle fibers; male – long dark brown
    moose mane
Body: female – rear one-third is cream poly, dubbed; front
    two-thirds is dark brown poly, dubbed; male – dark brown
    poly, dubbed and ribbed with a very fine light tan thread
Wings: white poly yarn, tied spent
Hook: 94840, #20–24

Nymph

Thread: black
Tail: dark brown hackle fibers
Body: dark brownish black fur
Wings: dark gray mallard quill section
Hackle: dark reddish brown
Hook: 3906B, #22

Blue-Winged Olive Dun

Copies *Drunella flavilinea*

Thread: olive
Tail: grayish olive hackle fibers
Body: light to medium olive poly, dubbed
Wings: dark gray hackle tips
Hackle: medium creamish olive
Hook: 94840, #14–20

Dark Olive Spinner

Thread: dark olive or black
Tail: moose mane (dark brown)
Body: dark olive poly (almost black with an olive cast)
Wings: pale gray poly yarn, tied spent
Hook: 94840, #14–20

Nymph

Thread: olive
Tail: wood duck
Body: dark brown angora tied over dubbed-in olive opossum

Wings: brown turkey
Hackle: cree, dyed olive
Hook: 3906B, #14–18

Pale Evening Dun

Copies species like *Heptagenia elegantula*

Thread: pale yellow
Tail: cream hackle fibers
Body: pale yellowish cream poly, dubbed
Wings: pale yellow hackle tips
Hackle: cream
Hook: 94840, #16–20

Pale Evening Spinner

Thread: cream
Tail: cream hackle fibers
Body: pale yellowish cream poly, dubbed
Wings: pale gray poly yarn, tied spent
Hook: 94840, #16–20

Nymph

Thread: dark brown
Tail: mallard flank fibers, dyed brown
Body: dark brown angora, loosely dubbed
Wings: dark mallard section
Hackle: grouse
Hook: 3906B, #14

Pale Morning Dun

Copies species like *Ephemerella inermis** and *E. infrequens.*

Thread: cream
Tail: cream hackle fibers
Body: varies from a bright olive to a creamish yellow. Use poly
and dub
Wings: very pale gray hackle tips
Hackle: cream
Hook: 94840, #16 and #18

Pale Morning Spinner

Thread: orange
Tail: tan hackle fibers
Body: tan poly

Wings: pale gray poly yarn
Hook: 94840, #16 and #18

Nymph

Thread: dark brown
Tail: mallard flank fibers, dyed ginger
Body: belly is amber angora or nymph dubbing with a darker
  brown back
Wings: brown turkey
Hackle: cree
Hook: 3906B, #16 or #18

*Note: Body colors on the dun vary tremendously in color from river
to river.

Order Plecoptera: stoneflies

Early Brown Stonefly

Copies *Strophopteryx fasciata*

Thread: dark brown
Tail: dark brown hackle fibers
Body: peacock (not eyed) stripped or brownish gray poly
Wings: mallard flank feather dyed brown
Hackle: dark brown hackle
Hook: 94840, #14

Light Stonefly

Copies *Isoperla signata*

Thread: pale yellow
Tail: cream ginger hackle fibers
Body: pale yellow floss ribbed with tannish yellow
Wings: mallard flank feather dyed pale tannish yellow
Hackle: cream ginger hackle
Hook: 94840, #12 or #14

Acroneuria Nymph

Thread: dark brown
Tail: light brown hackle fibers
Body: dark olive brown yarn, laid over top of pale yellow
  dubbing fur
Wings: dark brown turkey
Hackle: cree
Hook: 3906B, #10 and #12

Little Green Stonefly

Copies small-stream species like *Alloperla imbecilla*

    Thread: green
    Tail: short pale cream hackle fibers
    Body: medium green poly, dubbed
    Wings: pale gray hackle tips, tied down-wing
    Hackle: pale creamish green hackle
    Hook: 94840, #16

Nymph

    Thread: yellow
    Tail: pale yellow
    Body: use poly that is pale yellow with a hint of olive
    Wings: pale yellowish olive mallard flank
    Hackle: pale yellow hackle
    Hook: 3906B, #16

Yellow Stonefly

Copies species like *Isoperla bilineata*

    Thread: yellow
    Tail: short cream hackle fibers
    Body: pale yellow poly, dubbed
    Wings: cream hackle tips, tied down-wing
    Hackle: cree hackle
    Hook: 94840, #14 or #16

Nymph

    Thread: pale yellow
    Tail: pale yellow hackle fibers
    Body: pale yellow angora
    Wings: pale yellow mallard flank
    Hackle: pale yellow hackle
    Hook: 3906B, #14 or #16

Order Trichoptera: caddisflies

Green Caddis

Copies *Rhyacophila lobifera*

    Thread: green
    Body: green poly
    Wings: brown deer body hair

Hackle: tan hackle (optional with deer hair)
Hook: 94840, #14 or #16

Grannom
Copies *Brachycentrus fuliginosus, B. numerosus,* and *B. solomoni*
Thread: black
Body: gray fur dubbed
Wings: dark turkey tail or dark brown deer hair
Hackle: dark brown hackle
Hook: 94840, #12 to #16

Spotted Sedge
Copies *Symphitopsyche slossanae*

Thread: tan
Body: fox fur
Wings: pale deer hair
Hackle: ginger cream hackle
Hook: 94840, #14 or #16

Dark Blue Sedge
Copies *Psilotreta frontalis*

Thread: dark gray
Body: peacock herl (not eyed) or dark gray poly
Wings: dark bluish gray hackle tips or deer hair dyed gray
Hackle: dark brown hackle
Hook: 94840, #12

Little Black Caddis
Copies *Chimarra atterima*

Thread: black
Body: black fur dubbed
Wings: medium gray mallard quills or dark deer hair
Hackle: dark brown hackle
Hook: 94840, #16 or #18

Caddis Larva
Thread: appropriate color (most often dark brown or black)
Body: olive, green, brown, yellow, black, or tan fur dubbed and
    ribbed with fine wire, or use a rubber band of the appropri-
    ate color and tie in at the bend of the hook and spiral to the
    eye

Thorax: dark brown fur, dubbed; or an ostrich herl, dyed dark brown wound around the hook several times
Hook: 37160, #12–18

Emerging Caddis Pupa

Thread: same color as the body color you select
Body: olive, green, brown, yellow, black, or tan fur or poly nymph dubbing material
Wings: (optional) dark mallard quill sections shorter than normal, and tied in on both sides of the fly, not on top
Legs: dark brown grouse or woodcock neck feather wound around the hook two or three times
Hook: 37160, #12–18

TERRESTRIAL IMITATIONS

Recently, plastic foams like Polycelon have been introduced. This material is extremely useful when tying terrestrials and other patterns that you want to float high. The material comes in an assortment of colors and can be used for mayflies and caddisflies, as well as crickets, ants, beetles, and grasshoppers. Even if you can't tie flies, you can shape this material and tie it onto a hook. Barry Beck of Fishing Creek Outfitters in Benton, Pennsylvania, ties in a short piece of orange poly on top of some of the terrestrial patterns for better visibility.

Cricket Imitation

Thread: black
Body: black poly or black angora
Wings: black goose quills section tied down-wing
Hackle: black deer hair spun around the hook, just behind the eye
Hook: 94831, #10

The deer hair is buoyant and floats this large artificial rather well. The deer hair is spun around and clipped to form the head.

Grasshopper

Thread: olive, yellow, tan, or cream
Body: tan, yellow, olive, or cream fur
Wings: medium turkey wing tied down-wing

Hackle: brown deer hair tied similar to the cricket
Hook: 94831 or 9672, #10 to #18

Crowe Beetle
Hook: 94840, #14 to #18

Take a bunch of black deer body hair and tie on at the bend of the hook by the butt. After tying in the butt, wind the thread toward the eye of the hook. Now pull the tips of the deer hair up over the top of the shank. Tie in the tips just behind the eye and finish off, and clip off the end of the hair. If you want to imitate more closely the body coloration of the Japanese beetle, you can use peacock for the body.

Poly Beetle
Gerald Almy in *Tying and Fishing Terrestrials* suggests that the Crowe Beetle doesn't seem to stand up to the punishment of many strikes. A new, extremely simple, pattern Charles Meck developed does. To tie the Poly Beetle, use two to five strands (depending on the size hook you're using) of black poly yarn. Tie the yarn in well below the bend of the hook. Bring the yarn up over the top of the hook and tie in just behind the eye. Cut off the excess.

Ant
Hook: 94840, #14–20

Take a piece of black or brown polypropylene and tie it in at the bend of the hook. Make a few turns on the rear half of the shank of the hook to give it a humped appearance. Now take a black or dark brown hackle, tie it in at the middle of the shank, and make a few turns. Next, take the black polypropylene and make another hump on the front part of the shank. To imitate one of the many winged species of ants, add two pale dun hackle tips at the middle of the hook shank and place down-wing over the body.

You can also use black deer hair to tie the ant imitation. Tie the deer hair in at the bend of the hook similar to the beetle. Halfway up the shank tie in the deer hair, leaving some of the smaller, loose hairs as legs. Continue the deer hair to the eye and tie in at the eye. Clip and cement, and you have a realistic, buoyant imitation.

Western Stoneflies

Salmon Fly
Copies *Pteronarcys californica*
>Thread: orange
>Tail: dark moose mane
>Body: abdomen, burnt orange poly; thorax and head, bright orange poly
>Wings: creamish tan dyed mallard flank tied down-wing
>Hackle: brownish black hackle
>Hook: 94720, #4 or #6

Pteronarcys Nymph
>Thread: black
>Tail: black goose quill fibers
>Body: orange and black grindle chenille
>Wings: black goose quill
>Hackle: blackish brown hackle wound around front half
>Hook: 94831, #4 or #6

The Simple Salmon pattern is effective during the *Pteronarcys* hatch. *Charles Meck.*

Willow Stonefly

Copies *Hesperoperla pacifica*

Thread: tan
Tail: short brown hackle fibers
Body: creamish brown poly
Wings: creamish mallard flank
Hackle: brown hackle
Hook: 94720, #6

Golden Stonefly

Copies *Calineuria californica* (adult)

Thread: yellow
Tail: moose mane
Body: pale yellow poly ribbed with brown poly
Wings: pale tan deer hair
Hackle: cream and brown, mixed
Hook: 94840, #8

Family Perlodidae

Copies species like little yellow stonefly or yellow sally

Tail: very short yellow hackle fibers
Body: primrose poly, dubbed
Wings: pale deer hair, dyed yellow
Hackle: pale yellow hackle
Hook: 94840, #14 or #16

Western Caddisflies

October Caddis

Copies *Dicosmoecus* species

Thread: orange
Body: orange poly, dubbed
Wings: brown deer hair
Hackle: brown hackle
Hook: 94840, #6

Tan Caddis

Copies *Hydropsyche* species

Thread: tan
Body: yellow, tan, or olive poly

A midge pupa. *Charles Meck.*

A midge adult with a trailing shuck. *Charles Meck.*

Wings: dark brown deer hair
Hackle: brown hackle
Hook: 94840, #14–16

Order Diptera: Family Chironomidae (midges)

Emerging Pupa

Body: black, olive, or dark gray floss, ribbed with fine copper wire or Z-lon

Thorax: dubbed muskrat with guard hairs; tie in just behind muskrat a very short piece of white poly yarn or Z-lon. Pull poly or Z-lon over top of muskrat and tie off. A piece of poly or Z-lon should extend a short distance over the eye of the hook.

Hook: 94840, #14–22

9

Some Proposals for
Better Fishing

JOINING CLUBS AND ORGANIZATIONS

Recently we've seen enterprising individuals lease trout waters to interested anglers at unbelievable rates. Fishing on some eastern limestone waters runs as high as $150 per rod per day of fishing. Even at that price the landowner has had to turn away hundreds of would-be customers. Other landowners, seeing how successful this first farmer was, decided to lease their parcel of water out to anglers, and soon this cancerous growth of posting and leasing land spread to other fishing waters that had once been open to public fishing.

We're not telling a tale of what might happen in the future—it's happening right now! Once resourceful landowners realize generous returns from some of our better waters, they go private like a raging epidemic. Within a few years you'll have to either fish marginal trout waters and crowded public streams or join private clubs to enjoy top-notch fly fishing.

Thankfully, some states have been purchasing lands and access rights on some of the better streams and rivers. But they could—and should—go further: they should grant tax incentives to those landowners who allow public access. Think what would happen if a state gave an access-granting farmer or rancher a 50 percent reduction in real estate taxes.

Meanwhile, what can we as anglers do to preserve public trouting? First and foremost, as intelligent concerned citizens, we should become involved. Don't expect your state fish and game commission to do too much—they're limited by their budgets. You can join conservation and fishing-interest organizations or form one of your own. Here are some examples of what anglers thinking like conservationists can do.

Phantom Canyon, north of Fort Collins, Colorado, supports a wide array of flora and fauna unique to its area, and more than a mile of the North Fork of the Cache la Poudre River flows through this 1,600-acre property. Recently, citing its unique biological and botanical composition, the Colorado Nature Conservancy purchased this valuable piece of land. Now the Conservancy allows fly fishing on a limited basis to visitors. Without the Conservancy's foresight, Phantom Canyon would almost certainly have gone into private hands; but now it remains for all—naturalists and fly casters—to enjoy.

In 1975 the Nature Conservancy discovered that the 480-acre Sun Valley Ranch was up for sale. They purchased the land and opened more than 2 miles of Silver Creek, one of the top spring creeks in the nation, to fly fishing. All you have to do to fish this spectacular stream is sign in at preserve headquarters on the site. Thanks again to the foresight of this conservation-minded organization. As a dedicated fly fisherman, you should support this organization in every way possible.

The Big Wood River in south-central Idaho suffered from obdurate landownership, poor trout habitat, and occasional pollution problems. Enter an organization called the Friends of the Big Wood River, dedicated to the river's complete rehabilitation. These friends provided drop structures to create holding water for trout where there was none before. They continually lobby for legislation transferring water rights from agricultural use to in-stream use. They seek, as well, more and better access for angling.

The Anglers of the Au Sable is a unique group of conservationists, some 650 strong in number. They hail from many states across the country. Their newsletter, "The Riverwatch," is one of the best that we've seen. This group vigilantly monitors conditions in and around the Au Sable River in Michigan, and they need your support. Without them conditions on the river would not be what they are today.

Another conservation group in Michigan, the Manistee Restoration Committee, is one of the finest associations of its kind in the country. They have networked with the private sector, state and fed-

Members of the Anglers of the Au Sable monitor activities that may impact the water quality of the Au Sable River in Michigan. *Greg Hoover.*

eral agencies, and individuals to provide an excellent resource base to initiate appropriate decisions to protect and restore the Manistee River in Michigan. With leadership provided by Joe Kutkuhn, a retired fisheries biologist, this group has been very effective in its three years of existence. They have developed a ten-year action plan. Currently, they have placed sand traps in the upper Manistee to collect fine sediment that may impact substrate quality of the river. The committee has received a great deal of enthusiasm from governmental agencies. They have also enlisted the support of young men in a first-offender program. Direction is provided by a seventy-three-year-old man who in his lifetime has seen the program work in a positive way for both the young men and the Manistee. Conservation groups across the country would do well to emulate the Manistee Restoration Committee.

The Farmington River Anglers Association (FRAA) was founded in

1976 to further protect their river. FRAA is the watchdog for the quality of the fishing experience on the Farmington. Additionally, it has planted thousands of Bitterroot-strain brown trout eggs in the river and its tributaries. The organization is well informed regarding issues that may affect the water quality of the Farmington. They are one of the reasons that the Farmington is a high-quality trout fishery.

All of the above groups have several things in common. They stay focused on one or two goals; they have a well-informed spokesperson for their group; and they have enlisted the help of state and federal agencies, which makes their organizations much more effective. If you are initiating the formation of a group to protect your favorite trout water, you would do well to contact any of these groups. They have knowledge and experience to share that may reduce the frustrations of starting an effective conservation organization.

What can you as an individual do to ensure a future of excellent fly fishing for all to enjoy? You can join and contribute to worthwhile organizations like the Nature Conservancy, Trout Unlimited, the Federation of Fly Fishers, or the Izaak Walton League. Or you can form or join an organization dedicated specifically to the restoration and preservation of your favorite river or stream, the way the Friends of the Big Wood River did. If you do form your own organization, be sure to work for continued access to the water and better trout habitat.

You can also encourage your legislators to work on the problem of access. When rain fails to fall reliably, farmers and ranchers tend to request – and receive – federal drought assistance. Who ultimately pays for that assistance? You and I do. Notice then how sensible it is to enact laws allowing any farmer or rancher who receives federal assistance to open the land to the public.

Must anglers and landowners constantly squabble over access rights and water use? Look what FOAM (the Fishing Outfitters Association of Montana) did recently. Like many other western states, Montana, as big as it is, suffers from acute land-use and water problems. But unlike many other western states, Montana sportsmen's groups have allied with farmers and ranchers to overcome water problems and the associated obstacles to trout management. In 1987 more than a mile of the Ruby River went dry, and many blamed it on poor irrigation planning. The ranchers who use the Ruby agreed to cooperate with the Montana Fish and Wildlife Department to monitor the flow so it wouldn't run dry again. Here's an example of where two groups, rather than battling, agreed to work amicably.

Another example occurred on the nearby Big Hole River, where for years trout migrated up the irrigation channels only to be stranded and die. The ranchers' cooperative saw what was happening and agreed to shut down the water supply in three definite, equal stages. The trout left the ditches after the water began to lower during the first stage, and given this early warning, they survived. A conservation and water problem had been worked out in a civilized manner by the joint efforts of Montana Trout Unlimited, the Environmental Quality Office in Helena, local sportsmen's groups, and FOAM. In fact, all four organizations have formed the Alliance for Montana Waters to work with the state and its agricultural interests to maintain quality fishing in the state. Jack D. Hutchison, until recently president of FOAM and a guide for Tom and Sue Harmon's fly shop in Sheridan, credits his state with a unique approach to water problems: disparate groups combining their efforts to restore great fishing and to maintain the quality of their environment.

Let's examine yet another tactic for a moment. The Kootenai River near Libby, Montana, is still a fantastic river. Fly fish this wonderful tailwater during a little blue-winged olive hatch in May or September, and you will know the true value of this resource. Fly fish it when pale morning duns appear in late June or July, and you'll find it hard to leave. As you drift down to Libby along this productive river, you'll notice perhaps a dozen anglers fishing the shore. Look more closely and you'll also notice one more thing: each fisherman carries a white five-gallon bucket, which they fill with Kootenai rainbows and cutthroats to take home. The river can still support this loss, but not much longer. As it gains the fame it deserves, more and more anglers will kill more and more trout, and the Kootenai will soon suffer the fate of so many other once-famous, now-barren rivers.

What can we do to save such valuable resources? For one thing, we need more slot-limit and catch-and-release areas on our productive trout waters. Look at the McKenzie River near coastal Oregon. Until recently it, too, suffered from overkill. Then the state set a slot limit for the river and it has begun to prosper again. All McKenzie trout 14 inches and over must be returned to the river. Meanwhile, the state annually plants 100,000 trout up to 12 inches in the river. The 14-inch slot ensures that holdover and larger streambred trout will return to the river to breed. Although they return the breeding stock, anglers can still keep some of their trout—mainly stockers—to take home.

Recently Charles Meck suggested to some Pennsylvania authorities that the Commonwealth cut its regular daily-limit from eight to five trout. His reasoning: cut down on the number of fish stocked and spend the money saved to purchase access to some of the better streams throughout the state and to improve habitat. (Incidentally, if the number were cut from eight to five, more people would go home happy with a "limit.") The authorities scoffed at his idea. They know that the majority of anglers–their "constituency"–are interested only in catching a generous eight-trout limit. It seems that before we can truly protect our trout, some changes in thinking must occur among some of the authorities assigned to regulate trout fishing. This is where we–you and I–come in. We must coerce, cajole, and cooperate with authorities and encourage them to take unpopular positions designed to solve long-range problems and to preserve rather than simply plant and harvest trout.

Our precious streams and rivers are too valuable to be enjoyed by only a select few. They must be savored by everyone and preserved for future generations.

A Selected Bibliography

General and Aquatic Entomology

Barnes, R. D. 1968. Invertebrate zoology (2nd ed.). W. B. Saunders, Philadelphia.

Borror, D. J., C. A. Triplehorn, and N. F. Johnson. 1989. An introduction to the study of insects (6th ed.). Saunders College Publ., Philadelphia.

Chapman, R. F. 1976. The insects, structure and function (2nd ed.). Elsevier, North Holland.

Edmondson, W. T. (ed.). 1959. Freshwater biology (2nd ed.). John Wiley & Sons, New York.

Hart, C. W., Jr., and S. L. H. Fuller (eds.). 1974. Pollution ecology of freshwater invertebrates. Acad. Press, New York.

Hilsenhoff, W. L. 1975. Aquatic insects of Wisconsin, with generic keys and notes on biology, ecology and distribution. Tech. Bull. Wisc. Dept. Nat. Res. 89: 1–52.

Hynes, H. B. N. 1970a. The ecology of running waters. Univ. Toronto Press, Toronto.

———. 1970b. The ecology of stream insects. Ann. Rev. Entomol. 15: 25–42.

Lehmkuhl, D. M. 1979. How to know the aquatic insects. Wm. C. Brown Company Publishers, Dubuque, IA.

Macan, T. T. 1974. Freshwater ecology (2nd ed.). John Wiley & Sons, New York.

————. 1962. The ecology of aquatic insects. Ann. Rev. Ent. 7: 261–88.

McCafferty, W. P. 1981. Aquatic entomology, the fisherman's and ecologist's illustrated guide to insects and their relatives. Sci. Books International, Boston.

Merritt, R. W., and K. W. Cummins (eds.). 1984. An introduction to the aquatic insects of North America. Kendall/Hunt, Dubuque, IA.

Needham, J. G., and P. R. Needham. 1962. A guide to the study of fresh-water biology (5th ed.). Holden-Day, San Francisco.

Peckarsky, B. L., P. A. Penton, and D. J. Conklin, Jr. 1990. Freshwater macroinvertebrates of northeastern North America. Cornell Univ. Press, Ithaca, NY.

Pennak, R. W. 1978. Freshwater invertebrates of the United States (2nd ed.). John Wiley & Sons, New York.

Torre-Bueno, J. R. 1978. A glossary of entomology. N.Y. Entomol. Soc., New York.

Usinger, R. L. (ed.). 1956. Aquatic insects of California. Univ. Calif. Press, Berkeley.

Fly Fishing Entomology

Arbona, F., Jr. 1980. Mayflies, the angler, and the trout. Winchester Press, Tulsa, OK.

Berners, D. J. 1496. A treatyse of fysshynge wyth an angle. In the Boke of St. Albans. Westminster.

Blades, W. F. 1951. Fishing flies and fly tying. Stackpole Books, Harrisburg, PA.

Borger, G. A. 1991. Designing trout flies. Tomorrow River Press, Wausau, WI.

————. 1980. Naturals, a guide to food organisms of the trout. Stackpole Books, Harrisburg, PA.

————. 1979. Nymphing, a basic book. Stackpole Books, Harrisburg, PA.

Caucci, A., and B. Nastasi. 1986. Hatches II. Nick Lyons Books, New York.

Flick, A. 1966. Art Flick's new streamside guide to naturals and their imitations. Crown, New York.

Fox, C. K. 1967. Rising trout. Foxcrest, Carlisle, PA.

————. 1963. The wonderful world of trout. Telegraph Press, Harrisburg, PA.

Gaidy, C. 1986. Ephemeras – mayflies, naturals and artificials. Edicom, Inc. Publ., New York.

Goddard, J. 1966. Trout fly recognition. A. C. Black, London.

Gordon, S. W. 1955. How to fish from top to bottom. Stackpole Books, Harrisburg, PA.

Gordon, T. 1947. The complete fly-fisherman: the notes and letters of Theodore Gordon, John McDonald (ed.). Scribners, New York.

Grove, A. R., Jr. 1951. The lure and lore of trout fishing. Stackpole Books, Harrisburg, PA.

Hafele, R., and D. Hughes. 1981. The complete book of western hatches. Amato Publications, Portland, OR.

Hafele, R., and S. Roederer. 1987. An angler's guide to aquatic insects and their imitations. Johnson Publ., Boulder, CO.

Halford, F. M. 1910. Modern development of the dry fly. London.

———. 1897. Dry fly entomology. London.

———. 1889. Dry fly fishing in theory and practice. London.

———. 1886. Floating flies and how to dress them. London.

Harris, J. R. 1952. An angler's entomology. A. S. Barnes & Co., New York.

Harvey, G. W. 1990. Techniques of trout fishing and fly tying. Lyons & Burford, New York.

Jennings, P. J. 1935. A book of trout flies. Derrydale Press, New York. Reprint 1970. Crown, New York.

Koch, E. 1990. Terrestrial fishing. Stackpole Books, Harrisburg, PA.

———. 1988. Fishing the midge (2nd ed.). Stackpole Books, Harrisburg, PA.

LaFontaine, G. 1990. The dry fly, new angles. Greycliff Publ., Helena, MT.

———. 1980. Caddisflies. Nick Lyons Books, New York.

Leiser, E., and R. H. Boyle. 1982. Stoneflies for the angler. Alfred A. Knopf, New York.

Marinaro, V. C. 1950. A modern dry-fly code. Putnam's, New York. Reprint 1970. Crown, New York.

McClane, A. J. (ed.). 1965. McClane's standard fishing encyclopedia. Holt, Rinehart and Winston, New York.

Meck, C. R. 1991. Fishing small streams with a fly rod. Countryman Press, Woodstock, VT.

———. 1989. Pennsylvania trout streams and their hatches. Backcountry Publications, Woodstock, VT.

———. 1977. Meeting and fishing the hatches. Winchester Press, New York.

Mosely, M. E. 1921. The dry-fly fisherman's entomology. London.

Pobst, D. 1990. Trout stream insects, an Orvis streamside guide. Lyons & Burford, New York.

Rhead, L. 1916, American trout stream insects. Frederick A. Stockes, New York.

Richards, C., D. Swisher, and F. Arbona, Jr. 1980. Stoneflies. Nick Lyons Books/Winchester Press, New York.

Ronalds, A. 1836. The fly-fisher's entomology. London.

Schweibert, E. 1973. Nymphs. Winchester, New York.

———. 1955. Matching the hatch. Macmillan, New York.

Scotcher, G. n.d. The fly-fisher's legacy. Chepstow.

Skues, G. E. M. 1921. The way of a trout with a fly. London.

Solomon, L., and E. Leiser. 1977. The caddis and the angler. Stackpole Books, Harrisburg, PA.

Swisher, D., and C. Richards. 1971. Selective trout. Crown, New York.

Walton, I. 1653. The compleat angler. Rich, Marriot, London.

Wetzel, C. M. 1955. Trout flies (natural and imitations). Stackpole Books, Harrisburg, PA.

———. 1943. Practical fly-fishing. Christopher, Boston.

Whitlock, D. 1982. Dave Whitlock's guide to aquatic trout foods. Nick Lyons Books, New York.

Ephemeroptera (mayflies)

Allen, R. K. 1980. Distribution and reclassification of Ephemerellidae. In Advances in Ephemeroptera biology, J. F. Flannagan and K. E. Marshall (eds.), pp. 71–91. Plenum Press, New York.

Allen, R. K., and G. F. Edmunds, Jr. 1965. A revision of the genus *Ephemerella* (Ephemeroptera: Ephemerellidae). 8. The subgenus *Ephemerella* in North America. Misc. Publ. Entomol. Soc. Amer. 4: 244–82.

———. 1963a. A revision of the genus *Ephemerella* (Ephemeroptera: Ephemerellidae). 6. The subgenus *Serratella* in North America. Ann. Entomol. Soc. Amer. 56: 583–600.

———. 1963b. A revision of the genus *Ephemerella* (Ephemeroptera: Ephemerellidae). 7. The subgenus *Eurylophella*. Can. Entomol. 95: 597–623.

———. 1962a. A revision of the genus *Ephemerella* (Ephemeroptera: Ephemerellidae). 4. The subgenus *Dannella*. J. Kans. Entomol. Soc. 35: 333–58.

———. 1962b. A revision of the genus *Ephemerella* (Ephemeroptera: Ephemerellidae). 5. The subgenus *Drunella* in North America. Misc. Publ. Entomol. Soc. Amer. 3: 147–79.

————. 1961. A revision of the genus *Ephemerella* (Ephemeroptera: Ephemerellidae). 3. The subgenus *Attenuatella*. J. Kans. Entomol. Soc. 34: 161–73.

Argo, V. 1927. The North American species of the genus *Potamanthus*, with a description of a new species. J. N. Y. Entomol. Soc. 35: 319–28.

Banks, N. 1910. Notes of the eastern species of the mayfly genus *Heptagenia*. Can. Entomol. 42: 197–202.

Bednarik, A. F. 1979. Subgeneric classification in *Stenonema* (Ephemeroptera: Heptageniidae). J. Georg. Entomol. Soc. 14: 190–91.

Bednarik, A. F., and W. P. McCafferty. 1979. Biosystematic revision of the genus *Stenonema* (Ephemeroptera: Heptageniidae). Can. Bull. Fish. Aq. Sci. 201.

Bergman, E. A., and W. L. Hilsenhoff. 1978. *Baetis* (Ephemeroptera: Baetidae) of Wisconsin. Great Lakes Entomol. 11: 125–35.

Berner, L. 1978. A review of the mayfly family Metretopodidae. Trans. Amer. Entomol. Soc. 104: 91–137.

————. 1959. A tabular summary of the biology of North American mayfly nymphs (Ephemeroptera). Bull. Fla. State Mus. 4: 1–58.

————. 1955. The southeastern species of *Baetisca* (Ephemeroptera: Baetiscidae). Quart. J. Fla. Acad. Sci. 18: 1–19.

Berner, L., and M. L. Pescador. 1988. The mayflies of Florida. Univ. Presses of Florida, Gainesville.

————. 1980. The mayfly family Baetiscidae (Ephemeroptera). Part 1. In Advances in Ephemeroptera biology, J. F. Flannagan and K. E. Marshall (eds.), pp. 511–24. Plenum Press, New York.

Britt, N. W. 1962. Biology of two species of Lake Erie mayflies, *Ephoron album* and *Ephemera simulans* Walker. Ohio Biol. Surv. 1: 1–70.

Brittain, J. E. 1982. Biology of mayflies. Ann. Rev. Entomol. 27: 119–47.

Burian, S. K., and K. E. Gibbs. 1991. Mayflies of Maine: an annotated faunal list. Maine Agr. Exp. Sta. Tech. Bull. 142.

Burks, B. D. 1953. The mayflies of Ephemeroptera of Illinois. Bull. Ill. Nat. Hist. Surv. 26: 1–216.

Clemens, W. A. 1915. Mayflies of the *Siphlonurus* group. Can. Entomol. 47: 245–60.

————. 1913. New species and new life histories of Ephemeridae or mayflies. Can. Entomol. 45: 246–62.

Clifford, H. F. 1976. Observations on the life cycle of *Siphloplecton basale* (Walker) (Ephemeroptera: Metrotopodidae). Pan-Pacific Entomol. 52: 265–71.

Clifford, H. F., H. Hamilton, and B. A. Killins. 1979. Biology of the mayfly *Leptophlebia cupida* (Say) (Ephemeroptera: Leptophlebiidae). Can. J. Zool. 57: 1026-45.

Cooke, H. B. 1940. Observations on mating flights of the mayfly *Stenonema vicarium* (Ephemerida). Entomol. News 51: 12-14.

Daggy, R. H. 1941. Taxonomic and biological investigations on Minnesota mayflies (Ephemeroptera). Ph.D. diss., Univ. of Minnesota, Minneapolis.

Edmunds, G. F., Jr. 1982. Historical and life history factors in the biogeography of mayflies. Amer. Zool. 22: 371-74.

———. 1972. Biogeography and evolution of Ephemeroptera. Ann. Rev. Entomol. 17: 21-42.

———. 1959a. Ephemeroptera, p. 908-16. In W. T. Edmondson (ed.), Freshwater biology (2nd ed.). John Wiley & Sons, New York.

———. 1959b. Subgeneric groups within the mayfly genus Ephemerella (Ephemeroptera: Ephemerellidae). Ann. Entomol. Soc. Amer. 52: 543-47.

———. 1954. The mayflies of Utah. Proc. Utah Acad. Sci. Arts Lett. 31: 64-66.

Edmunds, G. F., Jr., and R. K. Allen. 1964. The Rocky Mountain species of *Epeorus (Iron)* Eaton (Ephemeroptera: Heptageniidae). J. Kans. Entomol. Soc. 37: 275-88.

———. 1957. A checklist of the Ephemeroptera of America north of Mexico. Ann. Entomol. Soc. Amer. 50: 317-24.

Edmunds, G. F., Jr., R. K. Allen, and W. L. Peters. 1963. An annotated key to the nymphs of the families of mayflies (Ephemeroptera). Univ. Utah Biol. Ser. 13(1): 44 pp.

Edmunds, G. F., Jr., S. L. Jensen, and L. Berner. 1976. The mayflies of North and Central America. Univ. Minn. Press, Minneapolis.

Flowers, R. W., and W. L. Hilsenhoff. 1975. Heptageniidae (Ephemeroptera) of Wisconsin. Great Lakes Entomol. 8: 201-18.

Fremling, C. R. 1970. Mayfly distribution as a water quality index. Wat. Poll. Cont. Res. Ser. U.S.E.P.A., Washington, DC.

———. 1960. Biology of a large mayfly, *Hexagenia bilineata* (Say), of the upper Mississippi River. Res. Bull. Iowa Agric. Exp. Sta. 482: 842-52.

Hall, R. J. 1975. Life history, drift, and production rate of the stream mayfly *Tricorythodes atratus* McDunnough in the headwaters of the Mississippi River. Ph.D. diss. Univ. Mich., Ann Arbor.

Horst, T. J. 1976. Population dynamics of the burrowing mayfly *Hexagenia limbata*. Ecology 57: 199-204.

Hubbard, M. D. 1990. Mayflies of the world, a catalog of the family and genus group taxa (Insecta: Ephemeroptera. Flora & Fauna Handbook No. 8. Sandhill Crane Press, Gainesville, FL.

Hubbard, M. D., and W. L. Peters. 1978. Environmental requirements
    and pollution tolerance of Ephemeroptera. Environ. Monit. Sup.
    Lab., Off. Res. Devel. USEPA, Cincinnati, OH.

Ide, F. P. 1935a. Life history notes on *Ephoron, Potamanthus, Leptophle-
    bia,* and *Blasturus* with descriptions (Ephemeroptera). Can. Ento-
    mol. 67: 113–25.

————. 1935b. The effect of temperature on the distribution of the
    mayfly fauna of a stream. Biology Series 39, Ontario Fisheries
    Research Laboratory 50: 9–76.

————. 1930. The nymph of the mayfly genus *Cinygma* Eaton. Can.
    Entomol. 62: 42–45.

Kennedy, C. H. 1926. The nymph of *Ephemera guttulata* Pictet with
    notes of the species. Can. Entomol. 58: 33–38.

Kondratieff, B. C., and J. R. Voshell, Jr. 1984. The North and Central
    American species of *Isonychia* (Ephemeroptera: Oligoneuriidae).
    Trans. Amer. Entomol. Soc. 110: 129–244.

Koss, K. C., and G. F. Edmunds, Jr. 1974. Ephemeroptera eggs and
    their contribution to phylogenetic studies of the order. J. Zool.
    Linn. Soc. Lond. 58: 61-120.

Koss, R. W. 1968. Morphology and taxonomic use of Ephemeroptera
    eggs. Ann. Entomol. Soc. Amer. 61: 696–721.

Lehmkuhl, D. M. 1970. Mayflies of the South Saskatchewan River:
    pollution indicators. Blue Jay 28: 183–86.

Leonard, J. W., and F. A. Leonard. 1972. Mayflies of Michigan trout
    streams. Cranbrook Inst. Sci., Bloomfield Hills, MI.

Lewis, P. A. 1974. Taxonomy and ecology of *Stenonema* mayflies (Hep-
    tageniidae: Ephemeroptera). U.S. Environmental Protection
    Agency, Environmental Monitoring Ser. Rept. EPA-670/4-74-006.

McCafferty, W. P. 1975. The burrowing mayflies (Ephemeroptera:
    Ephemeroidea) of the United States. Trans. Amer. Entomol. Soc.
    101: 447-504.

McCafferty, W. P., and B. L. Huff, Jr. 1978. The life cycle of the mayfly
    Stenacron interpunctatum (Ephemeroptera: Heptageniidae). Great
    Lakes Entomol. 11: 209–16.

McCafferty, W. P., and A. V. Provonsha. 1978. The Ephemeroptera of
    mountainous Arkansas. J. Kan. Entomol. Soc. 51: 360–79.

McCafferty, W. P., and R. D. Waltz. 1990. Revisionary synopsis of the
    Baetidae (Ephemeroptera) of North and Middle America. Trans.
    Amer. Entomol. Soc. 116: 769–99.

McDunnough, J. 1931a. The bicolor group of the genus *Ephemerella*
    with particular reference to the nymphal states (Ephemeroptera).
    Can. Entomol. 63: 30–42.

————. 1931b. The eastern North American species of the genus *Ephe-*

merella and their nymphs (Ephemeroptera). Can. Entomol. 63: 187–97.

———. 1931c. The genus *Isonychia* (Ephemeroptera). Can. Entomol. 63: 157–63.

———. 1925. New *Ephemerella* species (Ephemeroptera). Can. Entomol. 57: 41–43.

———. 1924a. New Ephemeridae from New England. Occ. Pap. Boston Soc. Natl. Hist. 5: 73–76.

———. 1924b. New North American Ephemeridae. Can. Entomol. 56: 221–26.

Minshall, J. N. 1967. Life history and ecology of *Epeorus pleuralis* (Banks) (Ephemeroptera: Heptageniidae). Amer. Midl. Nat. 76: 340–50.

Morihara, D. K., and W. P. McCafferty. 1979. The *Baetis* larvae of North America (Ephemeroptera: Baetidae). Trans. Amer. Entomol. Soc. 105: 139–221.

Murphy, H. E. 1922. Notes on the biology of some of our North American species of mayflies. Bull. Lloyd Library 22; Entomol. Ser. 2: 1–46. Cincinnati, OH.

Neave, F. 1930. Migratory habits of the mayfly *Blasturus cupidus* Say. Ecology 2: 568–76.

Needham, J. G. 1920. Burrowing mayflies of our larger lakes and streams. Bur. Fish., Bull. 36.

Needham, J. G., J. R. Traver, and Y. C. Hsu. 1935. The biology of mayflies with a systematic account of North American species. Comstock Publ. Ithaca, NY.

Provonsha, A. V. 1990. A revision of the genus *Caenis* in North America (Ephemeroptera: Caenidae). Trans. Amer. Entomol. Soc. 116: 801–84.

Spieth, H. T. 1938. A method of rearing *Hexagenia* nymphs (Ephemerida). Entomol. News 49: 29–32.

———. 1941. Taxonomic studies on the Ephemeroptera. II. The genus *Hexagenia*. Amer. Midl. Nat. 26: 233–80.

Thew, T. B. 1960. Revision of the genera of the family Caenidae. Trans. Amer. Entomol. Soc. 86: 197–205.

———. 1956. A list of the mayflies of Iowa. Museum Quarterly (Davenport Public Museum) 1: 1–6.

Traver, J. R. 1932. Mayflies of North Carolina. J. Elisha Mitchell Sci. Soc. 47: 85–181, 163–236.

———. 1931. Seven new southern species of the mayfly genus *Hexagenia*, with notes on the genus. Ann. Entomol. Soc. Amer. 24: 59–162.

Williams, D. D. 1980. Applied aspects of mayfly biology, pp. 1–17. In Advances in Ephemeroptera biology, J. F. Flannagan and K. E. Marshall (eds.). Plenum, New York.

Wright, M., and L. Berner. 1949. Notes on mayflies of eastern Tennessee. J. Tenn. Acad. Sci. 24: 287–98.

Trichoptera (caddisflies)

Betten, C. 1934. The caddis flies or Trichoptera of New York State. Bull. N.Y. State Mus. 292: 1–576.

Blickle, R. L. 1964. Hydroptilidae (Trichoptera) of Maine. Entomol. News 75: 159–62.

Blickle, R. L., and W. J. Morse. 1955. New and little-known *Polycentropus* (Trichoptera). Bull. Brooklyn Entomol. Soc. 50: 95–98.

Denning, D. G. 1943. The Hydropsychidae of Minnesota (Trichoptera). Entomologica Amer. 23: 101–71.

Ellis, R. J. 1962. Adult caddisflies (Trichoptera) from Houghton Creek, Ogemaw County, Michigan. Occ. Pap. Univ. Mich. Mus. Zool. 624: 1–15.

Etnier, D. A. 1965. An annotated list of the Trichoptera of Minnesota with a description of a new species. Entomol. News 76: 141–52.

Flint, O. S. 1960. Taxonomy and biology of nearctic limnephilid larvae (Trichoptera) with special reference to species in eastern United States. Entomologica Amer. 40: 1–117.

Gallepp, G. W. 1977. Responses of caddisfly larvae (*Brachycentrus* spp.) to temperature, food availability and current velocity. Amer. Midl. Natural. 98: 59–84.

Gordon, A. E. 1974. A synopsis and phylogenetic outline of the Nearctic members of *Cheumatopsyche*. Proc. Acad. Nat. Sci. Phila. 126: 117–60.

Harris, T. L. 1978. Environmental requirements and pollution tolerance of Trichoptera. Environ. Monit. Sup. Lab., Off. Res. Dev. USEPA, Cincinnati, OH.

Lloyd, J. T. 1921. The biology of North American caddis fly larvae. Bull. Lloyd Lib. 21: 1–124.

Mackay, R. J., and G. B. Wiggins. 1979. Ecological diversity in Trichoptera. Ann. Rev. Entomol. 24: 185–208.

Mecom, J. O., and K. W. Cummins. 1964. A preliminary study of the trophic relationships of the larvae of *Brachycentrus americanus* (Banks) (Trichoptera: Brachycentridae). Trans. Amer. Microsc. Soc. 83: 233–43.

Nimmo, A. P. 1971. The adult Rhyacophilidae and Limnephilidae (Trichoptera) of Alberta and eastern British Columbia and their postglacial origin. Quaest. Entomol. 7: 3–234.

Resh, V. H. 1976. The biology and immature stages of the caddisfly genus *Ceraclea* in eastern North America. Ann. Entomol. Soc. Amer. 69: 1039–61.

Roback, S. S. 1962. Environmental requirements of Trichoptera – Biological problems in water pollution. Third seminar, Publ. Health Serv. Publ., 999-WP-25: 118–26.

Ross, H. H. 1959. Trichoptera, pp. 1024–49. In W. T. Edmondson (ed.). Freshwater biology (2nd ed.). John Wiley & Sons, New York.

———. 1956. Evolution and classification of mountain caddisflies. Univ. Ill. Press, Urbana.

———. 1946. A review of the Nearctic Lepidostomatidae (Trichoptera). Ann. Entomol. Soc. Amer. 39: 265–91.

———. 1944. The caddis flies, or Trichoptera, of Illinois. Bull. Ill. Nat. Hist. Surv. 23: 1–326.

Ross, H. H., and D. R. Merkley. 1952. An annotated key to the Nearctic males of *Limnephilus* (Trichoptera: Limnephilidae). Amer. Midl. Nat. 47: 435–55.

Smith, S. D. 1968. The *Rhyacophila* of the Salmon River drainage of Idaho with special reference to larvae. Ann. Entomol. Soc. Amer. 61: 655–74.

Thut, R. N. 1969. Feeding habits of larvae of seven *Rhyacophila* species with notes on other life-history features. Ann. Entomol. Soc. Amer. 62: 894–98.

Vorhies, C. 1909. Studies on the Trichoptera of Wisconsin. Trans. Wisc. Acad. Sci. Arts Lett. 16: 647–739.

Wiggins, G. B. 1977. Larvae of the North American caddisfly genera. Univ. Toronto Press, Toronto.

———. 1976. Contributions to the systematics of the caddis-fly family Limnephilidae (Trichoptera). III. pp. 7–19. In H. Malicky (ed.). Proc. Int. Symp. Trichoptera, Lunz. 1, The Hague.

———. 1975. Contributions to the systematics of the caddisfly family Limnephilidae (Trichoptera). II. Can. Entomol. 107: 325–36.

———. 1973. Contributions to the systematics of the caddisfly family Limnephilidae (Trichoptera). I. Life Sci. Contr. Roy. Ont. Mus. 94: 1–32.

Plecoptera (stoneflies)

Baumann, R. W. 1975. Revision of the stone fly family Nemouridae (Plecoptera): a study of the world fauna at the generic level. Smithson. Contr. Zool. 211: 1–74.

Baumann, R. W., A. R. Gaufin, and R. F. Surdick. 1977. The stoneflies (Plecoptera) of the Rocky Mountains. Mem. Amer. Entomol. Soc. 31.

Claassen, P. W. 1931. Plecoptera nymphs of America (north of Mexico). Thomas Say Foundation, Entomol. Soc. Amer. 3: 1–199.

Frison, T. H. 1929. Fall and winter stoneflies, or Plecoptera, of Illinois. Bull. I81. Nat. Hist. Surv. 18: 343–409.

———. 1935. The stoneflies, or Plecoptera, of Illinois. Bull. Ill. Nat. Hist. Surv. 20: 281–471.

Gaufin, A. R. 1964. The Chloroperlidae of North America. Gewass. Abwass. 34/35: 37–49.

———. 1962. Environmental requirements of Plecoptera. Biological Problems in Water Pollution, Third Seminar, Publ. Health Serv. Publ., 999-WP-25: 105–109.

———. 1956. Annotated list of stoneflies of Ohio. Ohio J. Sci. 56: 321–24.

Gaufin, A. R., W. E. Ricker, M. Miner, P. Milam, and R. A. Hays. 1972. The stoneflies (Plecoptera) of Montana, Trans. Amer. Entomol. Soc. 98: 1–161.

Harden, P., and C. Mickel. 1952. The stoneflies of Minnesota (Plecoptera). Univ. Minn. Agric. Exp. Sta. Tech. Bull. 201: 1–84.

Harper, P. P., and H. B. N. Hynes. 1971a. The Leuctridae of eastern Canada (Insecta: Plecoptera). Can. J. Zool. 49: 915–20.

———. 1971b. The Capniidae of eastern Canada (Insecta: Plecoptera). Can. J. Zool. 49: 921–40.

———. 1971c. The nymphs of the Taeniopterygidae of eastern Canada (Insecta: Plecoptera). Can. J. Zool. 49: 941–47.

———. 1971d. The nymphs of Nemouridae of eastern Canada (Insecta: Plecoptera). Can. J. Zool. 49: 1129–42.

Hilsenhoff, W. L. 1970. Key to genera of Wisconsin Plecoptera (stonefly) nymphs, Ephemeroptera (mayfly) nymphs, Trichoptera (caddisfly) larvae. Res. Rep. Wisc. Dept. Nat. Res.

Hilsenhoff, W. L., and S. J. Billmyer. 1973. Perlodidae (Plecoptera) of Wisconsin. Great Lakes Entomol. 6: 1–14.

Hitchcock, S. W. 1974. Guide to the insects of Connecticut. Part VII. The Plecoptera or stoneflies of Connecticut. Bull. Conn. State Geol. Nat. Hist. Surv. 107: 1–262.

McCaskill, V. H., and R. Prins. 1968. Stoneflies (Plecoptera) of northwestern South Carolina. J. Elisha Mitchell Sci. Soc. 84: 448–53.

Minshall, G. W., and J. N. Minshall. 1966. Notes on the life history and ecology of *Isoperla clio* (Newman) and *Isogenus decisus* Walker (Plecoptera: Perlodidae). Amer. Midl. Nat. 76: 340–50.

Needham, J. G., and P. W. Claassen. 1925. A monograph on the Plecoptera or stoneflies of America north of Mexico. Thomas Say Found. Entomol. 2: 1–397.

Needham, J. G., and L. W. Smith. 1916. The stoneflies of the genus *Peltoperla*. Can. Entomol. 48: 80–88.

Ricker, W. E. 1959. Plecoptera, pp. 941–57. In W. T. Edmondson (ed.). Freshwater biology. John Wiley & Sons, New York.

Ricker, W. E., and H. H. Ross. 1969. The genus *Zealeuctra* and its position in the family Leuctridae. Can. J. Zool. 46: 1113–27.

———. 1968. North American species of *Taeniopteryx* (Plecoptera, Insecta). J. Fish. Res. Bd. Can. 25: 1423–39.

Stark, B. P., and A. R. Gaufin. 1976. The Nearctic genera of Perlidae (Plecoptera). Misc. Publ. Entomol. Soc. Amer. 10: 1–80.

Stark, B. P., R. B. Oblad, and A. R. Gaufin. 1973. An annotated list of the stoneflies (Plecoptera) of Colorado. Entomol. News 84: 269–77.

Stewart, K. W., and B. P. Stark. 1989. Nymphs of North American stonefly genera (Plecoptera). Thomas Say Foundation Ser., Entomol. Soc. Amer. 12: 1–460.

Surdick, R. F., and A. R. Gaufin. 1978. Environmental requirements and pollution tolerance of Plecoptera. Environ. Monit. Sup. Lab., Off. Res. Dev. USEPA, Cincinnati, OH.

Surdick, R. F., and K. C. Kim. 1976. Stoneflies (Plecoptera) of Pennsylvania, a synopsis. Bull. Penn. State Univ. Agric. Exp. Sta. 808: 1073.

Diptera (midges, mosquitoes, aquatic gnats, and flies)

Alexander, C. P. 1919–1920. The crane flies of New York. Part I (1919). Distribution and taxonomy of adult flies. Mem. Cornell Univ. Agric. Exp. Sta. 25: 765–993. The crane flies of New York. Part II (1920). Biology and phylogeny. Mem. Cornell Univ. Agric. Exp. Sta. 38: 691–1133.

Beck, W. M., Jr. 1977. Environmental requirements and pollution tolerance of common freshwater Chironomidae. Environ. Monit. Sup. Lab., Off. Res. Dev. USEPA, Cincinnati, OH.

———. 1976. Biology of the larval chironomids. St. Fla. Dept. Environ. Reg. Tech. Ser. 2.

Bryce, D., and A. Hobart. 1972. The biology and identification of the larvae of the Chironomidae (Diptera). Entomol. Gaz. 23: 175–217.

Byers, G. W. 1978. Tipulidae, pp. 285–310. In An introduction to the aquatic insects of North America, R. W. Merritt and K. W. Cummins (eds.). Kendall/Hunt, Dubuque, IA.

Curry, L. L. 1962. A survey of environmental requirements for the midges. Biological Problems in Water Pollution. Third Seminar, Publ. Health Serv. Publ., 999-WP-25: 127–40.

Deonier, D. L. (ed.). 1979. First symposium on the systematics and ecology of Ephydridae (Diptera). N. Amer. Benthological Soc.

Hamilton, A., O. Saether, and D. Oliver. 1969. A classification of the nearctic Chironomidae. Fish. Res. Bd. Can. Tech. Rept. 124: 1–42.

James, M. T. 1959. Diptera, pp. 1057–79. In W. T. Edmondson (ed.). Freshwater biology (2nd ed.), John Wiley & Sons, New York.

Johannsen, O. A. 1934–38. Aquatic Diptera. Pt. I (1934) Nematocera, exclusive of Chironomidae and Ceratopogonidae. Pt. II. (1935) Orthorrhapha-Brachycera and Cyclorrhapha. Pt. III. (1937) Chironomidae: Subfamilies Tanypodinae, Diamesinae, and Orthocladiinae. Pt. IV. (1938) Chironomidae: Subfamily Chironominae. Mem. Cornell Univ. Ag. Exp. Sta. 164, 71 pp.; 171, 62 pp.; 205, pp. 3–84; 210, pp. 3–80 (Reprint: 1969. Entomol. Rep. Specialists, Los Angeles).

Mason, W. T., Jr. 1973. An introduction to the identification of chironomid larvae. MERC/EPA, Cincinnati, OH.

Nowell, W. R. 1963. Dixidae, pp. 85–111. In Guide to the insects of Connecticut. Part VI. The Diptera or true flies of Connecticut. Fasc. 8. St. Geol. Nat. Hist. Surv. Conn. Bull. No. 93.

Oliver, D. R. 1971. Life history of the chironomidae. Ann. Rev. Entomol. 16: 211–30.

Roback, S. S. 1976. The immature chironomids of the eastern United States. I. Introduction and Tanypodinae-Coelotanypodini. Proc. Acad. Nat. Sci. Phila. 127: 147–201.

———. 1957. The immature tendipedids of the Philadelphia area. Monogr. Acad. Nat. Sci. Phila. 9: 1–152.

Saether, O. A. 1979. Chironomid communities as water quality indicators. Hol. Ecol. 2: 65–74.

Soponis, A. R. 1977. A revision of the Nearctic species of *Orthocladius (Orthocladius)* van der Wulp (Diptera: Chironomidae). Mem. Entomol. Soc. Can. 102: 187 pp.

Stone, A. 1964. Guide to the insects of Connecticut. Part VI. The Diptera or true flies of Connecticut. Fasc. 9. Family Simuliidae. Bull. Conn. State Geol. Nat. Hist. Surv. 97: 1–117.

Stone, A., and H. A. Jamnback. 1955. The black flies of New York State (Diptera: Simuliidae). Bull. N.Y. State Mus. 349: 1–144.

Teskey, H. J. 1969. Larvae and pupae of some eastern North American Tabanidae (Diptera). Mem. Entomol. Soc. Can. 63: 1–147.

Odonata (dragonflies and damselflies)

Corbett, P. B. 1963. A biology of dragonflies. Quadrangle Books, Chicago, IL.

Gloyd, L. K., and M. Wright. 1959. Odonata, pp. 917–40. In W. T. Edmondson (ed.). Freshwater biology (2nd ed.). John Wiley & Sons, New York.

Needham, J. G., and H. B. Heywood. 1929. A handbook of the dragonflies of North America. Thomas, Springfield, IL.

Needham, J. G., and M. W. Westfall, Jr. 1955. A manual of the dragonflies of North America (Anisoptera) including the Greater Antilles and the provinces of the Mexican border. Univ. Calif. Press, Berkeley.

Walker, E. M. 1958. The Odonata of Canada and Alaska. Anisoptera. Vol. 2. Univ. Toronto Press, Toronto.

———. 1953. The Odonata of Canada and Alaska, Part I, General, Part II. The Zygoptera-damselflies, Univ. of Toronto Press, Toronto.

Walker, E. M., and P. S. Corbet. 1975. The Odonata of Canada and Alaska. Anisoptera, Libellulidae. Vol. 3. Univ. Toronto Press, Toronto.

Westfall, M. J., Jr. 1978. Odonata, pp. 81–98. In An introduction to the aquatic insects of North America. R. W. Merritt and K. W. Cummins (eds.). Kendall/Hunt, Dubuque, IA.

White, H. B., and W. J. Morse. 1973. Odonata (dragonflies) of New Hampshire: an annotated list. N. Hampshire Agric. Exp. Sta. 30: 1–46.

Megaloptera (alderflies, dobsonflies, and fishflies)

Cuyler, R. D. 1958. The larvae of *Chauliodes* Letreille (Megaloptera: Corydalidae). Ann. Entomol. Soc. Amer. 51: 582–86.

Davis, K. C. 1903. Sialidae of North and South America. Bull. N.Y. State Mus. 18: 442–86.

Leischner, T. G., and G. Pritchard. 1973. The immature stages of the alderfly, *Sialis cornuta* (Megaloptera: Sialidae). Can Entomol. 105: 411–18.

Neunzig, H. H. 1966. Larvae of the genus *Nigronia* Banks. Proc. Entomol. Soc. Wash. 68: 11–16.

Parfin, S. I. 1952. The Megaloptera and Neuroptera of Minnesota. Amer. Midl. Nat. 47: 421–34.

Petersen, R. C. 1974. Life history and bionomics of *Nigronia serricornis* (Say) (Megaloptera: Corydalidae). Ph.D. diss. Mich. State Univ., East Lansing.

Riley, C. V. 1879. On the larval characteristics of *Corydalus* and *Chauliodes* and on the development of *Corydalus cornutus*. Can. Entomol. 11: 96–98.

Ross, H. H. 1937. Nearctic alderflies of the genus *Sialis* (Megaloptera, Sialidae). Bull. Ill. Nat. Hist. Surv. 21: 57–78.

Tarter, D. C., and W. D. Watkins. 1974. Distribution of the fishfly genera *Chauliodes* Latreille and *Nigronia* Banks in West Virginia. Proc. W. Va. Acad. Sci. 46: 146–50.

Tarter, D. C., W. D. Watkins, and M. L. Little. 1975. Life history of the fishfly *Nigronia fasciatus* (Megaloptera: Corydalidae). Psyche 82: 81–88.

Tarter, D. C., W. D. Watkins, M. L. Little, and D. L. Ashley. 1977. Seasonal emergence patterns of fishflies east of the Rocky Mountains (Megaloptera: Corydalidae). Entomol. News 88: 69–76.

Townsend, L. H. 1935. Key to the larvae of certain families and genera of Nearctic Neuroptera. Proc. Entomol. Soc. Wash. 37: 25–30.

Watkins, W. D., D. C. Carter, M. L. Little, and S. D. Hopkin. 1975. New records of fishflies for West Virginia (Megaloptera: Corydalidae). Proc. W. Va. Acad. Sci. 47: 1–5.

Coleoptera (aquatic beetles)

Arnett, R. H. 1963. The beetles of the United States. Catholic Univ. America Press, Washington, DC.

Boving, A. G., and F. D. Craighead. 1931. An illustrated synopsis of the principal larval forms of the order Coleoptera. Entomol. Amer., Brooklyn Entomol. Soc. 21 (N. ser).

Brown, H. P. 1972. Aquatic dryopoid beetles (Coleoptera) of the United States. Biota of freshwater ecosystems identification manual no. 6. Wat. Poll. Conf. Res. Ser. E.P.A., Washington, DC.

Leech, H. B., and M. W. Sanderson. 1959. Coleoptera, pp. 981–1023. In W. T. Edmondson (ed.). Freshwater biology (2nd ed.). John Wiley & Sons, New York.

Matta, J. F. 1974. The insects of Virginia: No. 8. The aquatic Hydrophilidae of Virginia (Coleoptera: Polyphaga). Bull. Res. Div. Va. Poly. Inst. State Univ. 94: 1–144.

Murvosh, C. M. 1971. Ecology of the water penny beetle *Psephenus herricki* DeKay. Ecol. Monogr. 41: 79–96.

Sanderson, M. W. 1954. A revision of the Nearctic genera of Elmidae (Coleoptera) II. J. Kan. Entomol. Soc. 27: 1–13.

———. 1953. A revision of the Nearctic genera of Elmidae (Coleoptera) I. J. Kan. Entomol. Soc. 26: 148–63.

———. 1938. A monographic revision of the North American species of *Stenelmis* (Dryopidae: Coleoptera). Univ. Kan. Sci. Bull. 25: 635–717.

Sinclair, R. M. 1964. Water quality requirements of the family Elmidae (Coleoptera) with keys to the larvae and adults of the eastern genera. Tenn. Stream Poll. Contr.

Lepidoptera (aquatic moths)

Lange, W. H. 1978. Aquatic and semiaquatic Lepidoptera, pp. 187–201. In An introduction to the aquatic insects of North America. R. W. Merritt and K. W. Cummins (eds.). Kendall/Hunt, Dubuque, IA.

Lange, W. H. 1956. A generic revision of the aquatic moths of North America: (Lepidoptera: Pyralidae, Nymphulinae). Wasmann J. Biol. 14: 59–144.

McCafferty, W. P., and M. C. Minno. 1979. The aquatic and semi-aquatic Lepidoptera of Indiana and adjacent areas. Great Lakes Entomol. 12: 179–87.

Hemiptera (true bugs)

Blatchley, W. S. 1926. Heteroptera or true bugs of eastern North America. Nature, Indianapolis.

Bobb, M. L. 1974. The aquatic and semiaquatic Hemiptera of Virginia. The insects of Virginia: no. 7. Bull. Res. Div. Va. Poly. Inst. State Univ. 87: 1–195.

Chapman, H. C. 1959. Distributional and ecological records for some aquatic and semi-aquatic Heteroptera of New Jersey. Bull. Brooklyn Entomol. Soc. 54: 8–12.

China, W. E., and N. C. E. Miller. 1959. Checklist and keys to the families and subfamilies of the Hemiptera-Heteroptera. Bull. Br. Mus. Nat. Hist. Entomol. 8: 1–45.

Davis, K. C. 1903. Sialidae of North America. Bull. N.Y. State Mus. 18: 442–86.

DeCoursey, R. M. 1971. Keys to the families and subfamilies of the nymphs of North American Hemiptera-Heteroptera. Proc. Entomol. Soc. Wash. 93: 413–28.

Hungerford, H. B. 1959. Hemiptera, pp. 958–72. In W. T. Edmondson (ed.). Freshwater biology (2nd ed.). John Wiley & Sons, New York.

———. 1920. The biology and ecology of aquatic and semi-aquatic Hemiptera. Univ. Kans. Sci. Bull. 21: 1–341.

Polhemus, J. T. 1978. Aquatic and semiaquatic Hemiptera, pp. 119–31. In An introduction to the aquatic insects of North America. R. W. Merritt and K. W. Cummins (eds.). Kendall/Hunt, Dubuque, IA.

Crustaceans (scuds, sowbugs or cressbugs, and crayfish)

Hobbs, H. H. 1972. Crayfishes (Astacidae) of North and middle America. Wat. Poll. Cont. Res. Ser., Cincinnati, OH.

Holsinger, J. R. 1972. The freshwater amphipod crustaceans (Gammaridae) of North America. Biota of Freshwater Ecosystems, USEPA Ident. Man. No. 5. Washington, DC.

Lorman, J. G., and J. J. Magnuson. 1978. The role of crayfishes in aquatic ecosystems. Fisheries 3: 8–19.

Williams, W. D. 1972. Freshwater isopods (Asellidae) of North America. Biota of Freshwater Ecosystems, USEPA Ident. Man. No. 7. Washington, DC.

Index

Note: References in italics represent illustrations.